THE COMPLETE IDIOT'S GUIDE® TO RVing

by Brent Peterson

ALPHA
A Pearson Education Company

For Loretta Sleeth, better known in some circles as "Nana."

International Standard Book Number: 0-02-864171-X
Library of Congress Catalog Card Number: 2001094729

04 03 02 8 7 6 5 4 3 2

Interpretation of the printing code: The rightmost number of the first series of numbers is the year of the book's printing; the rightmost number of the second series of numbers is the number of the book's printing. For example, a printing code of 02-1 shows that the first printing occurred in 2002.

Printed in the United States of America

Publisher
Marie Butler-Knight

Product Manager
Phil Kitchel

Managing Editor
Jennifer Chisholm

Senior Acquisitions Editor
Randy Ladenheim-Gil

Development Editor
Joan D. Paterson

Senior Production Editor
Christy Wagner

Copy Editor
Cari Luna

Illustrator
Jody Schaeffer

Cover Designers
Mike Freeland
Kevin Spear

Book Designers
Scott Cook and Amy Adams of DesignLab

Indexer
Amy Lawrence

Layout/Proofreading
John Etchison
Lizbeth Patterson
Nancy Wagner

Contents at a Glance

Part 1: To RV or Not To RV? **1**

1 Why RV? 3
Compelling reasons to jumpstart your RV life.

2 Who RVs? 19
A look into the world of the RVing community.

3 Where to Stay? 31
What to expect at a private campground, government park, or RV camped in the wild.

Part 2: Choosing Your RV **57**

4 The World of Motorized RVs 59
An examination of the various types of self-propelled RVs.

5 The World of Towables 87
An examination of the various types of towable RVs.

6 Narrowing Down Your Choices 115
What to consider before entering the buying stage.

Part 3: Buying Your First RV **137**

7 What to Buy? 139
Selecting the best RV for you.

8 The Art of the Deal 157
Navigating through the sale like a pro.

9 After the Sale 175
Insuring, taking delivery, and postsale musts.

Part 4: What's What Onboard? **187**

10 Electrical Systems 189
How to power up your RV adventures.

11 LP Systems 205
Learning the ins and outs of the RV's LP system.

12 Plumbing Systems 215
Managing water systems onboard.

Part 5: Your First Trip **229**

13 Towin' the Line 231
All of the essentials for towing an RV.

14 Drive Time 253
Driving techniques for motorhomes and towables.

15 How Much Does Your RV Weigh? 267
Managing the load, packing know-how, and weighing in.

16 Choosing a Campground 281
Knowing where to camp and what to do when you get there.

17 Roughin' It 301
Mastering life off the beaten path.

Part 6: Life on the Road 315

18 Travel Planning 317
Special considerations for traveling with families, pets, caravans, as well as full-timing.

19 Staying in Touch 333
Remaining in the loop when away from home.

20 Playin' It Safe 343
Avoiding crime, bad weather, and potential trip-busters.

21 Basic Care 361
Storage procedures and keeping the RV looking and running its best.

Appendixes

A Resources 373

B Glossary 381

Index 389

Contents

Part 1: To RV or Not To RV?

1 Why RV? 3

The ABCs of RVs 4
Different Strokes, Different Folks 5
Motorized RVs 6
Class A Motorhomes 6
Class B Motorhomes 7
Class C Motorhomes 8
Truck Campers 8
Towable RVs 9
Fifth-Wheel Trailers 10
Travel Trailers 10
Lightweight Travel Trailers 11
Fold-Down Campers 11
What's in It for Me? 11
Independence 12
Togetherness 13
Cost 13
Meal Deal 14
Hotel Hijinks 14
Tickets, Please 15
Commercial Break 15
Comfort 16
The Great Outdoors 16
Easy as You Please 16
Special Needs 17
What Can I Expect? 17

2 Who RVs? 19

Who's Doin' It? 20
All Aboard 20
Small Start-Ups 21
Howdy, Pard'ner 21
Hyper Active 22
Retirees 22
All in the Family 22
Motor Heads 23
Disabled Travelers 23
Pet-Lovers 24
Where the Wild Things Are 24

Snowbirds 25
Worker Bees 25
Athletic Supporters 26
Hobby Time 26
Types of Travel 27
Day Trippers 27
Weekend Warriors 27
We're Not in Kansas Anymore 28
Full-Timers 28
Restrictions 29
License to Chill 29
Driver's Ed 30

3 Where to Stay? 31

Campgrounds 32
Da' Basics 33
Welcome to Your Campsite 34
Hooking Up 34
Electric Avenue 34
Water, Water Everywhere 35
Sewer 35
Cable TV 36
Phone 36
Back That Thing Up 37
Length of Stay 38
'Tis the Season 38
Accessibility 38
What's to Do, What to Do? 39
Active Endeavors 40
Facilities 41
You've Been Served 42
Okay, How Much? 43
Discounts 44
RV Clubs 44
Franchise Clubs 44
AAA 45
You're How Old? 45
Length of Stay 45
No-No's 45
Types of Campgrounds 46
Private Campgrounds 46
Franchise Players 47
RV Resorts 47

Government Campgrounds 48
State Parks 49
National Parks 50
Bureau of Land Management 50
U.S. Army Corps of Engineers Projects 51
National Wildlife Refugee System 52
Camping Canada 52
Membership Parks 52
Members Only 52
Costs 53
Boondocking 53
You Get What You Paid For 54
Remember Your P's and Q's 54
Conventional Lodging 55

Part 2: Choosing Your RV

4 The World of Motorized RVs **59**
More Than a Motor 60
All-in-One Vehicle 60
Easy Street 60
Boondocking 61
In-Motion Access 61
One-Time Costs 61
Hitchin' a Ride 62
Motor Woes 62
Sticker Shock 62
Two Eggs, One Basket 62
Getting Cocky 63
Getting Around 63
Floor Plan-o-Rama 63
You Are Depreciated 64
Choices, Choices 64
Class A Motorhomes 64
What Is It? 65
Get Some Sleep 66
What's Cookin'? 66
Just Relax 67
Showering and Other Dirty Business 68
Behind the Wheel 68
Typical Specs 69

Price Tag 70
Final Analysis 70
Class B Motorhomes 71
What Is It? 72
Get Some Sleep 72
What's Cookin'? 73
Just Relax 73
Showering and Other Dirty Business 73
Behind the Wheel 74
Typical Specs 74
Price Tag 74
Final Analysis 75
Class C Motorhomes 75
What Is It? 76
Get Some Sleep 76
What's Cookin'? 77
Just Relax 77
Showering and Other Dirty Business 78
Behind the Wheel 78
Typical Specs 78
Price Tag 79
Final Analysis 79
Truck Camper 80
What Is It? 80
The Perfect Fit 81
Get Some Sleep 82
What's Cookin'? 82
Just Relax 82
Showering and Other Dirty Business 83
Behind the Wheel 83
Important Add-Ons 84
Typical Specs 84
Price Tag 85
Final Analysis 85

5 The World of Towables **87**

Tow: The Way to Go 88
Like the Bird Says, "Cheap, Cheap" 88
Double the Fun 88
Longevity 89
More Residential 90
Space: The Final Frontier 90

More Variety *90*
Second Home *90*
Towing Woes 91
The Big Tow *91*
Separation Anxiety *91*
No Rough Riders *92*
Meeting Your Match *92*
Accessorizing *93*
Types 93
Fifth-Wheel Trailers 94
What Is It? *94*
Life Onboard *94*
Sleeping Beauty *95*
Home Cookin' *95*
Inside Out *96*
Bathrooms and Showers *96*
Towability *96*
Typical Specs *97*
Costly Matters *98*
Final Analysis *98*
Travel Trailers 99
What Is It? *99*
Life Onboard *100*
Sleeping Beauty *100*
Home Cookin' *100*
Inside Out *101*
Bathrooms and Showers *101*
Towability *101*
Typical Specs *102*
Costly Matters *102*
Final Analysis *103*
Lightweight Travel Trailers 104
What Is It? *104*
Life Onboard *105*
Sleeping Beauty *105*
Home Cookin' *106*
Inside Out *106*
Bathrooms and Showers *106*
Towability *106*
Typical Specs *107*
Costly Matters *107*
Final Analysis *108*

Fold-Down Campers 108
What Is It? *108*
Life Onboard *109*
Sleeping Beauty *109*
Home Cookin' *110*
Inside Out *110*
Bathrooms and Showers *111*
Towability *112*
Typical Specs *112*
Costly Matters *113*
Final Analysis *113*

6 Narrowing Down Your Choices **115**

Talking the Talk 116
How Much Do I Have to Spend? *116*
Motorized or Towable? *116*
Who's Coming Along? *117*
Where Are We Going? *117*
How Much Room Do We Need? *117*
What's My Driving Mood? *118*
What Must Be Included? *118*
Even More to Think About 118
Slide-Outs or Not? 119
Bigger Is Better *119*
Resale *120*
Slip, Slide, and Away *120*
Overweight *120*
Room Service *121*
Breakdown *121*
Campground-Ed *121*
Gas or Diesel? 122
Today's Diesel *122*
Diesel Dilemmas *122*
Builder's Choice 123
Frame Job *124*
Wood *124*
Aluminum *124*
Steel *124*
Get Insulated *125*
Save Your Skin *125*

Raising the Roof 125
Rubber *126*
Aluminum *126*
Fiberglass *126*
What's Their Rep? 127
Wide-Body Designs 127
Walking the Walk 128
Showtime *129*
Kick the Tires *130*
Overdue Rent *130*
Take a Sunday Drive *131*
A Friend in Need *131*
Read All About It 132
Buyer's Guides *132*
The Horse's Mouth *132*
Campfire Chats *133*
New or Used? 133
Secondhand Views *133*
More for the Money *134*
They Don't Make 'Em Like That Anymore *134*
Used and Abused *134*
Buying Trouble *134*
Mechanical Difficulties *135*
New 135
Choice *135*
Rest Assured *135*

Part 3: Buying Your First RV

7 What to Buy? 139

Livability Tests 140
It Sleeps How Many? *140*
Food Fight *141*
What About My Ukulele? *142*
Going Through the Motions *142*
Live and Let Live *143*
Other Keys to Victory *144*
Take It Outside *145*
Storage *145*
Hookups *146*
Awnings, Steps, and Little Extras *146*

The Inspection 147

Inside *147*

Floor It *148*

Woodworking *148*

Furnishings *149*

Seals of Approval *149*

Appliances *150*

Exterior Inspection 150

Chassis *150*

Tired Out *151*

Sidewalls and Roofing *151*

Don't Get Hoodwinked 152

Gentlemen, Start Your Engines 152

The Towable Exception *152*

Prior to Take-Off *153*

The Course *153*

Warning Signs 153

Rentals *154*

Barely Driven Vehicles *154*

Lean and Mean *154*

Water, Water Everywhere *154*

Communication Breakdown *155*

Wish List *155*

8 The Art of the Deal **157**

The Hard Sell 158

Private Sellers 158

RV Dealers *158*

Dealer's Choice 159

Dollars and Sense *160*

Money for Nothing *160*

What's Their Rep? *160*

Service with a Smile *161*

Location, Location, Location *161*

Good Help Is Hard to Find *162*

Special Delivery *162*

Trade Ya *162*

Common Buying Pitfalls 163

Rush, Rush, Rush *163*

Don't Believe the Hype *164*

Falling in Love *164*

Pushy Salespeople *164*

Too Many Choices 164
Unreasonable Expectations 164
Wheelin' and Dealin' 165
The Give and Take 165
The Price Zone 165
The Fifteen Percent Rule 166
Patience Is a Virtue 166
Act Interested 167
Creative Bargaining 167
Extras, Extras 167
Factory or Aftermarket Company? 168
Viva Variety 168
Price vs. Service 169
Tradin' Time 170
Go Figure 170
Role Reversal 171
Warranties 171
You Break It, You Buy It 171
Stake Your Claim 171
Check, Please 172
The Finance Dance 172
Livin' on Borrowed Time 172
How Do They Rate? 173
To Serve and Protect 173
Avoid Borrow Sorrow 173
Interest-ed 174

9 After the Sale **175**

Taking Delivery 176
Final Walk-Thru 176
Follow-Up Meeting 178
Shakedown Street 178
A Little Insurance 179
RV Insurers 179
Types of Insurance 180
How Much Is Enough? 180
Crossing Borders 181
Finding the Best Deals 181
Discounts 181
Full-Timers' Policies 182
Roadside Assistance 182
A Little Help Here 183
Choosing a Service Plan 183

Lemon Aid 184
Defining a Lemon 184
The Write Stuff 185
The Killer Bs 185
The Ruling 186

Part 4: What's What Onboard?

10 Electrical Systems **189**
Straight to the Source 190
Engine Power 190
Coach Power 191
Coach Batteries 192
Hey, That's My Power 192
Shore Power 192
Rating Electrical Hookups 193
What Do I Have? 194
The Trickle Down (and Up) Theory 194
Generators 195
Is It for Me? 197
Camped or On the Go 197
Peak Performance 197
Generator Courtesy 198
Monitor Panels 198
Electricity: The Long and the Short(age) 199
Running Out of Juice 201
Hooking Up 201
Generators and Inverters 201
Drain in Vain 201
Solar Power 202
Blackout! 202
Important Add-Ons 203
Extra Shoreline Power Cord 203
Surge Protectors 203
Polarity Tester 203
Voltage Meter 204
Ammeter 204

11 LP Systems **205**
LP: It's a Gas 205
Refrigerator Madness 206
Mode-Us Operate-Us 207

The Heat Is On 207
Use the Force *207*
Catalytic Heaters *208*
You're in Hot Water *208*
Spaced Out *208*
Home on the Range 208
One in the Oven *209*
Water Heater 209
LP Containers 210
Container Types 210
DOT *210*
ASME *211*
Who Needs a Refill? *212*
What Do I Do? *212*
Gas Crisis *212*
Safety First 213
Handling the Tanks *213*
Happy Trails *213*
That Rotten Smell *214*

12 Plumbing Systems **215**

Water World 216
Fresh Water System 216
Water Sources *216*
Hose Job *217*
Handling the Pressure *217*
Tastes Great, Less Filling *218*
Going to the Store *218*
Fill 'Er Up *219*
Pumping Up 219
Avoiding the Cold Shoulder 221
Bathroom Talk 221
Wastewater Systems 222
When Good Water Goes Bad *222*
Runnin' on Empty 223
Sewer Hookups *224*
Down in the Dumps 225
Mr. Clean 227
Waste Not, Want Not *227*

Part 5: Your First Trip

13 Towin' the Line 231

How Much Can My Vehicle Tow? 232
How Do You Rate? 232
The Big Three 232
Unloaded Vehicle Weight 233
Gross Vehicle Weight Rating 233
Gross Combined Weight Rating 233
Matchmaker, Matchmaker 233
The Hitching Post 234
The Right Hitch 235
Conventional Trailers 236
Weight-Carrying Hitch 236
Weight-Distributing Hitch 236
What's What—Hitches 237
Hitching Up 238
Get Wired 238
Brake Time 240
Control Yourself 240
Safety Chain Gang 240
Breaking Up Is Hard to Do 241
Fifth Wheels 241
The Big Tow 242
Final Steps 243
Accessorizing 244
Mirror, Mirror 244
No Sway, No Way 244
Anti-Air 244
Stuff for Loners 245
Towing Behind a Motorhome 245
What Can My Motorhome Tow? 245
Towed Vehicles Come in Threes 246
Tow Bars 246
Hello, (Tow) Dolly 247
Trailers 249
Proper Wiring 250
Safety Chains 250
Give Me a Brake 250
Inspections 250

14 Drive Time **253**

The Only Thing to Fear 254
Start Your Engines 254
Take a Brake 254
Cornering 255
Lane Changes 256
Steep Grades 256
Parking 256
Clearance 257
Rush Hour 257
Life in the Fast Lane 257
Backing Up 258
It Takes Two 259
The Seven Deadly Driving Sins 259
Rush, Rush 260
Car Talk 260
Nervous Nellie 260
Lost in Space 261
Danger, Will Robinson 261
Overdoing It 262
Driving Under the Influence 262
Sleepy, Sleepy 262
Practice, Practice, Practice 263
A Class Act 263
Fuel 263
Dealing With … 264
You're Big 264
You're Slow 264
Must-Have Gear 265
Side Mirrors 265
GPS/Navigation Systems 265
Rear View Monitoring System 266

15 How Much Does Your RV Weigh? **267**

Weighty Concerns 268
Is My RV Fat? 268
Weight and See 269
Tipping the Scales 269
The Tale of the Tape 270
The Findings 271

Packing 271
When to Say When 271
What Weighs What? 272
Passengers 272
Tanks 273
Gear 274
The Leader of the Pack 274
Common Pitfalls 277
Chow 277
Cooking Supplies 277
Storage Pods and Nooks 278
Child's Play 278
Tools 279
The Loading Zone 279
Even Steven 279
Double-Duty 280

16 Choosing a Campground 281

Where to, Bub? 282
Location, Location, Location 282
Money Matters 283
Special Needs 283
Fun, Fun, Fun 283
Extras, Extras 284
Finding Mr. Right 284
Campground Directory 285
Internet 285
Tourism Agencies 286
Word of Mouth 286
Setting Up Camp 288
Checking In 288
A Site for Sore Eyes 289
Initiate Docking Sequence 289
On the Level 290
Hookups 291
Electric 291
Fresh Water 292
Propane 292
Sewer 293
Phone 293
Cable TV 294

What's Next? 295
Rules and Etiquette 295
Shhhh ... Quiet *295*
Gone to the Dogs *296*
Generating Ill-Will *296*
Don't Get Fired *296*
Trashy Behavior *296*
Walking the Walk *297*
Kids at Play *297*
Idle Engines Are the Devil's Workshop *297*
Breaking Camp 297

17 Roughin' It **301**

Why Oh Why? 302
Isolation *302*
More Than You Paid For *303*
Location *303*
No Vacancy *303*
Because I Can *304*
The Path of Most Resistance 304
Is It Legal? *304*
Is It Safe? *305*
Can the Rig Handle It? *306*
Ready for Action 306
Inspection *306*
Practice *306*
All Systems a' Go-Go *307*
Provisions *307*
Conservative Thinking 307
Power Outage *308*
Water Logged *308*
Waste Not, Want Not *309*
Don't Touch That Dial *309*
Cold-Weather Camping 309
One Cool Customer 310
Let There Be Heat *310*
Insulation *311*
Tanks and Pipes *311*
Tank Capacities *311*
Winterizing Hookups 312
Icy Conditions *312*

Part 6: Life on the Road

18 Travel Planning **317**

Kids and Families and Babies, Oh My 318
Get Them Involved 318
Man Your Positions 319
Take It Easy 319
Rules of the Road 320
Heavy Petting 321
Pack Animals 321
Cat Call 321
It's a Dog's Life 322
Campground Behavior 322
Abandoned Ship 323
The Group Mentality 323
Rally Ho 324
Tours and Caravans 324
Border Patrol 325
Oh, Canada 326
Mexico 326
The Full-Timing Life 327
Can I Afford It? 327
What Is My Purpose? 328
Will I Strangle My Spouse? 329
Can I Give It All Up? 329
How Do I Stay in Touch? 330
What RV Do I Need? 330

19 Staying in Touch **333**

Phone Home 334
Cell Out 334
Calling Cards 335
Campsite Hookup 336
Collect Calls 336
E-Mail 337
Computers 337
Internet Devices 338
Pagers 339
CB Radio 339
Mail Call 340
Mail-Forwarding Services 340
General Delivery 341

The Buddy System 341
Address Unknown 341

20 Playin' It Safe **343**

Weather or Not (Here I Come) 344
Wind Breaker 344
The Perfect Storm 345
Snow Day 345
Ice Capades 345
Pea Soup 346
Natural Disasters 346
The Accidental Tourist 346
Avoid 'Em 347
Oh-Oh 347
Protect Valuables—You 348
Don't Be a Hero 348
Motion Sickness 348
Circle the Wagons 349
Road Worrier 349
Twice as Nice 349
Mr. Fix-It 350
Camping Calamities 350
Pride Goeth Before the Fall 351
The Criminal Element 351
Troubling Behavior 352
Crime Fighter 353
Medical Emergencies 353
Sound the Alarm 355
House Warming 356
Animals and Critters 357
Trouble at Home 357

21 Basic Care **361**

Storage 362
An Idle World 362
Where Do You Want It? 362
Winterizing 363
Everybody Out 363
Plumbing 363
Mr. Freeze 364
Impenetrable Fortress 364

LP Gas 365
Assault and Battery 366
Tired Out 366
Engine 367
Spring Shakedown 367
A Quick Look Around 367
Systems Check 368
Motor City 369
Trailers 370
Drive-Thru 370
Clean Machine 370
Exterior Care 370
Interior Care 371

Appendixes

A Resources **373**

B Glossary **381**

Index **389**

Foreword

The first time I saw a motorhome, I didn't really know what I was looking at, but I sure was jealous. Here we were, four people in a tent trying to stay warm in sleeping bags on the ground on an unusually cold Central California summer night. I loved the fact that I was at one with nature, but my excitement was tempered by knowing that when I woke up in the morning, I'd have to get dressed, put on shoes, and walk about two blocks to find the nearest restroom. Our neighbors in the motorhome didn't have that problem. They were enjoying the great outdoors just as we were. In fact, we had shared a campfire with them as we counted the stars in the sky the night before. But while we wound up full of mud trying to wash our dishes under the campground spigot, they walked inside, put their dishes in the motorhome's sink, and listened to the radio while they cleaned up. I liked that. After a day of fishing and hiking, I could still find out if the Dodgers won that day. And the mere idea that they were sleeping in comfortable beds—not to mention the fact that their bathroom was about four steps from their bed—was very appealing.

There are lots of ways to camp, I've discovered, but RVing is the best of all worlds. You can go wherever you want—to a remote forest or a luxurious campground by the ocean—and you can go whenever you want. The weather no longer dictates the camping season because you have heat or air conditioning at the flip of a switch. You pack *your* favorite food since your rig has a fridge, and you have your own towels, sheets, and pillows on your bed because an RV is, in every sense of the word, your home on wheels. You can take as much or as little with you as you want when you go and spend a day, a week, or a month wherever you feel like it.

Of course, the type of RV you select isn't as easy as picking one out of a magazine and ordering it. There is a lot to learn—from reading the gauges on the monitor control panel to making sure your RV is level when you park—and price will be a factor, but the one aspect that has always impressed me is that RVers are just about the friendliest group of people you'll find. No matter where you camp or what style RV you pull or drive, your fellow RVers are eager to help you enjoy your journey. Often you don't even have to ask. There's an unwritten rule in campgrounds that says everyone should be comfortable, and if you can help make someone's stay more enjoyable, you are encouraged to do so. It's a camaraderie that I have not seen in any other industry.

RVing tends to be a lot of trial and error, but author Brent Peterson has thoroughly covered the lifestyle from beginning to end. *The Complete Idiot's Guide to RVing* takes away a lot of the guesswork and is a great tool for potential RV owners.

Rest assured that should you encounter something on your maiden voyage that you didn't anticipate, there will be a nearby RVer ready to help with a friendly smile.

Ron Epstein
Associate Publisher, *Highways*

Introduction

I knew enough about RVing to be dangerous, as the old saying goes. Okay, so I had never *actually* gone out and done it, but sitting behind my editor's desk, I was more than confident that I knew what was going on with my readers. Certainly, I had *read* enough about recreational vehicles throughout my various RV publications to be nothing short of a full-blown expert—or so I thought. Young editor's mistake number one.

My first RV trip was somewhat of a farce, like a gloating champion celebrating after a fixed prizefight. A big-time RV resort wanted me to visit their unveiling in the Florida Keys, providing me with the perfect platform to display my RV mastery. I piloted the awaiting 30-foot motorhome to the park with relative ease (I drove an ice cream truck for a summer, don'tcha know), an act that sent my confidence into overdrive. Of course, a guide had been hired to make sure I didn't get my hands dirty connecting the RV to the campground's electrical, water, and sewer hookups. And yes, he had even backed the motorhome into my campsite for me, so I didn't chip the paint bashing into a picnic table. He was also pretty useful, I must admit, when I couldn't figure out how to turn on the refrigerator or work the TV, but I'm sure I could have done so without him. My wife still rolls her eyes at that one.

However, returning to the office, I was now a man on top of my craft. I had walked the walk and lived to tell, and re-tell, and re-tell the tale. Like a modern-day Napoleon, I had to ask myself, "What was left to conquer?" Young editor's mistake number two.

Now fully believing that RVing was about as easy as opening up a sleeping bag and climbing inside, I arranged for a trip of my own. I'd even invited a few buddies along to witness my RV prowess at work. Driving the 38-foot motorhome was somewhat of a shocking adjustment, as evidenced by my white knuckles and cottonmouth. My ice cream truck never needed three guys scurrying around the back to help me back into the campsite. It only took me three tries to beach the rig in a somewhat awkward fashion. Our destination within a deserted national forest in Michigan's Upper Peninsula was a truly desolate place. Camping out of season meant that there wasn't a single person around. There were no electrical hookups, no water to drink. I had skipped right past RV kindergarten and moved straight to the advanced coursework—we'd be roughin' it now. I can attest that pride does indeed goeth before the fall.

Although it was 40 degrees outside, the first bead of sweat formed when I couldn't get a single appliance to work. The refrigerator made a rather terrifying noise and then clicked off. I had visions of the packet of sirloins spoiling right there on the counter. This brand new RV must be broken, I thought. When I later went to light the stove, I thought better of it. Will the RV explode? Thoughts of a flaming RV filled my head. When asked how to turn on the heat, I simply shrugged. My friends soon realized that I didn't know how to do much of anything except roll down the windows and whine a lot. When someone went to use the bathroom, I tackled them in the hall. "Are you crazy?" I said. "I have no idea how that works." After that point, I deemed anything water-related off-limits, a moot point since I had forgotten to fill up the water tanks anyway. The mood was deteriorating. Even the chipmunks laughed.

"Aren't you an RV editor?" mocked one of the crew as I fumbled with the lights. I decided to run the generator, but had no idea for how long or whether it might leave the rig gasless and stranded. I quickly turned it off to avoid any further calamities. Even the awning confounded me. Not only was my every move onboard stymied, but I had packed for the trip like a five-year-old. The lack of a corkscrew and bottle opener dampened our enthusiasm even further. No cooking supplies, either. My kingdom for a flashlight!

Despite having a $200,000 RV just feet away, we lived only slightly better than cavemen that weekend. Eventually, someone got a campfire going, which we huddled around for much of the trip. We burnt the steaks, froze at night, as I weathered the harsh looks of my comrades until slinking out of town, hat in hand.

What did I learn that day? That RVing, though wonderful and positively a blast when you know what you're doing, is not necessarily easy—especially for novices. It combines a list of unique driving and living challenges that aren't all-too-obvious for many of us. I realized that operating a recreational vehicle is a skill like any other and not a natural birthright. It takes understanding, practice, and know-how to begin.

Now I know what you're thinking. Who is this guy to tell us how to RV? That dope can't even work the fridge.

Before you start fishing around the house looking for the receipt to return this book, this story has a happy ending. You see, I got educated. So shamed was I by that experience, I re-dedicated myself to what I was doing. As a result, I became a more knowledgeable editor and, eventually, someone you wouldn't mind having along on an RV trip. You see, if there was ever a "complete idiot," it was me. I saw the proverbial light and got smart, and now I want to share it with you. My message doesn't come from the high, shiny pulpit of RV enlightenment, but from down in the trenches, where all of us begin when we embark on a new undertaking—this book is told from one "idiot" to another. Go ahead and take my former post on the dunce chair. I kept it warm for you.

Part 1, "To RV or Not To RV," is a closer look at the perks of RV travel, the kind of folks engaged in the RV lifestyle, and a rundown of where to camp.

Part 2, "Choosing Your RV," pares down the field from the countless recreational vehicles available to the one that best suits you.

Part 3, "Buying Your First RV," takes you through every step of the buying process from test drives to livability tests, finding the right seller to insurance and all those little extras.

Part 4, "What's What Onboard?" is a comprehensive look at what a recreational vehicle can do and how things work.

Part 5, "Your First Trip," details RV driving and towing, the importance of weights, choosing where to camp, and how to set up when you get there.

Part 6, "Life on the Road," explains everything you need to know to plan that perfect trip, stay in touch as you go, and overcome such trip-busters as bad weather, accidents, and breakdowns.

Special Features

In addition to the regular text, this book contains four extra features designed to help you learn about RVing.

Road Scholar

With all the complexities of a house and a vehicle, RVing presents many challenges. Fortunately, we've included lots of tips to help you through it.

RVocabulary

If you're gonna walk the RV walk, you gotta talk the RV talk. These sidebars contain important lingo to help you sound like a pro.

Pull Over

Travel is not without its share of possible dangers. Don't worry, we'll guide the way with a list of things to look out for as you go.

One for the Road

Ranging from the trivial to practical, this sidebar helps make sure RVers stay in the know.

Acknowledgments

Although I didn't fully comprehend the full meaning at the time, I now understand what my father-in-law meant when he said that nobody goes it alone. This book is evidence to that. None of this would have been possible without Bill Brophy, who obliged me when I sheepishly phoned the *Wisconsin State Journal* and said I wanted to be a reporter, and Ann Emerson, who, for some reason still unknown to me, gave me my first job in the RV business. Once there, I certainly wouldn't have lasted long without the tutelage of RV superstars Joe and Vicki Kieva. It was also in these early days that I met the great RV Doctor, Gary Bunzer, and wonderful Shelley Zoellick, the tag-team technical editors on this book. I cannot overstate their importance to this project, with each coming up with Herculean efforts in terms of knowledge, encouragement, and keen insights. Double thanks to Shelley for penning the chapter on towing and to Gary for his terrific photography found throughout this book. Lofty credit must also be given to Joan Paterson, for her skillful editing, Randy Ladenheim-Gil, for moving the book from concept to reality, and the whole Alpha Books team who worked on this title. And now to those who shared the trenches with me. First and foremost, my awesome wife Anne, who settled my rampant brain when it all seemed too much to handle. The fine makers of Trident Cherry Sugarless Gum, which I devoured nervously in bulk every day while writing the text, and Daisy the beagle, who contributed by taking me out for daily walks, which allowed me to collect my thoughts and regroup. NFL great Mike Alstott deserves some credit, too. And, of course, where would I be without my parents, who gave me the writer's itch and created a pretty good kid?

Special Thanks to the Technical Reviewers

The Complete Idiot's Guide to RVing was reviewed by two experts who double-checked the accuracy of what you'll learn here, to help us ensure that this book gives you everything you need to know about RVing. Special thanks are extended to Gary Bunzer and Shelley Zoellick.

Trademarks

Part 1

To RV or Not To RV?

The thought of owning a recreational vehicle is intriguing, isn't it? Perhaps you've dreamed of cruising down the interstate in your very own motorhome, not a care in the world. Or a meaningful vacation spent camping in Yellowstone National Park with the kids and a small trailer in tow. What better way to enjoy a sporting event or concert than tailgating with the guys in a fully stocked conversion van, complete with a kitchen, bathroom, and living area. These are just a few examples from the world of recreational vehicles (RVs), a lifestyle enjoyed by approximately 30 million people who want to live and travel on their own terms. In an RV, you go where you want, when you want—and your home on wheels comes along for the ride.

Chapter 1

Why RV?

In This Chapter

- Just what is a recreational vehicle?
- The different types of RVs
- Advantages of this kind of travel
- What you can expect from RVing

Your free time is precious. Whether it's a hard-earned vacation, an action-paced weekend away, or a spontaneous day trip, we all want to squeeze the most out of our time off. Time is short, money shorter, and every member of the family has a different opinion about where to go and what to do once you get there. What you need are choices.

Unfortunately, choices don't come sitting in an airplane re-routed to Sheboygan. And it's not much of a decision when debating between one overpriced hotel and the other. No matter whether your typical trips involve jumping in the family mini-van or flying off to warmer climates, the fact is, you're reliant on others for all your basic needs. Decisions about what to do, where to stay or eat, and how to get there can be limited—or virtually nonexistent. But they don't have to be.

Think of a recreational vehicle as the great equalizer. RVing is all about freedom. Camp, travel, and live in a bona fide home on wheels. There are no airlines, hotels, rental cars, or other budget-busting costs and impositions—just you and a wide-open itinerary. Take the family on an extended trip out West or simply down the road for a weekend at your favorite state park. If you want to stay longer, you can. Don't like the weather? Jump in the RV and head off in pursuit of golden sunsets. Eat out or cook meals in your very own kitchen. And best of all, everyone has his own stuff, his own place to sleep, and a comfortable way to get from here to there—and everywhere. Flexible travel means everyone's happy. You can visit an amusement park one day, the beaches the next, and a baseball game after that. It's living life on the go or on the slow. The choice is yours.

The ABCs of RVs

Simply put, an RV (recreational vehicle) combines transportation and living accommodations into one mobile package. Of course, that's a pretty loose definition. We never considered my parents' station wagon to be a "recreational vehicle," but we sure ate and slept in it enough during our epic family trips up north. Just think of the battles my brother and I could have avoided if we had only had the roominess of a 40-foot motorhome to divvy up instead of the ongoing turf wars in the back seat. But I digress.

To qualify as an RV, the vehicle must provide a place to sleep, basic cooking functions, and livable space. Sleeping on the floor of your mini-van dining on stale pretzels and warm soda from the travel plaza's vending machine doesn't count. But RVs usually go well beyond that simple definition, since most are loaded with many of the comforts of home. In fact, for many people RVing means pretty much life as usual, only with changing scenery.

Pull Over

Throughout the course of this book, the term "RV" will be used somewhat generically. Numerous types of RVs exist, in varying sizes, weights, methods of propulsion, room configurations, number of passengers, sleeping arrangements, onboard amenities, self-contained camping features, and cost. It's not uncommon for units to come in more than a dozen floor plans, and options can transform an inexpensive model into a costly one; a modestly appointed RV into a luxurious version.

Lounge about on your couch watching game seven of the NBA Finals. Prepare an ambitious meal in a kitchen equipped with running water, a gas stove, oven, and microwave. Work on your computer, play games, or chat around the dinner table. Feeling chilly? Adjust the thermostat (or put on a sweater, as my wife would say). A tad warm? Flip on the air conditioner and cool down in no time. Thirsty? Grab a beverage from the refrigerator or a glass of water from the kitchen faucet. Sleepy? Retreat to the master bedroom (if so equipped) or pull out the sleeper sofa into a comfy nook. Shower in your very own shower. Use your very own bathroom. Grab your golf clubs or fishing poles (you didn't forget those, did you?) and make a day of it. Not exactly roughin' it, is it?

Many deluxe models boast a list of entertaining options that would make Donald Trump giddy. Rooms may slide in and out at the touch of a button. Global positioning systems track your latest moves; satellite systems make sure you never miss your favorite show again. Multiple televisions, a VCR, and stereo keep you and the family entertained.

As we'll discuss in upcoming chapters, RVs come in all shapes, sizes, and budgets. Floor plans and sleeping capacities vary from model to model and one type of vehicle to the next. Some kinds are suitable to live in full-time, a way of life enjoyed by hundreds of thousands of people all across the country. Others are better utilized for shorter getaways, outfitted with everything to make for memorable trips for you and your family. No matter what your lifestyle, where you plan to go, or who's coming with you, there's a recreational vehicle built for you.

Different Strokes, Different Folks

To understand how and why people RV—and more important, if it's right for you—it's crucial to first learn what RVs are and how they are used. The best way to answer that question is to examine each kind of vehicle and its unique capabilities. Since RVing combines many of the accommodations of a small home, there is no shortage of available choices.

RVs come in two basic categories: motorized and towables. The major difference between these two groups is in the manner of propulsion, namely how you get from place to place.

One for the Road

The first versions of today's recreational vehicles were created in the early 1900s by those dissatisfied with—what else?—the state of commercial travel. Early models were essentially camping paraphernalia laden or pulled by horses. With the invention of the automobile, homemade tent trailers and car tents were created, adding free mobility to the rudimentary design.

Motorized RVs

Want to venture a guess as to what all these kinds of vehicles have in common? That's right, a motor. What gave it away? From the smallest, most entry-level unit to the most grandiose example in the lineup, every motorized RV comes equipped with its very own method for getting around—an engine. It might be a diesel engine or a gasoline version, located in either the front or back of the unit, but by golly, the only thing motorized RVs require to get going is the turn of the key, the right kind of fuel, and you're off.

Motorized RVs offer the noteworthy advantage of having all living and driving functions under one roof, in one vehicle. Unlike owners of towable versions, you will never have to hitch up to another vehicle only to have to unhitch yourself once the destination is reached. This is doubly validating when it's raining outside. Since you're only piloting one vehicle, many drivers find motorized vehicles much easier to navigate than towing a trailer. And with an appropriate hitch and a knowledge of tow ratings and vehicle weights, motorized enthusiasts may have the option to pull a second vehicle, or *dinghy vehicle,* behind their RV.

RVocabulary

A **dinghy vehicle** is a term borrowed from the boating world, used to describe a car or truck pulled behind a motorhome through the use of a tow bar, dolly, or small trailer. It is also known as an auxiliary vehicle and a toad or toad vehicle in some parts.

There are four types, or classes, of RVs within the motorized category: Class A motorhomes, Class B motorhomes, Class C motorhomes, and truck campers.

All of these RVs possess an engine, but after that, differences abound. Factors such as the number of passengers each kind can sleep and transport, onboard amenities, floor plans, sizes, weights, and costs can vary dramatically within the motorized category. The difference between an entry-level truck camper and an extravagant Class A motorhome is as different as choosing between a condo and a stately mansion—the basic living necessities are present but in varying degrees. However, all meet our working definition of a recreational vehicle, with at the very least a place to sleep, cook, and congregate. But rest assured, life onboard is far more interesting than that, as we'll see when we explore each motorized RV at length in Chapter 4, "The World of Motorized RVs." For now, here's a brief look at each.

Class A Motorhomes

The most common and most luxurious RV in the motorhome group, Class As simply have it all. Floor plans include a master bedroom in the rear of the coach, a large kitchen full of cooking appliances and storage for all your foodstuffs and cooking gear, a private bathroom and shower, a living area, and a cockpit where the driver and co-pilot sit.

A conventional Class A motorhome.

(Illustration courtesy of RVIA)

Many models include at least one slide-out, a room that extends outward several feet at the press of a button to expand the interior space; two or three such rooms, found throughout the coach, are becoming more and more common. Further sleeping areas are enabled through convertible sofas; dinette tables and bench seats unfold for additional bedding. Some Class As can accommodate up to eight passengers. Sizes range from 20 to 40 feet in length.

Class B Motorhomes

A van in RV's clothing, Class Bs look like an inflated version of the family van with one major exception—complete livability. These motorhomes might offer a standard queen-size bed or a dinette area that converts into one come nighttime. Some models can sleep up to four in relative comfort. A small kitchen, storage, bathroom and/or shower, and cockpit area take up the rest of the usable space.

A Class B motorhome, also known as a camper van.

(Illustration courtesy of RVIA)

The most versatile offerings in the motorhome class, camper vans, as they are sometimes called, also serve as a reliable everyday vehicle, with sizes averaging approximately 15 feet in length.

Class C Motorhomes

Although alphabetically the last of the three classes of motorhomes, Cs are bigger than Bs, and sometimes cheaper. The hallmark feature is the space hanging over the cab area, which is often used for a sleeping area, entertainment center, or additional storage. Otherwise, these motorhomes are condensed version of larger motorhomes, with everything onboard that the big boys have.

A Class C motorhome, also known as a mini-motorhome.

(Illustration courtesy of RVIA)

Sizes range from 20 to 32 feet, built on a conventional truck chassis with an attached cockpit area. Known also as mini-motorhomes, sleeping capacity can sometimes reach eight and slide-out rooms are fairly standard.

Truck Campers

The least expensive member of the group, truck campers are not bought as much as they are built. Start with a typical pickup truck (maybe even your existing one), add a hard-sided camper shell, and violà, you have a truck camper. The camper portion can be removed when not in use or left affixed to the truck bed for spontaneous getaways.

A typical truck camper.

(Illustration courtesy of RVIA)

Long the favorite of outdoors types for their go-anywhere attitude, truck campers can sleep two to four passengers and come complete with a small cooking area, dinette, storage space, and bathroom and/or shower. With camper attachment, overall size may only be several feet more than your standard pickup truck.

Towable RVs

The major difference between motorized and towable, of course, is that these RVs have no engine, and thus require a tow vehicle to move them around. Believe me, I've looked and there isn't an engine anyplace. Without a secondary vehicle, towable RVs would be about as useful for sightseeing and touring as your first apartment. Thankfully, the towing process is fairly simple, as we'll explore in Chapter 13, "Towin' the Line." And as is the case with motorized RVs, each of the four towable types offers a different set of onboard features and sleeping capacities, depending on size and weight.

Towable RVs require the aid of a tow vehicle to get them from one place to another. Not every kind of truck or automobile will work, however. Tow vehicles must be of a certain size and equipped with an engine and a hitch powerful enough for the job. The same family sedan capable of pulling a small fold-down camper couldn't budge a 20,000-pound fifth-wheel trailer. However, the opposite is true. Large vehicles can tow smaller towables. But more on this in Chapter 13.

Towable RVs enjoy the same levels of popularity as their motorhome brethren do, and many buyers find the lack of self-propulsion (okay, an engine) the most alluring feature. After all, no engine, no engine trouble. Break down in a motorhome and you experience the double unpleasantness of finding your home *and* your wheels in the repair shop. Towables are often cheaper than similarly sized and equipped motorized versions. The absence of a cockpit (who needs one?) even opens up more usable space for storage, a larger bedroom, or added furnishings. Since many folks already own a vehicle suitable for towing (we'll explain matching up your existing vehicles with a towable in Chapter 13), you already might have the perfect tow vehicle in place. Furthermore, once your destination is reached, towable owners can unhitch and head out to explore the area in a fairly mobile second vehicle.

There are four choices in the world of towables: fifth-wheel trailers, travel trailers, lightweight travel trailers, and fold-down campers.

While the manner in which they get from point A to point B is radically different than their motorhome counterparts, life onboard is pretty much the same, depending on the type you choose. Fifth wheels can reach 40 feet in length and outshine most condominiums in terms of luxury appointments, while fold-down campers, the smallest in the group, offer a relatively inexpensive entry into the RV lifestyle, but have all the basic features. We'll examine towable RVs more closely when they take center stage in Chapter 5, "The World of Towables." The following is a brief introduction to each member of the towable family.

RVocabulary

The area of a fifth-wheel trailer that hitches into the bed of a pickup truck or conversion vehicle to make a connection for towing is called a **gooseneck.** Inside, the gooseneck area is raised from the rest of the interior, reached by stairs, and almost always used as the master bedroom.

Fifth-Wheel Trailers

Fifth-wheel trailers, or fifth wheels, are to towables what Class A motorhomes are to motorized. They are the biggest, most expensive, and most well-appointed trailers available. In fact, they're the only RV with two levels, with the bedroom area stationed in the bi-level *gooseneck* area, which affixes to the cargo bed of large pickup trucks or conversion vehicle.

Typical fifth wheels come with deluxe cooking areas, abundant living space, a host of interior and exterior storage compartments, and fancy bathrooms and showers. Cavernous interior heights, multiple slide-out rooms, and large bay windows are also trademark features. Sleeping for as many as eight passengers is possible. Fifth wheels come in lengths ranging from 20 to 40 feet and must be towed by a large pickup truck or conversion vehicle.

A fifth-wheel travel trailer.

(Illustration courtesy of RVIA)

Travel Trailers

Versatile in terms of usage and floor plans, your average travel trailer suits full-time travelers and young families equally well. Sizes range from 12 to 35 feet. They can be equipped with bare-bones necessities in smaller models to luxurious accommodations in larger versions. Slide-outs are common on larger models, which might be able to accommodate up to eight passengers.

A conventional travel trailer.

(Illustration courtesy of RVIA)

Lightweight Travel Trailers

These RVs are lightweight and overall smaller versions of larger trailers. Weighing in at less than 4,000 pounds (we'll talk about the importance of weight in upcoming chapters), these towables are easily transported by many everyday vehicles, including mini-vans, trucks, SUVs, and, in some cases, large sedans. Families enjoy reasonably low starting costs and easy towing. Standard living amenities are provided in lengths ranging from 12 to 25 feet. Sleeping capacity usually ranges from two to six passengers.

A lightweight travel trailer.

(Illustration courtesy of Coachmen Industries)

Fold-Down Campers

Considered the perfect entry into the world of RVing, fold-down campers resemble hard-sided tents, capable of being towed even by smaller trucks and larger cars. Fold-down units, also known as pop-ups, tuck in during transit for aerodynamic travel and easy transport. Once the destination is reached, the unit is manually deployed, usually via a hand crank or with the push of a button, which expands the living space. Two bedding areas bookend a central living and cooking area. These can sleep up to six people.

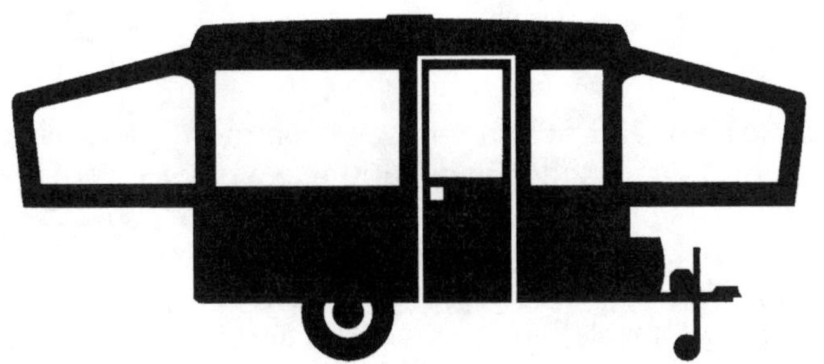

A fold-down camper, also know as a folding camper or pop-up.

(Illustration courtesy of RVIA)

What's in It for Me?

That's the real question, right? What is RVing really about, and is it for me? RV owners reap all the rewards of a home on wheels. You have all your crucial belongings because they travel with you. You sleep in the same bed every night, cut dining costs by cooking in your very own kitchen, and come and go as you please. Even the family dog or cat has a comfy spot to enjoy the ride.

One for the Road

The definition of a "mobile home" is one of the most misunderstood concepts around. Many folks use the term as a blanket reference to all recreational vehicles—after all, they are just that, mobile homes, right? In actuality, mobile homes don't live up to their nimble-sounding name, preferring to settle in one space as a permanent dwelling. Mobile homes are easier to tow than, say, a three-bedroom house, but not much. Like my brother Bruce, they *can* be moved, but get more than a little cranky when asked to do so. With no real get-up-and-go attributes, they fail to meet the RV definition, so let's just move on.

As we said before, RVing is all about choices. If you want to visit relatives in Ottawa, gas up the motorhome and go. Cold weather up north getting you down? Hitch up the trailer and head off in pursuit of sunshine. Always wanted to see the mountains, the desert, where Elvis lived? What's stopping you? Dream of quitting your job and living on the go like an air-conditioned gypsy? No problem. These are just some of the reasons why RVing is so popular. Here's more.

Independence

Trains, planes, buses, and cruise ships all have one thing in common—they leave on *their* schedule, not yours. One of the great advantages of traveling by RV is that you control your own agenda, an impossibility in the busy world of commercial travel. Again, RVing is about going where you want, when you want. Your itinerary is your own and can change on a whim. Want to extend your vacation another day, week, or year? Do it. Want to make your own meals? Put on an apron and pull out a cookbook. Spend a lazy day lounging reading a book, hike the Appalachian Trail, or see the country unfold in the ultimate touring vehicle. There are never any planes to catch, car rentals to return, or hotel check-outs to make or change. In an RV, you are the captain of your ship, your own pilot, the boss.

Togetherness

Spending time with family and friends is probably the reason the cavemen started vacationing in the first place. It's a time to reconnect with your spouse, children, siblings, and pals—not to mention a much-needed break from dodging those nasty T-Rex's and the humdrum of the whole hunting-and-gathering routine. The same is true with RVing, where a day can be as uneventful as sitting around a campfire, cooking s'mores, and watching the sky for shooting stars. Or it can be as jam-packed with side trips, outdoor activities, and a must-see list that would bring the Energizer Bunny to its knees. But in the end, it's about being together. You travel, eat, sleep, and enjoy things together as a family.

Cost

Here's a quick recipe to wind up in the poorhouse. Book expensive seats for your family to fly on its next vacation. Pony up the money for a large rental car, pay for separate rooms for parents and children, and dine out three meals a day. Be sure to add in plane tax, rental tax, food tax, vacation tax, and fun tax. Then just for kicks, throw in round-trip cab rides to and from the airport, generous tips for all those folks who helped you along the way, and the expense of shipping that replica of the world's largest ball of twine back home to Uncle Phil. While no one would argue RVing is inexpensive—after all, you're going to actually have to buy or rent some kind of vehicle—over time the savings can be dramatic. It also affords families choices—choices that can save big dollars over the course of many years' worth of adventures.

Road Scholar

There are many ways for RVers to save money on the road. Joining any number of travel or camping clubs entitles members to discounts on everything from overnight stays to fuel to RV insurance. Some campground franchises, such as Kampgrounds of America (KOA) and Yogi Bear's Jellystone Parks, offer discounts for repeat guests. Large gas station chains grant reduced fees for frequent fill-ups for their members. A full list of clubs can be found in Appendix A, "Resources."

Meal Deal

A lot of well-intentioned families spend piles of rainy-day money eating at restaurants while away from home. Eating out is great and exciting, but most vacationers don't have another choice. After all, most major hotels don't appreciate your attempts to barbecue in the master suite.

Don't believe eating out is all that expensive? Just do the math. Multiply the number of travelers by the cost of an average meal. Be sure to factor in the two desserts Aunt Martha always orders (who invited her, anyway?). Multiply that number times three for each meal of the day. Now factor in how many days you'll be away from home. Getting expensive, isn't it? That pain you're now experiencing in your chest is nothing like the overwhelming dread you'll feel upon returning home from your trip with credit card statements piled up like floats in the Rose Bowl parade.

What if you could cut costs by preparing some of your own meals, in your very own kitchen? Of course, we all know that preparing your own meals is cheaper than eating out (thank you, home ec). Prior to departure, the frugal RVer has already stocked up his or her pantry and refrigerator with a host of goodies to feed the troops. Meals are prepared onboard with the help of (in most cases), a stove, oven, microwave, running water, and space for all your cooking gear. Or head outside and grill out on your campsite's barbecue underneath the stars, or over the campfire. Of course, RVers can go out to dinner if they prefer, but the point is that they don't have to. Again, it's all about choices. And won't you enjoy yourself just a little more, secure in the knowledge that your vacation doesn't mean the children are forced to sell their shoes for college?

Hotel Hijinks

Lodging is the single greatest threat to any vacation budget. Even inexpensive motels can near $100 per room during a busy season; more if you really want to live it up in nice accommodations. Even if the whole family shares one room (your teenagers will love that), costs still proliferate. You do know it's not right to save money by sneaking the kids in the overnight bag, right?

One of the great benefits of RVing is that your bed travels with you. For many travelers, this alone is the justification to run down to their local RV dealer and purchase a new motorhome. Say good-bye to the lumpy, unyielding mattresses of your typical motel room, stocked with pillows that are too hard, too soft, too old, and blankets and sheets that might catch fire if you rub your legs together. After a long day of sightseeing, driving, or just taking it easy at the beach or around the campfire, RV owners are greeted by their very own bed, and in most cases their very own private bedroom, onboard.

Even the plushest RV resort, complete with pool, spa, manicured grounds, and a list of activities that would put the Love Boat to shame, rarely exceeds $40 per night.

And that's per campsite, not per person—meaning you only pay one modest fee. Did we mention that your campsite just may very well be overlooking majestic mountains, beachside with ocean views, or nestled amongst towering pines? Most campground stays cost between $20 and $35, depending on season, number of hookups (more on those later), and location. That number drops if you stay in a federally owned park such as those found at Yellowstone or the Grand Tetons. So let Bobby out of your duffel bag, okay?

Tickets, Please

The airport can be an expensive place. In the span of 50 yards, you've already dished out money to the cabby for the ride in, tipped the baggage handlers for making sure your luggage doesn't end up in Dubuque, and left your nest egg at the ticket counter in exchange for four tickets to Reno. No wonder your credit cards look so haggard. Luxury cruises and train tickets aren't cheap, either, which makes getting away more and more expensive.

If you're searching for the least expensive way to travel, there's no cheaper method than towing a fold-down camper. A family has everything onboard to make for memorable camping adventures—cooking functions, sleeping for four to six people, heating and cooling control, a place to relax—and all for less than the cost of a week at Disney World, mouse ears not included.

Commercial Break

Your flight gets delayed and is then suddenly cancelled. The hotel lost your reservation and your suite with a queen-sized bed and an ocean view is now a rickety cot next to the boiler room. The rental car costs how much? Where exactly are your bags? Can you possibly stand another night on Aunt Edna's couch? This vacation's costing you a fortune! The family's stressed out and no one's talking. You wish you had your own things—your dependable pillow, the sweater you forgot to pack, your autographed picture of Ernest Borgnine.

And I'll bet whoever said that getting there is half the fun never sat with their knees tucked underneath their chin stuck in economy class, eating day-old corn nuts and discussing industrial cleaning with that fabric softener salesperson from Omaha. They were probably never stuck in an airport for hours at a time, shuttled around like cattle from gate to gate, or forced to take out a second mortgage to pay for tickets for the family. Let's face it, getting there is often the worst part, full of unpredictability, sometimes outrageous expenses, and very little choices. But it doesn't have to be.

RVing provides a stable environment with only the landscapes outside subject to change. No matter where you go, you're home—same bed, same refrigerator stocked with all your favorites (yes, your wife remembered the Cheese Whiz), same TV to watch the football game. And you never, ever run the risk of getting bumped from this trip. That is, unless you forgot your anniversary again.

Comfort

Your husband's nodding off again, sprawled out like something out of a Rorschach Test on the couch. When is he going to wake up to put the steaks on the grill? The kids have reached a truce, enjoying a board game at the dinette table. Rex, the wonder dog, is curled up in the back bedroom, hoping no one will notice him burrowed underneath the blankets. You feel refreshed after that hot shower and are ready for a book or perhaps a check of your e-mail or maybe some TV in the back bedroom. A typical scene inside a recreational vehicle in Anytown, USA. Traveling by recreational vehicle is like owning a separate vacation home in every place you want to visit.

The Great Outdoors

Sure, the Discovery Channel is nice, but there's no substitute for seeing the real thing—nature in all its splendor. There's simply no better way to experience the profound impact of Maine's Acadia National Park or the breathtaking views of the Grand Canyon than by camping there in an RV. Your plans don't have to be that grand (pun intended) to see nature in all its glory. A short trip to your nearby state park or a rustic campground set amongst the trees is an easy way to shake off the hectic trappings of city life. An average weekend camping trip boasts more nature than most children see in a year's worth of cable TV. Sadly, our chances to observe wildlife in its natural environment (your brother-in-law, Joby, doesn't count) are becoming increasingly rare. Varieties of wondrous trees and plants, a spring-fed stream, mountains, and valleys void of development need to be experienced, and camping in the middle of it gives you a front-row seat.

Pull Over

There's a good reason why transporting passengers inside a moving trailer is against the law in many states. It's unsafe. Accidents happen, and passengers won't have time to react in case of sudden stops or quick turns, not to mention that general sway and bumps make for a very turbulent atmosphere inside. Towable travelers should always ride in the tow vehicle. Although its tempting to move about in your motorized RV while in transit, don't.

Easy as You Please

Race home from work on Friday night, load up the motorhome, organize the kids, wake the dog, grab a map, and head out to a weekend retreat. Wake up early, hitch up the trailer to the SUV, stop for groceries (yes, beef jerky counts), and start your vacation off on your terms. There are more than 2.4 million miles of paved roads, 16,000 private and public campgrounds, and hundreds of millions of acres to camp in the United States. I'll bet there's even a few greasy spoons along the way—and maybe a few interesting diversions. You don't want to ignore all of them, do you?

RVing is easy (or hopefully it will be when you've finished with this book). Just like your family car, you can keep your RV nearby, for whenever the need for adventure strikes. Some small towables and motorized models can fit in your garage or can be parked on your property. Large motorhomes and trailers can be stored in numerous RV storage facilities or your favorite campground, awaiting your arrival. Life is hard enough; your leisure shouldn't have to be.

Pull Over

Contact your city officials to find out if you can legally store your RV on your property. Some ordinances prohibit this practice, citing obstructed views and potential eyesores as the reasons. It's best to know beforehand if your RV is welcomed in your community or if other provisions for your vehicle must be made.

Special Needs

For the more than 50 million Americans struggling with disabilities or mobility issues, traveling by "conventional means" can be a daunting task. While ramps, automatic doors, and accessible bathrooms are common fixtures in public facilities, there is still a big world that doesn't always acknowledge the plight of those with any form of handicap. A doorway that's too narrow to accommodate a wheelchair, a bed that's too high or low for those suffering from crippling back pain, a staircase impossible to climb for those with debilitating arthritis—these are the kinds of unpredictable obstacles faced by those venturing into unfamiliar environments, challenges that can often curb the enthusiasm of even the most eager traveler.

For more and more folks, the reliable confines of an RV present a useful alternative. Some manufacturers can custom design and build a vehicle to a customer's exact specifications, complete with wheelchair ramps and lifts, roll-in showers, lowered appliances and cabinetry, and special driving mechanisms—even in-ceiling tracks to help passengers in and out of bed and around the coach.

What Can I Expect?

RVing can be unpredictable—if you want it to be. Just pick a point on the map and go. Damn the torpedoes, full speed ahead. If spontaneity is your thing, traveling by RV is a great way to be footloose and fancy-free, with your roving home along for the ride. But mostly, you can probably expect what you expected (sounds like something Yogi Berra might say, doesn't it?).

You might choose to visit relatives in Albany, walk the beaches of the Gulf Coast, or look for UFOs in Roswell. Spend the night in a serene campground, your favorite state or national park, a plush, five-star RV resort, or a place in the wild no one's ever been before. Even spend a few nights camped out in your in-laws' driveway or the local hotel if you want to.

Wake up camped out next to the pounding surf without owning a Malibu beach house. Enjoy the summits at 10,000 feet without the cost of an expensive mountain-top retreat. Tailgate with buddies before kickoff at the Penn State football game. Tour the beautiful backroads of America. Visit historical sites and enough must-see diversions to fill a hundred tour books. Live year-round in your rolling condo. RVers journey to every corner of North America—and beyond, if that's your thing. They visit friends and relatives, head south for the winter, or take day trips with their children. If you can plan it, you can do it. Repeat with me: RVing is all about choices.

The Least You Need to Know

- A "recreational vehicle" must have three basic criteria: a place to sleep, cooking facilities, and a living area—but most go well beyond that.
- Motorized RVs include Class A motorhomes, Class B motorhomes, Class C motorhomes, and truck campers. Towable RVs include fifth-wheel trailers, travel trailers, lightweight travel trailers, and fold-down campers.
- Varying floor plans, sizes, weights, methods of propulsion, onboard amenities, sleeping capacities, and costs mean every RV is different.
- RVers enjoy all sorts of advantages in terms of traveling and living onboard their vehicles. The biggest perk is the ability to go where they want, when they want. Cost, time spent with family, avoiding the hassles of commercial travel, and the option of a specially built vehicle for those with special needs are just some of the noteworthy advantages.
- Life in a recreational vehicle is what you make of it. The spirit of the traveler is much more impactful than the size of his or her budget when it comes to planning one's adventures.

Chapter 2

Who RVs?

In This Chapter

- The types of people who travel by RV
- The kinds of trips you can take
- Special licenses and restrictions for RVing

A young family, tired of cold and soggy nights spent roughin' it inside their tent, upgrades their camping adventures to a small fold-down trailer. A husband and wife quit their jobs, sell the house, and live onboard their RV year-round, going wherever their fancy takes them. A dedicated angler sets out on an early morning expedition, her truck camper loaded with fishing gear. A disabled traveler purchases a specially equipped camper van to take the unpredictability out of his travels. A family loads up the motorhome for a visit to Washington, D.C., the Florida Keys, or Las Vegas, and possibly all three.

You're probably now wondering if RVing is really for you. Perhaps you can't picture yourself behind the wheel of a large motorhome or speeding off to some weekend retreat with the kids and a trailer in tow. RV enthusiasts vary as much as the kinds of recreational vehicles built to take them where they want to go. People of all ages, backgrounds, and income levels enjoy this lifestyle, going where they want, when they want. But one thing is for sure, RVing is definitely not just for grandpa and grandma anymore.

There are nearly 10 million RVs on the roads of America today, and travelers represent lifestyles and histories too diverse to neatly categorize. As we'll examine in this chapter, RVing is for everyone.

Who's Doin' It?

Who's not? Many people are finding that traveling by motorhome or towing a trailer offers the kinds of qualities missing from vacations of old or simply lost in commercial travel. Retirees are flocking to RVs in the same numbers as couples with young children. Some folks stay in their vehicles full-time, while others hit the road only on weekends or for short vacations. Recreational vehicle manufacturers are doing their part by creating products for every need—basic or luxurious, expensive or inexpensive, capable of sleeping eight or just you and your spouse. The lifestyle is open to everyone.

The RV industry is coming off one of its best years in its 60-plus-year history, capping a recent growth boom. Orders for vehicles are up, campgrounds report brisk business during the summer and holidays, and RV wannabes are lured to dealers' lots and rental units by favorable publicity throughout much of the media. Otherwise, you might not be reading this book, wondering if RVing is indeed for you.

Pull Over

Some people believe RVing is for them and spontaneously buy an RV, sell all their earthly possessions, and hit the road—all without ever trying it out first. This is a dicey proposition. Make sure you like it—really like it—before making any major lifestyle changes.

The future of RVing looks equally promising. The baby boomer effect (the endearing name given to those born between 1946 and 1964, comprising 30 percent of the U.S. population) is only just starting to be felt, with more and more couples swarming over RV lots with disposable income and a burgeoning case of wanderlust. Retirees, many of whom are quitting their jobs at younger ages than ever before, have the time, money, and desire to hit the road and see what RVing is all about. Existing RV owners are trading up to larger models, just as they would their automobiles. However, it's an infusion of younger buyers that is reshaping the marketplace. More and more families are renting RVs, only to turn around and buy a small unit later on. A University of Michigan study revealed that nearly one in five households queried said they intended to purchase an RV someday.

All Aboard

If you're curious about the RV lifestyle, there's no reason to sit on the sidelines—get out there and do it. Vehicles are built for every type of traveler in mind, from the retired couple looking to spend their "golden years" in style, to the newlyweds who want to camp out in the boonies—and everyone in between. There's certainly no shortage of exciting places to go, people to visit, and things to do. And once there, there are thousands of campgrounds catering to a wide range of guests, with activities and facilities for every budget, every need, and every kind of traveler. In short, RVing is for everyone. Here's a closer look at some of the groups who make up the industry.

Small Start-Ups

One for the Road

More than 321,000 RVs were built and shipped in 1999, exceeding a total value of $10.4 billion. It was the highest margin of new vehicles ordered since 1978.

Admit it, you think RVing is just for senior citizens, don't you? Perhaps you fear that by joining their ranks, you'll spend slow-motion weekends playing bingo and swapping recipes for peanut brittle. At one time that might have been a fairly accurate portrayal of your typical RV traveler, but not anymore. Buyers are getting younger.

Would you believe that according to a study conducted by the University of Michigan, nearly half of this country's RV owners are between the ages of 35 and 54? And that number is expected to rise, thanks to the driving force (pun intended) from curious baby boomers, aggressive public relations efforts by the industry, and a more diverse line of vehicles from manufacturers. More and more families are realizing that for the modest investment of a small trailer or camper, their traveling and camping adventures can improve dramatically. Furthermore, with the unbelievable popularity of sport utility vehicles (SUVs), medium-size trucks, and mini-vans, most folks already own a likely tow vehicle, making the purchase of a towable RV more appealing—and less expensive.

It doesn't take a young couple with small children long to realize the benefits of a fully self-contained vehicle. Pulling a small trailer means that a comfortable bed is just feet away for unscheduled naps or nighty-night time. An onboard kitchen, with a refrigerator, pantry, range, sink, and microwave oven takes the logistical nightmares out of eating meals and snacks out away from home. The communal living area is suitable for relaxing, playing games, or just reconnecting with one another. All this and heat when it's cold, air conditioning when the temperature soars, and no shortage of onboard diversions to choose from. Can your tent or rental car do all that?

Howdy, Pard'ner

If it's true that the couples who play together stay together, then RVing qualifies as a genuine marriage re-vitalizer. Gas up the mini-motorhome, grab the travel atlas, and find yourself some adventure. Hitch up the travel trailer to the back of the SUV, point south, and go. Whether you're an active pair interested in hiking, boating, or snowmobiling, or simply looking for a quiet weekend retreat away from it all, the RV lifestyle is a perfect fit. By day you enjoy the perks of a mobile vacation home. Come nightfall, slip inside your queen-size bed, watch television, shower, prepare meals, send e-mails, or whatever. And since there's only two of you, any type of RV will work great, providing plenty of elbow room and creature comforts.

One for the Road

During the 1920s, four prominent Americans, Thomas Edison, Henry Ford, Harvey Firestone, and John Burroughs, enjoyed RVing together and became known as the "four vagabonds."

Hyper Active

Rock climbers need mountains, hikers need trails, and surfers most definitely need a good set of waves—or at least, a lot of space at the water park. Unfortunately, these locales are not always close by or easy to get to. And once there, the thought of staying at the local bed and breakfast might stifle your endorphin high just a tad. The choice of a four-wheel drive motorhome or conversion van can usually reach any of these off-the-path destinations. Or your turf-crunching SUV with trailer can provide a base camp for all sorts of interesting pursuits. RVs serve as the total package for adventure-seekers.

Retirees

Like RVers, retirees now come in all shapes and sizes. It could be the guy who took his Internet stock public or the couple living on a pension. People are retiring younger and younger, thanks to 401(k)s, an investing mindset, and that pile of Mickey Mantle baseball cards in the basement. It's not just the senior circuit now who's enjoying the good life. Of course, older travelers are still a mainstay in the industry. They finally have the time to take it easy, travel, and enjoy themselves without a schedule, boss, or teenagers. And they realize that RVing is a good way to do it.

Many retirees spend the rest of their lives traveling by RV. Others decide to try full-timing for a while, living in different parts of the country, or constantly staying on the go. Maybe they're scoping out locations for their true "retirement" or just collecting all the life experiences that their former 40-hour work week wouldn't afford them. Skip the long winters and frolic on the beaches of southern Florida. Visit the grandkids—all of them—at various points across the country. Caravan with friends up to Alaska, Baja, or even trips through Europe—and beyond.

All in the Family

Like Patton marching through Western Europe, vacationing with a large family can be a logistical nightmare. Planning (and paying) for everyone to enjoy a peaceful trip together and all the arrangements of traveling, eating, and sleeping that goes along with it are not for the squeamish. It's no wonder that RVing is popular with larger families, eager to rely on the known element of a stable number of beds, a stocked refrigerator, a full shower/bathroom, and plenty of usable space to make their time together easier. Larger motorhomes and fifth-wheel trailers can easily sleep six (up to eight in some models), and a sleeping bag or two on the floor increases the number of potential passengers that much more. Slide-out rooms expand the living space once the destination is reached so everyone has claim to some space. A roving vehicle means a loose itinerary, perfect for groups where reaching a consensus on anything is like a lost episode of *Mission: Impossible.*

Motor Heads

Winter comes and you have to put your Harley away. The weather warms and there's no longer any place to take your snowmobile. The in-laws want their lake house back, and your jet ski days are rudely interrupted. But what if you could enjoy these pastimes year-round or take them out to new landscapes for a whole new slate of adventures?

A relatively new crop of *sport utility trailers* (*SUTs*) feature an interior cargo area for transporting all your toys—motorcycles, jet skis, snowmobiles, dune buggies, ATVS, canoes—you name it. A deployable ramp makes for easy loading, and a quick way to hit the trails, surf, or wherever the thrills lie. Ever dreamed of taking the dirt bike to the desert or the kayak to the Gulf Coast? This kind of RV not only gets you there but also all your fun toys, too. Life onboard still features full living comforts, so you don't have to sacrifice living to make room for your pair of scooters.

RVocabulary

Sport utility trailers (SUTs) are towable RVs with a ramp and special cargo space for smaller motorized vehicles, such as jet skis, motorcycles, and snowmobiles. These are also known as sport patio-haulers or toy box models. Motorized versions exist as well. The rest of the RV still possesses plenty of room for living, sleeping, and cooking.

Or if you'd rather, many motorized RVs are capable of towing at least a small trailer, loaded with a boat, motorcycles, or whatever you can't live without. A speedboat behind the Class A motorhome? His and her jet skis towed by the camper van? Canoes for four, courtesy of a hard-working truck camper and a smaller trailer? Now enthusiasts can match their hobby with an easy way to get there.

Disabled Travelers

A host of manufacturers and retrofitting services can put those with mobility issues into a customized motorhome, van, or trailer. Vehicles can be built from the ground up, taking into consideration the buyer's exact needs and challenges. A less expensive method is to take an existing model and alter its features for easy access and adjusted living appointments. Either way, many of the estimated 2 percent of disabled RVers find the lifestyle accommodating.

Take, for example, the story of the husband and wife who loved to travel, especially if it meant a chance to watch the drag races in person. The fact that he was a quadriplegic, making it nearly impossible for him to get in and out of a conventional bed, shower, or bathroom without a lift system, forced the couple to drive back home every night. As a rule, they never ventured more than six hours away from home. That was until they bought their first accessible RV, with an in-ceiling tracking system, wheelchair lift, and roll-in bathroom and showers.

Pet-Lovers

Many consider their dog, cat, or pot-bellied pig an integral part of the family. After all, who else is going to chase away all your important packages from the UPS carrier or lick your face at 5 A.M. for breakfast? Just as you would never want to leave a child at home while you're off cavorting on vacation, there are those who will do whatever they can to make sure their pets come, too. (Okay, maybe I cried until I was breathless the first time I boarded my beagle. So what's your point?)

Pull Over

Pet policies vary from place to place. While many campgrounds allow well-behaved pets, most insist they are not to be left unattended, are picked up after, and remain on a leash at all times. Pets might incur an extra per-day fee. Check to make sure your next stop is pet-friendly ahead of time to avoid any surprises.

If you enjoy driving with a hound snoozing next to you in the passenger's seat, it's your choice. Like having the cat keeping your pillow warm for you? Great! Can't start your day without your parakeet singing "The Man from La Mancha"? Who can? Your RV, your rules. Just don't let your Boston Terrier, "T-Bone," work the pedals, okay? Most campgrounds permit pets, assuming they're not a disturbance—or lick *the campground owner's* face at 5 A.M. when they want to eat. Be sure to follow the standard protocol of picking up after your animals and keeping them on leashes. In some cases, dog runs are provided so your pooch can take you on your walk.

Where the Wild Things Are

It's been raining all afternoon and your camping trip is starting to resemble a scene out of *The Poseidon Adventure*. Your socks are soaking wet and now you're really miserable. The kids are fighting—ah, teenagers. Jake's mad because you couldn't fit his skateboard; Kaylee's upset because she can't watch TV, curl her hair, or e-mail the teen idol du jour. Even the family's hulking sport utility vehicle couldn't begin to fit everything your tenting trips need these days. Camping was never this difficult when the kids were small.

Camping at one of this country's thousands of state or national parks doesn't have to mean tent camping. Sure, it was great when the kids were little, but at some point sleeping on the ground lost a lot of its appeal. And, oh those freezing nights and lost days waiting for the rain to stop. RVs are as welcomed on our government lands as the bears, coyotes, and your Uncle Cutty. Wouldn't you rather treat yourself to a night in a real bed, dependable meals in your own kitchen, all in a comfort-controlled RV?

Snowbirds

One for the Road

Our National Park System is comprised of 380 historic sites, seashores, forests, and protected lands of all distinctions. More than 287,000,000 people visited them last year alone.

Like your Uncle Maury, snowbirds hate winter. The thought of freezing temperatures, shoveling snow, and spending another six months in mock hibernation are about as appealing to these folks as, well, shoveling snow in freezing temperatures. You get the picture. So, when the thermometer up north begins to drop faster than a panicky day on Wall Street, snowbirds vanish—loading up their RVs in favor of warmer climates, just like other birds of a feather. They might choose to spend six months sitting out winter at a Florida RV resort or busy themselves sun-tanning, star-gazing, and tofu-eating in Southern California. Or perhaps they'll try a little bit of both.

Snowbirds might travel toward their warm-weather destination in their own RV or rent a unit at their destination to stay in prior to departure. In either case, don't expect to see them back home until spring, when the weather is more suitable to their tastes. Since their travels might have them away from home for up to six months, snowbirds are most often retirees, or folks who take up a second vocation at their destination.

Worker Bees

Know the salesperson who keeps saying "My car is my office," or the woman who travels so much for work that you send her mail addressed to her license plate? Perhaps it's time for an upgrade. Why not put your office on wheels for real, with an RV built for the business traveler in mind? Instead of a "recreational vehicle," we can call it a "vocational vehicle." There are a number of motorhomes and conversion vans not much bigger than some of those trucks or SUVs you see—and every bit as drivable. But the big difference is they can be equipped with a computer station, fax machine, phone and modem hookups, and a host of career-friendly options. And, of course, you won't have to curl up in the backseat of your Subaru to sleep for a power nap before the big meeting. It's a good idea to ask your boss *before* you list a motorhome on your expense report, however.

An RV built for business may help keep the family together, instead of only seeing Mom or Dad on weekends due to a long commute or assignments that take them away from home. Artists might travel from show to show in a recreational vehicle, which offers an unrivaled mix of livability and a place for all their wares. An RV

Road Scholar

Manufacturers, such as Winnebago Industries, can custom equip an RV for companies or business travelers. These rolling offices might feature a conference table and chairs, computer workstations, phone and fax lines, as well as places to relax when the job is done. Fleetwood Enterprises developed the Smart Room, which converts from a bed to an office work space at the touch of a button.

One for the Road

NASCAR is the fastest-growing sport in America and a big hit with scores of RVers. There are many groups who follow the Bush and Winston Cup circuit from track to track in their RVs, caravanning to the next race, and camping out at the local facilities.

might become a traveling shop or business. Performers and vendors of all kinds realize that their vehicle, as well as its ability to transport their roving inventory, is indispensable to their way of life—not to mention a much-needed oasis from groupies. It's no wonder RVs are relied upon by actors, musicians, and NASCAR racers for their very livelihood.

Athletic Supporters

Take a look in the parking lot of your favorite college or professional sports team and what do you see? No, not the pummeling of the visiting team's mascot. RVs. Usually lots of them. You'll find them parked next to the fanatics in face paint, toasting sports legends of the past with a mighty skewer, grilling a wonderful concoction of pork and more pork. Certifiable sports nuts may quarrel over who to cheer for, but how to truly enjoy their pastime is never a debate. A fully stocked vehicle, loaded with tailgating goodies such as outside entertainment centers, a refrigerator full of typical parking lot fare, and plenty of storage space for chairs, grills, and the lucky Vince Lombardi shrine gives these folks plenty to cheer about—maybe even Bengals' fans.

In a roving fan base, you can travel with your team, devoting weekends to the everlovin' pursuit of football or the sport of the season. Never miss a game, never miss a meal. When the contest's over, throw the motorhome into gear and head on back home. Or live it up in the parking lot until the opposing team comes looking for you. In this case, lock the door and hide.

Hobby Time

Sometimes you just have to go where the action is. For example, for a Civil War buff, reading about Lee and Grant only takes you so far. What you really want is to see it for yourself. Every battlefield, every historic point of interest, like pages in a history book, unfold on trips and tours to the places where it all actually occurred, Antietam, Bull Run, Gettysburg. And an RV is the perfect way to enjoy this kind of extended trip.

Racing fans, staking out front-row spots in the infield of Talladega, Watkins Glen, or Daytona speedways, understand that watching the races on ESPN comes in a distant second when compared to seeing the action in person. It's no wonder that hordes of RVers tour right along with their racing heroes like one big racing caravan. The same could be said of bird-watchers, music-lovers, golfers, those interested in observing the foliage change, or any other circuit that caters to a passionate clientele.

Types of Travel

Hopefully, you're getting the picture that there is no right way or wrong way to enjoy your recreational vehicle. And that's the beauty of it. You never know who might be parked in the RV next door. It could be a family of eight on their way to the amusement park, a husband and wife revisiting their childhood, or a single woman on her way to Canada for a look around. The tales around the campfire come from every point of origin, every possible perspective. But the one thing each traveler has in common is the desire to take control, to pioneer his or her own trips, to create choices where there weren't ones before.

Most recreational vehicles are fully self-contained, complete with bathrooms, kitchens, and sleeping for the whole gang. They are capable of lasting extended lengths of time, for different purposes. And enthusiasts challenge that notion, using their vehicles for a variety of trips and duration. Some are prepped to work just as well in tough winter climes as on a beautiful summer day. Hundreds of thousands of people even live in their RVs full-time, opting for the freedom of a mobile existence. As you'll see in the following sections, there is no shortage of ways to enjoy this most unique, freeing way of life.

Day Trippers

Day trips are a great way to break your life's routine without spending a fortune or staying away from home too long. While most RVs work great for longer trips, they are equally useful for shorter getaways. There's simply no greater tailgating vehicle at the football game or better way to transport the kids to soccer practice than by a camper van or small motorhome. RVs serve as a wonderful base camp to take to the beach, a state park for a picnic, or even to grandma's house for the holidays. Maybe there's an art show or antique fair that you're dying to see—get there in style and comfort in your RV. And bringing home your white elephants is a whole lot easier than strapping them to the top of your Honda Accord.

Weekend Warriors

This is the most common type of trip for many people with careers and children. Again, this is what RVs were designed to do—get you away from it all for a few nights, no matter where the destinations lead you. And, since you're totally self-sufficient, just plan the day, pack the motorhome or trailer, gas up, and go. It sure beats piling into the station wagon, kids lumped one on top of the other, suitcases tied to the top of the car, doling out extravagant amounts of money for hotel rooms and countless meals out. Most medium-size motorhomes or trailers should be able to comfortably sleep at least four (two adults, two children) and possess enough storage, interior space, and cooking areas to make for memorable trips for families.

We're Not in Kansas Anymore

Two weeks of vacation per year just won't do it for some. Two to three months, now that's more like it. Extended travelers might want to spend a summer visiting every major league baseball park, visiting old college buddies, or soaking in the glamour of the Gulf Coast during the wintertime. These folks might be teachers, entrepreneurs, or retirees who want to spend some time away, and now have the time to do it.

Most RVs will facilitate living for several months onboard, depending on what you're willing to put up with. Some folks may find a small trailer or motorhome much too small for weeks spent living onboard, while others learn to make due with less. We'll explain how to select the right vehicle for you in Chapter 6, "Narrowing Down Your Choices."

Road Scholar

Since their RV is their home 365 days per year, the preferred vehicle of choice for full-timers is usually a large Class A motorhome, 30-plus-foot travel trailer, or larger fifth-wheel trailer, with the mantra being the more space, the better.

Full-Timers

These folks are serious about their travel—they live and travel in their RV year-round. In some cases, full-timers have quit their jobs or retired, sold or stored most of their possessions, bought an RV, and hit the road in search of adventure—or at least to answer the question of what's around the next bend. Or perhaps, a couple might have taken a leave of absence, keeping a residence until their wanderlust wears off. Since space is an issue, full-timers usually prefer a large motorhome or fifth-wheel trailer (more on these in Chapters 4, "The World of Motorized RVs," and 5, "The World of Towables"), providing plenty of storage and elbow room for all their adventures.

Full-timers may be constantly on the move, or may have settled down in a nice cushy spot where the weather is nice and the views are even better. They might continue to work, finding odd jobs in the places they go, or perhaps are able to continue their careers with e-mail, a computer, and a cellular phone. But basically, they're just like the rest of us, except they're truly mobile.

Full-timers are usually older, with enough savings to facilitate their newfound lifestyle, but more and more preretirees are opting for this way of life. A host of mail-forwarding services, automatic bill-paying software, and the trusty cell phone help acclimate their life as much as possible.

Restrictions

With all this talk describing the types of people who can and should RV, what about those who can't? Well, frankly, I haven't seen many of 'em. As previously proclaimed proudly, RVing is for everyone. I've witnessed every conceivable type of person, from all walks of life, come out of a recreation vehicle. People in wheelchairs, the ultra-wealthy, a husband and wife with seven kids, celebrities, my parents, a couple leading a pack of schnauzers headed to a dog show—even the little old lady from Pasadena, I suspect. If you can drive, you can travel by RV. And if you can't drive, find someone who can, and then you're off.

But this rosy picture can sometimes become clouded with a few vehicle restrictions imposed in a few places in the United States. RVs of certain lengths or widths may be in violation of state laws in some areas, but these cases are infrequent and usually only involve the very largest models available. We'll discuss possible legislative issues in Chapter 6.

As for drivers who have their doubts, read on. True, some folks just don't feel comfortable behind the wheel of a larger motorhome or towing a lengthy trailer. Others may have physical limitations that challenge this notion further. And, yes, there are a handful of states that might require something more than your regular driver's license to operate a big rig. Here's a rundown of possible exceptions to the RVing-is-for-everyone rule.

License to Chill

One of the great misconceptions about RV travel is the myth that a special driver's license is required. For the vast majority of RV owners, this simply isn't true. Your regular driver's license, the one you diligently earn every four years down at the DMV, is good for the operation of nearly every kind of recreational vehicle. However, at this time, there is one notable exception.

It might be necessary for owners of motorhomes rated to carry more than 26,000 pounds or tow vehicle/trailer combinations exceeding 26,000 pounds to take an additional written and/or skills test in some states. A motorhome that weighty would be among the very largest and most extravagant Class As offered, costing hundreds of thousands of dollars, and often nearing or exceeding 40 feet in length. (We'll examine weights and what they mean in Chapter 15, "How Much Does Your RV Weigh?") Unless you're anxious to take the helm of the very biggest of the big rigs, these laws simply don't apply to you.

Pull Over

Laws change, so it might be a good idea to check with your local DMV prior to purchasing a recreational vehicle to determine if any special licenses are required.

Driver's Ed

Think of driving a recreational vehicle as similar to watching a familiar movie in another language: Everything looks basically the same, but you'll need to concentrate a little harder to follow along. You're probably not going to see much if anything new in a motorhome's cockpit or behind the wheel of a large tow vehicle that you haven't seen before. You still steer with the wheel, brake and accelerate via pedals, and follow the same driving procedures as everyone else. However, operating a sizable motorhome or towing a large trailer requires more of you than your average trip to the mini-mart in your compact car. You will probably need to exert a little more muscle to maneuver, react more quickly to slow the larger loads, and muster up greater patience and poise during heavy traffic or rush hour. We'll discuss RV towing and driving practices in Chapters 13, "Towin' the Line," and 14, "Drive Time."

If you're in good health, drive with awareness, and don't have mobility issues that might make operating a recreational vehicle difficult, then nothing's stopping you. Hit the road and have fun. As mentioned before, many retrofitting services can outfit your rig with hand brakes and various controls to counter any disability or muscular weakness, opening up the world of RVing to more and more people.

The Least You Need to Know

- RVing is for everyone. Approximately 30 million people enjoy traveling and living in recreational vehicles, including small and large families, young couples and retirees, active and passive travelers alike.
- The RV lifestyle lends itself to any number of trips, from spontaneous weekend getaways to year-round living, also referred to as "full-timing."
- A special driver's license is rarely necessary to operate an RV. The one exception is a limited number of states requiring a special written and/or skills tests to operate RVs with weight capacities exceeding 26,000 pounds. Check with your local DMV to see if your state is one of them.

Chapter 3

Where to Stay?

In This Chapter

- Choices of where to stay and why
- Costs, recreation, services, and facilities offered
- What you can expect

Since your RV already comes with places to sleep, the question is not so much where to stay but rather where to park. Do you want to spend the night in a campground with water, electricity, and sewer hookups for all your onboard functions, or would you rather head out into the boonies, living off your vehicle's generator, batteries, and holding tanks? Do you want a full-service RV resort complete with cable TV, phone service, and days spent golfing, playing tennis, or hot-tubbing, or would you prefer the modest charms of a Ma and Pa campground in a rustic setting? Or maybe you'd like the low costs and big views found on government-owned lands in a state or national park. Of course, nothing's stopping you from parking the motorhome at the nearest hotel and spending the night there. In an RV the choice is yours, and you will always have plenty of accommodations to choose from.

No matter where you RV in this country, there's always going to be a place to stay. With more than 16,000 available campgrounds, and perhaps millions of suitable campsites, RV travelers can be as picky as they want to be in terms of where they stay. But just as nights in bed and breakfasts, hotels, motels, or curled up in a sleeping bag on the floor of your Aunt Bitsy's living room vary, so do campgrounds. Costs, amenities, recreation, services, sizes, settings, and clientele vary, too. And since where you stay determines a lot about any given trip, it's important you know what kinds of lodging are available.

Campgrounds

A campground is the preferred choice for overnight stopovers or extended stays for most RVers. Makes sense, doesn't it? After all, who better to cater to the unique needs of someone in a 40-foot motorhome or a travel trailer with three slide-out rooms and a tow vehicle than someone who understands the industry and those who enjoy it. Like recreational vehicles themselves, campgrounds differ in many ways. This relative unpredictability is part of what makes RVing so exciting. Of course, it also presents campers with the challenge of finding the most suitable one for them. But more on that later.

Life in a campground can be as rustic or elegant, active or laid back as you want it to be. You might pay less than $10 a night (or even nothing!) to camp on federal lands, home to majestic scenery, wondrous surroundings, and nature in its most preserved state. Or you can pay up to $50 per night at a premium RV resort for a beachfront location, spending your days shopping boutiques, swimming in a heated pool, getting massages, renting boats, or dining at their full-service restaurant. The park you choose might have an activity list a mile long or nothing to do but drop a fishing line in the water and wait for a tug. It might be equipped with modernized facilities with all the conveniences or a setting that hasn't changed since Watergate.

One for the Road

Is there a difference between a campground and an RV park? In theory, yes. Campgrounds are usually older, often built originally for tenters. As a result, individual campsites might be smaller. RV parks, on the other hand, are more likely built specifically for RVers, with larger sites, wider roads, and more advanced hookups. However, these terms seem to be used interchangeably, as we will use them throughout this book.

The perfect campground for you might exist just a mile off the highway, in the deepest part of a national forest, or within the limits of a large metropolitan area. It might be owned and operated by the federal government, a retired couple, or a large corporation. You might find yourself camped amongst thousands of people on a busy holiday weekend or have the run of the place during a winter stopover. Stay a day, a month, a year, or forever if you like it that much. As always, the choice is yours.

Da' Basics

For all their differences, most every campground or RV park has a few fundamental things in common. At the very least, it provides weary travelers with their own campsite, or site, for their RV. An office or ranger station usually greets guests for check-in. This is the place to ask questions and learn about rules and offerings of the park. A staff member, park ranger, or maybe even the owners themselves often direct guests to their campsites or supply them with a map to the location where they'll be camped. Sites are numbered and accessible by roads, although they may or may not be paved. Rustic or undeveloped parks might rely on a series of dirt or gravel roads, but don't worry—your RV can handle it.

Pull Over

Summer and holiday reservations fill up fast, particularly at campgrounds in popular areas. It's wise to call as far in advance as possible. Waiting lists for national parks can easily fill up three to four months in advance.

This campsite respresents the good life. A scenic view, plenty of shade, and a place to sit, relax, and take it all in.

(Photo courtesy of Newport Dunes Waterfront RV Resort)

Welcome to Your Campsite

The sizes and offerings of your campsite vary from place to place. Your typical government-run state or national park, perhaps established prior to the advent of RVs, may disallow vehicles over a certain length or width. Private campgrounds, too, may have limitations, but a 20 by 40 foot campsite is about average—large enough to accommodate most vehicles, with or without slide-out rooms. Overall sizes might exceed those dimensions at nicer or newer RV resorts.

Hooking Up

At some point during the process, someone at the campground will ask you about *hookups*. Hopefully, you answer correctly, since this decision dictates much of the quality of life aboard your RV, namely whether or not you want the air conditioning to kick in, the microwave oven to heat up leftovers, or perhaps the ability to watch your favorite *M*A*S*H* re-run. Hookups are what separate a campground from just another pretty landscape. There are five available hookups at any campground: *electric, water, sewer, cable TV,* and *phone*. Your campground may not offer all five types, but many offer a combination of them. Here's what to expect from each type.

Electric Avenue

Electricity from one source or another powers most of your RV's functions, including lights, most appliances, and temperature controls. Without it, you'll be flipping switches and turning on gadgets all day without any noticeable effects. And what fun is that?

Without getting too deep into this subject (oh, but how we will in Chapter 10, "Electrical Systems"), most of the onboard functions are powered by sweet electricity, which comes from three distinct sources. The first is your automotive battery. In a motorized RV, the automotive battery can charge and power devices such as headlights, in-dash air conditioning, and windshield wipers, just like your car does.

Second is the RV's coach battery. Found on all RVs, this separate battery powers everything from interior lights, water pump, furnace fan, and all 12-volt appliances.

Finally, the 120-volt system powers everything else, including all those big 120-volt appliances such as the air conditioner and microwave oven. Energize these devices either through the use of generator, DC-AC inverter, or, more applicable to this chapter, when plugged into an AC outlet like those found at a campground. This type of power source is often referred to as *shore power*.

RVocabulary

Shore power is a term used when receiving electricity from a standard campground pedestal, such as those found at campgrounds or even via a long extension cord plugged into an outlet in your very own home.

Plugging into an AC outlet at a campground, otherwise know as an electric hookup, is the greatest deal in town: You provide the electric cord, the campground supplies the juice. Each campsite should have a gray outlet box where the connection is made. Plug in and enjoy the sweet current to your rig. Your RV will reap the rewards of continuous power as long as you are connected.

Water, Water Everywhere

Just as your RV needs power to survive, you need water and lots of it, for things like showering, drinking, cooking, using the bathroom, and rinsing the dog's paws off in the sink. Bad doggie! A water hookup consists of a fresh water hose running from a spout at your campsite straight to a connection at the side of your RV. This allows for virtually unlimited fresh water for the length of your stay. Without this service, travelers must tap into their fresh-water storage tanks for their H_20 supply, propelled through the pipes via a water pump. Hot water (demanding, aren't you?) is secured by activating your RV's water heater. No need to call a plumber to explain. We'll tackle this slippery topic in Chapter 12, "Plumbing Systems."

Sewer

Sewer hookups allow wastewater to flow directly into the campground's septic system instead of remaining in your gray water holding tanks. *Gray water* is the used water from your sinks and showers, emptying into the gray water holding tank. *Black water,* the materials from your RV's toilet, empty into the black water holding tank. In any event, these tanks need to eventually be emptied, and many people prefer utilizing a sewer hookup for the job to visiting a *dump station* later on to perform the deed.

RVocabulary

The used water from your sinks and tub/shower is known as **gray water** and deposits in the RV's gray water tank. **Black water** is the polite way to refer to water and waste materials from your RV's toilet. Black water is stored in the black water tank. Both tanks have a limited capacity and must be periodically emptied. The **dump station** is the septic area where black and gray water is emptied via a sewer hose. Dump stations are found at most campgrounds or other special locations, such as RV service facilities, select LP dispensing locations, most truck stops, and some gas stations and rest areas.

The sewer connection is made from a hose running to a termination assembly that includes both tanks to a drain connection in the ground at the campsite. Admittedly, this is the hookup that no one actually wants to perform, but is a necessary evil in the RV world. For those who prefer to use the campground's facilities, or whose RV lacks a bathroom or shower, sewer hookup isn't necessary.

Cable TV

Can you still call it camping when you've got 25 channels including HBO? Sure you can. For some, this is a must-have option. Others could care less about watching television, which is probably the reason why they wanted to get away from home in the first place. The fact is, a lot of campgrounds don't offer it, or only do so in a fraction of sites. Premium RV resorts certainly will, but otherwise, this service can be hard to find. RVers will need a dedicated input jack onboard and a length of 75 ohm cable to connect.

Road Scholar

The actual cable for the cable TV hookup can be found at most electronic stores, including Radio Shack. Be sure to purchase one rated for exterior use, as it will hold up better over time.

However, you might still chance good reception without it. I once watched Game 5 of the World Series camped in the middle of 100,000 acres of pines in Michigan's Upper Peninsula without any such hookup. But good reception depends on your campground's location and the quality and range of your antenna. More on this in Chapter 16, "Choosing a Campground." For those traveling about with portable satellite systems, hundreds of channels are now your birthright, regardless of where you spend the night. Now you can politely tell the campground that no cable TV hookup (ha, ha, snicker, snicker) is required.

Phone

Although RVing and cell phones have seemingly forged the perfect relationship, you may be able to receive phone service at your site for your next camping outing. There are two methods for hooking up. The first is going directly through the local phone company, an option at many campgrounds. Unfortunately, the opportunity to speak to the grandkids comes along with a one-time connection fee averaging about $50. No one said Ma Bell didn't know how to make a fast buck. Long-distance calls and service charges are separate. Determine whether this expense is prudent before activation. Most RVers only opt for such services if their plans included staying put for several weeks or months.

The other alternative is an instant hookup controlled by the campground itself. For a daily fee (plus long-distance calls), travelers can phone home, close that lucrative book deal, or raise a ruckus on talk radio. Much like cable TV, phone service isn't offered everyplace, mostly nicer RV resorts and newer RV parks. However, availability is on the rise, thanks to a younger demographic demanding the need to stay in touch and more and more people desiring to go online.

One for the Road

Hooking up phone service is a nice, albeit expensive, option. A better decision is purchasing a cell phone, coupled with a nationwide calling plan easy on the long-distance costs and dreaded roaming charges. Cell phones grant users a permanent phone number to reach while out on the road. Their advantages of accessibility, safety, and staying in touch make them all but necessities in the opinions of most.

Hooking up a phone is easy, but you will, of course, need a phone and the appropriate jack onboard your RV. Once this is accomplished, presto—you're free to make and probably receive calls, surf the Internet, and check e-mails.

Back That Thing Up

Unless you opt for a *pull-thru site,* you're probably going to have to back your RV into your campsite upon arrival. This is a fairly common practice, especially in older campgrounds, originally designed only with the needs of tent campers in mind, rather than accessibility for larger vehicles. In most cases, landscaping or an adjacent site creates only one way in or out. Assuming you don't back into position, well, you're going to have to eventually throw your rig in reverse to leave, and many drivers just want to get it over with. Besides, backing allows for a better reach for your connections to the site's various hookups. And it just looks cool, too. Nervous about the thought of throwing your big motorhome into reverse? Who isn't at first? Don't worry, we'll tell you how to do it with style and grace in Chapter 14, "Drive Time."

RVocabulary

Pull-thru sites are campsites with access from more than one direction, allowing RVs to drive right through the site and gain access to a main road. This is popular with new RVers, as well as those traveling in large motorhomes, buses, or lengthy trailers that make for trickier back-ups.

You may be asked to park on a level, concrete slab (level is good) or find yourself in a more rustic spot of dirt or grass. In any event, your site might have its own fire ring for a nightly campfire and probably a picnic table for meals and a place to sit and relax. Other variables such as amount of shade, terrain, views, and proximity to the bathrooms or other facilities, depend on your location.

Length of Stay

A visit to that sunny Florida campground may result in your never, ever wanting to leave. Literally. The opportunity to live in an RV park full-time is often yours for the taking. Those making a yearly commitment receive tremendous discounts and a stable community of likeminded vacation-extenders. Long-term sites are called *seasonals,* which may be just for the summer, an entire season, or longer. Many warm-weather campgrounds thrive with long-term guests, since business stays open year-round. In northern climes, seasonals still exist, but may be shorter-term and interrupted for a winter closing.

RVocabulary

Seasonal describes a person who stays in a campground long-term, usually at least a month. Seasonal sites are only rented or leased for those interested in extended stays and are often situated in a separate area of the campground where only the long-term guests reside.

'Tis the Season

As you might have guessed, that Northern Wisconsin or Maine getaway is not terribly popular during January. For most Midwest, Mid-Atlantic, and Northeast private campgrounds, the average camping season runs between April and October. During the off-seasons, owners are enjoying the fruits of their labors, probably living it up in Florida just like you. Southern and western campgrounds earn no such vacations, often going year-round. Government parks, regardless of climate, may stay open all year, although cold weather might persuade most folks to stay home.

Accessibility

At this time, most campgrounds don't fall under the auspices of the Americans with Disabilities Act. However, that doesn't stop many places from adding accessible campsites, bathrooms, and facilities. It's wise to call ahead and determine if needs of those with disabilities or mobility issues will be met upon arrival. Even government campgrounds' attempts at accessibility can sometimes fail to address your specific needs, so it's best to verify all claims beforehand.

What's to Do, What to Do?

As you can guess, different places offer different things. But if campgrounds didn't offer a host of fun things to do, no one would stay there. Otherwise, you might as well camp out in the backyard. And you know how neighbors love that.

The breakdown between parks with lots to do and the others with minimal offerings usually stems from the philosophy of the owners about what kind of camping experience they want to deliver. Available resources, location, and the types of visitors and their expectations are also factors in this decision. However, most of the parks I've stayed at offer at least a swimming pool, and many offer a game room, camp store, sports fields (basketball, horseshoes, shuffleboard), and a rec. room for cards, television, and get-togethers. State and national parks, as part of an effort to keep the lands protected, and therefore, undeveloped, will almost never add to the surroundings in this manner. That's why you never saw a waterslide at Yellowstone or a miniature golf course chasing the alligators out of the Everglades.

RVocabulary

No one wants to come out and say no children, so an **adult-oriented park** is the next best way to deter families with youngsters onboard. Campgrounds under this banner are not trying to be malicious, rather they prefer to cater to an older clientele desiring a focus on adult activities.

Some parks cater to families and know the secret is to stockpile a long list of recreational pursuits to keep people happy and coming back. Here you might find a full-time activity staff to oversee games, outings, and classes for your kids. *Adult-oriented parks* might prohibit—or at least try to dissuade—children under a certain age, preferring to direct their efforts toward pampering the parents, retirees, and solo adult travelers.

A campground's surroundings also help to forge recreational pursuits. Some campgrounds rest in the middle of a pine forest, on oceanfront property, or within a beautiful summit and, therefore, play up their unique natural advantages of staying there. These types of environments might lend themselves to days spent hiking, biking, or horseback riding. A spot on the water might earn guests lazy days lounging on a fabulous beach, a choice of boat rentals, and terrific fishing. Urban settings with limited space may direct their efforts toward indoor pursuits such as a deluxe game room, movies, and a heated swimming pool and spa. Other parks are geared more toward convenience, perhaps located right off the highway for those who are just passing through. In these cases, there may be little to do since guests don't stay around very long. Or maybe that's why they don't linger?

Just as you won't find snowmobiling on the itinerary in the Florida Keys, snorkeling in Maine should be considered a rare find. Climate and weather certainly play a role in what you can do, which is why campgrounds in warmer locales such as Florida,

Texas, or California often offer a larger—and more consistent—array of year-round recreation. Again, the differences from park to park, state to state, are part of what makes RVing so enjoyable. You never know what's around the bend. Here's a list of what you might find during your next RV stopover.

- Basketball
- Batting cages
- Beaches
- Biking
- Boat rentals (canoes, kayaks, paddleboats, motorized)
- Bocce ball
- Cross-country skiing
- Driving range
- Golf course
- Fishing
- Hiking
- Horseback riding
- Horseshoes
- Jacuzzi
- Jet skiing
- Miniature golf
- Paddleboats
- Playground
- Putting green
- Scuba diving
- Shuffleboard
- Snorkeling
- Snowmobiling
- Softball
- Spas
- Swimming
- Tennis
- Video arcade
- Volleyball
- Waterslide

It's safe to say that a typical campground setting lends itself to a much wider array of recreational pursuits than your typical hotel or motel.

Active Endeavors

Since RVers are social by nature (it's true), group functions remain a popular practice in many campgrounds. Activities are usually scheduled in advance, catering to large numbers of guests at once. Such events might be aimed at kids, adults, or the entire family. Again, the list varies from place to place. As a rule of thumb, the larger the park, the greater the frequency—and types—of these kinds of offerings. Public campgrounds, with smaller staffs, offer very little in this regard. However, ranger-led programs, wildlife classes, and interpretive hikes may be on the agenda.

Activities reach their peak during the busy seasons, namely summer when the kids are out of school. Weekends and holidays are also popular times for bands, dances, and the ever-present theme weekends—park-wide events such as luaus, Halloween-related functions, and cooking spectacles of all descriptions. Admit it, you've always wanted to wear a hula skirt. Regular classes such as water aerobics, yoga, or line dancing may be offered at a set time every week. Here's a list of the kinds of activities that might be offered:

- Arts and crafts
- Bands
- Bingo
- Car shows
- Cards
- Church services
- Cocktail parties
- Cookouts
- Dances
- DJs
- Exercise classes
- Fireworks
- Happy hours
- Haunted houses
- Ice cream socials
- Luaus
- Magic shows
- Movies
- Pancake breakfasts
- Potluck dinners
- Storytelling
- Theme weekends
- Yoga

Of course, if you're the type who would rather avoid these kinds of situations, no problem. You certainly won't be ostracized as a detractor if you'd rather do your own thing.

Facilities

Facilities comprise the heart of any campground, and at some time or another, even the most self-reliant camper will depend on them for a variety of things. As previously mentioned, bathrooms and hot showers are available almost anywhere you might end up. Laundry facilities, too, are common in private campgrounds, as are rec. rooms, which serve as the hub of many activities, including dances, cards, or just agonizing over the afternoon Cubs game. An outdoor pavilion makes for a communal spot for outdoor activities or large clubs and family reunions. LP gas portals and dump stations are two important visits before heading out of Dodge.

> **Pull Over**
>
> You may be shocked to encounter pay showers during a trip to the campground's facilities, but it's bound to happen. A typical rate is $.25 for five minutes, a cost imposed to justify water consumption. Throw some loose change in your shower kit or ask the front desk if you can expect a pay-to-spray shower arrangement ahead of time.

Cabins or cottages are often available for rent of various durations for those traveling without an RV. One- and two-room units are common, usually complete with heat, air conditioners, and bedding. Kitchen facilities are sometimes included. Teepees, trailers, and large tents can sometimes make for a unique weekend stay.

Here's a sampling of common facilities you may experience on your travels.

- Adult lounge
- Bathrooms and showers (comfort stations)
- Boat landings
- Cabins
- Convenience stores (groceries, souvenirs, RV supplies)
- Cottages
- Dog runs
- Dump stations
- Fitness centers
- Fuel pumps (gas and/or diesel)
- Laundry
- LP gas stations
- Marina
- Modem center
- Pavilion
- Petting zoo
- Private mailboxes
- Pubs
- Rec. hall
- Rental trailers
- Restaurants
- Shops
- Snack shops
- Teepees
- Tenting

As a rule, the larger the campground, the more facilities it will have. If a laundry room, modem center, or rental units are important to you, be sure to call and check availability in advance.

You've Been Served

One of the purest pleasantries of RVing is that the majority of campgrounds are privately owned and operated. In many cases, visitors are greeted by the actual owners, people who obviously have a vested interest in the quality of your stay and your impressions of their facilities. They want you back, and it's plain good business to create a warm and congenial atmosphere. Many campgrounds are true family businesses, with siblings and extended family working in the park. Mom might be behind the cash register while Dad works the grounds. Sons and daughters might be found doing maintenance, working in the campground store, or planning activities for guests. With so many people's fortunes depending on the quality of your experience, you might find good service once again the norm and not the exception.

As for specific types of services offered, this, too, varies from place to place. Popular destination-type parks, with larger staffs, most always offer a longer list of services than smaller parks. Here's a sampling of what you might expect.

- Child care
- Complimentary hookups
- Concierge service
- Copy service
- Faxes
- Firewood delivery

- LP gas delivery
- Massages
- Message center
- Newspaper delivery
- On-site RV repair
- Rental vehicles
- RV storage
- RV washing
- Shuttle service
- Tours
- Twenty-four-hour security
- Valet parking

For those tired of inattentive service and the feeling that your very presence is an inconvenience, take note. You just might reconnect with the lost art of customer service at a campground near you.

Okay, How Much?

You can camp for free on some government lands or pay up to $50 per night at a five-star RV resort during a peak season. Just as hotels and motels charge by the room, RVers are charged by the campsite. And just like conventional lodging, location can make all the difference. For instance, a similarly equipped campsite overlooking a lake or adjacent to the ocean costs more than one next to the playground or near the camp store. Sites closer to popular facilities such as bathrooms, showers, or the rec. room might be pricier than other points within the park.

RVocabulary

Full hookup sites guarantee water, electric, and sewer connections. Some campgrounds also include cable TV and phone service in this package. **Primitive sites** most often suggest electric and water hookups only. However, the term can also be used to describe a campsite with no hookups of any kind, which is usually opted for by tent campers or RVers in search of a more rustic camping experience.

As discussed earlier, not all sites are created equal. Different sizes and availability of hookups (electric, water, sewer, phone, and cable TV) also affect costs. *Full hookup sites* come with a package of electric, water, and sewer connections. Upscale resorts often include cable TV and phone service in this definition. Definitions of *primitive sites* vary. The most common meaning is a campsite with just water and electric service. Others use the term to describe a campsite with no hookups of any kind. Primitive, to say the least. In these cases, guests are responsible for their own power (via gen-erator and holding tanks) and should have enough fresh water in their tanks for the duration of their stay. We'll examine how to pick the best campsite for you in Chapter 16.

Those traveling with larger groups of passengers might be charged an additional per-person fee. Some campgrounds base their prices on two persons per RV, others up to four. Additional vehicles at the site might incur a small charge, as well. Phone service can be a pricey upgrade, too, and is probably a better idea if you're planning on staying longer than a weekend. A down payment or credit card number is required for service. Running your air conditioner consumes a lot of electricity, something duly noted by park owners. In some cases, a minimal charge (say, a dollar per day) might be assessed if you plan on operating it during hot weather. Finally, your beloved pooch or feline might earn you an extra charge, per animal. Possibly more if it's larger than a pool table.

Discounts

Don't let these extra costs deter you. Even a campground that's quick to slap on extra charges can still beat the pants off a night at most any hotel/motel. Furthermore, campers can take advantage of a wide range of discounts, based on memberships in various clubs and affiliations, length of stay, and age. Here's a look at the various types of discounts honored by campgrounds.

RV Clubs

Many RVers find that enrolling in an established RV club yields a number of definite advantages, not the least of which are discounts at various RV parks nationwide. Most clubs aren't mutually exclusive, giving members the freedom to join as many groups as they like and thus, a greater chance of savings. For their part, campground owners, too, must decide whether or not to honor these discounts, which usually necessitates joining a particular club's network of places to stay. Whether or not a campground is affiliated with your particular club(s)—and cuts you a break on the price of staying there—may help narrow down where you stay and how often.

Memberships can usually save members 10 percent off the daily rate. RVers and campgrounds alike pay yearly dues to belong, and many other perks apply. (We'll talk more about the nature of clubs and the pros and cons of enrollment in Chapter 18, "Travel Planning.") The Good Sam Club, Coast to Coast, Camping World's President's Club, and the Family Motor Coach Association (FMCA) are some of the largest clubs in the RV industry.

Franchise Clubs

As mentioned, the majority of campgrounds are privately owned. However, as many as 10 percent are franchised, or members of a larger corporation with parks throughout the nation or perhaps even the world. Examples include Kampgrounds of

America (KOA), Yogi Bear's Jellystone Park Camp-Resorts, and Outdoor Resorts of America. And while each corporation is different, they're the same in one regard: They want your business. To win your favor, such places usually offer free or modestly priced club memberships, garnering cardholders discounts at parks throughout their system. Enrollment is a great idea for those who favor one franchise or another.

AAA

AAA had the right idea. If you honor it, they will come. Restaurants, hotels, and rental-car companies—and even many nationwide attractions—all got in the act of discounting rates for AAA members. Many campgrounds now honor the card as well. In addition to substantial savings, members receive roadside assistance, trip planning, and a host of valuable services on the go. An additional 10 percent off a campground stay is likely, and such affiliation can be plenty useful outside the RV world as well.

You're How Old?

Wisdom isn't the only perk of getting older—there are also discounts galore. The ubiquitous senior citizen discount is alive and well at many campgrounds, yielding anyone 65 years old or older (sometimes younger) a discount of up to 10 percent. Membership in the American Association of Retired Persons (AARP) is commonly accepted, too. So the kiddies aren't left out, junior members of your crew might not be charged or may be given a reduced rate.

Length of Stay

As described in Chapter 1, "Why RV?" RV travel isn't necessarily limited to just a quick weekend getaway. A snowbird might nest in a warm-weather campground for six months or more. Your full-timing in-laws could decide to settle in their favorite campsite for several weeks, perhaps finding one just miles from your very home. How did you get so lucky? Such demonstrations of loyalty to a particular place usually earn visitors some kind of discount, and not necessarily a small one either. Think of it as buying in bulk, like that 100-pound sack of potatoes you bought last year. Hash browns, anyone? Special weekly, monthly, and yearly rates may apply, saving you hundreds of dollars for a lengthy stay.

No-No's

You travel with a gaggle of ornery pit bulls. The RV takes up three campsites—four once the slide-out rooms are deployed. You brought your drums along and look forward to re-creating Woodstock all night long. That's all fine, but your campground might ask you to perform elsewhere. Owners tend to tolerate a lot of things, but excessive noise is not one of them. Since a few feet—and no doors—might be the only thing separating you from your neighbor's campsite, excessive noise is nonnegotiable grounds for the old heave-ho. Remember, sound carries, and annoying behavior carries even farther. Here, a few bad apples definitely spoil the bunch.

Parks may have provisions concerning anything from the size of RVs to pets to special policies concerning extra visitors at a site. Public drinking of alcohol may or may not be tolerated, but rowdy behavior is an easy way to be asked to leave. If you see a sign for an adult-oriented park, that's a polite way to ask you to leave your children at home. It's best to get an understanding of the rules and regulations prior to arrival to avoid any surprises.

Pull Over

Not every campground can handle the big rigs. Make sure your campground can handle your size RV during the reservation process. If you have a wide-body vehicle or slide-outs, make this known beforehand. As mentioned earlier, not every campground was created with the new *Titanic*-sized RVs in mind, so it's best to ask first. Such restrictions are most common at government parks and older campgrounds.

Types of Campgrounds

Classifying a "typical" campground isn't easy, but many follow similar characteristics based on the type of campground you stay in. There are three basic kinds: *Private, Government,* and *Membership*. The following is an overview of each kind and what might be offered to guests in the ways of recreation, activities, services, facilities, and cost. We'll discuss how to choose the best campground for you in Chapter 16.

Private Campgrounds

The majority of the campgrounds in the United States fall under this category. Many are family-run, handed down from generation to generation, or purchased by a couple tired of the rat race and looking to settle in to a less scheduled routine. A lot of passionate RVers decide to combine work and play by buying a campground of their own.

Quantifying your average private campground is next to impossible. Each one is unique, with different philosophies, rules, locations, and stuff to do. I've seen parks with 1,000 campsites, full of complex mazes of buildings, stores, restaurants, with everything to do under the sun across the street from a park with 50 great big sites and not much else.

Private campgrounds are open based on the owner's discretion, which may be open year-round or closed when the temperatures begin to dip. They might limit duration of stays or allow campers to live there for months, years, or forever. Costs typically range from $15 to $50, but $20 to $25 is about average. Most accept numerous club discounts in an effort to attract your business. Basic facilities usually include bathrooms with hot showers, dump stations, LP gas, a rec. room, campground store and/or office, and a variety of different sites.

Private campgrounds can also take the shape of two unique types: *Franchises* and *RV Resorts*.

Franchise Players

A small percentage of private campgrounds are operated under the guidance of a larger franchise, such as Kampgrounds of America (KOA) or Yogi Bear's Jellystone Parks. In these cases, facilities are often owned and operated by licensees following the policies set up by the parent corporation, much like a McDonald's or a Midas Muffler shop.

Those seeking a similar experience every time find staying within their favorite franchise park provides a fairly consistent camping experience. Services, facilities, and recreation are roughly the same throughout the nation, with variances coming in the park's overall size and location. Visitors to Jellystone Parks know that they'll be rewarded by a family-friendly philosophy, with most events aimed at children. And, yes, Yogi and Boo Boo will probably make an appearance, too. KOA Kampers can rely upon unique offerings such as Kamping Kabins and camp stores. Franchises reward repeat guests with reduced rates and other perks.

RV Resorts

Upon registration, a member of the staff might valet park your RV into your campsite. It may be overlooking the water, a beautiful mountain range, or some other scenic view. The grounds are immaculate; everything is well-kept. The landscaping is fabulous. As part of the arrival service, all your hookups are connected for you, including cable TV and phone service. This *is* a resort after all. Do you want to play a round of golf, swim in the heated pool, or take lessons from the tennis pro? It's been a long day of travel, so you opt for dinner down by the marina and a stroll along the water. Could a massage be in your future?

Pull Over

Seeing the term "RV Resort" in the name doesn't guarantee first-class accommodations. The proof is in the pudding, so to speak. When making reservations, ask about what's offered, such as services and amenities.

Scenarios like this are all too common at upscale RV resorts. Campsites are large and pristine, designed to handle the 45-foot buses often preferred by the wealthy clientele. These types of accommodations are among the least common in the industry and may attract travelers from many states away (across the country even) for a chance to experience the ultimate in luxury. Furthermore, guests also tend to stay longer, reaping the benefits for as long as they can.

Premium resorts are generally located in warm-weather climates, in order to create a year-round vacation experience. After all, it's easy to lose your ball golfing in the snow. Unfortunately, this may require guests to travel hundreds of miles to reach one. Another drawback is that bringing children is sometimes frowned upon. You probably won't find a playground or story time here. Campsites are also relatively expensive. Costs are on the high end of the campground range, averaging $40 per night. But for those desiring the finest in accommodations, RV resorts are the way to go.

Government Campgrounds

Our network of protected lands is the envy of the world. Hundreds of millions of acres fall under the jurisdiction of our state or federal government, safeguarding our natural treasures for generations to come. Most of our protected lands offer at least some kind of camping, although guests might struggle with the overall lack of facilities and hookups offered. For others, the chance to wake up amongst the Grand Tetons, hike the wind-swept shores of Maine's Acadia National Park, or camp overlooking the staggering views of the Grand Canyon is just too good to pass up.

Of course, the hallmark of this type of campground is the scenery. You can count on not being inches from a busy highway or having your jaw-dropping views obstructed by the local fast-food joint's gigantic billboard. If these areas weren't somehow special, pristine, or harboring rare species of wildlife or fauna, chances are they wouldn't be protected in the first place. It's for this same reason that junkyards or your neighbor's unmowed backyard with the rusted-out Chevy don't fall under government protection.

Nominal campsite fees and admission costs are also standard. While most private campgrounds average $20 to $25 per night, that's about the most you'd ever pay to camp on federal lands. One reason for the considerable savings is due to less staff and fewer amenities. The prevailing mandate is that our public lands should be made available to everyone and, therefore, should be inexpensive enough for anyone to enjoy. The government doesn't generally look at these parks as moneymaking entities, rather as a service to its citizens. Well done, Uncle Sam!

Full hookups are a bit of a rarity; electric sites are only sometimes offered, and it's not uncommon to have little or no services of any kind. You can probably count on fresh water, facilitated through a pump, as well as bathrooms and possibly showers. A visitor's center gets guests up to speed regarding information on the place, including rules, services, and what there is to see and do. Again, the point is to camp in a quasi-natural setting, so don't expect the red carpet treatment.

Just as our government has lots of branches, there are lots of different variations of government-run campgrounds: State, National, Army Corps of Engineer Projects, Bureau of Land Management (BLM), and National Wildlife Refugee Systems. Contact information for each kind can be found in Appendix A, "Resources."

State Parks

You probably won't need to travel very far to find one of these woodsy spots. Most states have a fairly large network of parks, in some of the most beautiful sections within state lines. Entry costs are often free, and campsite fees are fairly inexpensive, regardless of season. The upside is that you might find yourself camped in a truly natural setting, a growing rarity with rampant development in most areas. Their often nearby location, low costs, and natural environment make state parks very popular destinations with most RVers.

In most cases, campsites are small and fairly primitive. A site might be marked with a specific spot to park, complete with fire ring, shade, and picnic table, or offered on a first-come, first-served basis in an undeveloped, although sequestered, area. Larger rigs and trailers might exceed site size limits, and once there, might toil with an antiquated electrical system struggling to power their more sophisticated (and energy-hogging) onboard components. Again, it's best to call ahead and find out exactly what you're getting. Bathrooms and showers are likely, as is a place to dump your holding tanks. But overall, camping facilities are modest and about as close to roughin' it as most RVers ever come.

The good news is that there are a lot of natural activities to choose from. Active travelers find these areas among the best spots for hiking, with miles of challenging or easy trails to try out. Swimming and fishing are also popular, and many visitors tow canoes or a small boat to make the most of the local streams, rivers, and lakes. Wintertime opens up a new wealth of recreational pursuits, including cross-country skiing, snowmobiling, or snowshoeing. A camp store, boat rentals, and small food concessions are sometimes offered.

Pull Over

Check with park rangers about purchasing fishing licenses, as well as boat restrictions, drop-off sights, and motor limits, ahead of time. Regulations vary from park to park, and violators may be fined for any infractions.

The number of staff, or rangers, and services are minimal. After all, this is a state-run facility dedicated to protecting the environment; the comfort and conveniences of guests comes in a distant second. Don't expect too many man-made activities (mini-golf, swimming pools, water slides), either. A playground and a store are about it. Many state parks stay open all year.

National Parks

Certainly the best-known and most recognizable use of federal lands, our national park system is a testament to the diversity of natural landscapes in this country. Protected areas under the NPS (National Park Service) are some of the very best and most beautiful lands anywhere, the crème de la crème, better than ice cream and a snow-day rolled into one. And they're very, very popular with RVers.

Although the national park system boasts nearly 400 entries (380 to be exact), a great number of these locations are historic sites and monuments, which don't make for good—or legal—camping. You've never seen anyone lounging in front of the Lincoln Memorial roasting marshmallows, have you? (Okay, I did it once, but promised authorities that was the last time.) All told, there are more than 83 million acres governed by the NPS.

In most cases, camping is alive and well here, with scores of RVers making cross-country pilgrimages for a sight of Old Faithful or the chance to view Oregon's Crater Lake up close and personal. Reserving a campsite during peak seasons at the most popular national parks is extremely competitive. And if you're thinking you'll have the place to yourself, you may be disappointed by the hordes of like-minded vacationers, tenters, and tourists jockeying for position inside. But not even Disneyland can replicate the true power of many of these locales, and national parks routinely rank among the top destinations for RVers.

Road Scholar

A National Parks Pass ($50) grants cardholders free admission to any park within the system. For an additional $15, the Golden Eagle Pass adds free admission to sites managed by the U.S. Fish and Wildlife Service, the U.S. Forest Service, and the Bureau of Land Management. The Golden Access Passport ($10), for visitors 62 years of age or older, is a lifetime pass good for admissions and services. For more information, call 1-888-GO-PARKS (1-888-467-2757) or visit www.nationalparks.org.

Bureau of Land Management

Pssst. Want to camp for free? Yeah, that's right, zero, zip, nada. The freebie is alive and well at many areas governed by the Bureau of Land Management (BLM), a collection of recreational areas devoted to preservation for future generations. With more than 270 million acres within the system, many of which lack the name recognition of its national park counterparts, there are more than enough places to dock the RV for a short stay, often at no charge. And you definitely get more than what you pay for.

Pull Over

Although many federal lands offer rustic camping, visitors must use caution not to damage the very areas that we're trying to protect. Be careful where you drive, park, and hike. Take out all trash that you brought in. Observe rules about pets, campfires, and off-limit areas. Keep your impact to a minimum so the next visitors can enjoy the same preserved setting.

What travelers give up in terms of any hookups, services, and planned activities, they more than make for in the chance to use their RV like they probably have romanticized about since they bought it. Camp at the base of the Rocky Mountains or the high deserts of Arizona or New Mexico. You may find yourself all alone or among a social atmosphere of fellow campers. Hiking, fishing, hunting, birdwatching, and boating are just some of the fun diversions to partake in.

The one drawback is that BLM sites are found only in the western half of the United States and parts of Canada. Costs might be free, or you might be assessed a small charge. Facilities are usually nonexistent, so be prepared to live off your RV's self-contained capabilities (generator, LP gas, holding tanks). We'll visit this subject in Chapter 17, "Roughin' It."

U.S. Army Corps of Engineers Projects

And you thought you were too old to play soldier? There are thousands of places throughout the United States that fall under the jurisdiction of the Army Corps of Engineers, engaged in water reclamation, environmental relief, and civil works projects of every kind. As a result, there are plenty of campsites available (50,000 and counting), and these are some of the great camping bargains out there.

Facilities will most likely be limited to primitive campsites, places for picnics, trails, and boat ramps. The visitor's center is a good place to learn the rules, pick up maps, and discover what there is to do. Campsites are usually set near water (lakes, rivers, and oceans), and recreation is strictly of the natural persuasion. Great opportunities usually exist for hiking, fishing, boating, hunting, cross-country skiing, biking, birdwatching, and swimming. Permits are usually required for fishing and hunting. Sites are primitive, but the costs can't be beat. Visitors can expect to pay less than $10 per night. Some locations are free of charge.

National Wildlife Refugee System

Limited but spirited camping opportunities can be found within the system of federally protected wildlife refuge areas. Provided you don't interfere with the indigenous species and don't mind camping without most kinds of hookups, your overnight stay should resemble something out of *Jack Hannah's Animal Kingdom*. More than 400 protected regions, set amongst more than 90 million acres, are open to the public. Facilities are basic, if offered at all. Excellent bird- and animal-watching prevails, as do a host of outdoor activities usually found at government campgrounds. Cost is nominal. Expect to pay no more than $10 per night.

Camping Canada

Our good neighbors to the north enjoy their own system of protected lands, known as Parks Canada. The mission is the same as our own, namely to foster an appreciation and enjoyment of the natural world. Camping opportunities range from remote spots in the wilderness to pristine parks of a more popular design. As of this printing, there are 39 national parks in the system, comprising 2 percent of the country's land mass. As many as 14 others are planned in the years to come.

Membership Parks

Enrolling in a membership park plan is akin in some ways to that of a time-share arrangement. Spend a few weeks here, a few weeks there, and then go back to your home park or resort. Only in this case, you are not limited to a few locations to visit but rather a system of perhaps hundreds of RV parks across America. And since your agreement is not with individuals but a large corporation, you can schedule a visit at any time, during any season. Belonging to such an organization grants members drastically reduced daily fees at a network of campgrounds, maybe less than $5 per night in some cases. Compare that to the typical $20 to $40 per night fees for most commercial campsites, and you can see the advantages. Over time, this savings can add up, especially for full-timers always looking for a place to camp.

Members Only

In most cases, members must choose a "home park," which serves as their base between visits to other locations. Duration of stays at your home park may be limited to several weeks or several months during the year. The goal of these membership programs, of course, is to offer a network of available parks nationwide, with tempting accommodations offered in every state and place you might want to visit. Larger groups, such as Coast to Coast Resorts, Thousand Trails, and NACO, offer hundreds of places to visit; smaller companies might only contain a few dozen places in their network. Ancillary benefits usually include an RV park directory, club publication, and discounts on a range of RV services such as insurance and RV tours.

Costs

All this comes with a large price, however—usually several thousands of dollars or more to join the larger groups. This amount can be financed. After that, cost structures vary. You might be asked to pay a yearly maintenance fee or additional costs incurred at your home park. Activity fees may or may not be included and restrictions may exist. It's best to read the fine print carefully to determine your obligations over the course of the contract. Remember, your dues pay for membership only; you don't own the campsites.

Membership parks are best for those who plan to do a lot of RVing. High start-up costs are only offset if you plan to camp regularly. Hookups, recreation, and services vary from park to park, as do your length-of-stay agreements. You can live full-time in some parks or be limited to several weeks a year at others. Pets and children may or may not be allowed. Determine if other locations are viable trips for you, in areas of the country you want to visit.

The quality and accessibility of your home park plays a large role in determining your enjoyment. Make sure it's financially viable (so it won't disappear unexpectedly) and offers the kinds of things you'll want in a campground on a consistent basis.

Pull Over

Like any membership, there are risks. If the club goes belly-up, members might be out of luck, losing their camping privileges—and substantial investment—along with it.

Boondocking

You've been driving all day and your eyes are getting heavy. The coffee is no longer doing the job and that last Barry Manilow song didn't help matters. It's late. With little time and still a long way to go to reach the Amazing House 'o Cheese listed in all the brochures, you pull off the interstate and catch some zzzzz's in a deserted mall parking lot.

The prized fishing hole is hidden three miles off the dirt access road, through the forest of evergreens, on the left at the big rock. There's just enough space to squeeze your RV in. There's no one around for miles. You set up camp and spend a weekend enjoying the fish-in-a-barrel metaphor you've always dreamed about.

Your in-laws in Tallahassee want to see their grandchildren now. And, okay, you can come, too. You pack up the RV and head south, only to find that the local campground is just too far away for the baby-loving grandparents to endure. Instead, you spend the week in their driveway, granting Grandma and Grandpa 24-hour access to the newest member of the family. Oh, and you, too. (Yeah, right.)

RVocabulary

Boondocking, also known as "dry camping," means camping without hookups of any kind (electric, sewer, or fresh water). In these cases, you have to rely on your RV's various self-reliant features, including a generator, batteries, and holding tanks. Spending a night in a mall parking lot, a relative's driveway, or in the middle of a forest are all examples of this.

All three scenarios fall under the category of *boondocking*. Each example requires the use of your RV's self-contained camping features (generator, holding tanks, etc.) if you want lights, heat, water, and power to do anything onboard. These stopovers might last a night or for an extended stay, but no hookups are generally offered to tap into. You're on your own.

Pull Over

Driving late at night is rarely a good idea. Operating an RV (any vehicle for that matter) while drowsy puts you, your family, and fellow travelers at great risk. It's best to schedule your days to start early and end at a reasonable hour. However, if you must, pull off and take a quick nap. Better to be asleep on the side of the road than *on* the road.

You Get What You Paid For

However, boondocking is not without its risks. For starters, these areas can often be dark and vacant, which have always made me uncomfortable in terms of potential crime. Personally, I have never felt all that at ease with this practice and never sleep very well in such unsure surroundings. Many merchants aren't crazy about you camping on their property, either, and you may receive a 3 A.M. wake-up call from security to find another spot. It also may be in violation of local ordinances, meaning that police might be the ones performing the wake-up services. And many of these locations, such as truck stops, can be noisier than sleeping next to an airport runway.

Remember Your P's and Q's

Some establishments, such as some Wal-Marts and Camping World stores, view overnight tenants as potential customers, making these places popular with guests. However, it's important and just plain polite to secure the owner's permission before spending the night in their facilities. Don't be afraid to do a little shopping the night before or the next day as a thank-you for the impromptu accommodations. Don't make a scene by deploying awnings, activating slide-out rooms, or setting out lawn chairs for a wienie roast over the Hibachi. And don't stay more than one night in a commercial setting—this makes you a squatter and you're now just taking advantage of your hosts.

Conventional Lodging

Remember our mantra: RVing is all about choices. As such, you can choose to skip the campground routine altogether if you like. Can't live without the mints on the pillows? Need a break from the RV? Tired of all that fresh mountain air? There's no rule that says you can't dock the motorhome at the nearest Holiday Inn and spend the night as regular folk do. (Don't worry, we won't revoke your RV privileges.) Does that bed and breakfast look just too quaint to pass up? Want to treat yourself to a night at the Four Seasons? Longing for the springiness of your in-laws' sofa bed? Then do it. Campgrounds and conventional lodging aren't mutually exclusive. It is, however, a good idea to make sure you can find a spot to park your rig or trailer before signing on the dotted line for the night. Let the operators know during check-in so there are no surprises later on.

The Least You Need to Know

- RVers have a myriad of choices in accommodations, including private, federal, and membership campgrounds; boondocking; or any conventional lodging.
- Most campgrounds offer a choice of hookups, including electricity, fresh water, sewer, phone, and cable TV. The differences among campgrounds is determined by recreation, services, activities, facilities, costs, seasonality, size, length of stay, and locations.
- Boondocking is the term used when you camp independent of any hookups, usually in a remote location, parking lot, or driveway. In these cases, your RV's onboard systems must be self-reliant through the use of a generator, LP gas, and the various holding tanks.
- RVers always have the choice of staying in conventional lodgings (e.g., hotels, motels, resorts, bed and breakfasts), provided there's a place large enough to park their vehicle.

Part 2

Choosing Your RV

Now's the time to start thinking about what kind of recreational vehicle is best for you. Choosing the ideal RV requires careful consideration as to what you're going to use it for, who's coming along, where you're going, and for how long. Remember, this decision will, to a certain extent, dictate the kinds of trips you take, for better or for worse. Will your travels take you across the country or just to the local state park? Do you want to rough it, camping far removed from civilization, or is a lazy weekend at a plush RV resort more your speed? Is this vehicle for the whole family—the kids, the cat, and your next-door neighbor—or is this just for dad's weeklong fishing trips with the guys?

Chapter 4

The World of Motorized RVs

In This Chapter

- Pros and cons of motorized RVs
- In-depth examination of specific types
- Costs, specifications, and onboard features
- Who might benefit from each kind?

Life in a motorized RV is like a condensed version of life at home (although I recently drove a motorhome bigger than my first apartment). You can watch TV, listen to music, lounge about on couches and chairs, eat, shower, use the bathroom, sleep in comfort, play cards, write the Great American Novel (or the next great *Complete Idiot's Guide*), work, or do whatever. If you're a couch potato at home, there's nothing stopping you from assuming that vegetated state in your new motorhome, camper van, or truck camper. Family gourmets can knock themselves out in the galley, while the kids do their homework (yeah, right) in the living room or dinette area. Even the dog's 18 hours of daily sleep needn't be interrupted. It's basically life as usual—except, of course, for the fact that your house has a motor.

Ah, yes, the motor. Depending on whom you ask, it is the very source of the motorhome's undeniable appeal or the reason to take your business into the towable market. Prospective buyers must weigh driving ease and convenience against the added costs and potential longevity issues associated with such a purchase.

In Part 1, "To RV or Not To RV?" we briefly explored the two basic vehicle types: motorized and towables. In this chapter, motorized RVs take center stage.

More Than a Motor

The motor. The engine. The mechanical muscle that separates a fully packed, ready-to-hit-the-road motorhome from a trailer that's all dressed up with nowhere to go. This is the very heart of the matter—and the source of all the advantages and disadvantages of motorized RV ownership. Your fondness for life in a motorhome probably boils down to your comfort level with its associated costs, driving ease, and under-the-hood challenges, something we're going to explore in great length. But first, here are some of the unique perks of motorized RVs.

All-in-One Vehicle

No hitching, no connections, no need to learn just what the heck tongue weight is (see Chapter 13, "Towin' the Line," for the answer). The biggest advantage of motorized vehicles is that they're truly self-sufficient—everything needed is under one roof, in one vehicle, including the engine to take you there. Your motorhome is just waiting on you, your gear, and a full tank of gas (or sometimes diesel) to get your leisure time started. Walk triumphantly from driver's seat to refrigerator to bedroom, and never get your shoes dirty. When it's raining, say "Ha, I am King!" secure in the knowledge that your towable neighbors are scrambling between the raindrops while you're warm and dry. You are the king of a roving palace, ruler of all you survey, and most definitely free from the worries of "Just what's going on back there in my trailer?" Crown, flowing robe, and scepter not included.

The ability to make a quick getaway is especially nice during times of trouble. Did that black funnel cloud just turn in your direction? Turn the key and split! A plague of locusts descending on the campground? Then it's certainly time to go. Gonna miss the kickoff for the Packers-Bears game? By all means, floor it. Bank robbers, take note: Pick another vehicle for the next bank heist. Most motorized RVs are lousy in high-speed pursuits.

Easy Street

As a solo vehicle (a lone wolf, if you will), many folks find driving a motorized RV much easier than towing a trailer, especially when it comes to parking, backing up, and tight cornering. For starters, most trailer configurations are longer than most motorhomes; the combined length of the tow vehicle and medium-size trailer can easily exceed 40 feet. That's a whole lotta vehicle to take into the gas station, mini-mart, or weaving in and out of rush hour traffic. And when you consider the agile maneuverings of camper vans and truck campers, the driving benefits multiply rapidly. Motorized RVs only require positioning one vehicle into a campground space or parking lot during back ups, not two. Repeat after me: "One vehicle, one direction. Two vehicles, many directions."

Boondocking

In my experience, camping out in the boonies is much more practical in a motorized RV. For reasons previously stated, a maneuverable vehicle is key to traversing the tight roads (not to mention paths and makeshift trails) and tiny spaces often required for that perfect deep-woods spot. Truck campers, van campers, and mini-motorhomes—with low clearances and manageable lengths—are much more apt to get you there and still keep your paint job. An onboard generator (standard equipment or add-on in most cases) adds to the self-containment features once the destination is reached. And since generators are not commonly offered in most trailers, you're already one step up on the competition.

In-Motion Access

If I could watch *Buffy the Vampire Slayer* while my wife drove down the road, I wouldn't care where we ended up. The fact is, motorized passengers have access to all their RV's interior bounty while in motion. While I strongly discourage passengers in a motorized vehicle from spending much time moving about the coach—accidents happen—you certainly can reap the advantages of an onboard television, VCR, refrigerator, bathroom, and the like. Buckle up and play a game around the dinette table. Counter the "Are we there yet?" syndrome by letting the kids pop in a video game and work the controls from their recliners as you sail down the road. Make a sandwich, heat up the nachos, and pour a round of soft drinks as Mom makes time through the heartland. No, you can't drive the RV *and* watch *Buffy* at the same time. Sorry.

One-Time Costs

As my father-in-law likes to remind me, you should always know what your obligations are. He also says to never hand away your assets, which I guess means valet parking is out of the question. The sticker price is the only obstacle to beginning RVing. Motorized RVs require no extra equipment to start out—there's no pricey tow vehicle, hitches, sway bars, or connections of any kind (stay tuned to Chapter 13 to learn more). Think of your motorhome as an all-inclusive paid vacation, kind of like a Club Med, only without the flirty bartenders.

Pull Over

Most states disallow people to ride in a trailer while in transit, and you shouldn't do so regardless. It can be very turbulent and unsafe. You won't find seat belts inside for this very reason.

Hitchin' a Ride

All this, and the ability to tow a boat or secondary vehicle, too? In many cases, yes. The bigger the motorized RV, the more power it has, and the more weight it can support. After hauling around you, your crew, and all their stuff, your motorized RV just might even have enough gusto left over to tow a car, truck, or small trailer with a boat, snowmobiles, or a pair of jet skis. A hitch, a series of connections, and a firm knowledge of your RV's weight ratings and towing capabilities is all that's needed to bring such items along for the ride. We'll discuss how to tow a secondary vehicle or trailer with your motorhome in Chapter 13. True, this practice, of course, negates some of the benefits of drivability listed earlier. Ah, well.

Motor Woes

No, the honeymoon's not over, not by a long shot. However, to be fair, there can be (gasp!) disadvantages, or let's call them possible "setbacks" to the motorized life. Of course, these "problems" are only as troubling as you believe them to be. One person's dilemma is another person's gain. After all, you're the one who is going to be living in this RV, not me. That is, unless you bake cookies and throw in some comic books—then I'll come along, too. RV wannabes should be well-informed and consider the ramifications of any buying decision. Here's the potential dark side to motorized RVs.

Sticker Shock

For a similarly sized, similarly equipped towable, motorized RVs are more expensive. Yes, it's true, that pesky engine can affect your bottom line faster than a trip to L.L. Bean with your husband. How much more? The starting cost for a 20-foot conventional travel trailer is approximately $15,000 to $25,000; the same size Class C usually starts at $35,000 to $40,000. True, the difference can't all be blamed on the inclusion of an engine, but most of it can.

As a separate motorized vehicle, insurance costs fall under the requirements of automobiles and must be properly insured. For this reason, costs for these RVs always exceed those of any towable, no matter what discounts or tall tales you spin to your insurance company. Routine maintenance, in the form of oil changes, tune-ups, and any (cover your ears) breakdowns are more likely—and yes, more expensive—than what a motorless trailer will put you through.

Two Eggs, One Basket

Seeing your Class A motorhomes up on blocks at the mechanics is a dreadful experience. Did I say dreadful? I mean horrible. You know the terror that strikes you when your good old Chevy won't start? Combine that with the painful sensation of seeing a leak in your living room or broken disposal in the kitchen. Having your motorhome indisposed and out of action is like car trouble *and* house trouble all in one. Actually, that's *exactly* what it is. Passengers onboard a disabled motorized RV are going to have to find another place to sleep *and* a way to get there. This is why towing a secondary vehicle is an uplifting exercise.

Getting Cocky

We've referred to the place where the driver and co-pilot sit as the "cockpit" several times already. Why do we call it this? It's just fun to say, I guess. "Honey, I'll be in the cockpit if you need me." Admit it, you've always wanted your very own cockpit, haven't you? Well, don't kill the messenger, but when not in use, the cockpit is pretty useless. In fact, the rest of the interior must compensate for its very presence, jamming amenities and living areas into the remaining space. Sure, you can hang clothes to dry on the steering wheel or showcase your *Star Wars* figures on the dashboard, but you're basically wasting about 10 cubic feet of space when you're not behind the wheel.

Since RVing is definitely a game of inches, we like functional space. Trailer owners, pleasantly cockpit-free, incorporate this area into the rest of their design. The result is a larger bedroom, more kitchen space, or a spot to put their life-size replica of E.T. To counter this, many motorhomes feature swivel driver and co-pilot chairs, so you can join in on the action in the living area. This certainly brings some usefulness to the area.

Getting Around

You're thinking: "What? He just listed easier driving as one of the unique advantages of a motorized RV up above and now he's saying getting around is more difficult? Let's throw out this book and go see a movie instead." Wait! Give me a second chance. Have you lost weight? My, you are handsome/beautiful!

The thing is, once the destination is reached, the driving advantage swings back to towable owner. Why? That nifty car or truck that's been pulling their trailer around for the last 400 miles can now be disconnected and ferry the family around nice and easy. The trailer sits at the campground or Grandma's house until you hitch up again. Motorhomers who have decided against towing a second vehicle (or "dinghy," as explained in Chapter 1, "Why RV?") must make all side trips, errands, and sightseeing jaunts in their RV—and everyone must go together. Whether you're going to the movies or Mom's underwater basket-weaving class, everyone's along for the ride.

Floor Plan-o-Rama

Besides an engine and a cockpit, what do all motorhomes have in common? No, besides wheels. Besides a roof. And … I knew you'd be difficult. The bedroom is always in the rear of the coach. That's just the way it is. Add that to the fact that the cockpit is in the front (and we wouldn't have it any other way), and it leads to a fairly predictable series of floor plans to say the least. Sure, kitchens and bathrooms may move from one side of the coach to the other, and onboard standards and options change somewhat. But, basically, the room layouts are nearly identical, meaning fewer interior choices for prospective buyers.

You Are Depreciated

We've all heard the cautionary tale about depreciation. Buy a new car, drive a mile, try to sell it, and what do you get? Less money? Maybe even much less. Since it's now a *used* vehicle, it's suddenly worth less. Is that example kinda silly? Sure, but it doesn't make it any less true. Motorized vehicles have a dirty rat onboard in the form of their odometer. It tells new buyers everything they already suspected, dating mileage and creating doubt about the mechanical aspects of the RV.

Not only do motorized RVs cost more, but they also lose their value faster. An engine means more can go wrong. Try selling your two-year-old motorhome after logging a few cross-country trips and you'll experience this motorized bias firsthand. Trailers, with fewer mechanisms to wear down and break, endure the prying eyes of trade-in time much better.

Choices, Choices

Again, it can be difficult to speak generally of all RVs, and motorized RVs are no exceptions. Each kind is different, each with unique strengths to woo you from RV Wannabe to RV Addict. What might be right for you and the kids might never work for Grandma and her boa constrictor. And vice versa.

There are four types of motorized recreational vehicles: Class A motorhomes, Class B motorhomes, Class C motorhomes, and truck campers. An in-depth look at each is provided in the pages ahead.

Class A Motorhomes

Pretty much everyone knows one of these when he sees it. In a sea of trendy SUVs, kid-carrying mini-vans, and monster pickup trucks, Class A motorhomes are still the kings of the road, ranging in size from 25 to 45 feet in length and tipping the scales in excess of 20,000 pounds. Class As are fully self-contained vehicles, complete with a separate master bedroom, kitchen, bathroom with shower and/or tub, living area, and cockpit. You can also expect lots of interior and exterior storage for all your trip essentials. The majority have at least one slide-out room, and models with two or three are becoming increasingly common. They are the largest, most luxurious, and, therefore, the most expensive commercially made recreational vehicles on the road.

With sleeping for up to eight passengers and costs reaching up to a half-million dollars, the Class A motorhome is the biggest, most opulent motorized RV available.

(Photo courtesy of Monaco Corporation)

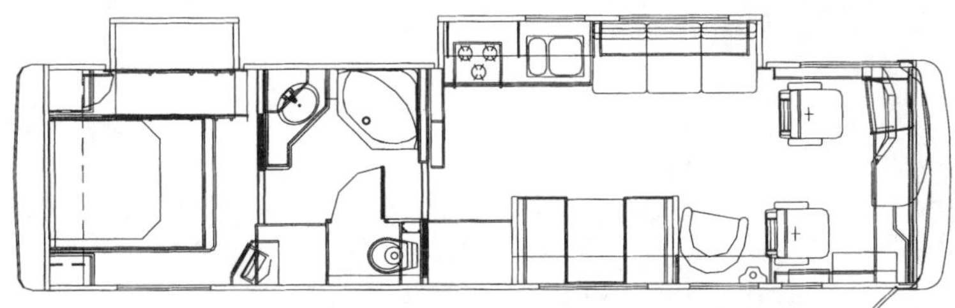

A typical Class A floor plan, with two slide-out rooms, a queen-size bed, and a bathroom, kitchen, and living area.

(Illustration courtesy of Monaco Corporation)

What Is It?

Class As are built on a specially designed chassis or existing bus chassis, powered by a gasoline or diesel engine. *Diesel pusher* models feature a diesel engine located in the rear of the coach, to better and more quietly propel you down the road. Engine noise is virtually eliminated in the cockpit area while riding in a diesel pusher model. We'll talk more about the differences between gas and diesel engines and the usefulness of wide-bodies in Chapter 6, "Narrowing Down Your Choices." *Wide-body* models are fairly common and boast an extra wide interior space. *Basement models* deliver lots of storage between the chassis and the floor of the interior. If a high-end Class A doesn't have what you need, you may need to reconsider if RVing is right for you. The range of onboard options should leave travelers with plenty to do and plenty of space to do it in.

RVocabulary

Motorhomes powered by a rear-mounted diesel engine, so equipped to propel rather than pull larger vehicles, are known as **diesel pushers.** They are generally found in motorhomes 35 feet in length and larger.

Any recreational vehicle wider than 96 inches, with 102 inches being the most common measurement, is a **wide body.** Most states limit vehicle width to 102 inches, and a few prohibit wide body RVs on some highways. This number does not include the added dimensions of expanding slide-out rooms.

Basement models are RVs with a separate storage section located between the chassis and the interior floor. Such designs allow for much greater storage capacity and accessibility to packed items.

Get Some Sleep

Mom and Dad are happy in their private master bedroom with queen-size bed. Other couples might share the sleeper/sofa and/or convertible dinette table and bench seats. Reclining chairs sometimes deploy into impromptu sleeping areas, often with mixed results. As always, numerous floor plans are available, with options such as bunk beds and double beds (instead of a queen-size), and other furnishings that might work in a pinch. Larger coaches are well suited for 6 to 8 passengers, and 10 is not out of the question.

What's Cookin'?

The abundance of riches continues in the galley, home to everything the camp cook could want. Standards include a three- or four-burner stove, oven, microwave, twin sinks, double-door refrigerator, and freezer. A pull-out pantry with built-in shelving, coffee maker, spice rack, and lots of deep cabinets and drawers are also common. Counter space, usually a premium in smaller RVs, should be as ample as the kitchen in your first apartment. Irritable landlord sold separately.

Pull Over

Examine and verify any claims in terms of sleeping capacity prior to purchasing any RV. Test out all bedding to see if it's fit for an adult or would be better suited for a small child. Sleeping capacity estimates do not follow any legal definitions. Some claims may be wishful thinking on the part of the manufacturer. Untested bedding may leave passengers cranky come nighttime.

Just Relax

Lots of living space makes larger motorhomes the most popular motorized RV in the marketplace. Nearly every model is offered in at least one living room slide-out floor plan. Two and three slide-outs may expand the kitchen, bedroom, and main living area.

The dynamic of the communal space follows that of the quintessential American living room—loads of comfortable furnishings revolving around a large color television. Of course, your house probably isn't equipped with a slide-out room if you're feeling a bit cramped. Couches turn into beds, recliners, well … recline—even the chairs in the cockpit most likely swivel to join in on the conversation. A host of side tables, interior lighting, and plenty of storage compartments in all shapes and sizes grace the coach.

One for the Road

Did you know there's something out there more extravagant than a Class A motorhome? How about a custom-made bus? The choice of the famous and the well-to-do, a 40- or 45-foot luxury bus starts where the ultra-nice motorhomes leave off. And so do the prices. The good news is that if you can afford one, you may equip it however you want. Water beds, his and her bathrooms, built-in karaoke machines, and state-of-the-art gadgetry are yours, assuming your wallet can handle it.

Motorhome designers rarely hold back in terms of luxury appointments for their Class A buyers. Carpeting is thick and interiors come in multiple color schemes. Mini-blinds cover the large windows scattered throughout the interior. VCRs, CD stereos with multiple speaker set-ups, and vanities and/or workstations (for computers or whatever) are usually offered as a standard or an affordable option. A powerful furnace and air conditioner—sometimes two—should come standard.

Road Scholar

RV buyers usually have their choice of several color schemes. Different colors for everything from the wallpaper, drapes, or blinds to carpeting and upholstery are yours to chose. However, enterprising consumers sometimes install other carpeting, re-hang blinds, re-upholster furniture, and the like if they can't find a style that suits them or their preferences change over time, just as they might in their own homes.

Showering and Other Dirty Business

A luxurious motorhome won't dazzle throughout only to leave the bathroom as an underachieving afterthought. In high-end models, the word glamorous comes to mind. Glass showers and tubs deliver regal looks and enough room for you and a rubber ducky of decent proportions. A skylight opens up additional light as well as initial insights into today's forecast firsthand. The shower and toilet often bookend either side of the coach, usually between the master bedroom and the rest of the interior. A separate vanity with sink, medicine cabinet, and additional storage sits adjacent to the shower. There should be no problems finding outlets, towel racks, and spots for all the little extras. The typical Class A bathroom simply outguns any other motorized vehicle in terms of spaciousness, aesthetics, and features.

Behind the Wheel

For those who enjoy riding up high in their SUVs, driving a motorhome is like that, multiplied by 10. Drivers look eye-to-eye with the truckers now, nodding in mutual appreciation of their mighty rigs. Pilot's (okay, driver's) and co-pilot's chairs are plush and comfortable, sometimes leather but always the nicest seat on the highway. A large, wrap-around window opens up a new world of scenery. Manufacturers take great pains to forge a smooth and comfortable ride. It feels like you're riding on air in most luxury Class As. Standard conveniences include electric mirrors, cassette/CD player, air conditioning, cruise control, and all the goodies of an expensive import.

Now don't panic, but the windshield-mounted rearview mirror is nearly always AWOL. It's simply useless in a vehicle of this size, revealing nothing but the kids in the back pulling each other's hair. But don't worry, you won't miss it. Backing up a large motorhome is accomplished in several ways. Large side mirrors reveal all the action behind the coach, or an add-on rear-mounted camera and monitor display all the happenings behind you. Or just ask someone to hop out and guide you in, which is the most common practice.

A taller exterior height—12 feet is average—means special attention should be paid to your motorhome's clearance height. A roof-mounted air conditioning adds another 6 to 10 inches. As a result, drivers must pay particular attention to low-hanging tree branches, overhead shelters at gas stations, and that occasional shorty overpass downtown.

More than anything, driving a Class A motorhome requires patience, not some untapped driving prowess. Extra time is needed to change lanes, stop, and accelerate. A motorhome is a 20,000-pound home on wheels, and often it drives like it. It might respond to steep mountain grades like a child without a nap—sluggish—or move about like a lumbering whale compared to your sports car back home. However, a quick glance behind you to see all your living space and furnishings should take the sting out of sometimes pokey travel.

Typical Specs

A larger RV allows for larger self-containment options. This means you can stay away from civilization (if you want to) for a greater length of time, boondocking without having to go into town to refill the propane container or empty your various holding tanks. Although I rarely see an expensive motorhome used for deep-woods adventures or other dry-camping escapades, they are in many ways more suited for it than any other RVs. Onboard generators create power where there is none, and are almost always listed as standards, fueled by a seemingly bottomless gas tank. Holding and LP containers are cavernous, allowing for greater periods between emptying and fill-ups.

Standard Specifications for a Typical Class A Motorhome

Self-Containment Features	Gallons
Fuel tank	75 to 200
Fresh water storage system	50 to 125
Gray water holding tank	40 to 100
Black water holding tank	40 to 100
LP gas container(s)	20 to 40
Water heater	6 to 10

Price Tag

Ah, yes, we had to talk about price, didn't we? A Class A may start at $50,000 for a small, "entry-level" gasoline model and evolve into as luxurious and pricey RV as you desire. A half-million dollars is not out of the question if you go hog wild, choosing the biggest version and loading it to the gills with goodies. And there's absolutely every kind of model in between. (I'm sure we can find you something nice in the $80,000 to $120,000 category.) Fortunately, just like your automobile and home, financing is available.

Fuel is the next major cost, as even the more fuel-efficient motorhomes (warning: oxymoron alert) might earn a dozen miles per gallon at best. A modest diesel engine may better that average by a few miles. A 100-gallon fill up at $1.50 a gallon is $150, no small change considering you might be making the gas station pilgrimage a couple times per week during longer trips. A more expensive RV purchase such as this also necessitates a larger insurance premium, storage costs (if necessary), and repairs. Unlike your serviceable everyday vehicle, routine maintenance in the forms of oil changes, tire service, and basic troubleshooting can only be performed by an RV service center, with facilities adept at handling the big rigs.

Final Analysis

The question is not so much who Class As are good for, but who can afford them. All that space and luxury comes attached with a fairly significant price tag, requiring a more serious commitment from their owners. Folks looking for casual weekends away might find a more suitable RV for their needs for less money, as might anyone just starting out and new to the lifestyle. A large motorhome demands thoughtful consideration to your types of usage. However, if you love RVing, with all its bells and whistles, you really can't do much better. Full-timers, eager for all the space and comforts possible, can justify the costs since it serves as their primary residence. Large families who love to camp and travel together might, over time, whittle down the costs compared to other forms of vacations.

The major drawbacks usually come down to drivability. Maneuvering a 35- or 40-foot motorhome is just too daunting a challenge for some folks. My 80-year-old Aunt Rite wasn't one of those, but buying a Class A does merit some attention in this respect. Finding a parking space large enough to accommodate your rig is also tough. Uncovering a spot in a residential neighborhood, that charming resort town, or within a metropolitan area is especially trying when you feel like you have the Seventh Cavalry in tow. Storing your motorhome for the winter requires a special facility (and special costs), which may or may not be located nearby.

A vehicle this size may require some sacrifices for your itinerary. Not every campground can handle the big rigs, which limits your choices somewhat, although not significantly. Some government-run campgrounds may lack the infrastructure for larger motorhomes. Navigating the narrow confines of a local park or rush-hour traffic might be nerve-wracking for some. And this is not the greatest vehicle to take four-wheeling off the beaten path. There also might be some attractions, businesses, and such that may not be able to accommodate a parked vehicle of this size. Remember, in a large motorhome, you should think like a mob boss—always plan a way out of any situation.

Class B Motorhomes

It looks like a van, drives like a van, but once you venture inside, it takes but a moment to realize you're not in Kansas anymore. These vehicles are popular with people who want to incorporate their recreational vehicles into their everyday lives. By day, a Class B serves as a dutiful second vehicle, great for shuttling the kids to school, running errands, and getting you wherever you want to go without the angst of lugging around an enormous RV. A large motorhome or travel trailer just seems strangely out of place at the PTA meeting. There's lots of space for all the kids (the whole soccer team, too), a menagerie of golden retrievers, and all those great buys you found at the antique auction. Class Bs drive like a dream and should easily fit in conventional parking spots and probably your garage. (Assuming you move your beer can collection out of the way.) Class Bs are also known as conversion vans, camper vans, and van campers.

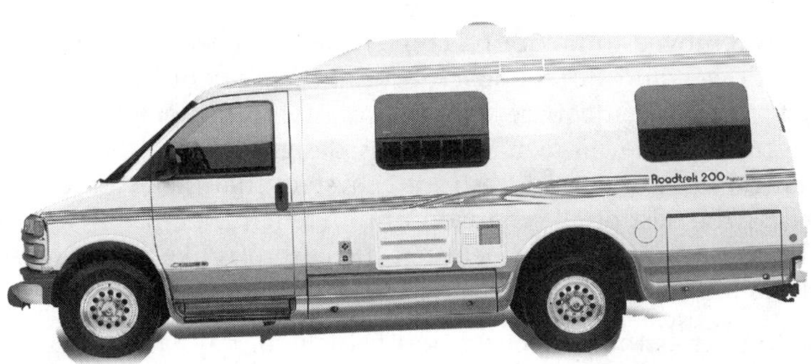

Class B motorhomes (camper vans) are known for their versatility as both a self-contained RV and an exceptionally mobile everyday vehicle.

(Courtesy of Home and Park Motorhomes)

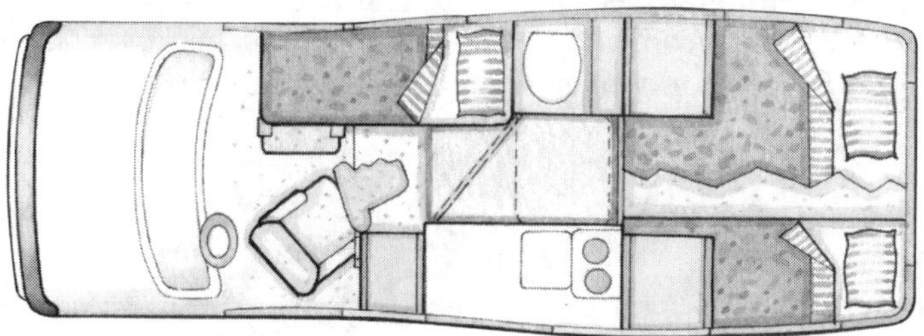

A typical van camper floor plan, complete with sleeping for two to three, galley, and small living area.

(Illustration courtesy of Home and Park Motorhomes)

When the weekend comes, look out. This is where these motorhomes really shine. Grab the kids, dogs, and gear and head north to the state park for a day of hiking, swimming, and picnicking. Arrive at the football game early for a little traditional tailgating, with a mobile kitchen to cook the feast, a refrigerator full of tasty beverages, and a TV to watch the pre-game show. Arrange a spontaneous getaway for you and the Mrs., confident in the knowledge there's always a place to sleep.

What Is It?

Credit the many Summers of Love of the late 1960s and early 1970s for the advent of these vehicles, when more and more people began customizing their vans with bedding and basic cooking equipment to accommodate their, ahem ... lifestyle. (Insert your own Grateful Dead joke here.) This craze led to the growth of conversion companies, willing to do the work in a more professional manner. Thus, the conversion van segment of the RV marketplace was born. These days, conversion vans fall under the category of Class B motorhomes.

Despite their sometimes everyday looks, Class Bs are card-carrying members of the recreational vehicle community. In fact, some strongly resemble the everyday van or mini-van perhaps parked right now in your very own driveway, only probably bigger, wider, and taller to accommodate all sorts of un-vanlike features. Underneath lies the same chassis as normal vans, with engines from such familiar names as Dodge, GM, and Ford. The cockpit area is virtually the same, too. But after that, all bets are off.

The conventional seating is removed in favor of a convertible or queen-size bed, small kitchen, bathroom, shower, and storage space. A drop floor might be installed and the rooftop extended to provide adequate standing room. Interior heights vary from five feet, five inches to nearly seven feet. Wide-body designs are common. The same holding tanks, electrical functions, and fresh water system that make an RV, well, an RV, are all present. And, best of all, you won't find French fries, pacifiers, and Legos imbedded in the backseats and jammed between the cushions like your van at home. At least not until the kids have at it.

My wife and I find these RVs act as the perfect support vehicle for days at the beach. Large outside storage compartments easily haul chairs, coolers, large towels, and all the must-have water toys. It's just not any fun unless you can tote along your inflatable pineapple raft, is it? When temperatures soar, we retreat back to the van, flip on the air conditioning, grab a few sodas from the fridge, and play a game of cards. And when the day is done, there's a condo on wheels to change clothes, wash up, and off we go, on to the next fun pursuit.

Get Some Sleep

Depending on the size of each passenger, most vans can sleep two people reasonably well. Four people is possible, depending on the model and floor plan. As always, the flexibility and willingness of kids to contort into a smaller sleeping area is a big plus. Bedding comes in many forms. The wrap-around sofa might pull out to make a double or two twin beds, or a queen-size mattress might sit unaltered in the back of the vehicle. In some cases, chairs lay completely horizontally, creating a usable night's sleep for the junior members of the crew. Many van owners sprinkle in hotel or motel stays if traveling with larger groups onboard. As always, different floor plans and manufacturers feature a number of ingenious uses of space.

What's Cookin'?

You won't lack for all the necessary appliances come mealtime. A two-burner stove, oven, sink, refrigerator, and microwave oven are common. However, counter space, cabinets, and drawers are at a premium. You may or may not have a pantry for stock food items. The amount of fresh water and LP gas, which powers heat and some appliances and governs drinking water, is limited, meaning additional fill-ups are sometimes necessary if you do a lot of boondocking. Preparing Martha Stewart–esque meals onboard in this relatively small area would be a triumph. More likely, Class B owners enjoy simpler meals, cook outside over the campfire or grill, or journey into town to eat. The amount and complexity of meals is determined by your willingness to work in a relatively small cooking area.

Just Relax

You might be lounging about on a sofa, sitting in leather chairs, or chatting around a dinette table in bench seats. Again, floor plans vary, but every camper van has a place for the family to talk, play games, and dine together. Spend nights watching TV or a movie through the VCR (usually listed as an option) or listening to music (either on a separate stereo system or using the one in the cockpit area). Windows slide open for breezes and views. A forced-air furnace and air conditioning keep you comfortable in variant temperatures. An optional generator keeps things going when shoreline power is out of reach. Life onboard is snug depending on the number of passengers, but certainly blows the doors off any other family vehicle in terms of functionality.

Showering and Other Dirty Business

The bathroom might be a separate hard-sided room or a section that pulls out of the wall and locks into position; the room recedes back into the sidewall when you're finished with it. Most every conversion van is outfitted with a toilet and shower, the latter of which might simply be a wrap-around curtain with a hand-held shower head and in-floor drainage system. Other models possess an outside shower, best reserved for muddy hands and feet or washing off the catch of the day. A water heater warms a few gallons of hot water with some advance notice. In any situation, space is tight. Some travelers favor using the campground's facilities instead, which is always an option no matter what type of RV you own.

Behind the Wheel

There aren't too many RVs you'd feel comfortable venturing through a drive-thru window or car wash in, but a camper van easily obliges. In fact, low overhead clearances and modest lengths make for easy trips no matter where you go. For those at ease operating a larger SUV or pickup truck, life behind the wheel of a Class B shouldn't be much different. Braking, turning radius, and overall acceleration may be lacking somewhat compared to your everyday vehicle, but the difference is negligible.

Since these vehicles are longer and wider than your car at home, backing up is more of a challenge. However, a clear view of the back window and full use of the rearview mirror remains, which makes the process easier than in most motorhomes. Overall, the conversion van ranks near the very top of drivable recreational vehicles.

Typical Specs

Easy driving, modest lengths and widths, and an optional generator make Class Bs as adept at surviving in the backwoods as Rambo. A few companies produce four-wheel drive models, kicking up such excursions to the next level of terrain and excitement.

Standard Specifications for a Typical Class B Motorhome

Self-Containment Features	Gallons
Fuel tank	25 to 35
Fresh water storage	15 to 35
Gray water holding tank	12 to 30
Black water holding tank	10 to 20
LP gas container(s)	5 to 30
Water heater	6 to 10

Price Tag

Camper vans aren't cheap, especially when you consider that some larger motorhomes offer much more livable space and amenities for less money. Prices range from approximately $40,000 to $80,000, certainly a great deal more than the commercial vans you're used to. Cost is factored by overall size, onboard amenities, slide-outs, and choice of engines.

Expect gas mileage to drift between 12 to 20 mpg. If you're planning on storing your van for the winter, your garage should work, saving you several months' rent at a dealership or storage facility. Otherwise, there are those costs to consider. Insurance is similar to the cost of your everyday vehicles, with adjustments made for type of usage.

Final Analysis

Nimble maneuvering, low profiles, and conventional looks make Class Bs 24/7 recreational vehicles. Their ability to adapt equally well to both life in the city and weekend getaways puts camper vans in a unique territory. No other RV functions as well as an everyday vehicle, a fact that should be considered into a somewhat inflated sticker price. While three to four passengers could get along okay onboard, Class Bs are better suited for singles, couples, and families with small children.

Gains in drivability and the perks of a usable second vehicle are somewhat tempered by the fact that life onboard can be fairly restrictive. Accessing the interior through the side or rear entry doors can necessitate an awkward entry. A few models, usually those boasting sleeker profiles, don't have enough room for taller passengers to stand up straight. A larger motorhome at roughly the same cost is much better suited for extended travel. Enjoying several extended weeks on the road is surely possible, assuming the lack of moving-around room doesn't bother you. But there is no better RV for tailgating, day trips, and weekends spent touring the countryside.

Class C Motorhomes

Think of a Class A motorhome and a Class B van camper zapped by a morphing laser from a mad science—or your local RV manufacturer—and you come close to what a Class C delivers: decent space in a very drivable vehicle. Getting around, not to mention parking and backing up, is just that much easier, making these RVs an all-around good bet. Class C motorhomes, also known as mini-motorhomes (ah, that's cute), are a nice compromise in the world of motorized RVs. These vehicles feature everything their larger counterparts do—bathrooms, bedrooms, kitchens, living area, storage, slide-outs, cockpit, and loads of standards—but at a reduced size. Although lengths usually range from approximately 20 to 32 feet, sleeping capacity can rival the big boys. Up to eight slumbering passengers is possible in some units.

Class C motorhomes deliver similar sleeping capacities and onboard amenities as larger Class A motorhomes, but in a smaller package.

(Photo courtesy of Winnebago Industries)

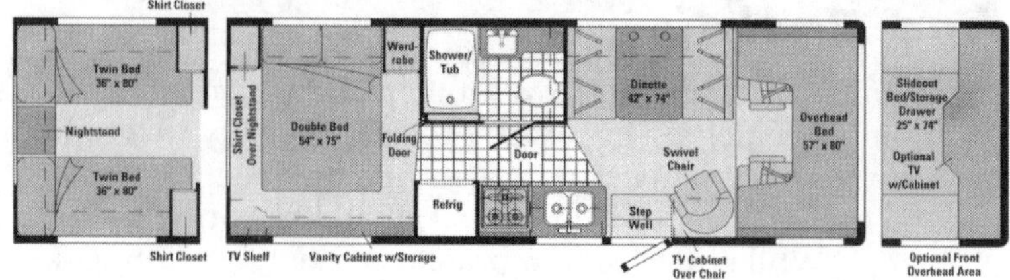

A typical Class C motorhome floor plan. Notice the over-the-cab sleeping area, a hallmark of this type of motorhome.

(Illustration courtesy of Winnebago Industries)

What Is It?

Mini-motorhomes start with the same basic van chassis as a Class B, nearly always courtesy of Dodge, Ford, or General Motors. However, a specially manufactured frame is then added, giving them a unique profile. Units are capped off with the trademark "*cab*-over" design, which creates an inhabitable space over the cockpit area and serves as a serviceable, albeit tight, sleeping area or spot to store larger items. Slide-outs are common, and some vehicles are beginning to affix up to three of them onboard. Diesel engines and four-wheel drive models also are available.

RVocabulary

The **cab** is another name for the cockpit. Class Cs are specially built so a portion of the shell actually hangs over the cab, providing an additional sleeping area or storage space.

Get Some Sleep

The rear private bedroom paired with a sleeping nook over the cab remains the dominant floor plan. Throw in a sleeper sofa and/or convertible dinette table and bench seats, and sleeping for six is a breeze. However, in recent years, Class C manufacturers loosened up and started creating more radical layouts. Wander into the back of some models and you might be greeted by the smell of bacon and eggs from a stocked kitchen, splitting the rear portion of the coach with a bathroom and shower. In fact, the master bedroom and its much-appreciated queen-size bed may have vanished, replaced by a sleeper sofa, expandable couch tandem, or other convertible bedding in the living area.

The debate over the usefulness of the cab-over sleeping area rages on. Assuming you can find someone to sleep in this smallish space, you'll be rewarded by a higher sleeping capacity and one less body to step over in the morning. Kids really seem to enjoy it, towering high above the rest of the crew in their secluded fortress. A privacy curtain and windows only add to this affect. Waking up to the rat-a-tat-tat of imaginary machine gun fire is likely.

Pull Over

The acceptance of the cab-over sleeping area is usually determined by the age of the guest. Youngsters seem to find the tiny area a space ship in the making and usually offer little resistance to sleeping there. Older passengers might struggle with the awkward ascent and find the crypt-like clearance somewhat troubling. Gauge the receptiveness of passengers to the area before assigning it for the night.

What's Cookin'?

The galley is reduced to scale, but still equipped with all the necessary cooking appliances to be dangerous come mealtime. A large refrigerator, two- to four-burner stove, oven, microwave, and double-sided sink are standard. However, the battle is won and lost in the extras. I've served as camp cook for four grumpy fishermen in a Class C that never disappointed. Of course, the menu was meat, meat, and more meat. I rallied thanks to generous countertop space, ample drawers and cupboards, and a pull-out pantry with adjustable shelves for a token can of vegetables. Other models weren't as gourmet-friendly, with little room to put a spatula, let alone my Pork ala Pork concoction. The majority of galleys, however, are quite functional for a small family. Determine the likelihood and frequency of onboard meals to help determine the best floor plan for you.

Just Relax

All the usual components and furnishings are included, with ingenious methods of incorporating a lot of onboard offerings in a relatively condensed package. The living room, often the benefactor of a slide-out room, usually features a dinette and sofa to enlist plenty of space to gather. In models under 25 feet, expect one or the other, but not both. A color television, VCR, stereo with multiple speakers, and cable TV and phone jacks are standard or available as relatively painless upgrades. All temperature controls (furnace and air conditioning) are present to keep you cool in summer, warm when temperatures plummet.

Interior and exterior storage compartments rank somewhere between Class As and Class Bs. Unless you're an insufferable pack rat (guilty as charged), finding a spot for all your "must-haves" shouldn't be a problem. Go ahead, bring your stack of Fantastic

Four comic books; most Class Cs can take it. Deep cabinets, a variety of drawers, wardrobe closets, and dressers should withstand most families' onslaught of provisions. Assorted exterior compartments, many of which are insulated, carpeted, and well lit for nightly rummaging, are best suited for durable fare such as golf clubs, folding chairs, and that gorilla suit for fun around the campfire.

Showering and Other Dirty Business

When it's time to pay the piper, your RV's bathroom often flips the bill. The bathroom/shower area is the first to get short-changed in smaller coaches, and the everyday Class C is no stranger to this. Expect snug fits in the bathroom and potential tight squeezes into the shower. A tub is unlikely, and if so equipped, probably not the sudsy paradise you envision. However, variances in these rooms occur, so be choosy if this space is important to you.

Behind the Wheel

Remember that time you rented that truck to move Uncle Jimmy to his condo in Florida? Minus the rough ride, his two angry pit bulls, and a cargo full of commemorative *Wizard of Oz* plates, driving a mini-motorhome is like that—only about a million times better. You won't see anything in the cockpit that you haven't seen before, and driving is a plus, not a liability, like some larger motorhomes. Units pushing 30 feet in length require patience, as acceleration, braking, and turning may take some getting used to.

Don't be surprised if a brawl ensues over who's going to drive. Class Cs are a blast to operate, with their often spirited acceleration, convincing stopping power, and relatively tight turning abilities. Go ahead, take that dirt path and see where you end up. Drive through the mall parking lot with confidence, and then park in a conventional space (better performed with smaller models). And when it comes time to throw it in reverse, ah, no sweat. Again, your rearview mirror won't be there to comfort you, but large side mirrors do the trick. Or send hubby out to help back you in. I'm proud to say that I've even managed to parallel park a Class C, and as the saying goes, if I can do it, anyone can. (Kids, don't try this at home.) However, it's best to stick to conventional parking spots. And keep it out of the drive-thru lane, okay?

A relatively low profile—typically 10 to 11 feet, 5 inches (add 8 to 10 inches more for a rooftop air conditioner)—reduces the possible clearance obstacles faced by larger motorhomes' owners. Still, drivers must be cognizant at all times of their rig's overall exterior height in the case of potential roof-scrapers that may damage your vehicle.

Typical Specs

A more agile alternative to larger motorhomes, Class Cs can squeeze through most awkward terrain to reach that remote camp-out location. Generators are usually standard, or, at the very least, wired for their future installation. Depending on the size of the vehicle and one's conservation practices, the various tanks and power sources should keep any hookup-free adventures running for several days without interruption.

Standard Specifications for a Typical Class C Motorhome

Self-Containment Features	Gallons
Fuel tank	55
Fresh water storage	30 to 60
Gray water holding tank	20 to 40
Black water holding tank	20 to 50
LP gas container(s)	7 to 40
Water heater	6 to 10

Price Tag

Do I buy that new Lexus or a mini-motorhome? Isn't the choice obvious? With a starting price of around $50,000, you, the kids, and the cat (and her scratching post) can travel, sleep, and eat your way across the nation. Larger and more expansive models might reach $85,000, still a bargain compared to bunking down in your pricey import. Take that, luxury automobiles.

A few smaller models might just tuck away nicely in your garage, thus eliminating the need for off-site storage expense. Insurance is a factor, probably somewhere between a Class A and a Class B motorhome, while routine maintenance should be relatively reasonable. Since your Class C started with a van chassis, larger repair shops should be able to handle many maintenance concerns. However, you might need to take it to a certified RV dealership or service center if your local garage balks at serving recreational vehicles.

Gas mileage is good, not great. Large models feast on fuel like a group of Boy Scouts at the local Dairy Queen; smaller versions may deliver up to 20 miles per gallon with a strong tail wind. But don't count on Toyota Corolla–like fuel economy here.

Final Analysis

Class Cs are useful for most any type of traveling situation. Call it the Goldilocks effect: Class As are too big, Class Bs too small, but these mini-motorhomes are just right for many. Their relative driving ease coupled with a surprising passenger capacity arms travelers with a multifaceted leisure machine. Factor in these pluses with reasonable start-up costs and the case for the mini gets stronger and stronger.

As a full-timing machine, Class Cs work exceptionally well. Everything is onboard—including enough elbowroom for you and the Mrs.—to create a truly memorable year-round living experience. Traveling in a 30-foot version with double slide-outs leaves nothing to be desired. A queen-size bed, along with the overall dimensions and appointments of the master bedroom, are sometimes sacrificed in smaller models in order to complete the rest of the interior. A dwarfed bathroom and cramped shower also sometimes come along with the territory. However, that's always the key to any RV—knowing what you can live with and what you can't.

Truck Camper

The rugged truck camper, also known as a pickup camper, provides a steady mix of comforts and nimble transportation to most any destination, in a very inexpensive package. This is simply one of the most economical ways to camp and play in all known creation, the ultimate for those who like to get off the beaten path and forge their own trail. Truck campers can go where other RVs—most any vehicle, for that matter—fear to tread.

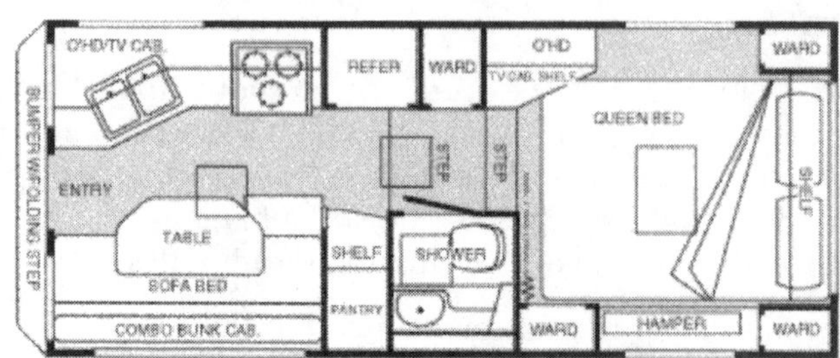

A truck camper boasts a number of features of larger motorized RVs in a fraction of the space.

(Illustration courtesy of Fleetwood RV)

What Is It?

A truck camper is essentially a pickup truck with a hard-sided camper, or cap, secured to the cargo bed. Then, presto, your everyday, hard-working vehicle is magically transformed into a genuine recreational vehicle. Who would have thought that the bed of that old pickup, formerly used only to haul around tools, firewood, and your boss's patio furniture, could suddenly transform into a year-round home on wheels. Neat, huh?

Inside plays host to relatively the same basic features of any other RV, only in a much smaller package. There are places to sleep, various cooking appliances, storage, and places to sit, relax, and plan your next camping escapades. Temperature functions are regulated with a heater and air conditioning; you can open the screened windows if the weather's nice or employ interior fans found in the ceiling. Nearly all truck campers have hot and cold running water, lighting, and are powered by the use of LP gas, or can run off the generator (if so equipped) when you're away from the conventional power source found at most campgrounds. Bathrooms and showers are fairly common. Truck campers usually sleep between two and six people, depending on the size, floor plan, and your passengers' willingness to cuddle.

The Perfect Fit

Trucks and the camper sections are rarely sold together in one package. Camper caps come in many sizes, so fitting it to your current truck, whether it be a monstrous or compact version, shouldn't be a problem. The most important criteria is not to exceed the truck's payload capacity, which should be listed in the owner's manual. To gauge this, add the weight of the camper itself (your dealer should know this, or it will be listed in the unit's owner's manual), plus the estimated weight of passengers, their gear, and fully loaded holding tanks. If this number is less than your pickup's carrying capacity, your truck can safely do the job.

Another factor is the overall center of gravity. It's not unusual for the camper to hang up to several feet beyond the end of the cargo area; however, make sure the overhang doesn't exceed three feet. Your dealer should help make sure you have the best fit for your existing vehicle.

For those without the necessary truck, you can either buy the camper first and match up a truck later, or vice versa. However, since your pickup truck will probably exceed the cost of the camper (far exceed in many cases, particularly if you purchase one with a diesel engine), it probably makes more sense to purchase the truck first. Caution, spouses: If your significant other has been toying with the idea of buying a truck, this may push him or her over the edge.

Truck campers are situated fully into the bed of the pickup and secured with turnbuckles and tie-down brackets—two on each side. Manually operated hydraulic camper jacks, permanently bolted to the

Road Scholar

One of the nice perks of a truck camper is its flexibility, offering the chance to install and remove the cap from the pickup with relative ease. Once the camping adventure is over, truck camper owners have the option of removing the cap, storing it away, and resuming their civilian lives until the call of the wild strikes again.

One for the Road

It usually takes a couple of people to dismount a slide-off truck camper model, so make sure if frequent off-loading is paramount, that you have access to a pal or two to help you. Campers may weigh several thousand pounds, making frequent loading a somewhat arduous task. Otherwise, hydraulic jacks make the job easier on newer versions.

four corners of the camper, make loading and unloading a breeze. Extending each jack eventually raises the camper above the level of the truck bed, providing plenty of maneuvering room to back the truck under or to pull the truck out. For safety, always have a buddy—or burly mountain man—help you.

Get Some Sleep

A large bed (sometimes a queen) is situated in the area over the truck cab, and should yield a comfortable, albeit somewhat cramped, night's sleep for an additional two passengers. Some floor plans boast additional bedding, either in the form of transformable couches, bench seats, dinettes, or double beds. RV manufacturers have a lot of clever ways to create beds out of otherwise functional space. Some campers claim accommodations for six, but I urge caution here. Six adults in this small amount of space will undoubtedly lead to calamities that would make even the Three Stooges blush. Bunk bed models are sometimes available for younger passengers.

What's Cookin'?

Gourmets need to make peace with the fact that their truck camper probably won't allow for many elaborate meals. Counter space is limited and storage is a valuable commodity. Your waffle iron, food processor, and deep fat fryer (for late night chicken wings, of course!) should probably stay at home. Most galleys consist of an oven and/or two-burner stove, a small refrigerator (perhaps a freezer, too), pantry, sink, and possibly a microwave oven. You might have to pay a little more to get these items as options, but that varies from manufacturer to manufacturer.

Pull Over

Many campers are not equipped with seatbelts. Even so equipped, passengers should ride in the truck's cab or in a separate vehicle. The ride inside is extremely rough and it may be illegal to do so in some areas.

Just Relax

A table with bench-style seats or wrap-around couch (both of which might turn into bedding) is common, creating a good spot to chat, plan the next day's events, or feast on the catch of the day (or frozen fish sticks if your luck went dry). TVs and stereos are sometimes offered. A host of interior cabinets and drawers house everything from silverware to clothing to all trip necessities. One model might feature a small wardrobe closet; another might be stocked with a storage chest and a row of overhead cabinets. Lights come on and off with a switch, temperatures are controlled via a thermostat, and an exhaust fan helps remove stale odors. You should find adequate lighting and enough room to move around without coming to blows with your fellow passenger(s). Year-round camping is certainly possible, thanks to adequate insulation practices and optional furnaces and air conditioning.

Interior height is problematic for your NBA pals, but adequate for most folks. An average height is approximately six feet, two inches, but this number varies from unit to unit. Some *pop-up* or *fold-down* models can expand (or pop-up) upward when not in transit, giving inhabitants more head room and space. The recent emergence of slide-out rooms, which expand a section of the room outwards, adds valuable inches onboard.

RVocabulary

Pop-up or **fold-down** truck campers lay flat in transit and must be deployed, usually by use of a hand crank, once the destination is reached. Advantages of these types of vehicle include less wind-resistance during transit, and, in many cases, increased headroom upon arrival. Pop-up models aren't as heavy and drive a little easier. These units are not to be confused with pop-up or fold-down trailers, which must be towed behind a vehicle.

Showering and Other Dirty Business

As if it weren't unbelievable enough that you could include a kitchen, bedroom, and a living room on the back of a conventional pickup, it's about to get more amazing. Many campers come equipped with a bathroom and shower, rivaling the big boy RVs as a totally self-contained experience. And while the bathroom accommodations may not rival the Taj Mahal, it's much preferable to those long, lonely trips out behind the oak tree. Deluxe units feature a private room complete with a marine-style toilet, shower, vanity, and sink. You might even get a cabinet or two thrown in for good measure. Or else, just a toilet and an external handheld shower outside the vehicle. This is also good for cleaning muddy boots, hands, and that lake trout that's been eluding you all these many days.

Behind the Wheel

You just passed the access road to the campground, now what? Motorhome owners might need to go miles ahead before finding a spot suitable to turn around. Truck campers, on the other hand, just, well, turn around. They drive like a pickup truck, because that's what they *are*. And in many cases, it's *your* existing truck, so driving should be a breeze. True, the camper attachment does add some height (roughly three or four feet) and several inches in width, but basic driving functions are the same.

Drivers won't have to concern themselves much with clearances, parking in conventional spots, or maneuvering the tight corners of city driving or those found in their favorite national park.

Be prepared, however, for more sluggish braking and less punchy acceleration, due to the extra weight of the camper. Remember, your pickup is now significantly heavier and, therefore, requires greater distances to stop and longer times to accelerate. You may also want to equip your truck with extendable mirrors to eliminate the larger blind spots, as well. Backing up is more difficult than when it was just your Ford or Chevy sans camper, complicated by the fact that your rearview mirror only shows the ubiquitous walls of the camper—or your Uncle Vinny's big head (why must he sit right there, anyway?). Fortunately, with a little help and practice, back-ups become routine.

Important Add-Ons

With the help of a few accessories, you can guarantee yourself an uneventful trip for both you and your camper. *Tie-downs* secure and fasten the camper to the bed or frame of the truck. Although well-intentioned, Uncle Maury is not qualified to hold the camper in place while in transit. Use these in conjunction with *bounce-aways,* shock-like devices attached below the cab-over section to the truck to reduce bouncing down the highway.

It is also necessary to invest in *electrical connectors* to operate your brake lights and taillights, which are obscured by the camper. Not having these is an easy way for the local sheriff to fill his monthly quota. These cords also serve to charge all the onboard functions while in transit. In some cases, depending on the overall length of the camper, *rear bumper extensions* may be necessary so the license plate is visible. Remember, the truck is licensed, not the camper, even though some come equipped with a plate bracket. The telescoping type simply extends when the camper is in place and retracts when using the truck as, well … a truck. Finally, make sure your truck camper comes with four mounted *jacks,* one on each corner. The purpose of these is two-fold: to keep the trailer off the ground when not in use, and to elevate them so you can back in your pickup between them for easy loading.

Typical Specs

Boondock away in the quintessential off-road camper. If you're serious about truly getting away from it all, opt for models with a bathroom and shower. Otherwise … well, you know. Relatively small tanks requires stricter attention to preserving available resources, but you should have the ability to stay away for a weekend if prudent with supplies.

Adding a camper to a four-wheel drive truck gives owners relatively endless possibilities in terms of where to travel. There are very few recreational vehicles that can compete with a truck camper's off-road capabilities.

Standard Specifications for a Typical Truck Camper

Self-Containment Features	Gallons
Fuel tanks	same as the pickup truck
Fresh water storage	10 to 50
Gray water holding tanks	10 to 25
Black water holding tanks	10 to 25
LP gas container(s)	5 to 5
Water heater	6

Price Tag

With a start-up cost between $5,000 and $20,000 for the camper portion, truck campers are among the least expensive recreational vehicles, ideal for "first-timers" with small families or a couple eager to get away for shorter trips. Of course, if you don't have a pickup, you will need to factor that price into the overall cost.

Truck camper enthusiasts enjoy consistently reasonable travel costs. Overall fuel costs, compared to your everyday pickup, will increase marginally due to an overall fattening up of the vehicle's weight, resulting in more work for the engine, and, thus, poorer gas mileage. Towing a boat or small trailer reduces fuel efficiency even farther.

Ancillary costs such as insurance are relatively minuscule compared to most recreational vehicles. Besides, in most cases, you were already paying insurance on your pickup, so the addition of a camper won't add very much. Most insurance companies might simply add the camper as a rider policy for a marginal fee. Again, most routine repairs and maintenance (tune-ups and oil changes, for example) are what you would have spent to keep your truck in good working order in the first place. A monthly storage fee probably won't be necessary, since campers are small enough to be stored in the garage, the backyard, or at your lucky in-law's house. All in all, truck campers are a bona fide travel bargain.

Road Scholar

Believe it or not, campers are also livable even when removed from the pickup truck, with legs to keep the unit off the ground, stable, and elevated. For extended stays in a truckless camper, it's best to support the underbelly or put the camper on blocks for additional support.

Final Analysis

Outdoors types love truck campers because these vehicles deliver a tough vehicle, capable of reaching the most remote places, like that deep-woods hideaway or that off-the-map backwater fishing hole. And depending on your pickup's towing capacity, it's still likely that there's enough power and carrying capacity to hitch up a small trailer to carry a boat, jet skis, motorcycles, or snowmobiles for even more active pursuits upon arrival.

For many, extended trips onboard a truck camper are out of the question. While these vehicles are surprisingly comfortable and livable considering their diminutive size, the accommodations do take some getting used to. Just as you wouldn't want to spend entire weeks at a time inside your tent, the same rule applies here. After all, you *are* eating, sleeping, and congregating in a space only slightly larger than the size of an average truck bed. Taller travelers will struggle with a relatively low ceiling, and it takes considerable effort for several passengers to intermingle onboard at once. All these factors make truck campers best suited for shorter getaways.

The Least You Need to Know

- Class A motorhomes cost from $50,000 all the way up to a half-million dollars. Sizes range from 25 to 45 feet and can sleep up to eight passengers. They are the largest and most well-appointed motorized RVs and a favorite with full-timers and large families alike.
- Class Bs, also known as conversion vans, van campers, and camper vans, are built on a standard van chassis, but customized with living quarters. Costs range from $40,000 to $80,000. Driving ease and their smallish size allow for everyday use.
- Class C motorhomes, or mini-motorhomes, cost between $50,000 and $85,000. Sizes range from 20 to 32 feet, and due to a special cab-over area, can sleep up to eight passengers. Minis feature everything large motorhomes do in a smaller and more maneuverable package.
- Truck campers combine a standard pickup truck with a hard-sided cap. Costs range from $5,000 to $20,000, not including the price of a truck. Truck campers are a long-time favorite for outdoors enthusiasts due to their rugged styling and nimble handling. Their compact dimensions make them best suited for short getaways.

Chapter 5

The World of Towables

In This Chapter

- Pros and cons of towable RVs
- In-depth examination of specific types
- Costs, specifications, and onboard features
- Who might benefit from each kind?

Abbott and Costello. Green eggs and ham. The Chicago Cubs and futility. Like all of life's great combinations, towables and the tow vehicles that love them comprise a tag-team for the ages. It's a partnership that has paid off in terms of lower costs, longer usage, and big-time creature comforts for owners and guests alike since the first commercially made trailers rolled off assembly lines more than 70 years ago.

The evolution of the towable enthusiast sometimes goes like this: With young children and faced with the expensive costs of getting out of the house, a couple purchases a fold-down camper to pull behind the station wagon. As the children age and everyone demands a little more space, a travel trailer is bought, perhaps splurging on one with a slide-out room, just for kicks. It won't be long before the parents, now empty-nesters, enjoy the luxury and easier towing found in a fifth-wheel trailer. However, others just jump right to the head of the class with a large first-time trailer purchase. As always, there's no right or wrong way to do it.

Affection for the towable lifestyle usually comes down to your comfort level with the thought of towing another vehicle. To some, the idea is peculiar and scary, especially when there's a perfectly good motorhome or camper van just waiting for a driver. But for others, the thought of RVing in any other manner and paying the higher costs associated with the motorized life is outrageous. In any event, it's usually a knee-jerk reaction to one way or the other. We'll take your interest in this chapter as a sign that towables might be for you. Here's a closer look at what's offered and the pros and cons of each.

Tow: The Way to Go

The choice seems so obvious for some: Towables are the way to go. One vehicle for driving, one for living. Sleep and eat where I drive? Don't be ridiculous. Put all my eggs in one RV basket? Never. Lug around a 40-foot motorhome? Are you crazy? Trailer aficionados want two distinct driving and livable vehicles, a separation of Church and State. As Rob Base sang, "It takes two to make a thing go right, it takes two to make it out of sight." With that thought freshly implanted, here are some of the obvious advantages of life with a towable RV.

Like the Bird Says, "Cheap, Cheap"

Looking for the travel deal of the century? Buy a fold-down camper (pop-up), hook it to your SUV or mini-van, and vacation on the cheap. When the kids get a little older—and less tolerant of you—opt for a 25-foot trailer, with room for four and all the goods. The price of *both* towables is less than the cost of most any *one* motorized RV. Small towables such as these provide the least expensive way to travel, hands down. Fact is, engines equal money, and big engines, like those found in medium- to large-size motorhomes, cost big money.

One for the Road

A recent study by PKF Consulting, an international travel and tourism firm, revealed that vacations spent in a fold-down camper pulled behind the family automobile were 50 to 70 percent cheaper than a similar trip requiring flying, rental cars, and hotels. It even beat out the family station wagon and hotel accommodations as the king of discount travel.

Your trailer never needs an oil change or tune-up, will never leak radiator fluid or blow a gasket. All things considered, the towable world is an uneventful one in terms of repairs and maintenance. (Onboard systems and appliances require regular upkeep, just as all RVs do.) Opening up your insurance bill won't send you into a Hulk-like rage, either. Towables are fairly inexpensive to cover, certainly lacking the automotive legalities of their motorized counterparts. In many cases, insuring the new trailer may be as easy as adding it as a rider to your existing automobile policy. We'll chat all about that in Chapter 9, "After the Sale."

Double the Fun

Yes, motorized vehicles only necessitate starting the ignition to kick off their adventures, leaving you in the dust as you hitch up the trailer. However, revenge comes in many forms. For starters, the vehicle doing the towing (a.k.a., the tow vehicle) serves double-duty as easy transport when the destination is reached. Once the trailer is set up, take the truck or SUV (whatever vehicle is up to the towing job) and head off for some fun. Enjoy a night at the movies, a gourmet meal at the local bistro, or day trips to scenic locales without a cumbersome motorhome to worry about parking in unfamiliar environments.

Two separate vehicles also deliver peace of mind during times of trouble. If anything were to ever happen to either your tow vehicle or the trailer behind it, you wouldn't experience the horrors of watching both home *and* transportation at the mechanics, a very real threat in the lives of motorhomers. Believe me, there is no worse feeling than witnessing your RV up on blocks while scrounging around for cab fare.

Longevity

No, the family pop-up doesn't have super powers. The trailer isn't impervious to harm or wear. Fifth-wheel manufacturers don't employ secret space-aged technology from NASA to add years to their products. But it may seem like it, since many towables outlast those members of the motorized world. Mechanical parts—engines, drive trains, and transmissions—break down over time. All moving parts do, which is exactly why your towable may surprise you, since the "box-on-wheels" design incorporates little in the way of breakable mechanisms. As previously mentioned, this is the reason why motorhomes are more expensive to buy and maintain. Don't be surprised if the same pop-up purchased for you and the kids has grandkids in it someday.

One for the Road

Park models aren't technically RVs. These residential-style structures are designed for set-up in one location for greater lengths of time. They resemble conventional travel trailers, but usually possess peaked, shingled roofs and wood frames, matched with vinyl and aluminum. Inside you'll find at least 400 square feet of space with appliances and furnishings straight out of a home. A second floor is common. Park models are more home than vehicle, *just* towable enough to lobby for true RV status, but really in a class by themselves. At 12 feet wide and with a turning radius akin to battleships, transport is best left to the professionals. Prices run between $15,000 and $50,000.

More Residential

Larger trailers and fifth wheels are more akin to condominiums than recreational vehicles, thanks to their residential styling. Walk inside, take a seat, and it can be hard to find evidence that you're *actually on wheels*. Towering interior heights, large bay windows, pleasing room layouts—even steps to the master bedroom (in fifth wheels)—all serve to create the familiar sensations of home. Many towable enthusiasts report that after a day's worth of driving, it's nice to retire to a place void of driver's seats, steering wheels, and other reminders of the long trip back.

Space: The Final Frontier

Did you know that a 30-foot fifth wheel delivers more space than a 30-foot motorhome? How can this be? Illusions? Smoke and mirrors? A clever plot by the government? None of the above. The motorhome's cockpit is to blame, taking up vital interior real estate, which is rendered virtually useless upon arrival to the campground. And with all towable RVs, the absence of a driving compartment results in more bang for your buck and more usable space for you and your crew.

More Variety

Motorized vehicles don't offer much in the way of flexibility, do they? Cockpits go in the front; the master bedroom in the back. But the good old travel trailer has no such obvious limitations, allowing designers to put things wherever they want. Bedrooms can go anywhere, front or back. The kitchen may be enormous (perfect for those who love to cook) and dwarf the rest of the coach. Or go with a rear living area with large bay windows and a slide-out, the center of all things inside. It's not unusual for a regular trailer to be available in double-digit floor plans. That's a lot of options for those looking for the perfect RV. And it gets better: More towable manufacturers means more models to choose from, too.

Second Home

Not everyone wants to roam the country, living life on the go. A job and a family may require more realistic vacationing, sometimes limited to weekends up at the lake or quick jaunts to a favorite campground. With this in mind, unhook the trailer and leave it full-time at a seasonal campsite or other purchased property a reasonable drive from home. Instead of worrying about towing, treat the trailer like that cabin in the woods or time-share, using your everyday vehicle to shuttle you and the kids up to your new "second home."

Towing Woes

Yes, there may be a few. Or perhaps none at all, if you are comfortable with the costs and traveling differences associated with this awesome, exciting, everyday-is-new-and-different lifestyle. Again, these are only disadvantages if you allow them to be. Here's a closer look at some of the potential pitfalls in the life of a towable owner.

The Big Tow

The pattern is simple: Big towables need big vehicles to tow them; small towables need smaller ones. Sure, it's a little more complicated than that rudimentary explanation, but in either case, you need something to pull your pop-up, travel trailer, or fifth wheel from place to place. Fitting a trailer to an existing vehicle truck or car (in a few cases) is great—it saves from writing a second check. However, you might fall in love with a real head-turner, an RV capable of keeping up on all the journeys planned in your mind. Then prepare yourself for the purchase of a tow vehicle—and the big ones ain't cheap. A pickup powerful enough to haul your dreamy fifth-wheel trailer might cost $30,000 to $50,000, so ready yourself for a run on your bank account if you go this route.

Pull Over

A seasonal or year-round spot is best in warm-weather locations, where travelers won't be faced with such issues as freezing pipes, unplowed driveways, and trailer insulation issues. Unless the property is yours, make sure it's okay to leave the trailer at the site for longer periods of time, such as seasonal sites, as discussed in Chapter 3, "Where to Stay?"

A medium-duty truck, sometimes referred to as a "baby-semi," is usually required for towing the largest fifth wheels and their Herculean weights of 18,000 to 22,000 pounds. Armed with 275 to 300 horsepower (HP), such diesel tow vehicles may include surprisingly nice sleeping and living quarters and usually make a powerful entrance at the supermarket or campground. True, this much muscle comes with a steep price tag, $60,000 to $90,000 if you go all out. However, this higher price tag is offset by its much longer life span. One of these trucks can sometimes outlast several pickups, so in the long run they may actually be cheaper.

Separation Anxiety

There are plenty of interested RVers who are simply fearful of towing a trailer. Certainly it's an unfamiliar situation for some, one that I compare to owning a beagle. As much as you'd like it, that towable, to behave and follow along, sometimes Daisy, err … I mean, the trailer, wants to do its own thing. Here you are turning down the sidewalk, and she's licking dirt off the mailbox. Of course, I've never seen a trailer that can catch a Frisbee.

This, of course, is an exaggeration to make a point. Towing is different, not difficult. Turns must be taken a little wider. Back-ins mandate patience and a Zen-like oneness with your surroundings. Winds and speed may cause your RV to sway, which can be disconcerting (and remedied in Chapter 13, "Towin' the Line"). Some RVers are willing to explore this challenge, while others say "No way, not for me." Hopefully, we can make this a less intimidating prospect in the chapters to come.

No Rough Riders

Talk about forbidden fruit. Owners must resist the temptation to ride in the trailer, with its comfy bed, fully stocked fridge, and that priceless collection of Paul Anka albums. It's too dangerous, and it's against the law in most states. As a result, all passengers belong in the tow vehicle, no easy task in a smaller pickup truck with limited seating. This also means you'll need to pull over to access the trailer, make any meals, use the bathroom onboard, or rummage around to find the game of Twister.

Meeting Your Match

Prospective buyers go giddy walking into an RV show. The choices are mind-boggling. The shiny trailers. The behemoth fifth-wheels. Or maybe think smaller in terms of a pop-up or lightweight trailer. For some, finding a husband was easier than choosing the perfect RV. And it gets harder. The towable you buy and the tow vehicle—be it a car, truck, or van—need to be properly matched, based on their weights, hitch, and towing capacity. In this case, opposites definitely do not attract.

Road Scholar

What good is a trailer that sleeps six when your tow vehicle can only accommodate your spouse, one child, and maybe his or her hamster? If future towing plans (fifth-wheel wannabes, take note) call for a pickup, entertain the idea of one with an extended cab with additional seating for everyone. Transporting six is not impossible, and customized vehicles may allow for even more passengers.

We'll break this down in detail later (Chapter 13), but here's the *Cliffs Notes* version: Your tow vehicle must have the ability (Tow Rating) to pull the towable in its loaded state (Gross Vehicle Weight Rating). Your hitch must also be rated to do the job. A tow vehicle's and trailer's fortunes and fates are intertwined, and a suitable match is the only way toward a safe RV experience. So whether you're buying a trailer to match your vehicle or a tow vehicle to match a would-be trailer, your choices are not as limitless as they might seem.

Accessorizing

A shiny new pickup sits ready in the driveway. Across the way is your beautiful new trailer or fifth wheel. They're like kids at the dance: interested, but not sure how to make that connection. The third-party matchmaker comes in the form of a hitch, which makes the introductions, and a series of connections (brakes, lights, safety chains), to seal the deal. After that, it's a good idea to purchase such *aftermarket* devices as an additional *anti-sway device* and other products to create a safer environment. All this, by the way, costs money, and should be factored into the bottom line. We will take a closer look at towing accessories in Chapter 13.

RVocabulary

RVers may choose to add options and accessories onto their vehicle during the buying stage or later on from separate companies and retail outlets, generally referred to as the **aftermarket.** Most products offered by the manufacturers themselves can be found throughout the aftermarket, allowing buyers to be patient with such decisions concerning add-ons and accessories.

Types

There are two schools of thought regarding the purchase of a towable RV. Either match up an existing vehicle (sedan, mini-van, SUV, pickup truck, or medium-duty truck) to a suitable towable, or vice versa. Of course, which route you take depends on a lot of things but starts with pondering what your needs are and how much you want to pay. As we've discussed, this vehicle tandem must be properly matched, based on your tow vehicle's tow rating and the towable's overall weight. Research and thought must be poured into this decision, something we'll assist you with in Chapter 13.

There are four types of towable RVs: fifth-wheel trailers, travel trailers, lightweight travel trailers, and fold-down campers (or pop-ups). An in-depth look at each is given in the pages ahead.

RVocabulary

An **anti-sway device** is an accessory that helps stabilize the connection between the tow vehicle and travel trailer and restrict motion while in transit. This is an especially useful item for negating the effects of high winds and turbulent conditions caused by traveling at higher speeds.

Fifth-Wheel Trailers

Fifth wheels are the granddaddies of the towable world. Walking inside, you may feel that you've crossed the threshold into a rolling condo—there's even a small set of stairs in the front of the unit, usually leading up to the master bedroom. There's no cockpit taking up valuable space. Fifth wheels, with their noticeable "goosenecks" (mentioned in Chapter 1, "Why RV?"), which hitch snuggly to within the bed of large pickups, deliver the most usable space of any type of recreational vehicle. Sizes go up to 40 feet, in which case a powerful one-ton or even a large hauler is needed.

Fifth wheels are to the towable marketplace what Class As are to motorized—the biggest, the most luxurious, and consequently, the most expensive. Interior heights are enormous, and slide-outs—as many as three per vehicle—are now the norm, not the exception. But that's not to say "entry level" models aren't offered, with smaller weights and lengths for easier towing—and prices to match. These days, there's a fifth-wheel trailer aimed at every type of buyer.

What Is It?

So how does a fifth wheel differ from your average travel trailer? And what about that goofy name? Both of these questions can be answered by examining the manner in which fifth wheels are towed. Instead of a conventional hitch and connection made at the bumper or frame of the tow vehicle, a specially designed fifth-wheel hitch, also the genesis for its name, rests in the cargo area in the back of the truck. Since this area must be open to store the hitch, pickup trucks, medium-duty diesels, and a few custom-made conversion vehicles are the only types of vehicles capable of towing a fifth-wheel trailer. The trailer's trademark "gooseneck" front end hangs over the truck's payload area, creating a much greater fit between the two vehicles, and a unique, bi-level recreational vehicle.

Fifth-wheel sizes range from 20 to approximately 40 feet, with weights sometimes tipping the scales at more than 22,000 pounds, fully loaded. Heavyweight models mandate a big-time truck or specially made conversion vehicle; the family station wagon or mini-van need not apply. Smaller models may or may not be compatible with your existing small- or medium-size pickup. Again, we'll get to that in Chapter 13.

Life Onboard

In addition to easier towing, the ramifications of the gooseneck overhang are felt throughout the interior of the trailer as well. Much in the same way that Class C motorhomes use their cab-over area as a supplemental sleeping or storage area, fifth wheels also make great use of this specially designed space. Of course, this area is a whole lot bigger, with dimensions large enough to accommodate a master bedroom, bathroom, tub/shower, closets, and nightstands. A few steps separate the front end from the rest of the interior, making for a nice oasis away from the noise of the television or conversations revolving around the disappearance of Disco in the living room. Interior heights are staggering when compared to other recreational vehicles.

Although not nearly as diverse as travel trailers (the undisputed kings of floor plans), varied fifth-wheel room layouts reward buyers with a wide range of interiors. As always, color schemes and choice of fabrics are offered, as is the obligatory long list of options, as found in most other RVs. Storage is usually immense, aided by multiple slide-out configurations and basement model floor plans, which are becoming more and more common in higher-end products.

One of the newest floor plan innovations is the emergence of the sport utility trailer (SUT). The growing appeal of extreme sports, a wallet-opening economy, and a go-out-and-have-fun mentality has opened up this new adventure market for RVs. After all, wasn't it our own Constitution that provided that every man, woman, and child needn't suffer without his or her own all-terrain vehicle? SUTs—available in both fifth wheels and travel trailers—feature a space for motorized vehicles in the rear, as well as a ramp or lift system for easy loading. Diamond-studded aluminum protects the flooring. And besides, it just plain looks cool. The rest of the fifth wheel appears as normal, only more compacted to make up for the cargo area. At the rate the industry is going, every fifth wheel and travel trailer dealer will have at least one model devoted to the SUT phenomena.

Sleeping Beauty

Sleeping four is easy and up to eight is possible, depending on the model and the contortion abilities and size of your passengers. The master bedroom, almost always outfitted with a queen-size bed, and a sleeper sofa perform the yeoman's work come nighttime. Some floor plans might even offer two bedrooms. A convertible dinette and bench seats and/or reclining loungers also transform into sleeping arrangements. Double beds can occasionally be substituted for the master queen-size, but it shouldn't be counted upon.

Home Cookin'

Most of the best kitchens anywhere in the RV world can be found in mid-range and high-end fifth wheels. Credit designers' willingness in some cases to dedicate the entire width of the trailer's rear to the galley, not just a small section pushed out of the way of the living room. The move can really pay off come mealtime. Ample counter space and enough drawers and cabinets for a lifetime of cookbooks means it might actually be fun to play chef for the entire family for a change. I recently test drove a fifth wheel with 15 deep storage compartments, including a five-shelf pullout pantry, in the kitchen alone.

Standard appliances include a three-burner stove, oven, double sink, microwave, and double-door refrigerator with freezer. The aforementioned pullout pantry with adjustable shelving is usually present or listed as a compelling option. Island kitchens, dishwashers, and convection ovens are also popular. Built-in spice racks, paper towel holders, coffee makers, garbage cans, knife racks, handheld sprayers, soap pumps, and ice makers can be homey touches, too. A kitchen slide-out sends the usable space and storage into overdrive.

Inside Out

An illusion is at work in many fifth wheels. No, David Copperfield isn't in the RV business—yet. Rather, awesome interior heights work on the psyches of these trailer owners, making rooms seem larger than they really are. True, the area between your head and the ceiling isn't exactly "usable" space, but it creates a more spacious, open feel. Smoke and mirrors are extra. As a result, taller closets, cabinets, and pantries can be added, holding everything from clothes to televisions to family heirlooms.

Furnishings come in the traditional forms of various couches, recliners, and a communal dinner spot, either a dinette table with bench seats or a free-standing table and chairs. Double and triple slide-outs are extremely popular, changing the dynamic (and size!) of the interior in mere seconds. Many fifth wheels now dazzle with opposing slide-outs in the main living area, which expand that total living area to 15 feet across. Amazing!

Bathrooms and Showers

One of the compromises of a smaller motorhome or towable usually comes in the form of a much smaller bathroom. Most RV designers seem to be in agreement that any vehicle concessions will be made in terms of size of the toilet, shower/tub, and vanity area. After all, it's much easier to use the bathroom and shower facilities of the campground than its cooking, living, or sleeping quarters. However, fifth wheels are generally impervious to such downsizing, since the gooseneck portion provides the obvious (and roomy) location for many of the industry's finest examples of bathrooms and showers. Toilets are often sequestered in their own private area across from the glass-enclosed shower/tub, sink, and vanity. Ceiling vents and skylights are standard features.

Road Scholar

The towing ease of fifth wheels as compared to travel trailers is a popular debate among towable enthusiasts. While most would agree the inherent configuration of the fifth-wheel mounting system increases overall maneuverability, a case can be made for trailers armed with a quality anti-sway device and an experienced driver behind the wheel.

Towability

Thanks to a more snug fit in the payload in the back of a pickup truck, and, therefore, less sway and overall length, fifth wheels help take some of the stigma out of towing. With the trailer's hitch mounted to the pickup truck's bed rather than the bumper or frame, fifth wheels generally ride smoother and are more maneuverable than conventional travel trailers. The symmetry between the two vehicles makes for easier back-ups, cornering, and parking, while reducing choppy movement and sway during transit.

The secret's in the geometry. The pivot point of a conventional trailer/tow vehicle combo is behind the rear bumper. The pivot point of the fifth-wheel hitch is directly over or slightly ahead of the tow vehicle's rear axle. The shorter the distance from the turning wheels of the tow vehicle to the pivot point, the easier it is to maneuver. Plus with a fifth-wheel trailer, the hitch weight is carried by the rear axle of the tow vehicle rather than having to be distributed mechanically, and therefore, less efficiently. It may sound like coursework from M.I.T., but the bottom line is an easier towing experience for all.

Since the truck and fifth-wheel combination "bends" in the middle, it can be more maneuverable than the larger motorhomes, and having the overlap of trailer and truck shortens the length and makes turning easier than with a travel trailer of the same length. Fifth wheels tend to be better built than travel trailers and are the choice of many full-timers. In fact, there are quite a few companies that focus on building full-time units exclusively.

Road Scholar

Portable generators, found in hardware stores, camping centers, or wherever appliances are sold, provide a useful alternative when onboard generators aren't offered. Raucous noise and awkward weights make some models difficult for some to bear so search out the quietest, lightest version you can. Portable models work equally well in terms of power output, as measured by kilowatts (kw).

Typical Specs

With exterior heights exceeding 12 feet, added to a fairly lengthy towing package, fifth wheels may struggle to reach the more elusive, exotic locales not listed (thankfully) in travel books. Places with low clearances, rough roads, and tight corners are problematic for larger models. Assuming, however, you can make it there, a series of large holding tanks allows for longer getaways than usual. An onboard generator may or may not come standard, so make sure your dream machine is equipped with one if you plan on camping away from shoreline power and covet the use of larger appliances, such as the microwave and air conditioner.

Standard Specifications for a Typical Fifth-Wheel Trailer

Self-Containment Features	Gallons
Fresh water storage	25 to 100
Gray water holding tank	40 to 75
Black water holding tank	30 to 50
LP gas container(s)	20 to 40
Water heater	6 to 10

Costly Matters

Sure, you can spend a not-so-small fortune on a roving palace, leaving you longing for nothing. But more realistically, fifth wheels average $25,000 to $30,000. Be prepared to open the checkbook for units with multiple slide-outs and lengths over 35 feet. Smaller, lighter-weight models start at as little as $15,000 and may be towed by a smaller pickup truck, saving you another costly trip to the local truck dealership. Unfortunately, the most difficult part may be the decision of what to tow it with. As explained, the flexibility of choices afforded most trailer owners is narrowed down to what type of pickup truck is up for the job. As mentioned earlier, for those who haven't priced a medium-duty truck lately, they're not cheap. Expect to pay at least $60,000 for one to safely haul the largest fifth wheels. Otherwise, a 3/4- or 1-ton truck can be had between $20,000 and $35,000.

Since there's no motor, there's no need to spend any time under the hood. (Besides, there isn't a hood anyway.) Towable owners won't need to waste another Saturday changing belts or plugs, driving down to the RV dealership for a costly tune-up, or searching for the origin of that brown puddle collecting underneath the engine. Insurance premiums are relatively low—contingent on the sale price—so pat yourself on the back for your frugal purchase.

Final Analysis

Ample space and storage make fifth wheels popular with full-timers, as well as families with more than a couple of kids. Your canary will love the high ceilings, and the edginess that sometimes accompanies life in a confined space should be blissfully absent from days onboard. As previously mentioned, the resemblance to a rolling condominium is uncanny in higher-end models. Manufacturers do their best to dazzle buyers with loads of luxury appointments. Large windows, plush fabrics and carpeting, and the quality hardwoods continually position fifth wheels among the most livable RVs in the industry. You'll also discover some of the finest and most thorough examples of kitchens and bathrooms in the marketplace. The rest of the interior ain't too shabby, either.

Unfortunately, relatively modest start-ups costs must be tempered with the possible purchase of an expensive tow vehicle. If you've already got that truck in your driveway, you're in luck. The fifth-wheel lifestyle is closer than you think. However, it's best to price both the trailer and tow vehicles to make your accountant happy—the combination can cost more than a suitably sized motorhome. This cannot be overstated. Upon scanning prices for the medium-duty trucks at a recent RV show, I nearly fell into a coma.

Fifth wheels have the greatest price variances of any RV. Such a purchase can easily vary from the cost of a small automobile to four years at Harvard, which takes discipline when exposed to the full gamut of options. You don't want to be the couple budgeted for a modest duplex ending up with a five-bedroom manor with an English butler named Chauncey.

Travel Trailers

The backbone of the towable marketplace, travel trailers come in all shapes and sizes, from basic to luxurious, super lightweight to those requiring a larger tow vehicle. It's for this reason that we've created a sub-group, lightweight travel trailers, in the pages ahead. Travel trailers are also the oldest forms of recreational vehicles, with manufacturers such as Airstream now in their eighth decade of building them.

One for the Road

Horse-drawn wagons served as the blueprint for the earliest examples of recreational vehicles. After the invention of the automobile, more and more travelers began pulling small trailers, loaded with small beds and various camping equipment.

Free of a cockpit and lacking the gooseneck area of fifth wheels, designers are free to create a full gamut of varying interiors. Like a crazed Dr. Frankenstein bent on showing his unbridled genius (a slight exaggeration, perhaps), manufacturers mix and match layouts in ways that would make Picasso proud. Bedrooms may be front or back—or both. Kitchens can take up the entire rear of the unit, share space on either side, or be scattered about, refrigerator here, pantry there. Bathrooms range from lean and functional to spacious and opulent. You also may find up to three slide-out rooms onboard.

What Is It?

A box on wheels is as good a description as any I've heard. Travel trailers lack the slopes and quirks found on most other RVs, although many have been rounded over the years somewhat in an effort to maximize aerodynamics. Unlike fifth wheels, these trailers attach to a frame-mounted hitch, with the load distributed over anywhere from one to three axles of your dutiful tow vehicle. Conventional travel trailers vary from 24 to 40 feet. A good-size truck or SUV with a V-8 engine or better is often capable of handling the towing duties, assuming it is equipped with a compatible hitch.

For inclusion in the category, travel trailers should exceed 4,000 pounds, unloaded. Anything less makes them a *lightweight travel trailer*, as described in the following section. That weight does not include your portly cat, your collection of shot glasses from all 50 states, or that supplemental canned ham in case the fish aren't biting—just the trailer and nothing else. More on calculating these numbers and their importance will be in Chapter 15, "How Much Does Your RV Weigh?"

Road Scholar

When comparing various RVs by size, it's important to know how vehicle lengths are calculated. Fifth-wheel measurements are taken from the tip of the front extension (gooseneck) to the back bumper. Travel trailers start at the end of the trailer tongue (where the connection to the hitch is made) to the back bumper. In both cases, this adds several feet of superfluous space to the number. Motorized RVs are measured bumper to bumper.

Life Onboard

Don't be alarmed, designers remembered to include a couch and a television. So relax, your reruns of *Charlie's Angels* aren't in jeopardy. In fact, everything you've come to expect of the RV lifestyle should be present no matter what size travel trailer you favor; but as always, in varying degrees based on the size and weight of your chosen model. Cooks continue to work their magic in the kitchen, bathrooms and showers are standard, and everyone remains free to fight over who gets the master bedroom.

Sleeping Beauty

Sleeping capacity can hit as high as eight in larger models. Of course, this mark is easiest reached if passengers aren't overly finicky in terms of where they lay their head at night. Four to six sleepers is a much safer number. A master bedroom with a queen-size bed is common, although double beds and bunk beds are routinely offered. I did a double take when I spotted a triple bunk bed configuration recently. The usual cast of convertible furnishings transforms the living space into a nightly snoozefest.

Home Cookin'

If cooking is important to you—better yet, if eating is important to you—opt for a kitchen-friendly vehicle. Some models devote the entire rear of the trailer to cooking appliances, countertops, storage, and pantries. Yes, you can wear that funny white hat and apron that says "Kiss the Cook." For a few extra pennies (don't quote me on that), a kitchen slide-out may allow you to finally open up that French bistro onboard that you've always dreamed of owning.

Of course, dining out is nice, too. When in Rome, eat like the Romans do, I always say. In fact, I say it so much, my wife has asked me never, ever to utter that phrase in her company again. It stands to reason that escaping the perils of mealtime might be why you're vacationing in the first place. For those who like cooking about as much as a tax audit, tour floor plans with smaller kitchens, meaning more room for the things that you do like.

Inside Out

Buyers worried about interior space—not to mention a trailer full of bored teenagers—should feel at ease after kicking a few tires at the local RV show. Large televisions (sometimes two), with or without satellite programming, VCRs, CD players with surround sound, telephone and cable TV jacks are common, albeit listed as options in some cases. Various sized sofas, loveseats, and recliners also help champion the cause of true leisure and contented passengers.

Bench seats around a dinette table continue to be the perfect place for eating dinner, playing games, or writing angry letters to the mayor for your town's lame-brained RV storage laws. And since there's no cockpit, every inch of the interior is utilized, whether it takes the form of larger rooms, expanded furnishing, or greater storage. Interior heights average a respectable six and a half feet.

Bathrooms and Showers

Every travel trailer in this class comes with a toilet, shower and/or tub, and bathroom sink. Whether it's a tight fit or you find yourself swimming in all the space depends on the particular model. A vanity, medicine cabinet, roof vents, towel bars, and skylight (for waving at passing 747s) are fairly common.

Towability

There's no way to sugarcoat it. Most would agree that a lengthy travel trailer is the hardest of all recreational vehicles to command. However, that's not to say that operation is necessarily difficult, only different. Millions of people tow these babies every day, and travel trailers continue to rank among the most popular RVs in the marketplace.

Unlike fifth wheels, which attach snuggly to their tow vehicles like teenagers during a slow dance, travel trailers rely on a lone undercarriage hitch receiver or frame-mounted hitch. As a result, a 40-foot trailer and a 15-foot tow vehicle combine to form a whooping 55 feet of vehicle, cruising down the highways, parking lots, and campgrounds of America. Back-ups might take longer, as the trailer might want to veer to one side or the other. Since the tandem is less than aerodynamic, head winds affect fuel economy worse than any maniacal oil baron ever could, while heavy cross-winds can unleash more trailer rock 'n' roll than Elvis on the *Ed Sullivan Show*.

Road Scholar

Most, if not all, truck manufacturers publish a yearly tow vehicle ratings guide to help you in determining how much each vehicle can safely tow. Information can be had for every engine and transmission combo listed. Another good source is the towing guide put out each year by *Trailer Life* magazine, showcasing vehicles of all kinds and their towing prowess.

Worried? Having second thoughts? Want to jump ahead to the lovable fold-down camper and forget all about it? Don't be silly. These potential problems can be lessened with the aid of a couple of products and some advice we'll dispense in Chapter 13.

Remember, tow vehicles and trailers must be matched to the job. I can't think of any regular automobile capable of hauling a trailer of these proportions. This is a job better left for your pickup truck, van, or SUV, especially if you fall head over heels in love with a 40-foot model with enough slide-outs for a roving block party. In the case of such lofty purchases, a walk to the diesel side of the truck lot might be required. Otherwise, a muscle-bound pickup truck or SUV with a V-8 engine should do it.

Typical Specs

Travel trailers, regardless of size, boast fairly lofty self-contained specifications. Holding tanks are comparable to motorized RVs and fifth wheels of similar size. LP tanks, a standard 20 to 40 gallons in most cases, may be removable or permanently installed to the front end, so keep that in mind come buying time. A generator might be a no-show, due to the fact that space for it as well as the separate fuel supply (like that found in a motorized vehicle's gas tank) might be lacking. As a result, boondocking gets a little more complicated. However, we'll talk about potential solutions in Chapter 17, "Roughin' It."

Standard Specifications for a Typical Travel Trailer

Self-Containment Features	Gallons
Fresh water storage	30 to 60
Gray water holding tank	30 to 45
Black water holding tank	25 to 40
LP gas container(s)	20 to 40
Water heater	6 to 10

Costly Matters

Compared to a similarly sized motorhome, travel trailers—all towables for that matter—always win in terms of initial sticker price. Remember the mantra: Motors equal money. Inch for inch, trailers are the blue-light specials of the industry, provided that there's a nice shiny truck in your driveway eager to meet the towing challenge. Expect to pay somewhere from $15,000 to $70,000 for a trailer in the 25- to 40-foot neighborhood. Extra costs rear their ugly heads for such importances as a tow vehicle (assuming you don't have one), $500 to $1000 for a hitch, and a few bucks to equip it with the extra gear we're recommending in Chapter 13.

As mentioned during our chat about fifth wheels, less expensive, motorless vehicles skirt the heavy insurance premiums and required automotive coverages of motorhomes. You can expect fewer trips to the mechanics, too. Routine maintenance is mostly limited to the refrigerator, air conditioner, and like appliances, saving owners more than a few bucks over the lifetime of the trailer.

Final Analysis

A 30-foot trailer is a one-size-fits-most situation. The right floor plan dares most families to try and outgrow it, and it works as well for year-round living as it does for the Boy Scouts' trips into the mountains, merit badges included. The variety of types and sizes gives buyers unparalleled options and buying power. Don't like one? Move on to the next. There are literally thousands of floor plans within the trailer marketplace to choose from. Be choosy. Be picky. Be happy with your purchase.

Trailers do equally well towed or settled down as a vacation home. Tour the nation with your apartment on wheels behind you, or plop down stakes at a nearby seasonal campsite, commuting back and forth to your new second home via the family vehicle. Ever wanted a spot in the mountains, amongst the tall pines, or adjacent to a wonderful lake? Their ability to serve as permanent housing without fear of mechanical failure from idle engines is a great plus. Travel trailers go where the family cabin or high-priced motels never could.

The knee-jerk reaction of some is to dismiss the idea of towing a separate vehicle altogether. It's too hard, they say. I've never done it before. My trailer will get mad and run away. Don't fall prey to such rash judgments. Towing is just like any new skill—strange at first, made easier over time. Travel trailers can provide you and your family years of inexpensive and fulfilling travel. A frugal purchase saves you tens of thousands of dollars over an equally stocked motorhome, so don't be too quick to dismiss it. Just find the right vehicle to tow it and let the adventures begin.

One for the Road

The early 1970s was one of the worst periods in the history of the RV industry. High gas prices and a tight economy resulted in poor sales and lackluster interest in both motorhomes and trailers alike. The era signaled the deathknell for many manufacturers, while renewing the thinking of smaller recreational vehicle designs.

Lightweight Travel Trailers

In an attempt to woo (don't you just love that word?) young families, the RV industry has spent much of this decade building hybrid towables known as lightweight travel trailers. Weighing in at less than 4,000 pounds, the majority of them can be towed by the many mini-vans, small- and medium-size trucks, and the scores of SUVs on the road today. And America simply *loves* their big vehicles, which routinely surpass the forgotten automobile in terms of annual sales. This trend means more and more families are just a hitch and relatively inexpensive towable away from enjoying the RV lifestyle.

We've been down this lightweight road before. During the 1980s and early 1990s, this class was nearly extinct. Larger motorhomes and trailers took center stage, while automobiles, not terribly useful in terms of towing, got smaller and more fuel-efficient. The mini-van and SUV enjoyed only a fraction of the popularity each has today. During the fuel shortages and staggering prices associated with a full tank in the mid- and late 1970s, lightweight towables came into vogue as an alternative to gas-guzzling motorhomes. Sporting modest sticker prices and lesser tow vehicle requirements, this market segment enjoyed some popularity as the RV industry floundered.

Some would call putting these towables in their own category splitting hairs. Perhaps. But humor me anyway. Otherwise it proves too difficult to single out their advantages among the countless entries in the travel trailer market, and you wouldn't want that, would you?

What Is It?

Lightweight travel trailers fall somewhere between a fold-down camper and conventional travel trailer in terms of size, weight, cost, and amenities. Sizes generally won't exceed 25 feet since the extra materials would tip the scales into the next weight division, the conventional travel trailer.

Unlike the standardized looks of fifth wheels and larger towables, lightweight versions can look, well … a little peculiar. Some models sprout "wings" upon arrival, extending the bedding outward in a tent-like material; others must be manually deployed, or popped up, via a hand crank to access the interior. There are even a few that resemble spaceships from an Ed Wood movie. If little green men are camped out in one next to you, you know you have a problem. However, most are simply shrunken versions of a larger trailer design, built using wood and aluminum instead of fiberglass shells and steel carriages to keep weights low. Many are just plain cute, with adorable names like Scamp, Kiwi, and Koala. Ah, Mommy, can I keep it?

Life Onboard

Perhaps only a supermodel understands the plight of the poor lightweight trailer. Just how does it stay desirable to consumers without exceeding its waifish physique? I'm sure this problem has kept many an RV engineer up at night. In the world of 30,000-pound motorhomes, you can imagine the limitations imposed on a 4,000-pound trailer. In fact, some units may only be a piece of chocolate cake away from losing their good standing in the lightweight community. But kudos to manufacturers who continually make it work—a durable trailer with just enough functionality for the average family to enjoy for years to come.

Larger models reflect all the comforts associated with conventional travel trailers. Heat and air conditioning, full kitchens, adequate bedding, bathrooms, and living space are usually all included. Interior heights average six feet, five inches, which is about the norm for any RV. Even slide-outs are sometimes offered. Miniaturized versions can be more unpredictable. Once standard appliances can be downshifted to options; separating walls can be removed for a more communal feel inside. However, no matter how small—and some can get pretty tiny—they continue to provide the basic requirements of cooking, sleeping, and congregating.

Sleeping Beauty

The "master bedroom" often achieves martyr status, sacrificed for the greater good of the interior. In these cases, expect substitutions to take the form of convertible sofas, unfolding mattresses (also known as bunk ends) that extend beyond the perimeter of the unit, or more ingenious designs. Sleeping capacity reaches six in larger models, but that's a lot of people and belongings sharing a 20- to 25-foot space. Finding a traditional floor plan, with the bedroom in the rear, shouldn't prove difficult for those desiring a private room, a respite from the television and Uncle Lou's version of *Swan Lake*. A double bed might take the place of the preferred queen-size version, however.

Road Scholar

Lightweight trailer owners must accept the fact that fewer onboard conveniences are offered than those found throughout larger towables. A careful review of available floor plans and a few well-placed accessories alleviate some of this loss, however. If the sacrifice in terms of overall space and amenities is too much to bear, you and yours might be happier in a larger travel trailer or fifth wheel.

Home Cookin'

I've seen models with countertops that struggle to fit a six-pack and a bag of chips. Serious cooks can get a little squirrelly when faced with the space and storage obstacles inherent in smaller designs. Say good-bye, fancy food processor, hello Mr. Handbeater. Stately kitchens are casualties of smaller interiors. A two-burner stove, sink, and small refrigerator remain standards. However, the oven and trusty microwave might not make the cut. Offset this by supplementing some of the meals with the local cuisine and grill fare at the campfire. Or use the money saved on your smaller investment to dine on fresh lobsters in Maine, fish tacos in Baja, or beer-soaked bratwursts in Sheboygan.

Inside Out

Like Forrest Gump says, "Life is like a box of chocolates. You never know what you're gonna get." The same can be said about any "typical" interior. Many times, the entire unit acts as the living area. Other floor plans appear as if they were pureed in a blender, creating a wonderfully unorthodox collage of rooms rolled into one. The main living area sometimes moonlights as the bedroom. Several additional feet may be granted thanks to a small slide-out room. Couches can encase the entire front end, work in conjunction with a dinette table, or be absent altogether. The only thing we know for sure is that numerous floor plans are available, so keep looking until you find the best one for you.

Road Scholar

Bathrooms and showers can be found at most campgrounds, removing some of the urgency of having them onboard. Using such outside facilities means hot water is more abundant, water pressure more consistent, and gray water tanks needn't be emptied as often.

Bathrooms and Showers

A full bathroom may or may not be present, or may be reduced to a simple marine-style toilet in a closet-like space. How can I put this delicately? Some of these rooms are terribly cramped for "huskier" passengers. Showers come and go, but you can count on a water heater to keep icicles from forming. Travelers looking for fancier appointments often find them in trailers in the 25-foot range.

Towability

We saved the best part for last. Smaller and lighter towables only require the services of—you guessed it—smaller and lighter tow vehicles. For many models, vehicles with a six-cylinder engine should do, provided it possesses the necessary hitch. That means even the family sedan may get a crack at the RV life. And in a world of trucks, SUVs, and vans (maxi and mini alike), most families already own the tow vehicle to do the job. Congratulations, you're halfway there.

Despite their scale-pleasing weight, towing lightweights is not unlike conventional travel trailers. Be prepared for up to 25 feet of trailer to maneuver, in addition to the tow vehicle's length. All this can add up to 35 to 40 feet of recreational vehicle, about the same length as most luxury motorhomes. This combination can cut quite a figure when backing in or driving through a new city, although give the nod to lightweights and their "bending" capabilities.

Typical Specs

Passengers lack for none of the usual onboard offerings. Standard electrical systems prevail, as does a fresh water system, holding tanks, and propane gas containers for fueling the furnace and stove. However, space and fuel limitations leave a generator off the list of standards—even optional equipment in most cases. Power 120-volt appliances through the aid of a portable generator in the event of camping in remote locations, void of shore power.

Standard Specifications for a Typical Lightweight Travel Trailer

Self-Containment Features	Gallons
Fresh water storage	15 to 35
Gray water holding tank	20 to 35
Black water holding tank	10 to 35
LP gas container(s)	5 to 14
Water heater	6

Costly Matters

A few hundred pounds may be all that separates a lightweight trailer from a trip to a higher weight class. In these cases, costs are similar to those of travel trailers. Otherwise, expect these reductions in size and weight to pay off when making out the check to the local RV dealership. Fully loaded and pushing the 4,000-pound weight limit, a handful of models might flirt with a $20,000 sticker price. However, $8,000 to $17,000 is more likely.

Again, engineless living benefits owners with a virtual blackout on any major exterior repairs. The biggest concern is probably the tires, which are susceptible to wear and tear just like any others. As with all RVs, some preventive maintenance will need to be performed inside. Routine tinkering with the unit's air conditioner (if so equipped), furnace, and refrigerator rounds out the list of likely interior projects, some of which can be undertaken by most backyard mechanics.

The amount and degree of insurance is up to you, but, like all towables, costs are relatively cheap and coverage can often be attached to an existing automobile policy. Save additional cash by storing trailers in the garage or on the premises when not in use. Fuel costs will rise for the tow vehicle, now asked to pull a heavier load. However, costs should be among the most reasonable in the towable class.

Final Analysis

Lightweight towables are hot. Nearly every RV manufacturer has scurried over the past several years to gain entry into this competitive new arena. Buyers are blitzed with choices ranging from stripped-down versions of larger and, therefore, heavier models, to brand new creations to fit the family station wagon.

Pick the right trailer and it should deliver many years of faithful service. This is the first (and sometimes only) RV some families will ever own, thanks to low starter prices and upkeep expenses. A week-long trip with the kids should easily save you the equivalent of the down payment. The availability of many likely tow vehicles grants easier entry into the lightweight trailer fraternity than ever before. Add a suitable hitch and you're in business. In fact, I'll bet there's a vehicle in your very driveway more than up to the job.

Couples and small families can't do much better. Multiple floor plans with emphasis on cooking, sleeping, and living space means there's something out there for everyone. True, lightweights pale when compared to the onboard offerings of most fifth wheels and motorhomes. However, RVing isn't about one-upmanship, rather providing a comfortable and functional way to compliment your leisure. Groups of five or over quickly expose the limitations of this category. This may be asking too much of a 20- to 25-foot trailer. For everyone else, the reemergence of the lightweight signals an easy and satisfying entry into the world of RVing.

Fold-Down Campers

Or maybe you know them better as pop-ups, camping trailers, or tent trailers. We used to call them Big Macs as kids (still do, actually), because of their boxy shape while in transit. I was young and it was kind of cute in a five-year-old way. Despite the name, fold-downs serve as the best and most cost-effective way for young families to camp and travel. For starters, they are easily towed, ranging in weight from 1,500 to 4,000 pounds, and form a terrific pairing to most SUVs, trucks, mini-vans, and some larger automobiles. After that, you're free to roam the country, confident that a dry bed, storage for your gear, and a hot meal (or cold one, if you prefer) await you.

What Is It?

Pop-ups deliver a major upgrade from a tent and sleeping bag, not to mention a much more reliable and durable barrier against the elements. Resembling ... okay, Big

Macs in transit, you wonder just how anyone could possibly get, let alone live, inside. However, that question is quickly answered upon arrival at the family's favorite campsite or for a true getaway in the back country. The once modest 12- to 18-foot box unfolds (pops up!) via a manual crank or push-button deployment system, now assuming the appearance of a tent on wheels. Unfolded lengths can exceed 25 feet. Not a bad little trick, is it?

Your standard pop-up features a mix of hard walls and durable fabrics, resembling a tent with wings once it's completely set up. Nearly all models feature two identical sleeping areas that bookend the middle living and cooking space. More expensive units boast a shower, toilet, a manual slide-out room (which greatly expands the roominess inside), and more deluxe cooking features. Travelers are protected from the elements by a combination of heavy canvas and hard-sided roof.

Life Onboard

Space is at a premium, with most units totaling under 20 feet in length. Be prepared for communal living, with all passengers sharing one small living space for cooking, eating, and hanging out. Labels like "kitchen," "bathroom," and "living room" are misleading here, since these are all simply offshoots, not separate entities. Say adios to the walls and doors that divvy up larger trailers and motorhomes, serving to create a private oasis. Think of a pop-up, rather, as like life in that first efficiency or studio apartment you rented after graduation. When my wife-to-be and I had an argument, one of us would have to go into the bathroom and shut the door to get away from our tormentor. Many a lonely night spent in the bathroom evolved me into a much more agreeable partner. At least in a fold-down, you can tell the other person to "go take a hike" and really mean it.

Many pop-up owners are transplanted tent campers, so dealing with small space is not really an issue. After all, they're used to much less room, with only a zipper and light fabric separating them from the rest of the world—not to mention angry grizzlies. A night in a pop-up feels like the penthouse at the Four Seasons after a few seasons of soggy tenting. Interior height is often surprising, averaging six foot, six inches for most units. Some manufacturers achieve a whopping eight feet, though this cathedral-esque height is not always present throughout the entire interior.

Sleeping Beauty

Remember the old Wrigley chewing gum jingle, "Double your pleasure, double your fun"? What that had to do with gum, I have no idea. But it's extremely appropriate to most fold-down floor plans, since matching sleeping areas are found on either end of the unit. I say "areas" instead of bedrooms because of the lack of true, closed-door privacy, and the fact that a mattress is usually all that's involved. No nightstands, fancy vanities, or hulking wardrobe closets are present. Typical bed dimensions average 70 by 80 inches, which is doable for most couples.

Further bedding may come in the form of a convertible dinette and/or a sofa bed. A few select models can sleep eight, assuming there are some youngsters in the mix. Otherwise, four is a safe bet and six is possible.

Home Cookin'

Engineers must make tough decisions about what stays and what goes in an RV of this size. In no place is this more apparent than the fold-down's "kitchen." A sink with hot and cold running water is standard, but after that, the cooking methods vary. A dorm-sized cooler may replace the large refrigerator found on nearly all RVs; a two-burner range, instead of three or four. Some models offer ovens and microwaves as standards, while others provide neither. Some models are equipped with an exterior propane stove, which hooks up to the outside of the trailer.

All this may be too rustic for some, but not for those just starting out on the road to more luxurious RV living. Most of the pop-up owners I've observed do a fair share of cooking the old-fashioned way—over the campfire, underneath the stars. I don't recall hearing anyone complaining about that fact, either. Besides, a ready tow vehicle is there to scoot you into town for more complex culinary delights if the steak and potatoes routine gets a little tiresome.

Pull Over

Although sinks are almost always present, holding tanks to collect the gray water aren't always installed on smaller towables. In these cases, water from the sink empties out the side of the trailer into a bucket or other receptacle for later emptying. Travelers are required to collect and empty gray water in a safe and responsible manner. Be sure to follow all campground rules and city ordinances regarding proper disposal.

Inside Out

Don't expect too many—if any—variations from the traditional floor plan, beds on either end, living area in the middle. That's the way it's been for decades, and that's the way it's probably gonna stay. However, dimensions are starting to grow, thanks to manual slide-out areas adding crucial feet of living space.

A dinette table with bench seats serves as the chief locale to eat, work, and rally the troops for another day of fly-fishing or another trip up the mountain. A couch is offered in larger models, so Dad and dog can assume their most natural state—napping, and dreaming of playing centerfield for the Yankees or chasing rabbits (whatever the case may be). Storage is often catch-as-catch-can, with smaller compartments dotting the interior. Relief usually comes in the form of one larger interior cabinet or storage compartment. Enlist the tow vehicle to store extra items such as firewood, patio chairs, and that set of *World Book* encyclopedias. A small furnace and air conditioner (sometimes optional) help control temperature fluctuations.

Unfortunately, the chances of finding a unit with the big three—TV, VCR, and stereo system—is somewhat remote. However, true campers won't be too put out by this fact, since the outdoors isn't just another setting to watch the 6 o'clock news and get the latest stock tips. Besides, David Letterman and the great outdoors is an unsettling combination. For those who must get their TV fix or can't travel without tapes of the 1984 Rose Bowl game, a quick trip to the local electronics store for a few necessities can remedy all that. Just bring a credit card or two.

Bathrooms and Showers

Assuming the fold-down has one or both, great. But don't count on it. Until recently, scores of manufacturers shied away from even attempting to install a toilet and shower onboard. Where would they put them? The challenge of location, privacy, and would anyone even want to contort to use them daunted designers for years. However, convenience is the new battle cry for buyers, and manufacturers are only happy to create a manageable system ... with mixed results.

Pull Over

Water restrictions at campgrounds vary, but a few standard rules apply. Some parks disallow the washing of vehicles, which quickly muddies the area, consumes a lot of resources, and presents disposal problems. Washing dishes or clothes at the campsite is sometimes prohibited for the same reasons.

In some cases, a lone marine-style toilet, such as those found on most RVs, resides in a thin-walled closet at either end of the unit. Black water empties into a traditional holding tank. Others feature a porta-potti with re-circulating system, filtering and reusing black water, with material waste collected for later emptying. These types of set-ups may sound grim to some. If this describes you, purchase a unit without a bathroom and get acquainted with those at the local campground.

Showers come in many forms, sometimes included with the lavatory, with gray water running down into an installed drain. An outside hose with handheld nozzle and hot and cold running water presents travelers with the dilemma of just what exactly they want to use it for. A public shower? I'm not sure that's its intended use, as much as washing muddy children, dogs, and a cooler full of trout.

Towability

Look around the highways and what do you see? Pop-ups towed behind smaller trucks, vans, and sedans. There are even smaller automobiles up to the job, bolstered by the trailers' low weights. Rarely will a pop-up exceed 3,500 pounds, and 1,500 to 2,000 is about average. This is good news for folks eager to get started and hoping the everyday vehicle is up to the job. The right hitch, either bumper- or frame-mounted, is usually all that separates many decent-size vehicles from doubling as tow vehicles.

Fold-downs are the easiest vehicles to tow in the RV world. The biggest challenge owners face is probably backing into their campsite. Just take it slow and have your co-pilot hop out and give you directions. Or better yet, opt for a pull-thru campsite and skip the whole process altogether. Cornering, turning, and parking is much more easily accomplished than in any other towable, with common sense and patience the most vital ingredients. But more about that in Chapter 13.

Typical Specs

As previously mentioned, the presence of a toilet and/or shower dictates what—if any—type of holding systems are found onboard. Even the water heater is a possible no-show, so conduct a thoughtful search if these attributes are important to you. An onboard generator is extremely rare, as is LP gas and fresh water capacities capable of lasting more than several days away from civilization. However, fold-downs commute reasonably well to off-the-beaten-path locations. Agile maneuvering is complemented by small traveling lengths and virtually nonexistent traveling heights.

Standard Specifications for a Typical Fold-Down Camper

Self-Containment Features	Gallons
Fresh water storage	5 to 18
Gray water holding tank	N/A to 20
Black water holding tank	N/A to 15
LP gas container(s)	5 to 10
Water heater	N/A to 6

Costly Matters

You can buy most new pop-ups for between $5,000 and $10,000, a bona fide bargain considering its livability. A family of four, particularly if the kids are still young enough to consider sharing a bed fun, should have little problem eating, sleeping, and dressing onboard, provided you don't spend countless hours in a space that is still relatively tiny. Aside from the cost of the hitch, a pop-up adds little in the way of extra expenses. Your tow vehicle's gas mileage will suffer somewhat, but only marginally, and insurance and maintenance costs are a fraction of higher-end towables.

A recent study declared camping by fold-down camper the least expensive way to vacation. When compared to other forms of travel, including planes, cruises, rental cars—even motorized and towable RVs—each failed to deliver as much bang for the buck as the Big Mac–looking, bank account–saving, plenty-of-good-living pop-up.

Final Analysis

A sign hung above the office window of a car service center read: "Cheap, fast, and good. Pick two." Had it not been my vehicle on blocks, the slogan would have been hilarious. But pop-ups meet all three criteria. Low sticker prices and virtual maintenance-free living establish them as the cheapest way to RV, by far. Since most folks already have a usable tow vehicle, you and the family are just an RV show away from finding the right vehicle for you. Standard floor plans and uncomplicated offerings hasten search time. Finally, is it good? Absolutely. What's not onboard, you won't miss. And the money saved can help put the kids (or my kids: please, please?) through school.

As a full-timing choice, well, it is not so good. We're talking about a 365-day home, so it's best to get the biggest RV possible. Pop-ups are also easily outgrown. Once those adorable kiddies start to "mature," preferring a set of headphones and a video game to conversation with Mom and Dad, it might be time to upgrade to a travel trailer or fifth wheel. Furthermore, winter and fold-downs really don't mix. Most lack proper insulation, and the heavy canvas and tent-like fabrics aren't much consolation come December. Finally, it only takes a few adult bodies to cramp everyone's style onboard. Factor in who's coming and for how long prior to any such purchase.

Families who spent one-too-many camping trips suffering through cold nights and gear mishaps often soon find themselves on an RV dealer's lot scouting out these "entry-level" units. And for many, buying a pop-up represents a couple's first foray into the world of RVing, with the purchase of a larger trailer or motorhome not far behind. RV manufacturers know this, and hope travelers use a pop-up as a springboard to a larger, more expensive RV later on. Until that time, however, enjoy these small camping wonders, the best value in the industry.

The Least You Need to Know

- Fifth-wheel trailers are the largest, most luxurious, and most expensive tow-ables on the market. Costs vary from $15,000 to $100,000, with sizes ranging from 25 to 40 feet. Multiple slide-outs are common. Their gooseneck design and special hitch require a pickup truck to serve as the tow vehicle.
- Travel trailers offer the greatest flexibility in terms of manufacturers, models, and floor plans. Sizes range from 24 to 40 feet, and double and triple slide-outs are common. The price range is $15,000 to $70,000. Travel trailers can usually be towed by vehicles with a V-8 engine or greater.
- Lightweight travel trailers weigh less than 4,000 pounds, allowing for most trucks, SUVs, and mini-vans to perform the towing duties. They are extremely popular with buyers, thanks to low costs ($8,000 to $17,000), large sleeping capacities (up to eight in some cases), and sizable amenities.
- Fold-down campers are the quintessential family-friendly RVs, with low start-up costs, easy towing, and a major step up over tents. Most units cost under $10,000. The box-shaped unit seen in transit deploys via a cranking mechanism once the destination is reached. Most sleep four to six passengers and are popular with couples with young children.

Chapter 6

Narrowing Down Your Choices

In This Chapter

- How to choose the best RV for you
- Key factors in this selection
- New or used?

Still with me? You didn't go to the basement to air out the tent, did you? Don't tell me you're spending the next family vacation in a Ramada? Assuming your travel agent isn't holding on the other line with cruise recommendations, making it this far suggests that RVing is more than just a passing fancy. The idea is taking hold.

So far, we've talked about recreational vehicles in the abstract. You learned that RVing provides a comfortable, reliable, and affordable way to live and travel and is loved by all different types of people. We've asserted that RVing is all about choices, with plenty of options regarding where to stay and the variety of vehicles to launch your family getaways. You understand the uniqueness of a motorized as opposed to a towable RV and the various selections within these two categories. As one of my mentors used to say, you now know enough to be dangerous. It's time to put that knowledge to good use.

The goal of this chapter is to provoke a discussion about which RV is right for you. The brand, the exact size, or who makes it isn't what we're after here, just what kind. Is it a small motorhome or a whopping fifth wheel? Do you want to put the family SUV to use with a lightweight trailer or is a camper van or truck camper more your speed? Could it be that a 40-foot diesel pusher is in your future? Let's find out.

Talking the Talk

In the RV equivalent of *Fantasy Island,* such decisions would be easy. In the absence of such reality, we'd probably all just take the biggest and the best. Money would be no object. Other "little" annoyances such as weight, towing ability, and where to park wouldn't factor into the decision in the slightest. But sadly, we awake to the real world, with a beagle licking our face, hungry for breakfast, and maybe a quick walk around the block while we're at it. Alas, narrowing down the RV choices requires a little work. Pondering the following questions should help narrow the search.

How Much Do I Have to Spend?

Every other part of the decision-making process comes second to this key determination. Believe or not, the local RV lot wants more than a smile and a handshake to close the deal. It takes money, and sometimes a great deal of it. Buying an RV is just like buying a car. Assuming your proverbial ship didn't come in, financing is the way to go. How much money can you afford to part with every month? How much can you scrape together for a down payment? Be sure to leave a little stipend in the budget for some actual trips, invoking fuel, toll, insurance, and campground costs. We'll discuss such matters in the chapters ahead.

Pull Over

Good common sense regarding any big purchase applies here. Be realistic with your bottom line. Know what you can spend, and don't deviate. Looking out of their price range only serves to leave buyers frustrated and complicates the matter further. Remember, there's an RV made for every budget. Put that motto to the test and you won't be disappointed.

Jumping into the high-end world of an ultra-extravagant motorhome or towable just might not make financial sense at this point. Besides, it's never a bad idea to start small and work your way up to a nicer vehicle over time. As is the case with any major purchase, overbuying creates a sense of dread and remorse. Would you rather spend your free time rationalizing an expensive RV or enjoying it? A $5,000 fold-down camper can provide the same bonding and fellowship any larger towable can—and at a fraction of the price. Plenty of memorable outings can be counted on in a small motorized (and its more reasonable costs) as any Class A motorhome.

Motorized or Towable?

Chances are, you made this decision 50 pages ago. Most people fall into one of the two camps (pun intended) early on. Like the idea of operating just one vehicle (a.k.a. a motorhome) with easier driving and trips free of hitching up? Already have that tow vehicle in place and just an inexpensive towable away from launching your next big camping adventure? We discussed the pros and cons of each type of RV in

Chapters 4, "The World of Motorized RVs," and 5, "The World of Towables." Deciding on the motorized or towable route will make all other decisions a little easier, and thus help narrow your search.

Who's Coming Along?

Most any RV is great for just you and the spouse, or excuse me, you and the girlfriend. (When are you gonna make an honest woman out of her already?) Traveling solo? Even better. Absolutely any RV on the market should be more than roomy enough if it's just for you. However, for those traveling with the boys' choir, the Harlem Globetrotters, or a pack of fluffy kittens, a careful examination of the situation must be made. Believe me, even the seven brides for seven brothers won't be so cordial in a 22-foot travel trailer.

The probable headcount should make all kinds of decisions for you. Generally, the two-parent, two-children dynamic lends itself to most kinds of RVs. Truck campers and smaller Class Bs may or may not oblige, but most others should. Add an adult or two to that mix—or a brood of growing teenagers—and choices shrink to larger trailers and Class A and C motorhomes. Think at least 30 feet of vehicle for five or more passengers and their gear. Six to eight passengers shrink your options to the largest motorhomes or fifth wheels.

Where Are We Going?

While it's mostly true that RVs do well in all kinds of environments, some versions are better suited for specific activities than others. For the family planning on sticking to the highways, opting for local campgrounds and major attractions, any RV should suit. However, those wanting to off-road and just basically go where none have gone before, this requires a highly maneuverable, rugged, and well-equipped machine. That lengthy fifth wheel or monstrous motorhome may struggle when compared to hunting and fishing trips utilizing camper vans, truck campers, and smaller towables. More active types, dreaming of side trips aboard motorcycles, snowmobiles, and the like, might consider a trailer or Class C equipped with a special cargo area to store their motorized goodies.

Road Scholar

Stop me if you've heard this one before. Since passengers are *strongly* discouraged from riding onboard a trailer while in transit, your tow vehicle, therefore, is really what determines how many people can come along. Sleeping for six aboard your new trailer is only useful if the tow vehicle can get them all there. Have I harped on this point enough? I think so.

How Much Room Do We Need?

I've met full-timers who were happy as clams touring the country in their camper van as well as those who felt claustrophobic aboard a 40-foot motorhome with multiple slide-outs. Towables are cheaper per foot than motorized vehicles and further aided by the absence of a cockpit. As you inspect any new RV, ask yourself one question: Can I live here? Large amounts of time spent indoors are probably worth the investment of a bigger vehicle. A few rainy days in tight quarters raises everyone's annoyance level a few degrees. Conversely, making do with less requires a less costly investment.

Pull Over

Is the spouse afraid to operate the new fifth wheel or motorhome? Situations where one member of the family does all the driving invite trouble down the road. What if the perpetual driver gets hurt, sick, or needs a rest? What then? A true driving partnership is always the goal of any new purchase, so buy only what both of you feel comfortable with.

What's My Driving Mood?

It's an irrefutable rule: The smaller the overall length of your RV, the easier it is to move around. And since many hours are spent in transport, careful thought should be given to this most underrated consideration. Is the extra space of a Class A worth the extra diligence required finding a parking space, backing up, or changing lanes? Is the lesser expense of a travel trailer worth the added sway and towing considerations over most fifth wheels? Opting for a camper van amortizes its initial expense with use as a second vehicle. If so, is this what you envisioned as your everyday, 24/7 vehicle?

What Must Be Included?

Deluxe showers and fold-down campers are mutually exclusive. Triple slide-outs and truck campers simply cannot be. Camper vans cannot accommodate a washer and dryer, a gigantic kitchen, or bunk beds for the kids. Thinking about what, if anything, you can live without should break through a decision deadlock. Again, roomier—and more expensive—RVs reward buyers with added options and accessories. Motorized buyers, be sure there's a place to sit and a seatbelt for every member of the family.

Even More to Think About

Making any progress? Is the soul-searching paying off? Before I unleash you at the local dealership for the buying stage (soon, in Chapter 8, "The Art of the Deal"), a consensus should be reached about the type of vehicle you covet. Is it a towable or motorized? Fifth wheel or trailer? Class A, B, or C? Lightweight travel trailer or fold-down camper? Ideally, you also know what you want to spend, how many people the RV must transport, and what kinds of things you'd like to see onboard (besides the Swedish Bikini Team). Get closure on these issues before proceeding. Go ahead, I'll wait.

Great, glad that's decided. But there are a few more things to consider before busting open the piggy bank. Again, we want to avoid impulsive decisions on the dealer's lot. A little forethought can go a long way to making a good buying decision. Here are a few other wrinkles in the decision-making exercise.

Slide-Outs or Not?

It's like something straight out of science fiction, a magical expanding room that creates extra livable space onboard your RV. Come one, come all, see the amazing motorhome gain valuable feet in every direction. It's the extraordinary slide-out room, a relatively new innovation that has kept many marriages afloat, giving couples and families more than just the elbow room they were used to. Picture the living area, the couch you were idly sitting on, able to expand horizontally at the touch of a button, past the confines of the RV's shell, opening up several new feet of valuable space. Slide-outs can be found in any room onboard, and most people love 'em. However, despite the liberating roominess offered and a little more square footage for everybody, slide-outs are not without their drawbacks. Here's a closer look at the pros and cons.

One for the Road

The first slide-out room appeared on motorhomes built by Newmar Corporation in 1990. The advent of the slide-out turned the RV industry on its collective ear. Vehicle lengths had plateaued for many years, so the chance to expand outward threw buyers and dealers into a collective frenzy. Slide-out rooms are now so common that it's unusual to see a model without at least one onboard.

Bigger Is Better

Obviously, a slide-out room treats passengers to a profit-sharing situation: Everyone gains. A larger kitchen means no more excuses for the camp cook to recycle that mac 'n' cheese recipe ... again. More space in the bedroom helps to create the "private sanctuary" always promised in the RV brochures. And if The Who decide to reunite and stop by for a jam session, you'll appreciate the several new feet gained once these rooms are deployed. Slide-outs are easy to activate and reward the extra money with the remarkable return of more room for you and yours. Now even the in-laws can come. Or, er, not.

Pull Over

A little forethought should prevent slide-outs from any unnecessary damage. Survey the landscape around the RV prior to deploying any slide-out. Trees, picnic benches, and the next-door neighbor make for inviting targets to a room that is aimlessly deployed. Park the RV so as to clear the path of any and all slide-out rooms. And don't use the sliding room as a weapon against Uncle Harry.

Resale

Remember when the real estate agent cautioned you against buying a house you couldn't resell? And then you went ahead and bought that Norman Bates replica house anyway, complete with scary figure in the window? The same truths apply in the world of recreational vehicles. Although you might be ambivalent about their presence, prospective buyers might quickly dismiss a rig without a slide-out. Expect the salesperson's exuberance for your trade-in to deflate somewhat upon the news that it is "slide-free."

Slip, Slide, and Away

Alas, for all its good, a slide-out can cause its fair share of headaches. Or maybe that was Uncle Lou's bagpipe playing that caused your head to hurt? No one's arguing that additional space is bad. I mean, it does give the family pet another spot or two to lounge around in. But problems associated with their added weight, the potential for mechanical breakdown, and size restrictions should be considered before purchasing a slide-out model.

Overweight

Unlike our nation's obsession with weight, worrying about the portliness of your RV is a good thing. Too heavy a load, and things start to wear down, falter, and break. Furthermore, driving an overloaded vehicle is against the law and harder to control. The inclusion of a slide-out (or three) chips away at the total weight your RV can carry, meaning tough decisions must be made about what stays at home. At approximately 500 to 1,500 pounds per slide-out room, it doesn't take long before the foosball table, food processor, and two of your three kids are left on the curb. More on this matter in Chapter 15, "How Much Does Your RV Weigh?"

Room Service

Ever order room service in a nice hotel? I'll bet you didn't know there was such a thing as a $50 breakfast, did you? Who knew corned beef hash was so posh-posh? Like eggs Benedict at the Hilton, slide-outs are expensive. Expect a steeper-than-usual bill when ordering a unit with a couple of slide-outs than a similarly equipped model without one. The markup can easily knock your carefully prepared budget for a loop, something to keep in mind while crunching numbers. Fortunately, there's no gratuity involved.

Breakdown

Put this criticism into the "glass-is-half-empty" category, but adding another mechanical doohickey onboard means another device to care for, worry about, and possibly repair. Yes, a slide-out could break, make weird noises, or generally leave you dreading the day the room fails to retract properly. I've heard a few stories about the mechanism becoming misaligned after bouts with particularly bumpy roads. Like all RV appliances, slide-outs require a little preventative maintenance and care when using. Poor sealing around the room itself can lead to leaks, drafts, and debris interfering with its operation. And when it snows, guess what you'll be shoveling before retracting?

One for the Road

The expansion and retraction of slide-out rooms is powered by your RV's 12-volt coach system. Repeated operation of such an electricity-hogging device can drain the coach's battery, leaving a room partially deployed. This is really only a problem when dry camping and failing to replenish the batteries. Fortunately, in the event of a power failure, a manual backup system is almost always offered, usually via a hand crank.

Campground-Ed

Size restrictions might cause slide-out owners about as much difficulty getting in at a few campgrounds as if they were traveling with a swarm of bees, smoking stinky cigars, and talking politics. This sometimes occurs at older campsites, such as those found at a portion of some federal lands and campgrounds not updated since the pet rock last blew into town. In these cases, travel to another facility or simply keep the room retracted. As discussed in Chapter 3, "Where to Stay?" it's always a good idea to call ahead when traveling with an extra long, wide, or slide-out happy RV.

Gas or Diesel?

You've decided upon the motorhome or tow vehicle of your dreams and just one question remains: gas or diesel? Most Class A manufacturers offer at least one model with a diesel engine; it's even occurring somewhat in the Class B and Class C marketplace. These extra choices (with larger price tags) beg the question, which type of engine is indeed better?

A good rule of thumb is to seriously consider a diesel engine for any RV greater than 35 feet in length. This is doubly true if your driving adventures take you through much hilly terrain, where a rear-mounted diesel engine's extra power comes in handy. The reason has to do with the length of the driveshaft and its ability to transfer power to rear wheels. Of course, I just test drove a 37-foot gas-powered motorhome, and it did just fine; but generally the rule is still a good one.

Today's Diesel

A few of the old stigmas of the hard-starting, noisy diesel engine still apply, but their effects have been greatly reduced. Today's diesel engines are quieter, harder working, and more efficient than ever before, as best exemplified from the latest offerings from Cummins and Caterpillar. With today's diesel pushers (rear-mounted diesel engines), noise is almost a nonfactor. Noise may be a different story when sitting in the cab of a diesel pickup, where passengers are much closer to the engine.

The diesel smell is also not the greatest, and cold-weather start-up problems can still hamper engines when the temperature dips below 30°F. However, electronically controlled engines, properly maintained, shouldn't really be hard-pressed until temperatures plummet below 0°F.

Diesel Dilemmas

Consider the cost factor. Diesels are more expensive, whether it's for your RV or tow vehicle. Fuel costs usually run higher, but are offset by better fuel economy than its gasoline counterpart—a very big perk for a motorhome struggling to earn double-digit miles per gallon.

With cold weather comes a set of fuel considerations for diesel owners. Icing and gelling in the fuel tank, associated with the changing of temperatures, often necessitates special care. A number of additives are available to remedy these problems if they should occur. Travelers also have to be sure their diesel fuel is fresh since it doesn't share the popularity of unleaded fuels, and thus, runs the risk of being old.

It's probably best to fill up along the interstate, where the hordes of 18-wheelers keep the diesel supply fresh and the turnover rate higher than at other locales. Many RVers prefer truck stops, offering plenty of room, sizable overhead clearance, and a chance to fill up with the big boys.

Your diesel engine will probably need less routine maintenance over time (no tune-ups or spark plug changes necessary), but when work is required, it will definitely cost more—and not every shop can do the job. A $100 oil change is very possible. However, diesel engines are extremely durable and should last a long time. Stories about pickups besting 500,000 miles are not uncommon. This workhorse reputation should serve you well come trade-in time.

One for the Road

Diesel engines surely have gasoline versions beat in terms of overall lore. Ever heard the one about the owner who got 500,000 miles out of his medium-duty pickup? I personally have seen countless examples of diesels exceeding 200,000 miles and look primed for more. How about the motorhome that rolled out 300,000 miles and is still going strong? True or false, such tales are certainly a part of the diesel mythology.

The best answer to the eternal question of engine type lies in a comprehensive test drive. Compare your gas and diesel models for acceleration, hill power, noise, and smell. Be realistic about the costs as well as your commitment to diesel fuel, obligating owners to a somewhat different mix of maintenance procedures and filling up with the big rigs.

Builder's Choice

Your sixth grade tree house provided a lifetime's worth of lessons in the building process. True, the sheet wood was easier to carry, but it didn't exactly hold up well over time; metal was too heavy, and Dad would never allow it to wrap around his beloved maple. The materials used to build RVs undergo a similar evaluation. All RVs start with a stainless steel chassis, which includes the axles, wheels, tires, and suspension system. In the case of motorized vehicles, an engine, transmission, and drivetrain are added. The materials and manufacturing processes used to construct the RV's

RVocabulary

Stick and tin is the term used to describe an RV built on a wood frame and covered with an aluminum "skin." Stick and tin construction is inexpensive and lightweight, the two magic words for Mr. and Mrs. New Customer.

interior shell vary. As always, the goal is low weights matched with durability and reasonable costs. The materials employed in building directly affect the vehicle's longevity, insulation, and safety of your RV.

Frame Job

A user-friendly floor plan and the standard features inside are key considerations for new buyers. However, an equally important story is what's behind all this and how will it hold up over time? Wood and aluminum are the most common materials for the framework of your RV, often encompassing a mix of each. You might occasionally see steel, more so on older units. The characteristics of each are unique and important to realize before progressing much further into the buying process.

Wood

The rigorous demands of road travel require a solid element, and for the most part wood construction obliges, securing a steady base for your RV's shell. Wood also flexes with movement, a good thing since most trips commute through areas of rough terrain. It's the more insidious factors that affect wood the most. Leaks are an unfortunate byproduct of so-so building, ill-fitting seals around doors and windows, and multi-seamed roofs worn down over time. Unfortunately, wood frames often take the worst of water damage, causing possible rotting in severe cases. On the plus side, wood construction is much cheaper to repair, since a skilled welder or expensive equipment isn't needed to do the job. Owners with basic carpentry skills may be able to do the work themselves.

Aluminum

Aluminum is inexpensive, durable, and lightweight. It's impervious to rot and bugs, while shielding the RV from the sometimes rough-and-tumble life on America's byways. The knock against aluminum is its difficulty in repairing (as opposed to the hammer and nail approach for wood), possible breakage from poor welding, and some claims that it is much more likely to condensate in cold weather (helped by lackluster insulation).

Steel

We all know about steel's legacy of strength and durability. They didn't call Superman the Man of Ceramics, did they? Shark cages aren't made of plastic for a similar reason. However, the Kryptonite in this case comes in the form of possible corrosion and rust. This added protection also comes with a price: extra weight. This means some onboard amenities must be sacrificed to prevent overloading the chassis. It could be that easy chair, awning, or your collection of sock puppets. Steel is also more expensive to repair, unless you are the proud benefactor of a degree in welding.

Get Insulated

Give a little thought to what's inside the walls. For RVers caught in the crossfire of bad weather—or just preferring the solitude of a nice wintry campground—insulation is important to keeping the cold out and spirits up. Some RVs have regular insulation (the pink stuff) in the walls and between studs, while others have vacu-bonded walls, meaning the wallboard, foam board insulation, and outside skin are stuck together. As with many things in life, the more insulation, the merrier you'll be.

Save Your Skin

The final step is the RV's exterior or the "skin." No, this isn't meant to be creepy, although it sorta is the more I think about it. Fiberglass, aluminum, and plastic (a.k.a. Filon), believe it or not, are the three prevailing materials used to safeguard your investment from dings, dents, and that heat-seeking grocery cart. Lighter weights and toughness are what we're really after, qualities these materials provide in their own way. A nasty collision with a mailbox or your son's mountain bike may leave an aluminum exterior dented whereas a fiberglass may crack. Pick your poison, I suppose. Each material requires regular cleaning to remove salt, debris, and possible corrosion-causing items. Wax is also a good idea.

Raising the Roof

You wouldn't think such a benign-sounding topic as the RV's roofing would be so lively. Oh, yes indeed. Back in my days as editor for *RV View* magazine, the single greatest response we ever received was to an article on rubber roofs. Hundreds of letters and e-mails poured in, reporting the virtues of the old faithful aluminum types. Conspiracy theorists suggested that the advent of rubber roofing in the 1980s was a great ruse by manufacturers, passing on an inferior product to save a buck. One man said the first RV to roll off an assembly line with a rubber roof was the darkest day in the history of RVing. Geez. Months after the story came and went, the debate raged on and still probably does around a campfire near you.

Once upon a time, aluminum roofs were king. That is, until EPDM rubber (Ethylene Propylene Diene Monomer, for those of you keeping score at home) crashed the party. Today, it's virtually a moot point. You get what you get, and manufacturers seem to prefer rubberized versions. However, let's throw a little more wood on the fire, just for fun. Here's a look at the differences between the two, which for RV purists may affect their buying decisions one way or the other.

Rubber

The center of the anti-EPDM hurricane lies in the fact that rubber roofs can tear. A low-hanging tree branch (common) or walking around the roof in your golf spikes (uncommon) can rip, disfigure, or otherwise mar an RV's uppermost protection. Stains from tree sap, not-so-friendly birds, and debris can be tough to remove. This was never a problem when aluminum was up there, proclaim RVers nostalgic for the good old days. Oxidation is also a problem, brought about by the ravages of the sun. Over time, owners might see a chalking or flaking effect of the rubber compound, which could lead to mostly cosmetic disturbances such as streaks down the side of the unit.

The good news is that frequent cleaning remedies this problem, and scores of aftermarket repair kits can help patch and contain any problems. With a little preventative care, a quality-made rubber roof should last 10 to 15 years. They also hold up well under harsh weather conditions, including excessive heat and cold.

Aluminum

Aluminum is tough, lightweight, and relatively low-maintenance. Just install it and forget it. There's never been much need for frequent washings and excessive stain-removal. You can probably then understand why rubber seems like a step in the wrong direction to some folks. You'd have to do something truly awful to tear an aluminum roof; denting is possible but can be remedied. A quality-made aluminum roof can last and last and keep Sunday afternoon trips to the car wash or RV store to a minimum.

Of course, some believe it's more prone to damage from the barrage of elements—wind, sand, hail, and road debris chief among them. And you will surely hear every raindrop tink, tink, tinking away overhead. Some aluminum roofs are not solid, but simply aluminum stretched over rafters and soft insulation. Needless to say, this is very easy to damage when checking seams, sealing vents, or just poking around up there. In these cases, a "walking board" is commonly used to keep from puncturing it. This practice is more common in low-end trailers.

Fiberglass

The rarest of the bunch, fiberglass roofing, boasts strong proponents of its own, more common to high-end units. Sure, they're heavier and more expensive but are redeemed somewhat by managing to hold their good looks over time. Where rubber roofs fall victim to dinginess, an occasional wash and wax is usually all it takes to keep fiberglass looking marvelous.

Road Scholar

Leaks are one of the greatest threats to the sanctity of your recreational vehicle. They're also very annoying and difficult to track. Faulty seams in the roof are the greatest culprits, expanding and weakening over time. Next thing you know, that innocent trickle resembles the Love Canal. If given the choice, a one-piece or seamless roof is better than one that is pieced together. Inspect seams regularly and reseal them with aftermarket products if problems develop.

What's Their Rep?

Unlike the automobile industry, limited to a few giants and their subsidiaries, there are loads of RV manufacturers. A few can boast 70-plus years in the business; others started last Thursday. Company XYZ might build every type of RV under the sun, while another focuses on one or two kinds. Every manufacturer brings something new and different to the table in terms of design or engineering, presenting the dilemma of who to trust to build yours.

At some point, the choice might boil down to an RV from company X and company Y. The prices are competitive. Each passes all your tests as far as livability (as we'll see in Chapter 7, "What to Buy?"). Even your goldfish seems impressed. I recommend letting the manufacturers' reputations break the tie. Listening to the opinions of customers, the media, and even wacky Cousin Al reveals certain patterns about a company's products, accountability, and commitment to the customer. Question that RV owner at the rest stop or gas station for his thoughts on his particular unit. Ask your local RV dealer why he carries the products he does. Read as many publications as you can, particularly ones conducting RV road tests. Go online and solicit opinions from members of various RV-related chat groups and message boards (that is, if you can get them off the subject of *Star Trek* long enough). Useful sources for your search are listed in Appendix A, "Resources."

Wide-Body Designs

Wait a minute. Unclench those fists. Nobody's saying that your RV's fat. Please, put down that tire iron. Actually, the term "wide-body" is quite complimentary. With an exterior width of more than 96 inches, any recreational vehicle can be one, allowing more space for you and your crew. Many RVs extend up to 102 inches (wide-bodies), which is a nice 6-inch boost to those inside. These slightly plumper vehicles yield other advantages besides just added space. Like slide-outs, wide-body designs are quickly becoming the norm and not the exception in everything from camper vans to diesel motorhomes to the long list of towables. You'll notice the difference come resale, too. The downside is that wide-bodies might cost a little more and affect vehicle weight.

Road Scholar

If you're worried about violating state laws concerning width, stick to the interstate, which falls under the auspices of the wide-body-friendly federal government. Contact the state's Department of Transportation to learn which roads are suspect to violation if you're nervous about venturing off the main highways. A lot of noise has been made as of late about the duality of such policies, so don't be surprised if these contradictory laws are eventually overturned.

Probably the single biggest fear of wide-body owners is possible legal issues. Once upon a time in America, 96 inches was the limit on all state and federal highways. It wasn't until recently that Uncle Sam loosened up on that restriction, upping the ante to 102 inches on interstates. However, the decision of how to deal with the thousands of two-lane roads and lesser highways was left up to each individual state. As you might expect, laws—and levels of enforcement—vary from place to place. While it's true that wide-bodies are legal in all 50 states, that doesn't account for every stretch of road, only the federally controlled interstates.

It is my experience that this is all but a nonissue for most travelers. Seldom do you ever hear of a ticket being issued. You'll also notice the hypocrisy of *selling* wide-body trucks and RVs, which happens freely in all 50 states. Strange, isn't it?

Walking the Walk

It's time to leave the nest. Hitch up the horses. Polish up the shoe leather. In short, this part of your quest cannot be accomplished in your favorite easy chair. Okay, you can bring the remote control if it makes you feel better. It's time to hit the streets in search of answers. The best way to truly narrow down your choices is to tour the RVs themselves—lots of them. If a picture is worth a thousand words, what then is an afternoon spent looking at vehicles worth? The answer could put me out of the book-writing business.

Examine the floor plans, see how a slide-out really works, get behind the wheel and make loud driving noises. Compare the living quarters of one type of RV to another. Ask questions. Listen. Repeat. Eliminate the vehicles you can't afford, drive/tow, or those that are too big or too small. You're not here to buy, that comes later. Leave the checkbook at home, or that wad of cash safely tucked away in the mattress. No transactions today, only fact-gathering and lively discussions between you, your spouse, and the family about what type of RV is best for the group. The following is an itinerary of sorts, a list of places and ways to refine your opinions in an effort to, say it with me, narrow down your choices.

Showtime

Want to see a grown man cry? Set him in front of the diesel trucks or motorhomes at the RV show. It's a truly sad spectacle to see men huddled around in an impromptu support group, lamenting about their vehicle's lack of power, how the Mrs. won't let them walk around with the checkbook, and how they would champion the causes of all that's good and true if only they could possess such a manly vehicle. Don't get caught up in this (yet), you're here to do your homework.

There's an RV show happening somewhere nearly every week of the year. The local convention center or football stadium is awash in a sea of recreational vehicles, a sight so profound for those who love the lifestyle, that traveling hundreds of miles to attend is not unheard of. I know couples who struggle to name the date of their anniversary, but are quick to drop the date and time of the next big show. Events such as these are created with three goals in mind: sell, sell, and sell some more. Area dealerships showcase their wares, with salespeople in a frenzy to make a deal.

In addition to a bunch of shiny new RVs, exhibitors may offer entertainment, food, and events to lure potential buyers. Representatives from nearby campgrounds and resorts, the latest accessory products, food, and probably a juggler or two are also common RV show sights. But remember your mission: to tour every RV you can, and make some decisions about which is best for you. There is simply no greater opportunity than this to survey the RV landscape. Okay, you can have some cotton candy, too.

Show dates and times can usually be found in the local newspaper. The travel or auto section is the best bet. Otherwise, the Recreation Vehicle Industry Association (RVIA) features a comprehensive listing of RV shows nationwide. Visit www.rvia.org/rvshows/ for a comprehensive listing.

Kick the Tires

The next best way to sample RVs is to visit area dealerships. Of course, you may be spoiled rotten after the head-spinning selection at the RV show. Instead of hundreds of units on display, most medium-size dealerships might have less than 50 available to tour. The price and space requirements of inventory minimize the amount of overhead most can handle.

RV dealerships vary from their automotive counterparts in several ways. Unlike the massive Honda, Ford, or Mercedes dealerships you're used to seeing, most RV lots feature a scattering of different manufacturers and a mix of vehicle types. For example, Dealer X might sell fifth wheels by one manufacturer, travel trailers from another, and a few lines of motorhomes thrown in just for fun. Meanwhile, Dealer Y offers three kinds of fold-down campers, a number of lightweight trailers, and truck campers from several different makers. Be sure to call ahead to eliminate unnecessary visits. For example, if you've ruled out motorized vehicles all together, then only coordinate visits to those selling towables.

Overdue Rent

Since the driving/towing segment of RV life is crucial to your level of comfort and enjoyment, it's prudent (if at all possible) to take your preferred type of RV out for a spin. Renting a vehicle for a few days takes this one step further, offering consumers the chance to actually live onboard and experience the lifestyle firsthand. The benefits of such a trip are two-fold: first, to determine how much you like traveling by RV; and second, if this is the right kind of vehicle to do it in. Sure, the differences between a 35-foot motorhome and small camper van are fairly obvious upon first review, but an extended trip reveals key insights into the strengths and weaknesses of each. Buyers often discover a great appreciation for what they're looking for after a weekend sleeping, cooking, showering, using the bathroom, and lounging about an RV. Fortunately, rentals are available for such introspection.

Pull Over

Rental companies are notorious for some rather oddball—and pricey—provisions found within the fine print. Beware of extra charges for cleaning the unit, refilling water and LP tanks, and emptying the holding tanks. Hammer down any possibly extra mileage costs or per-diem insurance before you leave the premises.

The good news is that rental companies exist. The bad news is that towables are rarely on the menu. The deliberations required to match up a tow vehicle correctly to the trailer du jour is more fuss than most customers and renters want to endure for a spontaneous getaway. Opportunities for fifth-wheel and travel-trailer owners are few; smaller fold-down campers and lightweights are more common, but still a minority of the nation's rental fleet. Life on the motorized side is much better, since nearly everyone rents Class Cs. Larger Class As, camper vans, and truck campers are also available, although to a lesser degree.

The drawback is that renting isn't cheap. Expect to pay $100 to $200 a night for the vehicle itself, possibly more depending on when and where you rent. Campground costs, fuel, tolls, a per-diem insurance, dumping fees, and miscellaneous costs might appear in the contract. A mileage fee may or may not be included.

The nation's largest RV rental chain, Cruise America (1-800-327-7799; www.cruiseamerica.com) is a sure bet. At this time, the company rents various-size Class Cs, including a Fun Mover model with a ramp and cargo area for dirt bikes, snowmobiles, and other motorized goodies (Cruise America rents motorcycles, too). A deluxe truck camper is also available. Otherwise, the local Yellow Pages or an online search is warranted. For a complete catalog of rental companies, contact the Recreation Vehicle Rental Association (1-888-467-8464; www.rvra.org).

Take a Sunday Drive

Test-driving a little beauty off the dealer's lot is another option. This is only really of use to get a feeling for "how she handles" and not for gauging the living quotient onboard. Walking around in your PJs, drinking milk straight out of the container is usually frowned upon. However, a decision between a 35-foot Class A and a 30-foot Class C motorhome might just come down to the driving ease of each. Maneuverability, parking, and whether or not your anxiety level behind the wheel causes you to break out with hives might set your sights to a mini-motorhome or even something smaller.

Towable enthusiasts fare only slightly better here than in the rental sector. In cases where matching up an existing vehicle is a potential influence on a buying decision, some dealers might allow you to hitch up the trailer to your existing tow vehicle and take it out for a spin. Otherwise, don't expect a loaner vehicle on the premises to transport the fifth wheel or travel trailer you've been eyeing. A dealer's fears over liability and low overhead for such superfluous vehicles are the main reasons behind this.

Road Scholar

Our good friends at RVIA offer a number of ways to aid your decision-making process. Call 1-888-GO-RVING for a list of local RV dealerships, rental facilities, and information about the lifestyle (although I'd like to think this book is helping in that regard). A free video about how to get started is also included.

A Friend in Need ...

With more than 10 million RVs on the road, somebody you know has to own one. Perhaps they may even let you take it out for a spin. An in-law, a cousin, the neighbor with the black socks and the Bermuda shorts. The boss's nephew who you helped move last summer? What about Grandma and her quarter-million-dollar diesel pusher with three slide-outs? Maybe your close personal friend John Madden will let you borrow his? (You didn't hear that from me!) Once you've located that person, bend his ear, and see if you can't arrange a visit. Two words: Ask nicely.

RVers are some of the nicest, most outgoing people around. And why shouldn't they be? They are enjoying a very liberating and thrilling way to live and travel. The joy is evident on their faces. The other thing we all have in common is how we love to talk about—and show off—our vehicles. These nickel tours and candid discussions are the real deal, the truth in a world full of spin and misinformation. If you're fortunate enough to know someone with the type of RV you're desiring, do whatever you can to hear their opinions. And if they're really nice, you might even get to borrow it some weekend and learn firsthand for yourself. Two tickets to Sunday's football game wouldn't hurt this negotiation.

Read All About It

There's also no shortage of up-to-date information about the RV lifestyle, whether it be online, on magazine shelves, or through scores of publications devoted to specific RV travel clubs. Check out an Internet discussion group, post a barrage of questions on bulletin boards (the cyber kind, not the one at work), and question fellow RVers about their RVs and preferences. Be prepared for forthright and eager responses, as my experience is that we RVers love to talk. Sure, some folks have an axe to grind or may be ill-informed, but such candid discussions are still usually beneficial.

Several larger magazines such as *MotorHome, Trailer Life, Camping Life,* and the various titles from Woodall's Publications feature monthly RV road tests and industry news. These are good sources to get you thinking about specific vehicles or the advantages of one type over another. A list of RV-specific publications can be found in Appendix A.

Buyer's Guides

More comprehensive information can be found in an RV buyer's guide, available on an annual basis from *Trailer Life* and *Woodall's*. These guides feature detailed information on a wide range of RV offerings for the upcoming year. Sizes, weights, floor plan choices, standards and options, prices, and a shiny photograph is the least that is offered. RVs are broken down into classes, allowing for an easy glimpse of many of the hottest new designs in one specific category.

The Horse's Mouth

After a lengthy investigation, everything might start to blur together into a never-ending collage of fiberglass, rubber, and wheels. Taking in this much new information should leave your brain more fried than a chicken sandwich from KFC. Grab brochures of favorite models and scribble down notes and costs. At some point, you'll begin to recognize the makers of a specific RV by their unique features. Eventually, the pendulum might swing in favor of a couple of specific manufacturers, perhaps due to their aesthetics, user-friendly floor plans, or obvious quality. You may not know what RV you want, but perhaps company XYZ is the answer.

Pinpoint your search by going directly to the manufacturers themselves. Visit their Web sites and tour their product galleries. Send away for brochures and read everything printed about that company, their reputation, and customer service.

Campfire Chats

The mood is serene. A parade of campfires flicker away in the summer night. Kids are passive, watching the burning embers and readying marshmallows for a thorough torching. The smell of hickory dances in the air. And then someone starts talking about his RV. It never fails. RVers love to talk about their vehicles. During my various road tests, it's common for curious strangers to approach me about what I'm driving. Come on in, I'll say. Have a look around. This kind of RV showcasing isn't braggery, rather an inquisitive look at what the other folks have. Surely, they'll return the favor and walk you through their motorhome or talk about what they love about their 10-year-old trailer. Ask your neighbor for opinions. Next thing you know, you'll be sharing beef stew talking about why she prefers this brand of Class C or another. Bring over dessert and school is in session.

New or Used?

The new or used debate is a classic one, for everything from CDs to RVs. Many owners treat their recreational vehicles as luxury items, subjecting them to relatively low mileage, wear and tear, and light periods of use. As a result, it's not unusual to see 20-year-old rigs out on the road (avocado interior included). Factor this in with the expense of the latest models, and the appeal of a previously owned unit becomes obvious. However, a secondhand product comes with a fair share of risks. Why are they selling? How did they treat it? What if it breaks a mile down the road? Determining whether to cut a larger check for a new RV or roll the dice on an older model is a major decision. Let's look at some of the key factors.

Secondhand Views

That sinister little foe, depreciation, makes buying a used RV very attractive. Purchase a new vehicle, drive it around for a while, re-sell it, and what have you got? About 10 to 20 percent less money than you started with. This is especially true for motorized units, with an engine and more mechanisms to wear down from use. Of course, you probably don't need me to tell you that lower price is the single biggest advantage to buying used.

More for the Money

Depreciation affects all those neat do-dads onboard, too. Those pricey upgrades—the leather sofas, dishwasher, and the undercarriage rust-proofing the dealer sold you on—are also used, and, therefore, should be less expensive, too. That one-year-old global positioning system and the awning you just installed also fall under this category.

They Don't Make 'Em Like That Anymore

I love old RVs. Some of the earlier motorhomes resemble something straight out of Moon Base Alpha rather than something camped out at the KOA. You wouldn't believe some of the creations out there: one-of-a-kind prototypes, goofy designs that never caught on, classic head-turners replaced by a fickle public. Just like my beloved 1972 Nova, they don't make 'em like that anymore, which is why they're so appealing to some. The added perk is that classic RVs are a fraction of the price of today's models.

Road Scholar

It's worth the money to have an RV service technician look over any used RVs you're serious about buying. Undetected trouble doesn't stay that way long, which is why it's best to have the pros take a look see.

Used and Abused

The dream is that you'll find that little old lady who only drove her RV to church. The reality is that like you, a used RV has a past, one that may reflect a history of abuse and little respect for itself, kind of like you back in college. Did the owner(s) take care of it or were they too busy chasing squirrels off their lawns? Was routine maintenance performed on the appliances, electrical and LP systems, and plumbing? Was the vehicle properly stored when not in use and eased back into service in the spring? Did they drive it like a government mule—or worse, like a rental car? As we'll discuss in Chapter 7, there's a lot we can do to verify the overall condition of a vehicle. Unfortunately, unlike Al Capone's vault, Geraldo Rivera won't be there to uncover all of its secrets for us. There are some things about a used RV that you may never know.

Buying Trouble

It can be said that there are few assurances in life. And sadly, the few givens out there just aren't any good—death, taxes, and the Cubs losing 100 games. Who wants those things? Buying used is risky. A private seller will offer no quarter in terms of warranties or a nice return policy when it starts coughing up antifreeze. An RV dealership may or may not offer such consolations on their older models, either, but will assuredly work harder to satisfy a paying customer.

Mechanical Difficulties

Back to the 1972 Nova. I loved that car ... that is, until the day the gas tank sprung a leak. I knew the duct tape wouldn't be enough this time. Actually, my friend had to talk me out of welding the gas tank back together. "What's the big deal?" I asked. Sadly, a replacement tank was nowhere to be found, revealing an important lesson: The older the vehicle, the harder it is to find parts. In an age where mechanics need computer degrees just to pop the hood, servicing an older RV can be problematic.

New

Price. Plain and simple. That's the one solid argument against buying new. A higher sticker price and higher insurance premiums await all new buyers. If cash is short and you're feeling frisky, a terrific case can be made for a preowned unit. I would rather have you out there RVing, living life on your terms, reaping the rewards of spending time with your family, than sitting at home pondering all the what-ifs. Now, here's what's good about buying new.

Choice

Face it, new RVs come with more choices. Size, color, engine, etc., it's a smorgasbord of opportunity. Just visit an RV show to know what I mean, much more tempting in terms of driving out in a new 40-foot diesel than the slim pickings found on the waiver wire of the weekend classified section. While frugal buyers comb the used dealer lots and Web sites for deals, you've got the pick of the litter. Hundreds of choices await, and dealers are more than happy to show you all around. Play eenee, meenee, minee, moe to determine a favorite. This is doubly true for floor plans, with multiple variations in every unit, from every manufacturer.

Rest Assured

The RV is brand new. Plastic is draped over the furnishings; the floor is unspoiled, pristine and beautiful. The odometer is fresh as a daisy. The driver's seat lacks the butt groove of any previous owners. A sparkling clean engine radiates under the hood. Appliances sit clean and shiny. Everything is untouched, unspoiled. Inhale deeply. Notice the smell of honest clean. That is what you're paying for.

Not only that, but newer is usually better in terms of quality. Newer materials like Corian, gel coat fiberglass, and Thermopane windows (to name a few) are superior to their predecessors. With every production year, RVs get better made, safer, more aerodynamic, and probably more durable than a unit made 5 or 10 years ago. You won't find air bags or the top-of-the-line innovations on some older vehicles. Nor will your investment be protected by a warranty as comprehensive, giving new buyers a level of confidence.

The Least You Need to Know

- Determining such factors as budget, driving or towing abilities, the number of passengers, and types of usage are paramount to picking the best type of RV for you.
- Wide-body vehicles and slide-out rooms deliver extra room, but at additional cost and weight. An RV manufacturer's reputation is also worth investigating before a purchase is made, as are the RV's building materials (roof, shell, and exterior), insulation, and gas vs. diesel.
- Visiting RV shows, touring dealer lots, renting, and taking test drives help many buyers discover their needs and further narrow down their list of must-haves for their future RV.
- A used RV might work better for smaller budgets or for those wanting the distinguished looks of an older vehicle. New RV buyers pay more for the confidence of the latest product designed, with warranties, floor plan choices, and a clean driving history.

Part 3

Buying Your First RV

Call the accountant, notify the bank, wake the dog—it's time to buy. A close financial inspection revealed that there is indeed a little money in the reserves to jump into the recreational vehicle fold. Congratulations. Your hard work has paid off, and now you, the family, and relatives you've never heard of can soon hit the road in search of … well, whatever. So what's it gonna be? A 35-foot motorhome for you and the wife? A fold-down camper for use behind the family SUV? A medium-size trailer that sleeps six? Hopefully, some sort of a decision about that has been reached, since this part of the book is dedicated to pulling the proverbial trigger on a new RV.

Chapter 7

What to Buy?

In This Chapter

- Inspecting a new or used RV
- Testing the livability index
- The test drive

New or used. RV dealer or private seller. Motorized or towable. Assuming you're not going to inherit an RV from Grandma Ruth or find a shiny new rig underneath the Christmas tree, you've got to go out and get one. Any RV purchase requires a comprehensive evaluation, both in terms of the quality of its construction and the usefulness of the interior. Like boot camp marines, we're gonna put each and every vehicle through its paces. The more legwork you do in the early stages, the less likely you are to ask yourself, "Why did I buy this?" later on. We definitely want to avoid that lonely utterance if we can help it.

By now, you should have a working model of what you're looking for, or, at least, what you definitely *don't* want. A financial summit has produced an acceptable budget, and a headcount has determined just how many people your future RV needs to transport and sleep. If not, go back to Chapter 6, "Narrowing Down Your Choices," and get a handle on these most important factors. Believe me, it's a lot easier to find the perfect travel trailer under $25,000 capable of sleeping six than it is finding, say, "whatever towable that will work." Otherwise, you may wilt under the pressure of a charismatic salesperson. A sort of RV-show paralysis is all too common for those unfocused in their buying decisions.

Now hop aboard, the perfect RV awaits.

Livability Tests

Your eyes meet from across the lot. Could it be love at first sight? A thoughtful glance at the sticker price only strengthens your resolve—you can afford it! You walk inside, trying to imagine the whole family in a peaceful co-existence. After a slow walk-thru you're still smiling. You like it. Now it's time to get serious. Every vehicle claim will be tested, every nook and cranny thoroughly examined. The purpose of such a "livability test" is to determine how user-friendly this new motorized or towable truly is. Can it really sleep eight passengers? Is the shower of adequate size? Can you see the TV from the couch? Is there enough storage for all of your bowling trophies? Remember, this is your hard-earned money. Make sure your new RV is worthy of this investment.

Let's start inside, since this is the make-or-break spot for most of us.

Road Scholar

You might look at dozens of RVs before settling on one you like best. As such, keeping the details straight from one unit to the next can be difficult. Most dealers carry brochures on each RV—make sure you grab one. Take deliberate notes. Circle the floor plans you've toured, including prices and noteworthy points. Some buyers employ a video camera to record their findings for later review.

It Sleeps How Many?

For the most part, RV manufacturers do a reasonably good job with their sleeping claims. Of course, there are a few that are a wee too optimistic. If a unit says it sleeps up to six, make them prove it. Is that six adults or six children? Can your sister who played center for three seasons in the WNBA fit anywhere? Start in the master bedroom (if applicable), the most important bed in the place. Why? Because it will most likely be *your* bed, that's why. Lie down. Ask your spouse to come along, too. Is there room for the two of you, or would this tight fit create a nightmarish situation for the both of you? Is there a spot nearby for the alarm clock, journal, and eyeglasses?

Don't stop there. Test out every sleeping configuration the RV has to offer. Deploy the sofa bed, convert the dinette table sleeper, crawl up in the cab-over area (Class Cs only) and lie down. Are these spaces comfortable, easy to deploy and access? Do you fit? Will cousin Benny? I'm constantly driven crazy during RV road tests when my feet hang over the bed. I'm six feet tall. Personally, I don't think the problem is me. After all these tests, determine just how many the RV can sleep—and sleep comfortably.

Food Fight

Assuming cooking—and eating—are important to you, then the kitchen area should definitely be somewhat chef-friendly. Consider space issues. Is there enough storage for pots, pans, and place settings for everyone onboard? How about the sink? Can it hold more than two dirty plates at a time? Do you have enough counter space to chop vegetables, set bowls for mixing, or prepare sandwiches for the gang? Where will the garbage go (most RVs don't come with a garbage can)? What about recycling (ditto here as well)? Is the underneath-the-sink storage a usable space, or dominated by plumbing fixtures? Are the drawers decorative or functional? How about outlets, lighting, and a place for larger or awkward cooking items?

One for the Road

Most, if not all, convertible dinettes are too short for adults. Sofa beds vary a lot in terms of overall mattress size and comfort. Be sure to watch that metal bar underneath (you know the one) that can make for long nights for your guests.

Check out the appliances. What comes standard and which are options? Will two burners be enough, or can you find three or more in your price range and vehicle type? Can the oven accommodate anything larger than a tray of cupcakes? A small refrigerator and a large family equals trouble. Visualize all the usual staples—an endless assortment of soft drinks, cumbersome leftover dishes, and the catch of the day. And maybe just enough space for a few supplemental canned hams, a Peterson family tradition. Do you have a freezer or icemaker? Do you need one? Is the microwave standard or an option? Do you care? Would a convection oven be the best of both worlds? Where will paper towels, silverware, and spices go? Give adequate attention to these small, but ultimately significant issues.

One for the Road

Don't forget about the most underrated cooking area, the campfire. Many RVers without deluxe kitchens (or those opposed to messing up the interior) cook over hot coals and never miss a beat. Others rely on the portable grill, along for the ride tucked inside an exterior storage compartment.

Perhaps cooking and the complexity of the kitchen is the last thing on your mind. You didn't buy an RV to scramble eggs and labor over a hot stove, after all. You're on vacation! In this case, less is definitely more. Don't waste money and interior space on an RV with a deluxe kitchen when the local steakhouse or roadside diners will be doing most of the work. Accordingly, look for floor plans that use the leftover space to benefit the rest of the coach, affecting the rooms that you care more about.

Pull Over

The bigger the vehicle, the larger the kitchen. In this case, you usually get what you pay for. If the budget calls for a fold-down camper, don't expect the island kitchens, double-door refrigerators, and dishwashers found in some high-end fifth wheels. The question, rather, should be whether or not there's a *reasonable* mix of storage, space, and functionality present. If not, perhaps the next model will work better. Unrealistic expectations can plague the buying experience.

What About My Ukulele?

Keep tabs on all interior drawers, cabinetry, and storage compartments. Open each one. Are they there for show or are they ready to serve? Are they skinny or deep, tall or tiny? Is there a wardrobe closet onboard? Does that matter to you? Does each room possess enough storage to prevent the endless searching for your gear? I once saw an interesting trailer where the largest concentration of storage was found in the bathroom. Would such a situation work for you?

Are there larger compartments for blankets, cleaning supplies, and bulkier items? A great development is the advent of underneath-the-bed storage, where the bed easily lifts to provide a sizable, out-of-the-way compartment. Plenty of overhead storage onboard is also great, but really only useful for lighter items. Heavier stowage belongs closer to the floor, to prevent a top-heavy condition. We'll discuss proper packing and what to bring along in Chapter 15, "How Much Does Your RV Weigh?"

Going Through the Motions

I guarantee that you're going to feel goofy standing in the shower with your clothes on and a curious salesperson looking on, but do it anyway. Step inside and go through the showering motions (no water required here). Otherwise, this watery tomb may prove to be a constant source of annoyance after the purchase. A roomy shower is a joy; conversely, a tight squeeze should be reserved only for orange juice. In the case of smaller RVs, often lacking their own paneled showering room, it's doubly important to "try it out." How does it work? Does a curtain wrap around the middle of the camper van, with water going down an in-floor drain? Just because a shower is offered, doesn't mean it's a satisfactory experience. Walk the walk so you know what you're in for.

You know what's coming next, don't you? If a bathtub is present, go ahead and test it out. Ask the salesperson to scrub your back if you like. Can you spread out? Is it worth the extra cost? Showers with tubs can be more difficult to access than flat-floor showers. Keep this in mind for passengers struggling with mobility issues. Garden tub/shower combinations are becoming more and more common. They don't take up as much room as a full-size bathtub, yet feel quite roomy.

Is there a spot for soap, shampoo, conditioner, and rubber ducky? How about towel racks and outlets for the hair dryer? How do the sink and vanity rate? Generally, bathrooms don't possess too much storage, so a medicine cabinet is a nice touch. Actually sit on the toilet (yes, I know how this looks). Do your knees knock against the walls? Are you constricted like a Houdini stunt? One of the nicest fifth wheels I ever saw didn't have a roll for toilet paper. Certainly not a deal-breaker, but it's important to think about the little things. An annoyance now only grows in frustration over time.

Road Scholar

Space aboard smaller RVs such as fold-down campers, truck campers, and Class Bs can be tight. In some cases, bathrooms and showers aren't offered. Judge for yourself if such a convenience is important to you or whether or not you're willing to sacrifice the space to bring it onboard. The majority of campgrounds feature bathrooms and showers. Most are free to use or offered for a nominal fee.

Live and Let Live

My first several trips RVing were spent mostly outside. I cooked over the campfire, roasted marshmallows, and frolicked around town and saw the sights with my awesome wife. At night, we might climb the rear-mounted ladder to the roof for a nightly star show. The thought of turning on the TV or spending much time indoors seemed kind of strange to us. Longer trips and occasional bad weather eventually forced us inside for greater lengths. It wasn't too long before the remote was in hand, the TV antenna raised, and the smell of microwave popcorn filled the air. I can't say I didn't enjoy that part of RVing, too.

One for the Road

Back in the day, a small "step" between the slide-out and the room itself was an unfortunate by-product. Today, many manufacturers utilize a "flush-floor" slide-out room, with no noticeable difference between the two rooms. Better yet, no stumbling about with hot coffee in your hand.

Road Scholar

Color schemes vary, and most interiors give choices of carpeting, tiles, fabric, countertops, and woodworking. It's a good idea, especially if traveling with several passengers (or energetic children) to opt for medium colors and patterns; light and soft colors tend to show every smudge and speck of dirt. If you can afford it, leather is extremely durable and easy to clean.

No matter how sporty you are or how active the itinerary, spending *some* time lounging about the interior is inevitable. During these times, the comforts of the couch and size of the TV matter a whole lot more than whether or not the fish are biting. High-line RVs come with all sorts of entertaining options; that list is whittled away somewhat as you move down to the more entry-level offerings. But a few key questions remain. Are the chairs and couches comfortable? Does the swivel chair swivel, the recliner recline, and the expandable table, well, you get the picture. Can everyone see the TV? Do you require a second one in the bedroom? In many motorhomes, the cockpit chairs swivel around to join the conversation, for additional seating. Is this important to you? Would a slide-out living area provide the finishing touch?

Where will drinks go? How's the lighting for reading? Got enough headroom? Interior heights and widths vary, so don't settle for dwarfish dimensions. Keep looking, you're bound to find a manufacturer capable of getting the most out of every inch. Would a freestanding table, capable of being moved, be better than a stationary dinette with bench seats? I was just in a travel trailer where all the furnishings were movable, in stark contrast to the nailed-down furnishings of most coaches. Would a J-shaped couch be better than a loveseat? Does the motorhome have enough seat belts? Where will the laptop go? Deploy all slide-outs to gauge their impact in terms of space.

Other Keys to Victory

Honor your first impressions. Does the interior feel homey and welcoming? Can you picture the family running around within, husband snoozing away peacefully on the couch, the dog licking her chops in front of the refrigerator? Is there enough light? Are there enough windows and skylights to allow the sunlight to radiate throughout? Are overhead lights, outlets, and heating ducts abundant? What about jacks for phone and cable TV hookups, a TV antenna for better reception, or a place for newspapers and magazines? Is the décor something that reflects your tastes or Minnie Pearl's?

Take It Outside

Since you won't be living outside (unless you forgot your wife's birthday again), poking around the exterior isn't technically a livability test. That doesn't mean you won't be spending some quality time rummaging out there, however. Expect plenty of moments rummaging through the various exterior compartments, hooking up to the campsite utilities, deploying the awning, and the like outside your new RV.

Storage

Go outside and open up the storage compartments. In nicer models, expect to see carpeting, insulation, lighting, and the ability to be locked for safekeeping. Is this the case? Is there enough room for bulkier items such as fishing poles, life vests, and lawn chairs? Believe me, bags of charcoal and firewood don't make for great chaperones inside. A pass-thru storage means gear can be accessed from either side of the unit. Basement storage models, as discussed in Chapter 4, "The World of Motorized RVs," are cavernous and great for those traveling with larger numbers.

You cannot have too much storage space in an RV. Ask any seasoned RVer what his biggest gripe is, and the majority will side squarely with the "place-to-put-stuff" issue. Some of the fancier coaches feature nice, sturdy, slide-out trays that extend from outside storage compartments (think of it as an industrial-grade spice rack). Of course, slide trays are also available in the aftermarket as an upgrade for your existing storage space. And don't overlook the possibility of adding a roof-mounted storage pod when that below the floor or in the basement area isn't quite voluminous enough.

Road Scholar

Slide-outs are truly amazing—that is, until you need to get at something located in a compartment stuck underneath the extended room. Your choices are but few—go inside and retract the room, or crawl on your belly to get that meatball recipe. Thankfully, a few manufacturers patented systems where exterior storage compartments expand right along with the room. This may be worth a look if a slide-out is in your future—and you love meatballs.

Hookups

Hooking up to a campsite's utilities requires a series of hoses, cords, and mechanisms to make things go. Is a fresh-water hose and in-line water pressure regulator included? They should be. Is the hose approved for RV use? It should be. Is the connection easily accessed and easy to make, or do you need a circus contortionist to make that connection for you? How about the sewer hose attaching point? Are the termination valves (a.k.a. dump valves) located in an easy-to-get-to location? Do they hang too low, thereby creating a problem accessing driveways or traversing speed bumps? A key indicator is the presence of new ABS drain plumbing or new dump valves (or scrape marks on the bottoms of older valves). When buying a new RV, a new sewer hose and attaching adapter with clamp should be provided as part of the package.

Are the LP tanks permanent or removable? When you run out of LP gas, will you be forced to take the RV to the propane station or just a couple of tanks? Does the electric shoreline cord extend far enough to reach potential outlets? Is it retractable, recoiling in a nice, easy fashion, or is a wad of cord provided that requires a complex series of twists and shoves to get inside? More on what all these goodies in the electricity, propane, and plumbing systems are in the chapters ahead.

Pull Over

Just because there's a ladder doesn't mean going topside is entirely safe. More than a few unwilling participants have tap-danced their way off their rubber roof after a morning rain. Please be careful. Wear rubber-soled shoes, as if you were boarding a slippery sailboat. Watch the air conditioner, antennae, and seams. Don't let children transform the top of the motorhome into a treehouse.

Awnings, Steps, and Little Extras

Plan to spend any quality time on the roof (not a good idea with a pop-up or small RV)? A rear ladder is your gateway to impromptu roof inspections or watching meteor showers, not to mention a great seat at the races. Expect a few extended horn blasts from those behind you if you expect to take this lofty perch at the drive-in movies, however. Otherwise, consider yourself grounded. What about the entry step? Is it strong and resilient, or spongy, propelling you in and out of the coach like an

Olympic diving competition? Electric and manual models are available. Handrails in the entryway are a must for older passengers and generally a good idea anyway.

Awnings—sometimes gigantic versions—are included as standard on many RVs to create shade and shelter from the rain. Is yours easy to deploy or a bear to operate? Some older models required the patience of Job to operate, negotiating a never-ending series of latches, clasps, and a supplemental pole for extracting. These days, more and more manufacturers are going the motorized route, which removes most of the ill will from the process. Does your RV have one? Do you care? Aftermarket awnings aren't cheap, so try to get one in the buying process if you can.

The Inspection

Any RV that passes these livability tests is probably in the running for your hard-earned dollar. You liked what you saw, went through the appropriate examinations, and this RV should be considered a finalist in the single-elimination tournament that is buying an RV. But a final hurdle still awaits—the inspection. Get out the magnifying glass and overcoat, Sherlock, it's time to see what makes this baby tick. What we're looking for now is quality—quality craftsmanship, proven materials, and a product built to last. Basically, a job well done. Or as the great RV Doctor, Gary Bunzer, likes to say, "fit and finish."

I don't believe in assumptions, especially when it requires signing over a great big hunk of money. The quality of a new RV isn't necessarily a given. Just because the motorhome has less than 100 miles on the odometer and has a pretty pink ribbon on top, doesn't mean we should let it off easy. Was it built right? How long has it been sitting on the lot? Was it professionally crafted or does it resemble work done by a monkey with a caulking gun (another classic Bunzer quip)? Is that bluish puddle underneath sign of a leak or just the remains of your husband's snow cone?

Make doubly sure all previously owned RVs receive a close inspection, both inside and out. Sure, such examinations will undoubtedly favor the used-RV buyer more, but it's important that all would-be consumers not accept things at face value. With that said, I will agree that today's RVs are built better than anytime in their history. Computer technology, refined building practices, and decades of learning what works and what doesn't has helped manufacturers construct the finest RVs ever. However, I *still* favor leaving no stone unturned come buying time. Repeat after me: Every RV purchase demands a close inspection.

Inside

Ascertain the maker of a prospective RV's dedication to quality building and craftsmanship. This is nice place to begin when searching for a new RV. If either quality is lacking, don't even bother with the rest. Move on and find another. Depending on what you are looking for, this can rule out a lot of units and really save time. Start your inspection inside-out. Poor engineering of the roof, sidewalls, or windows and doors will undoubtedly result in future leaks, electrical and plumbing problems, and other sneaky damage.

Floor It

Look down and what do you see? Is the carpeting plush and springy or beaten down by life? How is the coloring? New patches or cut-outs indicate work has been made to that area. Was it a leak, a hole, or what? Walk the coach, taking careful note of any spongy or tilted areas beneath you, all possible indications of rotten floorboards or other looming problems. Examine around baseboards, underneath doors and windows, and near appliances where leaks are most likely to develop.

Though some squeaks may be inevitable, listen for excessive noises as you walk the floor area. Improperly secured flooring may manifest itself as squeaks or groans. If the galley or bathroom area is tiled, look for cracked or loosened tiles that may indicate a sub-flooring problem.

Woodworking

Don't shortchange the importance of durable woods and craftsmanship, affecting everything from drawers, cabinets, closets, doors, tables, and chairs. Nothing dooms resale faster than shoddy work and flimsy materials. As a rule, solid woods are better than particleboard; screws and glue superior to staples. Open and close the drawers and tug on cabinets. Is the woodworking rugged or set to come apart five miles outside of Albany? Do the side tables, bookshelves, coffee table, and magazine racks feel like they can go the long haul?

Road Scholar

Follow your nose, it always knows. Involve your sense of smell in the search, with a whiff of mildew being a prime giveaway of leaks. In such events, determine what, if any, maintenance has been performed to correct the problem, or if it's the responsibility of a new owner. In any event, you've got damaged goods on your hands. It's now just a matter of gauging the damage and deciding whether you want such an undertaking.

Don't let the price fool you. One of the most beautiful (and expensive) RVs I ever tested had marble (yes, marble) countertops on top of cheap and amateurish woodworking. The same brand-new RV concluded my three-day road test with several broken drawers, an end table with a bum leg, and a pair of wobbly side mirrors. I didn't do it, I swear! Moral of the story—you *don't* always get what you pay for.

Furnishings

Most folks know quality when they see it, and cheap fabrics are about as obvious as a $4 necktie. Are the fabrics strong and durable or already showing signs of wear just from a few walk-thrus and sit-downs? Is this the couch that will take you through countless Sundays watching NFL football? Can the chairs hold up against your six-year-old with the penchant for biting? Do the cushions spring or sag?

As you manipulate the sofa hardware, listen for any squeaks, rattles, or rumblings that may be a precursor to spring or support problems to come. Will that fold-down table really fold down? As for convertible dinettes, as mentioned earlier, be sure the cushions configure as they should in any and all positions.

Seals of Approval

Improper sealing around doors, windows, roofing, and slide-outs are the most likely culprits for future leaks and other problems. Inspect doorways and windows for a tight fit. Wetness or incoming air suggests a less than snug situation. Double-check rubber seals for fading and cracking. Inspect the seams in the walls, where pieces are joined. Any spots, buckles, or fading? Any mismatched wallpaper or paint jobs, clear signs of past repairs? Watch the slide-out as it expands and retracts. Does it keep the debris, air, and moisture out, or bring it back in when it's through?

Road Scholar

If possible, tour prospective units during inclement weather, namely rain. This is the surest way to determine an unforeseen leak problem. It's not a bad idea to take your test drive under less than favorable situations as well. Wind, snow, and rain are a part of life, and how this RV handles at its worst can be very telling. Now if only I had listened to this advice when I bought my house.

Appliances

You must be convinced that all appliances and onboard systems are in proper working order. Don't take anyone's word for it, see it for yourself. This goes double for used units. RVs with faltering heating or cooling, batteries that won't hold their charges, or drains that won't send gray water promptly away are about as fun as ants at the family picnic. At the very least, you should ask for a full rundown and showing of all appliances, how they work, and troubleshooting information prior to taking possession. More on this in Chapter 9, "After the Sale."

Let the seller know ahead of time that you intend on checking everything onboard. Yes, everything. This should give him or her the opportunity to fill the tanks (water and propane), fuel the generator, and precool the refrigerator. At this stage of the game, a cursory look into each of the following is highly recommended.

- ❑ Furnace
- ❑ Air conditioner(s)
- ❑ Generator
- ❑ Water pump
- ❑ Holding tanks (gray and black)
- ❑ Fresh water storage tank
- ❑ Shower
- ❑ Sinks
- ❑ Flushing toilets
- ❑ LP tanks
- ❑ Refrigerator
- ❑ Water heater
- ❑ Batteries
- ❑ Interior/exterior lights
- ❑ Cooking range
- ❑ Microwave
- ❑ Awning
- ❑ Oven
- ❑ Monitor panel
- ❑ Carbon monoxide detector
- ❑ LP gas detector
- ❑ Smoke alarm
- ❑ TV(s)
- ❑ Stereo
- ❑ VCR

Exterior Inspection

Leave the white pants at home, it's time to get dirty. A careful examination of the exterior—roof, chassis, sidewalls, etc.—should reveal whether or not this vehicle can keep up with all your heavy-duty plans. True, you won't always know what you're looking for, but it's worth the effort anyway. Surely, you can spot obvious trouble when you see it. Crawl around underneath, go on top, look at the RV from every angle. What you detect now might save you trouble down the road.

Chassis

Just what exactly is going on underneath that thing anyway? Leaks, puddles, critters' nests, dangling wires, rust, and more obvious signs of damage should cool off the trip to the ATM machine for your down payment. Follow the exhaust system for cracks and rust. Take your time and maneuver underneath as much of the rig as possible. Shiny new parts on an older unit indicate a new repair. What was the work for? Is this the sign of things to come?

Inspect tenaciously for cracks or openings into the living portion. Critters, especially mice, can enter and exit through the tiniest of holes or gaps between the floor and sidewalls. Check closely around the drain pipes that extend below the floor line also.

Tired Out

Check the tires for wear, cracking, and fading. Even relatively new, undriven tires fall victim to oxidation from that pesky ozone and UV radiation. Uneven tread may mean an alignment problem. Use a flashlight and a mirror if necessary to inspect the sidewalls between the rear dual tires on a motorhome. The sidewalls are the most vulnerable and any cracking mandates replacement regardless of the age of the tire. Better to find this out now, as a trip to the tire store is an expensive outing.

Sidewalls and Roofing

Unsightly seams and excessive caulking are red flags of a rushed job or poor work. Be skeptical if your new RV looks hastily put together, which just might be the sad truth. Various viewing from aft and stern discloses any problematic tilts, leanings, or bulges in the sidewalls. Such findings are significant enough to cause you to rethink this purchase. Follow the line of all seams, looking closely for a tight fit. Rust, new paint or panels, and stucco are calling cards for Trouble, Inc.

Pull Over

No matter how hard we look, most of us only possess the skills to detect the more obvious problems (e.g., loose wires, colorful puddles, gaping holes). That's why it's probably worth the investment to have a professional RV specialist appraise a prospective purchase. Upon narrowing down the field, make an appointment with an RV technician to shake down the vehicle for any signs of trouble. This is a must for all preowned vehicles.

In the case of larger vehicles, get on the roof and have a careful look around. Again, question excessive caulking and sealant. Reexamine seals, particularly around roof-mounted air conditioners and antennas. Tears, rips, and cracks can usually be easily repaired, but the extent of the external damage caused could be worrisome.

Road Scholar

In the event of used RVs, I prefer a seller with a comprehensive record of vehicle maintenance and repairs. Such dutiful record-keeping demonstrates care and integrity and gives buyers the chance to reexamine those areas in question. Make sure you cross-check any obvious areas of work with the owner's records for consistency.

Don't Get Hoodwinked

Pop the hood on motorized RVs and take a peek inside. As always, we're searching for the usual suspects—leaks, rust, and worn seals and rubber. A new motorhome's engine should be clean and fresher than a new shirt taken out of the dryer. Evidence of corrosion or excessive wear here should send you scurrying off the lot. On the contrary, a new-looking engine doesn't necessarily guarantee prime working condition since engine washes are easy and inexpensive. Check belts, hoses, and plugs. Are the fluids sagging dangerously below levels, suggesting the owner is less than faithful in his or her upkeep?

On some older motorhomes it is near impossible to check the brake fluid reservoir without the aid of a trained monkey wearing a miner's hat with light. Some had access plates under the carpeting near the driver's feet. On motorhomes with engine access covers inside the coach, inspect closely the seals around the cover.

Gentlemen, Start Your Engines

The purpose of the test drive is two-fold: first, to access your comfort level piloting this particular RV; second, to gauge the likelihood of any mechanical problems that could snafu your adventures. Both goals will be accomplished with one or two reasonable-length outings behind the wheel. Sellers who lobby hard to limit the trip to a spin around the block and five minutes of road time might have something to hide. It's best to bring a co-pilot as another set of eyes and ears and to get their input on things from their vantage point.

The Towable Exception

As we'll see in Chapter 13, "Towin' the Line," trailer operation requires a well-matched tow vehicle with a suitable hitch. Assuming you already have these things in place on the lot and ready to go, a "test tow" can probably be arranged. However, for whatever reason, such tests aren't very common, and most dealers won't have a tow vehicle to loan you provided your existing vehicle isn't up to snuff. It's a moot point anyway, since all tow vehicle configurations are different. What *is* paramount, however, is learning 1) What, if any, nifty new pop-up, travel trailer, or fifth wheel your existing vehicle is able to tow? or 2) What size tow vehicle do you need to haul away the towable you've got your eyes on? The answer to both questions lies in Chapter 13.

Prior to Take-Off

Start the engine and have a listen. Does the rush of power sound triumphant, followed by a steady purr, or rather like the sound the neighbor's cat makes when someone steps on his tail? Soak in all the sounds for a moment before taking off. In the meantime, adjust the seats and side mirrors, and buckle up. We don't want any distractions, so turn off the radio. Besides, there's no reason to listen for the Cubs score; they lost 10 to 0. Turn on the dashboard heat and air conditioning. How fast does it warm up/cool off? Send the co-pilot out back to test the break and backup lights. Make sure all doors are closed, the slide-out is retracted (you couldn't operate the vehicle if it was), and do a quick walk-thru to make sure everything is battened down. Now it's time to hit the road.

The Course

Your motorhome is only as good as the terrain it can cover. Mountain grades, crowded city traffic, Autobahn-like highways, and trips to the market are all parts of the RV experience. Make it clear to the seller that you want to sample a mix of road situations and plot a course accordingly. If they hem and haw, restate the fact that this is an expensive proposition and you want to be very sure of your decision. And then remind them that the dealer down the street had no problems with the idea of an extended test drive.

Keep a careful account of the following:

- ❑ **Stopping:** Are you comfortable with the stopping power?
- ❑ **Acceleration:** An underpowered RV can leave you lacking during inclines.
- ❑ **Cornering:** Do you feel like you're at the wheel of an aircraft carrier?
- ❑ **Turning:** A vacant parking lot is a good place to test the turning radius. Backups, too.
- ❑ **Clearance:** Does the high clearance make you wary?
- ❑ **Handling:** Is the steering responsive?
- ❑ **Gadgets:** Are the controls user-friendly?

Warning Signs

New buyers can't be expected to stroll onto a dealer's lot with an advanced mechanical degree. At some point, most of us must trust that our new vehicles will act as such and the careful preparation and examinations will pay off in the form of a well-built unit. A nice set of warranties should help erase some fears, too. There are, however, a few telltale, don't-walk-but-run-away signs to avoid any particular unit. Follow these and your odds of buying a clunker reduce dramatically.

Rentals

You know that expression, "It's been driven like a rental?" It evolved from the fact that most of us drive such vehicles, shall I say, a little differently than our everyday autos. Okay, most of us drive rentals fast, hard, and with little regard for their well-being. Rental *RVs* are no different, with scores of novice drivers jumping curbs, backing up into mailboxes, and navigating the learning curve behind the wheel. When rental RVs outlast their effectiveness, they go to dealerships, sporting a "for sale" sign and a nice discount. Many come with an ugly history of overuse coupled with long periods of sitting around. It may just be a personal bias, but leave rental re-sales alone.

Barely Driven Vehicles

My prized 1972 Nova was coming off two long years of virtual nonuse. I saw it as a good thing—lower mileage, less wear and tear, fewer incidents at the drive-thru. It turns out that dormancy is one of the worst things that can occur to any vehicle, especially when improperly stored, as we'll reveal in Chapter 21, "Basic Care." Within a year I had replaced every hose and seal; the bugs who lived in the engine fought my every move; the tires were shot; and it never, ever came close to the tremor-inducing street machine it once was. Just imagine if it had contained the complex plumbing, electrical, heating, and cooling systems that your RV does, along with an array of appliances and sensitive components. Rarely used RVs are often neglected, meaning more maintenance duties for the new owner: you.

Lean and Mean

As previously stated, an RV shouldn't lean like a high school kid working at McDonald's. Rather, it should stand up straight and tall like a fresh graduate from officer training school. Awkward tilts reveal some not-so-subtle foundation woes, problems best left for the next sucker, I mean, buyer.

Water, Water Everywhere

Wayward leaks are the single greatest threat to an RVer's sanity as well as your vehicle's foundation. As your soggy basement at home consistently proves, water can be a slippery foe, with the origins of leaks difficult to track and even harder to remedy. When faced with the foe of wallet-plucking scent of mildew, squashy floorboards, and buckling paint, repeat after me: "Thanks, but no thanks."

Communication Breakdown

Do your simple questions about the history of the trailer go unanswered? Are there creative gaps in the history of this particular Class B? Is the slow learning process starting to resemble a courtroom scene out of *Kramer vs. Kramer?* Sellers unwilling to part with important information about the unit are hiding more than their people skills. Furthermore, lackluster attention to the vehicle's upkeep, a dirty unit, poor records, and one too many "Hey, don't look in there!"s are good indications that this RV probably has another zero in the odometer—and definitely another zero for a seller.

Wish List

There's nothing scientific about this list, just a collection of the "I-Wish-I-Had's" from the many travelers I've heard from over the years. Learn from their mistakes, and find the best RV you can.

- ❑ Garbage can
- ❑ Dirty clothes hamper
- ❑ Larger refrigerator
- ❑ Towel racks
- ❑ Place for recyclables
- ❑ More interior storage
- ❑ Bedside stand
- ❑ Deeper sink
- ❑ Larger windows
- ❑ Full-length mirror
- ❑ Separate room for toilet
- ❑ Washer/dryer
- ❑ Computer desk/workstation
- ❑ File storage
- ❑ Places for shoes and coats
- ❑ Icemaker
- ❑ Phone jacks
- ❑ End tables
- ❑ Storage, storage, storage

The Least You Need to Know

- A comprehensive series of "livability tests" is the fastest way to determine if this RV is for you. Lie down in the beds, pretend to shower, move about the coach as if you owned the place. Going through the motions provides a sneak peek into the possible challenges of your future home on wheels.
- RVs still in the running for your dollar should be carefully inspected inside and out. Check the interior for quality woodworking, premium fabrics, the evidence of leaks, and the possibility of previous repairs. Go underneath the chassis and inspect the sidewalls and roof for rust, leaks, and evidence of future trouble.
- Test all appliances to make sure they're in working condition. Notify the seller ahead of time to fill up all tanks, start the generator, and prepare for a close examination of all onboard systems and components.
- An elaborate road test is the final factor in gauging if an RV is right for you. Listen for signs of engine trouble. Take note of the stopping, starting, and turning abilities. Head out on the highway, through city traffic, and through a parking lot to determine your comfort level behind the wheel.

Chapter 8

The Art of the Deal

In This Chapter

- Choosing the right seller
- Avoiding buying pitfalls
- Getting the best deal
- Financing, trade-ins, warranties, and taking delivery

You're getting dangerously close to the big "C." Commitment. Hopefully, you know exactly the RV you're looking for or have at least shortened your dance card to just a couple of possibilities. It's now just a matter of making it all official, finding the right seller and reaching a deal you can live with.

Some folks regard the buying stage as an epic battle, them versus the dealer. Like Gary Cooper in *High Noon,* they feel it's time to put on their white hat and prepare to shoot it out against a most unsavory foe. Others succumb to a more passive outlook, shrinking away from a situation they find uncomfortable and confrontational. They prefer to go meekly through the process; just wake them when it's all over. My advice is to approach the sale with realistic expectations and a reasonable point of view. Both buyer and seller want the same thing: to get you RVing. When you think about it like that, negotiations take on a different light. Of course, it comes down to who wants it more, and what each party is willing to do to get there. That's where this chapter comes in.

Of course, there's more to it than finding a trustworthy seller and an affordable product. Other questions arise. Where and how do I finance? What extras must I have? How do I redeem a warranty? What about my trade-in? You sure do ask a lot of questions. Good thing, since the answers are coming.

The Hard Sell

Choosing the right seller is important for a number of reasons. Unlike your prom date, this may turn out to be a fairly lengthy relationship, especially if your RV ever needs service or repairs. Financing through the dealer might also ensure some future dealings, so thoughtful consideration should be given to the kind of people you're doing business with. Remember, a check with a whole lotta zeroes is the prize for the seller meeting all of our criteria. However, to earn it, all questions must be answered, all expectations met. A deliberate investigation rewards buyers with peace of mind—and a fruitful business relationship in good times and bad.

Basically, there are two types of sellers: private sellers and RV dealers.

Private Sellers

As stated in Chapter 6, "Narrowing Down Your Choices," private sellers offer a somewhat tantalizing proposition. You might find the deal of a lifetime, the perfect used vehicle at an unbelievably low price. Much like that vase bought at the garage sale that turns out to be a lost treasure from the Ming Dynasty, these situations are somewhat rare. More frequently, buying from a private seller requires a small act of faith on your part that the RV isn't a clunker. No warranties or returns will be honored, and there may be some lingering doubt about the possibility of breaking down outside Anchorage. The inspections discussed in Chapter 7, "What to Buy?" should help assuage some of that concern, and good deals can certainly be had. Your comfort level of gambling on a less-than-sure thing, as well as your troubleshooting abilities in the event of problems, probably determines the appeal of a private seller.

The newspaper is still the best spot to find regular folk ready to sell, with the weekly auto section (most often Saturdays) being the best bet. Otherwise, regional buyer's guides such as the *Trader Times,* found at mini-markets, grocery stores, and the like, might feature an RV section. A quick search online should uncover other sellers in your area. Try www.rvsearch.com for starters.

RV Dealers

If a new RV is on the docket, then shopping through an established dealership is a must. The upside is that unlike private sellers, these people are running a business, with a reputation at stake with every transaction. Consequently, they're less likely to take advantage of their customers—at least, we would hope so. In addition, dealerships offer a greater selection and a deeper inventory, and most likely a service center, financing, a parts department, warranties, and possibly a trial money-back period. You might be able to score a hot dog and some cotton candy, too, but let's not get distracted.

One for the Road

Much like the rest of the RV industry, most dealerships are small, independent businesses. Many of these operations are family-run, with a loyal customer base and handshake-type approach to doing business. The recent wave of consolidation has resulted in the emergence of the RV superstore, offering incredible inventory, volume discounts, and massive staffs who might not remember your name. It's worth a look at each type to determine which situation you favor.

Unlike their automotive counterparts, RV dealerships are not found in every town. In fact, buyers might have to travel a significant distance to find one that carries their specific RV, particularly if it's produced from a smaller manufacturer with a tiny network of sellers. But according to a survey sponsored by Woodall's Publishing, readers said they were willing to travel up to 200 miles to find the best deal. Now that's dedication.

The Yellow Pages is still the best place to find local dealers. A call to a specific RV manufacturer should put you on the path to the dealer carrying their products. Otherwise, keep your eyes open for one of Woodall's regional publications (see Appendix A, "Resources," for a complete listing), a long-time home to regional dealer advertising, as well as your daily newspaper's weekly auto section.

Dealer's Choice

A nearby dealer is the best kind of dealer. In the event of service or a breakdown, a short trip down Main Street for warranty-related repairs or routine service is preferable to heading back across the state. Service and repairs can be performed at most any service center, but nearby is always better. For this reason, start any search locally and spread out accordingly, branching out only as far as you feel comfortable commuting. Determining what the important factors are in your search is up to you. Price is the first and last word for most, so start there. If customer service, knowledgeable staff, repair facilities, and financing are important, then audition sellers based on these concerns.

Incorporate proven techniques here as you would for any big purchase. Be patient. Ask questions. Keep looking. Be assertive—it's a lot of money we're talking about here. If you're unsatisfied, go elsewhere. An uncooperative or shady salesperson might be indicative of the way this company does business. Take careful notes. And remember, these people are working on your behalf, not the other way around.

Dollars and Sense

If your decision simply comes down to who has the lowest price, you've heard it all before. The mantra is comparison shop, comparison shop, and comparison shop. Making a few calls for quotes is still the fastest route to saving thousands of dollars. It saves dealers time, too, since they don't need to show you around and dust off their standard pitches. Ask each dealership for their rock-bottom price on vehicle XYZ, ask exactly how long this dollar amount is good for, get the name of the person who quoted you this figure, and repeat this process at as many places as you can. I also like to add: "You're not just quoting me this price to get me to walk in there, are you?" in case they're doing just that. Have them fax you the quote in writing so there's no misunderstanding. Repeat these steps until you've found the best couple of deals and work with these sellers exclusively.

Conventional views suggest late in the year ranks among the very best times to buy new RVs. Fall through the first of the year is a transition period, when new models bump last year's versions to the back of the lot. Many sellers historically drop prices on year-old units and good deals are likely. Otherwise, buying out of RV season works well, or when the weather is relentlessly crummy and foot traffic at the dealership is low. Timing and comparison shopping are the keys to great deals.

Money for Nothing

Congratulations—you found the RV you wanted, and didn't break the bank in the process. So why are you still worried? If it were a can of soup or a clock radio, I would say great. However, RVs cost considerably more, and there are other important issues to consider in addition to sale price. What about repairs and service? Is there follow-up after the sale, or are buyers on their own? Will the dealership be around in two years to honor any warranties or contractual obligations? Certainly, price is of the utmost importance, no argument there. There's no sense paying more than you have to. But the savings reaped can quickly disintegrate if there are problems later on. Here are some other criteria to include on your next shopping trip.

What's Their Rep?

Know whom you're buying from. Question friends, members of the local camping club, or online chat rooms for their preferred dealerships. Why do they recommend them? Did their sweetheart service change after the deal was reached? What salesperson did they like? Did the staff descend on them like a pack of vultures at a carrion convention? Was it like pulling teeth to schedule service?

Finalize your list and start visiting some lots. Does the inventory look scattered, battered, or haggard, suggesting money problems and a possible red flag on the SS *Chapter 11?* Remember, a bankrupt dealership complicates matters after the sale. Buy from the healthiest company you can to avoid getting stuck with promises unkept and services unfulfilled.

Save a few questions for the salesperson, too. How long has this dealership been in business? Are they members of RVDA (Recreation Vehicle Dealer's Association)? Why not? Ask for the names of several recent customers to get their important feedback. Be skeptical if the dealership refuses. There's no truer portrayal than from those who have undergone the process before you.

Road Scholar

Let the findings from the Better Business Bureau help you decide. A long list of complaints and charges probably means an unwillingness to work with the customer. While a "clean record" doesn't necessarily guarantee a perfect buying experience, it does serve as further evidence that you might have found yourself a winner.

Service with a Smile

At some point, even the finest vehicles need some service. It could be a routine repair, preventative maintenance, or a sizable undertaking, but it's gonna happen. Many buyers prefer to return their RV to the dealer they bought from to have any work performed—and dealers may oblige with perks such as free washings, inspections, etc. for their existing customers. What services and repairs can and can't they do? Can they handle the big jobs, such as engine repair, transmissions, and chassis trouble? What if the refrigerator breaks, pipes burst, or leaks develop? Can they fix most problems there, or is everything just sent back to the factory?

Do customers get special treatment, or are they thrown into the mix with everyone else? How many service bays and technicians are on the premises? What are their qualifications, certifications, and areas of expertise? Are their hourly rates outrageous or reasonable? Is a towing service provided? A large parts inventory means fewer delays come fix-it time. Find out now, before there's trouble.

Location, Location, Location

How far are you willing to travel for this transaction? As we've discussed, closer is always better, but it may be worth throwing the husband, kids, and mother-in-law in the station wagon to scout out nicer deals. Big savings on the RV of your dreams might be enough reason to make a weekend of it a few hundred miles away from home. Factor in any cost breaks with distance required to make the sale. Conversely, are you favoring a local dealership too much, unwilling to journey for the lowest price?

Good Help Is Hard to Find

Good salespeople can work at bad dealerships and vice versa. However, a lack of understanding or shady practices can reflect the culture of the company, so be careful. Does your salesperson know what he's talking about? Does he or she RV? How long has he worked there? Is this his career or was he selling lawn mowers yesterday? Is he or she demonstrating a strong knowledge of their products or using the brochures like a crutch? Get them talking. Some professionals don't know a hitch from hot chocolate, so it pays to be a little skeptical at first. Ask questions. Listen. Then decide if this person is for you.

What is his attitude? Friendly? Confrontational? Interested? Your salesperson is your main liaison before, during, and after the sale. Do you feel comfortable with this person and what he's telling you? If not, leaving the dealership isn't necessary. Politely ask to work with a more experienced employee. Don't mess around with bad service or a mule cart full of BS. Remember, the typical motorhome costs as much as four years of college; the average towable as much as a luxury automobile.

Special Delivery

Get a sense of the delivery process *before* signing on the dotted line and pocketing the keys. Will the salesperson walk you through every inch of your coach, explain all warranties, run through each and every appliance, and demonstrate the inner workings of the new unit? Or are customers just a check to cash? Some dealerships have a goodwill period of 30 days to work out the kinks of a new RV. Does yours? What about a follow-up meeting to discuss any problems associated with the new vehicle? A hands-off attitude after the sale is a symptom of poor customer service down the road.

Although still rare, some dealerships pride themselves on after-the-sale instruction in the form of seminars and customer clinics. Classes might range from driving and towing, troubleshooting onboard systems, boondocking, and various how-to's for their customers—usually at no charge. These sellers are demonstrating a commitment to their customers, and such opportunities shouldn't go to waste.

Another growing practice is the emergence of the dealership/campground, giving new and prospective customers a safe haven to acclimate themselves to their new RVs. Smart dealers and buyers know that there's simply no substitute for the experience of spending a few nights in a new purchase. Provisions such as these show a seller's willingness to work with you after the sale, instead of the hurry-to-buy, hurry-to-leave approach taken at some places. We'll explore what steps to take before taking delivery in Chapter 9, "After the Sale."

Trade Ya

I like someone who will bend over backward to make the sale. For instance, consider the Florida dealer who prides himself on accepting all sorts of unusual items as trade.

Lore has it that he's taken classic cars, boats, even a pair of tigers to help grease the wheels of a transaction. True, most businesses won't accept your lama and pair of dancing chimps, but an existing RV might do the trick. Trade-ins are usually accepted as a means to secure your business. Those uncomfortable with selling their RVs themselves should gravitate toward dealers with a kind and loving attitude toward previously owned models.

Pull Over

Skip the folks selling RVs in the abandoned lot or along the side of the road. Sometimes know as "gypsy dealers," these sellers promote unbelievable deals, hoping for an impulse buy. Avoid these situations, as this is no way to make such an important investment. If a seller looks like a fly-by-night company, it probably is. Where did these vehicles come from? Resist the knee-jerk reaction to getting a "once-in-a-lifetime deal."

Common Buying Pitfalls

Many folks want to get the buying process over as soon as possible. They know what RV they want and dislike the adversarial process of negotiating. Besides, the sooner you buy it, the sooner you can hit the road and start enjoying it, right? Resist the urge to make a quick sale. If the first dealership was great, the second one may be better. And the fifth one might blow the first two away, saving you thousands of dollars in the process. To avoid a nasty case of buyer's remorse, visit as many lots as you can. Listen. Gain insights from salespeople. Take notes. Record prices. Ask questions. Be patient. Repeat as necessary. Most of all, prepare yourself for a lengthy process. A purchase this size demands it. And most important, resist each of the following.

Rush, Rush, Rush

Avoid quick decisions. "Today-only sales" and "limited-time offers" may or may not be for real. But in either case, don't allow the seller to dictate the pace. Buy only when *you're* ready, even if it means missing out on a special offer. Sales promotions are like boomerangs, they have a tendency to come back around.

Don't Believe the Hype

Big sales events with balloons, hot dogs, and all the soda you can drink certainly breed goodwill and make the process more enjoyable. However, this generosity fails to address your primary concerns of "Is this the seller for me?" A festival-like atmosphere might be all sizzle and very little steak, designed to get you in the door only. Stick to the mission of buying from the best, most thoughtful, and service-oriented place you can. You can get a hot dog at the ballgame.

Falling in Love

The lyrical question was once asked, "Why do fools fall in love?" My only answer is that they like paying full price. Love makes you do funny things (I got the wedding ring to prove it), and reveling in an RV that sends your heart all a-flutter is dangerous come bargaining time. The easiest way to louse up a deal is fretting that the RV might suddenly vanish if you don't scoop it up today. Forget it. These are RVs, not Judy Garland's ruby red slippers. There's a thousand more where that came from. Leave your emotions back at the car. This is business.

Pushy Salespeople

In the presence of an aggressive salesperson, some people fold like a three-card Monty game in Times Square. Who's in charge here, anyway? You are, so stay the course. If a seller comes on too strong, tell him or her so. Be candid about your pace, stating that you're in the looking stage and dislike the in-your-face style. If he or she continues, ask for another person. If you wanted the hard-sell, you would have stayed home and chatted with all those lovely telemarketers.

Too Many Choices

Feeling paralyzed with all these options? Then it's time to regroup. Remember, it's a dooming prospect to approach buying with a scatter-shot approach. Get your bearings and revisit Chapters 6 and 7 to determine exactly what it is you're looking for. Perhaps in the search for a modest camper van you begin to fancy a mini-motorhome. Then it's time to refocus on those sized vehicles, or you might find yourself then poking around the 40-foot diesel motorhomes. Next thing you know, you've overbought and are forced to work a night job to pay for fuel.

Unreasonable Expectations

Transactions are a two-way street, so be reasonable. Dealerships cost money to run and must show something from each sale. Demanding the invoice prices on a unit is unreasonable. For the dealer's part, the price to run the dealership must be factored into each sale (e.g., inventory, salaries, utilities, real estate). Salespeople have to eat, too.

Wheelin' and Dealin'

Now it's time to save yourself some money, perhaps lots of it if you're patient and persistent. At this point, you've found an RV you like and can afford, as well as a seller you're comfortable with. But unlike the game show, the price *isn't* right. Maybe we can do better. Peeling away the extra costs associated with the sticker price isn't an exact science; there's no magic formula or secret password to make the seller cave in to your demands. Short of hypnotism, the next best thing is a little psychology, knowing the facts about the RV in question, and good timing.

The Give and Take

Although haggling isn't encouraged when buying shoes or knocking long-distance calls off the phone bill, it's a well-established practice in the field of RV buying. The best deal won't fall into your lap; rather, it is an act of erosion. If you want to save some money, you're going to have to play the game.

There are two starting points for negotiations. The first is to take the sticker price and work your way down. This number should be fully disclosed, usually pasted on the vehicle itself. The second is to learn the *real* cost of the RV, the invoice price, or the sum the seller actually paid for the RV. Finding the true cost is more difficult. There are a few companies that sell such information, such as the RV Consumer Group (1-800-405-3325; www.rv.org). In this case, the goal is to stick as closely to the invoice price as possible.

Pull Over

Realize that the seller must make a profit. You are never "doing them a favor" by "taking an RV off their hands." Clinging too tightly to an invoice cost is the surest way to arrive at a stalemate. If you can find it, the invoice price serves as a valuable bit of knowledge brought to the bargaining table, but it serves only as a starting point.

The Price Zone

With invoice price in hand, examine the sticker price. Subtracting the two amounts will determine the range of negotiations. For example, an invoice price of $50,000 and a sticker price of $60,000 means there's $10,000 to work with. Obviously, the closer the final sale is to the invoice cost, the more successful your transaction. The difference could be tens of thousands of dollars for an expensive RV; much less for an entry-level unit. However, every dollar counts, and this range is where you should concentrate your efforts.

The Fifteen Percent Rule

When forced to deal from the sticker price, take their best offer and reduce it by 15 percent. Expect shock, horror, and utter disbelief. Your salesperson might even grab his or her chest, as if mortally wounded. Will they go for it? Probably not. However, you have established a price zone of your own, ranging from your low-ball offer to their negotiable sticker price. Work within these parameters and pound out a satisfactory deal. However, this strategy only works if you believe in the principle that ...

Patience Is a Virtue

What's your hurry? Take it slow. I have found a little persistence mixed with a relaxed approach can whittle down a significant percentage off any new purchase, whether it be a dream house, RV, or prized Superman comic book. The key, however, is to remove the sense of urgency and slow down the pace. Operating at breakneck speed only aids the seller, propelling you into a rash decision. Here's the magic formula to remember:

Time + Persistence = The Best Deal

Chances are excellent that you may hit an impasse over price. You and the seller are dug in; neither party is willing to budge. Given the lofty prices of some higher-end vehicles, the two of you might be several thousands of dollars away from common ground. At some point, the seller will say no way, can't do it, no chance, have a nice day. Be patient. Tell them to sleep on it—while you visit the nice dealer down the street. The sight of you walking out the door might be enough to make them reconsider. Otherwise, call them back in a week when their attitude might have changed. Perhaps your offer will look better after a few slow weeks and a mountain of new inventory sitting idle. Since most salespeople work on commission, most reasonable offers are considered.

One for the Road

My sister demonstrates how *not* to make a purchase of this type. Arriving on the lot with a car on the edge of total collapse, Lauri frantically embraces the nearest salesperson. Stating that she *must* buy a car *tonight,* that her poor Mazda can't go another day. The salesperson smiles. The next day she finds herself the proud new owner of an overpriced, overfinanced, underpowered Chevrolet.

Act Interested

Sellers deal with a lot of half-interested customers, just there to kick the tires or do a little "window shopping." After a while, this effect can transform even the most do-right salesperson into a kind of walking zombie when a new couple enters the lot. True, taking the emotions out of the sale maintains a level-headed approach, but it's equally important to show that you are indeed interested in buying and not just blowing smoke.

State that you're a serious buyer and want vehicle XYZ. A letter of loan preapproval in that amount from your bank should capture their full attention. However, it's now a question of price. And since you want the best deal, you're willing to shop around and take your time. This declaration works in two ways: First, it lets the seller know his or her time isn't being wasted; second, it sets a forthright tone for the negotiations.

Road Scholar

As the old saying goes, "Always dance with the gal who brung ya." If you've found a salesperson you like and you intend to buy his product, work directly with him until the sale is reached. *Don't* show up on his day off to close the deal with someone else, leaving him commissionless for all his efforts. Reward a professional by taking his card and asking for him for all future dealings.

Creative Bargaining

When the going gets tough, the tough ask for leather upholstery, cruise control, or a rear-mounted camera with cockpit monitor. Extras cost money, too, and can play a role when the money talks deadlock. If they won't come down another $500, how about adding an awning, convection oven, or towing package? What about adding to the extended warranty or granting free oil changes or washings?

Extras, Extras

Most every new recreational vehicle comes with pretty much the same stuff. Sure, floor plans vary, as well as size, price, and sleeping capacities, but as features go, well … they are more alike than different, a galley with a stove and fridge; a living space with a TV and a few comfy places to sit; sleeping areas for you and your crew. Power doors and windows, and a nice adjustable seat for you and the Mrs. are typical cockpit fare. Some RVs and their manufacturers are stingier about what's included than others, but the line between *standard* and *optional* is usually pretty well-defined. But that shouldn't stop you from wanting as much stuff onboard as you can get.

Separating yourself and your new RV from the Jones's isn't very hard. All it takes is an open mind—and a checkbook to match—to crack the vault to a world of alluring add-ons, ranging from the latest technological gadgets to the "must-have" accessory du jour. There are no shortages of things to buy. However, where and when to buy such things—and the ramifications of such purchases—require a little forethought.

Factory or Aftermarket Company?

Choosing the RV was the hard part. Deciding what little extra goodies to install is fun—it's the gravy on top of the mashed potatoes. However, a few irresistible, albeit expensive, options can easily transform a once frugal investment into a bank-draining albatross faster than you can say "heated mirrors and electric awning." Deciding *who* to buy these goodies from can make all the difference. Should I have it installed at the factory or wait and secure it in the aftermarket world?

Don't think all final decisions must be made on your dealer's lot. If you're unsure of whether or not you need—or can justify the cost of—an expensive option, then wait. The marketplace is ripe, full of companies that will gladly fill your vehicle with any and all must-have items after the point of purchase. If you should decide six months later that a global positioning system or high-end generator is a must, don't worry—a quick trip to Camping World (1-800-626-5944; www.campingworld.com) or any number of RV parts and accessories suppliers should remedy that. RV publications are jam-packed with advertisements and editorials showcasing all sorts of exciting gadgets and gear, so keep your eyes open.

Pull Over

Consider the weight of each item before buying. Remember, an RV's chassis can only carry so much, whether in the form of a slick new global positioning system, living room chair, or bowling lanes. We'll explore the perils—and prevention—of overloading in Chapter 15, "How Much Does Your RV Weigh?"

Viva Variety

An RV manufacturer might only equip its vehicles with one brand of CD player, leveling system, or backup monitor, accounting for only a small portion of the total suppliers in that given field. If your heart is set on a specific brand-name product, chances are you'll have to buy it from someone else later on.

However, the flip side of that coin is that compatibility isn't usually an issue with a factory-installed item. Installations made at the assembly stage virtually guarantee a correct fit, serviced by professions used to working on recreational vehicles. This is especially true when debating such electric upgrades as inverters, generators, and big-time electronics. The local superstore may quiver at the challenge of equipping that pricey stereo system inside the confusing world of an RV's cockpit. In these cases, it's probably wise to let the manufacturer do the work.

Price vs. Service

Is the lowest price always the top consideration? Maybe, maybe not. While the purchase price for small options (CD stereo, awning, etc.) is usually cheaper in the aftermarket sector, the dealer's price most likely includes installation. (If you're not sure if there's a separate installation fee, be sure to ask.) Remember, labor is often the most expensive part of any job, so factor these cost differences into the final equation, as well as the time and hassle of finding another company to do the work. Factory-installed prices are usually competitive for big-ticket items such as generators, air conditioners, and high-end appliances.

Features typically listed as options from RV manufacturers, if available, can include:

Cockpit

- ❑ Cruise control
- ❑ Leather pilot's seats
- ❑ Multi-position seats
- ❑ CD stereo
- ❑ Larger refrigerator
- ❑ Backup monitoring system
- ❑ Global positioning system
- ❑ CB radio
- ❑ Fog lights
- ❑ Engine brake
- ❑ Daytime running lights
- ❑ Flood lights

Bedroom

- ❑ TV
- ❑ Stereo
- ❑ Safe
- ❑ Ceiling fan
- ❑ Lift-up bed storage
- ❑ Cedar-lined closets
- ❑ Vanity

Living Area

- ❑ Leather seating
- ❑ TV antenna
- ❑ Satellite dish
- ❑ VCR
- ❑ Computer desk/workstation
- ❑ Stereo surround sound
- ❑ Ceiling fan
- ❑ Larger air conditioner
- ❑ Gas fireplace

Kitchen

- ❑ Corian countertops
- ❑ Ice maker
- ❑ Convection oven
- ❑ Built-in coffee maker
- ❑ Dishwasher
- ❑ Water purifier

Bathroom

- ❑ Full-size bathtub
- ❑ Washer/dryer
- ❑ Tiled floors
- ❑ Brass fixtures

Exterior

- ❑ Generator
- ❑ Hydraulic leveling system
- ❑ Ladder
- ❑ Spare tire
- ❑ Tinted windows
- ❑ Exterior shower
- ❑ Outside entertainment center
- ❑ Side awning
- ❑ Screened-in room
- ❑ Extra insulation
- ❑ Thermopane windows
- ❑ Aluminum wheels
- ❑ Hitches (motorized RVs)
- ❑ Security system
- ❑ Electronic entry step
- ❑ Keyless entry
- ❑ Solar panels

Tradin' Time

Like the two cranky kids in the back seat, keep the trade-in and the new RV transaction separate. Such dual negotiations only serve to swing the pendulum of control back to the seller while complicating the issue of price. Forge a sale price for your new rig or towable *before* any talk of an existing vehicle arises. In my mind, these are two separate transactions and should be treated as such. If the dealer balks, you can always sell the used RV on your own.

Go Figure

Determining the value of a used RV is as easy as a phone call. Did you know there's a way to value older RVs? Kelley's Blue Book produces two such price guides, *The Motor Home Guide,* which covers 20-plus years' worth of models, and the *Travel Trailer Guide,* for most kinds of towables. The costs are $54 and $50, respectively. Call 949-770-7704 or visit www.kbb.com for ordering information. Unless there's a convincing argument against it, demand the same price from the seller.

Add-ons are worth money, too. Be sure to factor in the cost of any and all added features such as leather upholstery, multiple slide-outs, and your gifted child's artistic crayon markings on the walls (probably worth some money some day).

Role Reversal

You have more options than you think regarding a used vehicle. Assuming a satisfactory trade-in arrangement can't be reached, then it's up to you to put on your salesperson hat and sell it yourself. A well-placed ad in the weekly transportation section of a large daily newspaper should generate interest. Sunny days and warm temperatures are better times to sell than when the doors are frozen shut and the vehicle is trapped underneath a foot of snow. Local vehicle trading guides are another useful spot for a classified ad, and some dealers sell on consignment.

Warranties

A drawer full of warranties is one of the main advantages to buying a new RV. A one- or two-year bumper-to-bumper warranty is common. After that, expect a structural or roof warranty and perhaps coverage on some of the larger items. The refrigerator is governed by a different set of terms and conditions than the drivetrain or water heater. As such, expect different lengths of coverage and repair procedures for just about every moving part onboard your RV.

One for the Road

Warranties vary, but three years/36,000 miles is typical for the chassis. Onboard appliances are usually governed by a policy limited to 12 to 24 months. The roof may be covered for periods ranging from 5 to 10 years—or longer.

You Break It, You Buy It

Expect to void a warranty if the product breaks and you were the one doing the breaking. Manufacturers are testy about laypersons tinkering with their products, and as such, may not honor a warranty if you're the reason behind its sudden nonworking condition. Read the terms carefully before trying to perform repairs yourself or jamming that screwdriver in with reckless abandon. In the event that the heater went south for the winter without any help from you, you probably have a reasonable claim.

Stake Your Claim

Just what are the procedures for making a claim? Although most service centers can probably handle the work, who pays to fix it, ship it, and reinstall it when it's well? In the event of a possible challenge to your claim, who has the final say? In the event the manufacturer refuses a reasonable claim, your original dealer can act as a strong advocate. After all, an unhappy customer is bad for repeat business. Be sure to follow the claim procedures to the letter and get the salesperson involved in case of problems. Since warranties are offered from the manufacturers directly, don't expect terms to vary from seller to seller.

Check, Please

It's time to settle up. Pay the piper. Break out the checkbook and starting writing until somebody tells you to stop. But where's the money coming from? Ah, good question. Whether it's time to break into the piggy bank, sell off the IBM stocks, or head down to the bank for a loan, don't expect the keys to the RV kingdom until everyone has been properly paid. Which begs the question: Where are you gonna get the money?

Road Scholar

Motorized buyers may be offered a service contract on their new motorhome or camper van. Like warranties, these were devised to offer added protection, only in this case, against mechanical breakdowns. Questions about accountability, length of coverage, and repair procedures should be answered, as well as an analysis of costs versus potential savings.

The Finance Dance

Unless your last name is Trump or Gates, chances are good that financing is in your future. Fortunately, there are all sorts of folks who want to help you pay for your RV. A good thing, too, since without the deep pockets of such lenders, most of us would still be confined to getting around on our bikes with baseball cards tucked in the spokes. But just because there are those willing to lend us a few bucks doesn't mean all the deals are the same.

Livin' on Borrowed Time

You didn't get this far in life without realizing that borrowing money costs money. It's not like Popeye's friend Wimpy, who would gladly pay you Tuesday for a hamburger today. In the eyes of a money-lender, that original burger now costs a hamburger plus cheese to repay. Anyone else hungry?

At the heart of the matter lies the interest rate, which varies due to the stinginess of the various lenders. I'm sure you've played the interest rate game before during such purchases as a house or car. In addition to banks, savings and loans, credit unions, and typical lending institutions, a number of RV-specific finance companies are jumping up and down to get your attention. Larger RV dealers might sway you toward their in-house loan departments in order to help close the deal.

How Do They Rate?

Compliment your careful search for the perfect RV by finagling the best financing deal possible. Again, the rules are simple: Shop around. RV shows and publications reveal a host of industry lenders experienced at navigating through such purchases. Since RVers boast a famously low level of default (approximately 1 percent), coupled with the fact that RVs are longer-lasting and depreciate more slowly than automobiles, expect a better deal than what you scored for your little red sports car. A 10- or 15-year agreement is fairly standard, with 10 to 20 percent required for a down payment.

To Serve and Protect

Low rates are important, but so is service. Like any contract, know what you're getting into. Make sure all the terms are carefully explained and easy to understand before you comply with a signature. Consider the significance of a prepayment penalty, which prohibits paying off the loan early. What are the fees to refinance? Does the company offer automatic payment service? How long have they been in business? What is their reputation? Do they service the loans themselves? Rates should be competitive enough among lenders to let their range of services break the tie.

Road Scholar

Consider arranging for a loan *before* buying that new RV. For starters, this "voucher" lets you know exactly what you can and—aw, shucks—can't afford. As important, finding a lender early eliminates the rush-rush of financing once the deal is reached. This unnecessary practice might send you scurrying into a bad deal and 10 or more years to stew over a bad decision.

Avoid Borrow Sorrow

Bad loan arrangements come in many forms, but usually stem from not devoting time to a quality search. Taking the first deal is a sure-fire way to overspend. Remember, even a $^1/_4$ percent rate difference may end up costing several thousands of dollars more over the life of a loan. Avoid the impulse to just go through your local bank. Chances are there's a better deal out there. An online search should yield a host of possible suitors, in addition to current rates and range of services.

Interest-ed

This is one time when you won't mind calling the IRS. One of the great perks of RV ownership is that interest on most any type of RV loan is tax-deductible. Sound the cannons. Ring the bells. You're getting a tax break! This savings is based on a recreational vehicle's role as a second home (whether it actually is or not). Some special provisions apply, so it's best to contact the IRS (1-800-829-3676; www.irs.gov) for more information. Ask for a copy of "Home Interest Deduction" and "Selling Your Home," and you might actually be smiling for a change on April 15.

The Least You Need to Know

- ➤ A private seller might offer a lower price but no warranties or returns. Audition RV dealerships based on price, knowledge of staff, service facilities, and reputation.
- ➤ Learn the invoice price to reap the best deal. Adapt a slow pace for negotiations and be persistent with price. Throw in optional accessories when talks stall. Discuss any trade-in vehicles only after the deal is done.
- ➤ New RVs come with myriad warranties, covering everything from the mechanical parts to appliances. Extended warranties are available through many companies and only worth the extra costs if they provide peace of mind.
- ➤ Shop around to get the best loan rate. Avoid easy routes of working through dealers and your local banks until after you've scoured the marketplace. Clean up your financial records and reevaluate the purchase if you're turned down.

Chapter 9

After the Sale

In This Chapter

- Important steps when taking delivery
- Insuring your new purchase
- Why roadside assistance is a must
- Protecting yourself from a "lemon"

Strike up the band. Uncork the champagne. Wake the neighbors. You've just purchased a recreational vehicle. A dedicated search yielded a go-go machine, one that hopefully you and the family will enjoy for countless adventures. Congratulations, you're almost ready to reap all the benefits as a card-carrying member of the RV community. However, in the postsale euphoria, there's still some work to be done.

The sole purpose of this chapter is protecting you and your investment. Before driving off the lot in a hail of confetti and dancing bears, we want to make certain of a few things. For starters, the act of taking delivery should be more involved than "Here are your keys, what's your hurry?" Making the most of this process can make a lot of difference (for the better) in the early stages of your RVing life.

Then there's the matter of insurance. Surely, it's nobody's favorite subject, but it's imperative. Regardless whether you're pulling a towable or snuggled in the cockpit of a new camper van or motorhome, a costly purchase mandates coverage. And if that wasn't reason enough, well, it's the law. We'll even cover why roadside assistance is such a no-brainer, examine your rights under existing "lemon laws" if things aren't working out, and discuss how to deal with a nasty case of buyer's remorse.

Taking Delivery

Like proud new parents, expect to feel a combination of excitement and relief over the family's new addition. The long buying process is over, and you'll probably be anxious to get home and start living it up. Don't be in such a hurry. Once you're off the lot, an ugly sort of transformation occurs: You're now a *customer* instead of a *potential* customer. Big difference. A quality dealership takes the time to walk buyers through their purchase, demonstrating how everything works, explaining warranties, and answering any and all questions before shaking hands and bidding adieu. Buying from a seller with a strong after-the-sale commitment will reduce the anxiety many new buyers feel with a new RV.

Final Walk-Thru

No, the seller didn't paint the interior lime green while you were off signing the ownership papers. Nor did they replace the tires with pothole covers or short sheet the bed when no one was looking. The primary reason for the final walk-thru is to make sure you know how everything works. And I do mean everything. Plan to spend a minimum of one hour with the salesperson or service technician for this tutorial on the inner workings of your new vehicle. A larger motorhome or fifth wheel may take considerably longer, but it's time well spent.

Have this person show you how something operates (refrigerator, water heater, awning, etc.), and then repeat it yourself. Get involved. Don't just observe, but go through the motions. Take notes. Ask questions. Ask more questions. Film it if that makes you feel better. Yes, we'll cover how everything operates in upcoming chapters, but doing it yourself—in your specific RV—is the best way to learn.

Road Scholar

No new purchase would be complete without parting gifts in the form of a mountain of warranties and service manuals. Don't treat them like family heirlooms, actually hold on to these. Study manuals for operating tips and preventative maintenance. Keeping these materials together and intact will pay off when you really need them.

The following checklists were created to make sure you don't forget anything on your final walk-thru:

How Do I?

- ❑ Take a shower?
- ❑ Get running water?
- ❑ Get hot water?
- ❑ Activate slide-outs?
- ❑ Transform all sleeping areas?
- ❑ Deploy the awning(s)?
- ❑ Work the satellite TV, backup monitor, or TV antennae?

Test Appliances

- ❑ Stove burners
- ❑ Oven
- ❑ Microwave oven
- ❑ Refrigerator (on all settings)
- ❑ Furnace
- ❑ Air conditioner
- ❑ Fans and roof vents
- ❑ Water heater

Learn the Systems

- ❑ Filling the fresh water tank
- ❑ Learn the ins and outs of propane container(s)
- ❑ Emptying the gray and black water tanks
- ❑ Hooking up to shoreline power
- ❑ Working the generator (if applicable)
- ❑ Examine all batteries and their fuse locations
- ❑ Locate the 120-volt AC breaker box/identify all circuits

RV-Specific Questions

Towable RVs

- ❑ A full run-through of hitching and unhitching

Fold-Down Campers

- ❑ Deploying and retracting the unit

Truck Campers

- ❑ Installing and removing the camper

Motorized RVs

- ❑ Towing a car or trailer

In the event that a postsale inspection uncovers a problem, have it fixed immediately. Don't take possession of a faulty RV. Expect to go to the head of the line to get this problem righted immediately.

Follow-Up Meeting

Only after you're completely satisfied that everything's in working order—and that you won't be scratching your head when it's time to deploy the sleeper-sofa—should you hit the highway. But before heading off into the sunset, schedule a follow-up meeting with the salesperson for a few weeks later. This second meeting is devoted to answering the questions and addressing concerns that you no doubt will be having after your first "shakedown trip" (see the following section). A quality seller may offer a goodwill period to return the RV if there's a problem or if it needs service. Schedule the meeting within 30 days.

Shakedown Street

Plan a weekend away from home within a week (sooner is better) of taking delivery. As the old saying goes, this is where the rubber meets the road; there's simply no better way to see what your new RV can do than by, well, doing it. Choose a campground far enough away to get the feel for life behind the wheel or your towing aptitude. Since we want to test all the onboard features, a full hookup site is necessary. This allows you to evaluate the water, electric, and sewer systems, as well as practice hooking up and dumping the tanks. Consider phone and cable TV service a bonus if you can get it.

Load up your rig with what you'll need for a weekend away from home. Prepare to do all the cooking onboard, so a trip to the grocery store is in order. Yes, you can have a candy bar. If you didn't already do so at the dealership, fill up on propane and fresh water (see Chapters 11, "LP Systems," and 12, "Plumbing Systems," respectively). Fuel up at the gas station (remember to go to the diesel side if your motorhome is of that persuasion) and take a trip to the weigh station to make sure you didn't overpack, something we'll discuss in Chapter 15, "How Much Does Your RV Weigh?" As previously stated, every RV has its weight limitations, and a weighing-in is good practice against stuffing your new purchase like a beef burrito.

One for the Road

In an effort to ease buyers into their new RVs, some dealerships feature overnight camping facilities on the premises for customers to get acquainted with their vehicles. This is an ideal way to learn the ins and outs of your new RV, backed by knowledgeable personnel nearby if you should have questions or problems.

Plan to spend the first night living off the hookups and the second night running off the coach batteries and/or generator (if applicable), giving you a taste of both ways of RV life. Make lists with problems and questions about procedures to ask the dealership. Meanwhile, ask the folks in the next campsite for assistance if you forget how something works. You'll be surprised at how willing fellow RVers are to help a traveler in need.

A Little Insurance

Insurance isn't a matter of choice, rather one of degree. The lending institution that probably made this purchase possible will demand a full-boat policy to protect their investment, which basically makes the discussion of why to insure an RV a moot point. A minimum level of insurance is also the law, so there's no getting around it—every vehicle must be insured. Besides, it just makes good sense, whether you're involved in an accident, theft, or liability issues raised when simply parked at the campsite.

The good news is that RV insurance isn't the budget-busting practice one suffers at the hands of their automotive premiums. This is doubly true for less-expensive towables, which dodge their fair share of lofty payments. You can thank historically low accident rates among the RVing population, as well as less overall usage and incidences of vehicle thefts, for that. Since RVers tend to be older and more experienced drivers, they tend to stay out of trouble ... unlike your 16-year-old with that souped-up Camaro.

Road Scholar

Make sure you brought everything needed for hookups prior to camping out. A sewer hose and shoreline electrical cord should come with a new RV, but many folks lament that neither is ever long enough. A fresh water hose, designed especially for RVers, is usually the responsibility of new owners, as are the various adapters for the different kinds of electrical hookups.

RV Insurers

Expect a cold reception from your automobile insurance provider at the subject of a new RV. Chances are excellent that even the most open-minded agency will balk at the thought of insuring it, perhaps adding a giggle or two for good measure. Most consider RVs unprofitable and outside their level of expertise. Besides, wouldn't you rather go with someone who knows a thing or two about it? Frankly, most automotive carriers don't know the difference between a slide-out and a submarine sandwich and should be left to manage the things they know best. In the case of smaller towables, however, it may be possible to simply add a rider to an existing policy. Be sure to call for answers.

Road Scholar

Buyers must show proof of insurance before taking ownership of a new RV, so get it beforehand. The finance company and state laws say so. Besides, an uninsured wreck on the way home is no way to begin this exciting new way of life. Start comparing quotes when you have settled on a particular make and model, and finalize the policy after the deal is reached.

The case for enlisting an RV-specific insurance company is obvious. Not only do they understand the industry and the lifestyle, but they also can make recommendations based on your level of use, type of vehicle, and specific situation. A couple living full-time aboard their fifth wheel requires a decidedly different batch of insurance than a family taking sporadic trips in a small motorhome. RV insurers excel at these differences, crafting the best policies for you.

Pull Over

Carefully read over your policy to ensure coverage for any number of scenarios. Provisions for damage from weather as well as replacement costs for stolen or damaged personal possessions can be overlooked. Also, avoid doubling up coverage already provided by your homeowner's policy, such as medical costs.

One for the Road

In some cases, coverage might fall under an existing policy, with no modifications required. A new pop-up, lightweight travel trailer, or truck camper may only require a rider to your existing auto policy. Check with your auto carrier or policy for answers. Be sure to ask about onboard possessions and whether you're covered when parked or just in transit.

Types of Insurance

Good coverage protects owners both inside and out, while in transit and when camped for extended periods of time. RVers can be just as liable when that youngster injures herself tripping over your fresh water hose as when causing an accident on I-80. Since an RV is a combination home and vehicle, special care should be taken to protecting yourself in each type of situation.

A look through a typical RV policy includes all the usual suspects: liability (bodily injury and property damage); collision; medical payments; comprehensive coverage; and clauses for uninsured motorists. However, replacement costs for interior furnishings, appliances, and your personal possessions should also be included, as should living expenses (hotels, rental cars, etc.) in the event you and your rig are sidelined due to an accident. Terms covering you in the event of a breakdown can also be added, including roadside assistance, towing, and rental options. As you can see, there's a lot to think about. Most RVers would agree that gaps in coverage are less likely to exist when working with a knowledgeable RV insurer.

How Much Is Enough?

In the eyes of most carriers, you can't have too much insurance. Friends might advise carrying the bare-bone amount mandated by your state. As usual, my advice is to take a middle-of-the-road approach, favoring proper coverage somewhere in between these two extremes. Again, your lending institutions will be very vocal about their coverage demands, establishing a starting point to work from. Your state's insurance laws play a role in this decision, too. After that, it's up to you to decide how deep you want to go. Factor in the age, value, and usage of your RV, your financial situation, and peace of mind (or lack thereof) associated with different policy levels.

Crossing Borders

Aside from hungry grizzlies and those funny Mountie uniforms, there's nothing unusual involved when crossing Canada's borders. Pull up to the border, answer their questions, and make tracks to the nearest Canadian bacon outlet. The same insurance that's good enough for American soil is honored (and appreciated) up north (even way north). Mexico, however, is a different story. Our friends to the south require specific documentation stating in no short order that your coverage extends within their country. Unfortunately, a quick call to your insurer may reveal that they don't, forcing you to buy insurance from one of a number of companies found near the border.

One for the Road

Consider the case of the disappearing deductible. More and more insurers are rewarding customers for every claim-free year with a lower deductible. For instance, a couple starting off with a $1,000 deductible may find it shrink by $250 per year, finally vanishing completely.

Finding the Best Deals

By now you know the drill to getting a good deal. Comparison-shopping is what separates the inflated-price-know-nothings from a company built to serve you well during both good times and bad.

Owners willing to assume more of the risk receive lower premiums by carrying a higher deductible. True, if something goes wrong, you'll be asked to chip in more moolah. However, the monthly savings can add up to a pleasing sum. Choose a dollar amount that you can live with provided this figure ever comes a-calling. Determine the cost savings by switching the payment schedule from monthly to bi-monthly, quarterly, or semi-annually. Reducing coverage during periods of non-use such as RV storage is also a good idea. This practice is referred to as *suspension coverage*.

RVocabulary

Suspension coverage is a type of insurance policy allowing you to cancel or reduce vehicle coverage during periods of dormancy, including storage.

Discounts

Even the best rates have some flexibility, based on a number of eligible factors. Here are a few:

- Defensive driving course
- Onboard safety features such as air bags

- Anti-theft devices
- Good driving record
- Special senior rates
- Rural versus urban residency

One for the Road

The RV Driving School (909-984-7746; www.rvschool.com) is the oldest and most comprehensive of its kind. Participants can attend at a number of school locations or receive behind-the-wheel training at or near their homes. Graduates of the two-day course learn and/or reinforce their driving skills and may benefit from lower insurance rates for their matriculation. I strongly recommend the school even for the most experienced drivers.

Full-Timers' Policies

Full-time RVers fall under a different class of RV owners. Since their RV serves as a permanent home, and they spend a majority of the time there, an insurance company assumes more risks. Some insurers deem participants "full-timers" if they live in the vehicle for more than 150 days per year. Qualifications vary, so ask around. Of course, this status means you'll pay higher premiums, something a few folks are unwilling to do. A little white lie to Mr. Insurer won't hurt anyone, they believe, as they claim to use the RV only "sporadically." However, if an accident should occur and it's proven that you do indeed fit their definition of a full-time RVer, your coverage might be voided, leaving you a big (and potentially expensive) problem.

Roadside Assistance

You're headed down a deserted stretch of road when the cautionary lights on the dashboard start glowing like a Christmas tree. Or perhaps a tire blows or a much more subtle calamity transpires, such as steam from the engine or a horrendous sound coming from underneath. It's late and there's no one around. Your spouse flashes you a look as if to say, "This isn't happening, is it?" Best-case scenario, you dial for help on the cell phone and wait for a tow or on-the-spot fix-it from a qualified RV service technician. Worst case, you're stranded, baffled at how to fix things or unable to do so, without a clue of whom to call. This is why roadside assistance was created, to shield you and your family from trying and potentially dangerous situations like these.

Think changing your SUV's tire was tough, wait until you try grappling with one the size of a fourth-grader found on your motorhome, in the rain, with all your earthly possessions onboard, without a jack. A better idea is to let the pros handle it. Since a breakdown now strands the family's home as well as their transportation, it's doubly important to have a good service waiting on the speed dial. Anyone doing any RVing at all should have *some* form of roadside assistance, designed to meet the specific needs of these kinds of vehicles. End of story.

Pull Over

Your current auto club may not cover your new RV, even for routine saves for such misfires as a dead battery or lockouts. For those unwilling to switch or add on to their regular auto club, make sure of what is and isn't covered ahead of time.

A Little Help Here

Do you know the old saying, "Don't send a donkey to do the work of a buffalo?" No? Well, I might have made it up. How about, "Don't send a boy to do a man's job," which is what you're doing when you call the local gas station or auto mechanic for help for a stranded rig. Conventional tow trucks are powerless against large motorhomes; transporting the fifth wheel to safety is beyond the grasp of most dispatched trucks from the local towing company. And then who's going to fix it? The mechanic at the Amoco station? Not likely. Trouble, in this case, is best left to a certified RV service technician, not to the same guy who's a whiz working on 1970s muscle cars. (Although these folks are my heroes, nonetheless.)

In addition to heavy-duty towing equipment and a knowledge of RV mechanisms, RV roadside assistance companies usually belong to a large network of troubleshooters. If they can't do the job, they should be able to locate someone who can, saving you a lot of grief (not to mention roaming charges) when you're phoning frantically for help, stuck at the side of the road.

One for the Road

Towing and roadside assistance can often be added to an RV's insurance policy and sometimes for less than the yearly premium of a separate club. Call your insurer for details and carefully review the services offered to determine if it's comprehensive enough for your needs.

Choosing a Service Plan

With most roadside assistance plans costing less than $100 per year, the battle for the consumer dollar comes down to services. If road troubles were confined to running out of gas or jump-starting a dead battery, then there would be no shortage of would-be heroes. Unfortunately, it's not always that easy. See "Murphy's Law" for more explanations.

Pull Over

Beware of hidden charges, most likely found within the towing section. Watch for mileage and cost restrictions. A 10-mile towing limit might only get you to the nearest town and not to a qualified RV repair center. It might be worth it to spend a little more in membership costs to avoid getting underserved during crunch time.

A good service plan offers heavy-duty towing equipment for both motorhomes and trailers as well as provisions for ancillary vehicles, such as the car you're towing behind your Class A. Affiliation with a comprehensive network of RV service centers is also warranted, with locations throughout the country. Subscribing to a company lacking West Coast towing services does you little good when you're watching the steam pour from the radiator outside Reno. Nationwide plans are better than regional providers; regional plans better than local ones. Tire changing, lockout service, and the traditional battery jumping and gas filling should be included. Upstart companies might provide trip-planning services and discounts for other services.

Lemon Aid

That citrus smell onboard was a dead giveaway. Far be it from me to dash the good feelings of any new RV owner, but a frank discussion on what to do in the rare event your RV is defective—okay, a lemon—is in order. This fruity label is slapped on any vehicle that fails to live up to the warranty after repeated attempts to remedy a problem(s). In the eyes of the law, declaring a vehicle a lemon is the scarlet letter, a nasty brand for all the world to see. A busted radiator cap won't garner much sympathy from the courts, but that chronically underperforming engine, leaky roof, or uncorrectable brakes are good examples. (Well, not really *good,* but appropriate candidates.) Invoke your state's lemon laws when reasonable steps have failed to correct a problem with the manufacturer.

Pull Over

The trailer bias continues, as evidenced through many states' legal dealings. Towables do not frequently fall under most states' lemon laws umbrella. In these cases, the burden falls on the owners, who can still argue their case in the traditional courts or work through the Better Business Bureau for resolution.

Defining a Lemon

Laws vary from state to state concerning the definition of a "lemon." However, many share similar legal themes, including the amount of repairs within a 12- to 24-month period; number of days confined to the service center within a period of time; and defects that are deemed a threat to safety, which remain unfixed. The more serious and debilitating the problem is, the more leverage you have to slap a lemon tag on any particular vehicle. Determine your state's laws by contacting either the Department of Transportation or Consumer Protection Office. The Better Business Bureau (www.bbb.org) features a searchable database of lemon laws organized by state.

The Write Stuff

That X#%@% transmission has been in the shop three times in six months and you've had enough. Proper documentation is the key to either resolving a dispute or championing your case as hard evidence if the matter goes to the courts. Always start with the dealer that sold you the vehicle, regardless of the problem. Although they didn't build the unit, dealers can be powerful advocates when lobbying a manufacturer for justice. An unhappy customer—a yelling one at that—can be quite damaging to a small dealer's reputation, so involve them in your fight.

Record all the events that transpired in detail: when the vehicle was purchased, when and where it was repaired, mileage, and days spent in the shop. Get names and include those whenever you can. Be sure to save all copies of work receipts and any correspondence about the problems in question. An angry customer armed with a paper trail is as formidable as Darth Vader wielding a lightsaber to many manufacturers.

Road Scholar

Send complaints and important correspondence via certified mail with a return receipt. This makes absolutely sure the participant receives each document and moves these letters to the top of the mail bin, which should expedite matters. It also sends a message that you're serious about getting satisfaction.

Any phone calls should be backed up with a letter re-stating the points of the conversation. As the old saying goes, a verbal agreement isn't worth the paper it's written on, so don't rely solely on verbal correspondence. List the actions you want taken. Keep the tone professional. Whether deemed a nuisance or better yet as an important customer, customers are much more likely to get issues resolved by talking to the top people. And always, always get the names of all people you speak with, and involve them in your fight. The more people aware of your problem and working on your behalf, the better.

The Killer Bs

Repeated letters and calls go unanswered, or the manufacturer's attempts at appeasement are far from satisfactory. Going to court should be your last resort. In case you haven't heard, lawyers are costly (news flash). A better alternative is to invoke the aid of the Better Business Bureau's Auto Line program (1-800-955-5100; www.bbb.org). If both parties are willing, a neutral arbitrator oversees the case and provides a ruling. Technical experts may also be involved in the process if needed. The arbitrator calls a hearing to determine fault, rules on a settlement, and oversees that the decisions are carried out. Of course, the mere act of involving the Better Business Bureau's might be enough to garner a quick settlement.

The Ruling

Like a pair of old ski boots, the arbitrator's decision is only partially binding. Both parties must agree to abide by the final ruling ahead of time, usually limited only to covering warranty violations, replacement procedures, and their costs. No punitive damages or monies for personal injury, fraud, or angst can be awarded. If you're still unsatisfied, consumers can pursue one of the great benefits of a litigious society …

The Least You Need to Know

- Don't take delivery of a new unit until all questions are answered and you know how to operate all onboard systems and appliances. Schedule an appointment for a walk-thru with the salesperson, and arrange for a follow-up visit after you take the vehicle camping.
- Operating an RV without proper insurance is against the law. Towable and motorized RVs fall under different guidelines, as mandated by your state and the finance company that loaned you the money. Many travelers discover that an insurer specializing in RVs is definitely the way to go.
- Modest costs and a network of qualified RV service professionals make membership in a roadside assistance company a must. Automotive clubs often lack the heavy-duty equipment for towing and the technicians to work on RVs, so join a club that specializes in recreational vehicles.
- Lemon laws vary from state to state but are worded to replace, repair, or repurchase defective vehicles. Meticulous record-keeping and persistence is how such battles are won. Otherwise, take the matter to the Better Business Bureau or the courts.
- The excitement over a new RV sometimes gives way to doubt when the check clears. Relax. You made the right decision. Plan a trip as soon as you can and start enjoying this wonderful way to live and travel.

Part 4

What's What Onboard?

Don't be like I used to be. Don't drive an RV completely oblivious as to the inner workings of the unit. I started my first forays into the "field" as a pampered RV editor, completely unaware of how and why the lights came on, if the heat would ever stop pouring out of the ducts, and believing the fresh water would surely last as long as I wanted it to. I camped at sophisticated RV parks, chose full hookup sites, and didn't use the bathroom onboard because, well, I didn't want to make a mess.

Whoever said ignorance is bliss never spent a frigid night inside a perfectly wonderful high-end RV. The following section is devoted to learning what's what onboard, why things work the way they do, and how to skip the hapless beginnings of yours truly.

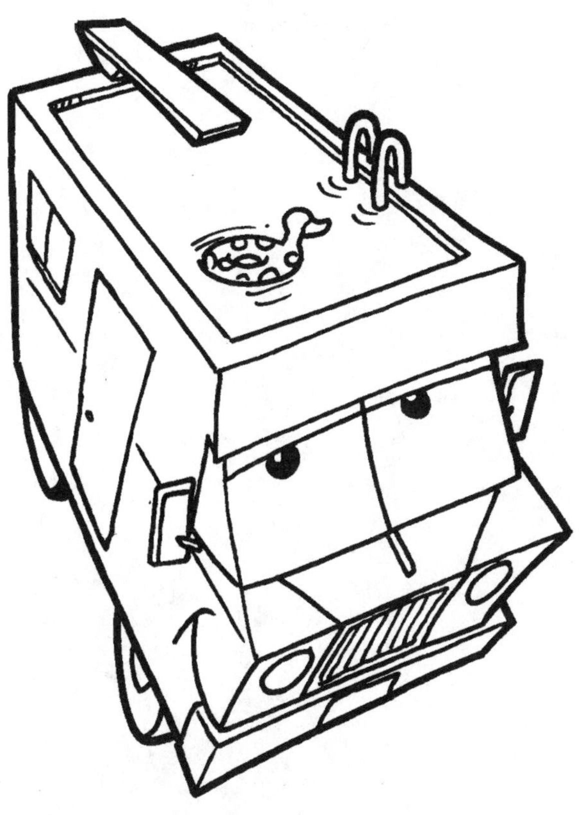

Chapter 10

Electrical Systems

In This Chapter

- The various sources of an RV's electricity
- Tapping into adequate power no matter where you go
- Tips for safe and efficient operation of appliances

Repeat after me: All RVs are self-contained. Now they wouldn't exactly be the home on wheels we've described for the last nine chapters if they sat dark and powerless upon arrival. Sweet, wonderful electricity surges through every RV, from the least expensive pop-up to the multimillion-dollar bus. All that onboard lighting and temperature controls, cooking appliances, and entertaining options aren't just for show. There's real bona fide electricity flowing though those outlets, just looking for something to do.

If powering up all these electrical doo-dads was as easy as it is at home, this chapter wouldn't be necessary. Just flip a switch and expect the lights to come on. Run all the appliances at once without giving a single thought to consumption or limits. Fall asleep with the TV on, wrapped in your electric blanket, while your spouse vacuums and the kids stare longingly at the burritos sizzling away in the microwave. RVing is pretty happy-go-lucky, but it's not *that* happy-go-lucky. The laws of cause and effect are still in play, and every RV has its limits.

A basic command of the RV's electrical systems is the difference between pleasurable and efficient travels and coach blackouts, dead batteries, and a considerable amount of wear and tear on your appliances. Is it important to learn every single term and earn the equivalent of a master's degree in electronics? No, and there won't be a lengthy essay to write later on. But a little knowledge on the subject couldn't hurt and will make you a more confident and able RVer.

Straight to the Source

Before you learn to wield your electrical know-how, it's important to know where the stuff comes from, or better yet, how electricity is generated. Onboard electricity is available through three basic sources, found on any motorized RV or tow vehicle/ trailer combination: engine power, coach power, and shore power.

Engine Power

This is also known as the 12-volt DC (direct current) automotive system. Like "The Force" within a young Luke Skywalker, engine power rests inside, in this case, your motorhome or tow vehicle's engine (accomplished for towable owners via wiring connections made during hitch-up or through the trailer electrical connector cable). The dynamics at work here are basically the same witnessed in your automobile. Start the ignition and what happens? Power. Not only power to drive, but power for the interior components as well. The dashboard lights up. The radio belts out your easy listening station (come on, admit that you like Kenny G!). Interior and exterior lights are ready for action. Windshield wipers, the lovely horn, even the cigarette lighter are all ready to go. The same is true with your RV. Turn the key in the motorhome's cockpit or inside the tow vehicle and a number of things come to life.

Equipment controlled by engine power include:

- Engine
- Windshield wipers
- Horn
- Dashboard lights
- Headlights
- AM/FM radio (cassette and CD, if so equipped)
- Power doors, mirrors, and locks
- Dash-mounted heat and air conditioning
- 12-volt appliances plugged into cigarette lighter or separate outlet
- Electric brakes (trailers only)

The heart of this system rests in the *automotive battery,* which sparks the engine into action when the key is turned. An *alternator* is responsible for maintaining the battery's charge, and as revealed momentarily, the core between the two DC battery systems (engine power and coach power).

RVocabulary

Similar to those found in regular cars and trucks, the **automotive battery** provides the power to start the RV or tow vehicle's engine and keeps the 12-volt equipment running. The **alternator** works in conjunction with the automotive and coach battery systems to maintain a positive charge whenever the engine is running. The condition and the state of charge in each of the batteries determine how hard the alternator must work.

Coach Power

Watching the wipers drag across the windshield and tooting the horn at fellow campers gets pretty boring after a while, which is why there's a second batch of power for the RV's other assorted 12-volt equipment. We call this the coach power, or the auxiliary battery system, since its range extends far beyond the simple dashboard delights provided by engine power. This is also referred to as the 12-volt DC coach system.

Equipment controlled by coach power include:

- Interior lights
- Water pump
- Furnace fan
- Exhaust vans
- Roof vent fan
- Exterior lamps
- Power awnings
- Alarm systems
- LP and CO leak detectors
- Roof-mounted evaporative cooler
- Radio/stereo/CD player
- Monitor panels
- TV antenna booster
- Slide-outs
- Leveling jacks, hydraulic or electric
- 12-volt appliances
- Inverter

In this case, a *deep-cycle battery* is used, one capable of supplying a greater amount of current and holding its charge longer than the smallish battery residing in the engine. The alternator is enlisted here as well, but this time it works feverishly (okay, maybe not *that* hard) to recharge both sets of batteries, meaning more current to go around.

RVocabulary

Your RV's **deep-cycle battery,** also known as a marine-style battery, provides a greater supply of power for the coach's 12-volt electrical system. These larger batteries are capable of withstanding a "deeper" charge than their automotive counterparts.

Coach Batteries

Coach batteries come in several sizes, each with a limit to the available current it can store, measured in amps. Obviously, the greater the amp rating, the more power available to run your onboard systems—and the less often it must be recharged. Two six-volt golf cart batteries are usually included in larger RVs. When wired in a series configuration, the two heavy-duty six-volters combine to yield approximately 250 total amps of storage capacity but delivered at the user-friendly 12-volts.

Automotive and deep-cycle batteries are separate but very unequal. Automotive models are designed for a high-current output, but for a short duration, like when starting the engine. Deep-cycles are designed for a low current rate, but for a longer duration. These batteries should never be swapped and only be replaced with another similar battery capable of doing the job.

The Most Common Examples of Deep-Cycle Batteries	
Group 24	70 to 85 amps
Group 27	90 to 105 amps
4D	180 amps
8D	250 amps
Golf cart	250 amps at 6 volts

Hey, That's My Power

Just what prevents the automotive battery from draining the reserves of the deep-cycle batteries and vice versa? Is it the honor system? This type of electrical embezzlement between the two batteries is thwarted by an *isolator,* which effectively splits the alternator output to each battery system and never allows them to be connected together.

Shore Power

Don't be confused by the nautical terminology—you won't need a boat and no awkward docking is required. Shore power works the other side of the proverbial street, in the form of AC (alternative current), found at electrical hookups at the campsite and even your home or garage. In fact, it's the very same juice powering the ole homestead right now. In a pinch, an onboard or portable generator can do the trick if no electrical hookups are available, allowing for use of the full range of appliances when camped in remote locations.

This electrical system, also known as the 120-volt AC electrical system, powers all the big-time consumers of electricity onboard. The 12-volt systems previously mentioned simply don't possess the necessary muscle to power larger appliances, such as the air conditioner or microwave oven. If the equipment plugs into an outlet, chances are it falls under the umbrella of the 120-volt system.

RVocabulary

The **isolator** maintains battery separation, to prevent one from taxing the reserves of the other.

Equipment controlled by shore power include:

- Roof-mounted air conditioner
- Microwave oven
- Hair dryer
- Vacuum cleaner
- TVs (unless 12-volt)
- Computer
- Toaster
- Coffee maker
- Converter
- Refrigerator (runs on more than one power source)
- VCR
- Washer/dryer
- Portable heaters
- Ice maker
- Anything that plugs into a typical house receptacle

Is a piece of equipment 12-volt or 120-volt? Following the previous lists should help determine what equipment falls under what power source onboard your RV. However, in the cases of some appliances, it's not always clear, such as TVs, commonly available in either 12-volt DC and 120-volt AC versions. Check the label, which should reveal the exact voltage, or the owner's manual.

Rating Electrical Hookups

Available current from a campground electrical hookup comes in several forms: 15-, 20-, 30-, or 50-amp service. As you can see by the accompanying figure, the outlets' shapes reveal the extent of their electrical output. Although the process for hooking up is the same (connecting the electrical cord to the outlet within the campsite's pedestal box), an adapter plug might be needed to secure a proper fit, assuming your power cord doesn't match.

A 15-amp connection means, you guessed it, there are only 15 amps of electricity to supply current for your onboard goodies. Some older and antiquated campgrounds continue to offer this lackluster power source. However, the vast majority of campgrounds deliver 30- and 50-amp service, which is usually plenty for most onboard equipment.

Left to right: a 15-amp outlet, a 20-amp outlet, a 30-amp outlet, and a 50-amp outlet.

Road Scholar

The wise RVer carries adapters to fit each kind of outlet, as electrical hookups vary from campground to campground. Adapters are inexpensive and can mean the difference between powering up and petering out.

What Do I Have?

Most new RVs should come with a power cord suited for 30-amp hookups. More deluxe models offer 50-amp service. What happens when I plug in a 30-amp cord (with adapter) into 15- or 20-amp service? Connections work on the theory of the lowest link in the chain. In this case, you can expect 15- or 20-amp service. Conversely, attaching to 50 amps when you're only rated for 30 amps yields just 30 amps of power.

The Trickle Down (and Up) Theory

Plug into a 120-volt receptacle (such as that found at the campsite) and all your equipment will thank you. Not only are your larger appliances working steadfastly but the smaller, 12-volt components are feeding off the same electrical scraps, thanks to a *converter*. The name almost says it all. A converter transforms (okay, converts) existing 120-volt AC power into 12-volt DC, thus getting the RV's 12-volt system in on the act. Now everything's powered. The coach's deep-cycle receives a boost via an integrated battery charger, which helps to eliminate drain. A converter is standard equipment onboard most RVs.

Not one for charity, the 12-volt system also does its part by aiding the 120-volt system. An *inverter* says "right back at ya'," allowing for larger appliances to now be run off the 12-volt system. Who needs a generator when there's an inverter to be had? Indeed. Some folks forgo the generator route all together, relying on an inverter to summon up the energy to heat that pot of coffee, microwave a couple of spuds, or cool off (thank you, air conditioner) in desert climes. Like generators, inverters have their limits, listed as *watts.* Exceed these ratings and your RV will do its best impression of a prehistoric cave—after the circuits are tripped. The downside of this amassed power is that an inverter really taxes the battery, so be prudent with its usage. This is part of the reason why they're usually listed as options and are more common in the aftermarket sector.

RVocabulary

A **converter** transforms 120-volt AC into usable 12-volt DC electricity. Converters are standard onboard most RVs. An **inverter** is the opposite of a converter. Inverters turn 12-volt DC into 120-volt AC power for use in running larger equipment. Power is listed in terms of watts, which governs the output of each device. Prevalent in the aftermarket sector, inverters are usually listed only as an option on anything less than high-line motorhomes.

Generators

The secondary means to infuse 120-volt power to your RV, a generator can be your best friend when camped off the beaten path. If you're one of those who likes remote locations while maintaining the more civilized equipment, make sure you have one at your disposal. Camped away from hookups and without an onboard inverter, it's the only way to activate larger equipment, such as the air conditioner, hair dryer (right, Mrs. Peterson?), and microwave oven. As mentioned in our RV round-ups in Chapters 4, "The World of Motorized RVs," and 5, "The World of Towables," generators are fairly standard on motorized vehicles and less common in towables, particularly smaller models lacking the necessary space, fuel source, and big-ticket appliances (in some cases) for which they are used. Portable generators are available in the aftermarket.

Road Scholar

A portable generator is a nice substitute for an installed version when travels begin to take on a more rustic tone. However, some burdens do apply. Portables must be stationed outside the RV (rain, anyone?) and are even louder than RV-equipped models. Prepare for a manual start, like your lawnmower, and less overall power. Although small, they're usually plenty heavy. Be sure you're up to the heave-ho of moving them around.

A typical generator, found on most motorhomes and higher-end towables.

Most generators run on gas, but diesel and propane models are available. In many cases, installed generators tap into your motorized RV's fuel supply, making for a steady fuel source, but may bear watching to prevent the accidental draining of the tanks, leaving you stuck out in Nowheresville. Fortunately, most onboard models are designed to quit running when the fuel levels dip below a quarter tank.

A generator's power is measured in watts. Just how many watts are needed for all your stuff is up to you, based on your appliance needs. Larger onboard models put out between 4,000 and 7,500 watts, slightly larger on the really big rigs. Smaller motorhomes generally range between 2,000 and 3,000 watts. These ratings are important: Exceed them and you'll trip the breakers and the flow of energy will be interrupted. This then involves putting on that raggedy robe that should have been donated to the Salvation Army years ago, turning off all the 120-volt appliances, resetting the breaker, waiting a fair amount of time, stewing over your mistake, and starting it all again, now a much more power-savvy traveler. We'll talk about knowing your power limits in the following sections.

Road Scholar

Generators that share fuel with your RV's engine know better than to consume that last important drop of gasoline or diesel. Most shut down when the fuel levels dip to 1/4 tank, signaling a trip to the gas station. Otherwise, keep an eye on the supply via the fuel gauge.

Is It for Me?

Generators aren't cheap, so consider their possible role in your camping adventures before plunking down extra money for one. Staying at traditional campgrounds means constant access to electrical hookups, so you won't need a secondary power source there. If you're a less-is-more kind of family, wishing to leave the computers, blow dryers, and such at home, you probably won't need it. Generators best serve those who boondock or have heavy power requirements. Otherwise, you may not miss it.

One for the Road

Would you rather have a 3,000-watt generator or a 3.0 kW version? They're the same, as one Kilowatt equals 1,000 watts. For example, a 4.0 kW generator is another way of saying its output is 4,000 watts; 4.5 kW is 4,500 watts. This is just another way the metric system inches ever closer to mainstream America.

Camped or On the Go

Don't think there won't occasionally be energy needs while in transit. Larger motorhomes are nearly impossible to cool down on a hot day utilizing just the dashboard air conditioner. Generators work equally well when you're on the go, whether the coach's cool AC is in order or someone wants to heat up leftovers in the microwave.

Peak Performance

Generators are like beagles: They need attention. Run them at least once a month (generators, that is; beagles like daily exercise) under a substantial load (a few appliances at a time), whether you need to or not. This action helps recirculate stagnant fuel while cleaning the lines, the carburetor, or fuel injectors. Try to run the generator at heavier loads, rather than just on and off to warm a cup of coffee or some other small chore. Allow even new models to warm up, at least a few minutes, before activating any 120-volt equipment. Repeat this courtesy when the task is completed, letting it "cool down" without any load before turning it off. Routine maintenance such as changing the spark plugs, filters, and oil should be performed based on the operating instructions of the particular unit.

Generator Courtesy

While any normal flow of electricity features a slight, pleasing hum, generating power fills the air with a noisy racket and some carbon monoxide (CO) to boot (expelled through an exterior exhaust vent). Take special care to make sure you're not annoying your neighbors—or blasting lethal byproducts through a vent into an open window. Many campgrounds prohibit generator use during quiet hours or disallow them altogether. It's generally bad form to excessively run a generator, which parallels a chronically barking dog or loud reruns of *Barney* to all your campsite neighbors.

Pull Over

Carbon monoxide is one passenger you don't want along for the ride. As stated, a generator produces enough of it to merit attention. Make sure the unit's exhaust vent is clear and that wind isn't blowing the gas back inside the RV. Every new RV comes with a CO detector. Make sure it works and test it often. While these steps should avert trouble, I also recommend never sleeping with the generator running.

Monitor Panels

Most RVs feature the electronic equivalent of the Magic 8-ball found somewhere inside in the form of a *monitor panel*. Want to know how much fresh water is in fresh water tanks? Need to gauge how soon the wastewater tanks need to be emptied? For the purposes of this chapter, a monitor panel also displays the state of the charge within the deep-cycle battery(ies). Nicer versions might also give the status of the water heater (on/off) or the fresh water pump (on/off). Monitor panels reside in conspicuous places, such as the kitchen, with a quick examination relaying all this information (usually in cool-looking LED light display) so you always know the status of the systems onboard.

Be forewarned: Monitor panels offer ranges, not exact levels. Use them only as a guide, and don't let important items like battery charges drain or holding tanks exceed capacity.

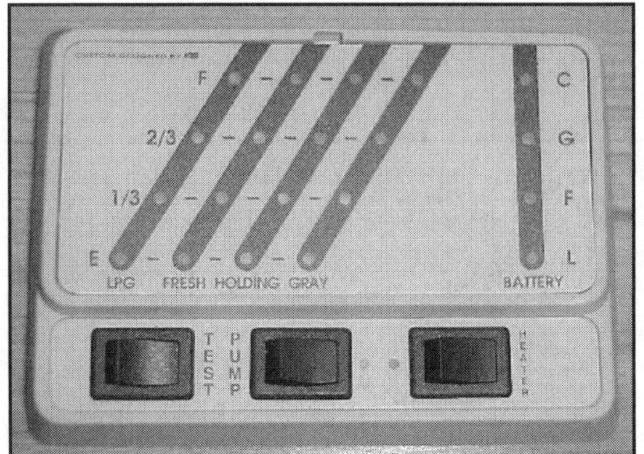

An interior monitor panel displays important information concerning the levels of your RV's holding tanks, LP gas container, and battery voltage.

RVocabulary

The **monitor panel** relays important information about the levels of your RV's onboard systems. Readings usually include the amount of fresh water, battery voltage, LP gas, and the status of the gray and black water tanks. It may also tell you whether the water pump and/or water heater is on. Usually found in the kitchen area, monitor panels should be used as a guide, not a precise rating.

Electricity: The Long and the Short(age)

As you can see, recreational vehicles are electrical dynamos, capable of powering lots of complex equipment through different electrical systems. A combination of engine, coach, and shore power, teamed with an understanding of what is responsible for what, should keep you from sitting in the dark wondering why the lights won't come on. For some, plugging into the campsite's electrical hookups is all they're concerned with. However, for others, the question of just how much power they need consumes them.

Everything has its limits. You've experienced this fact at home when you blow a fuse, sending your spouse scurrying to the basement to fumble with the circuit breakers. A recreational vehicle is no exception, with limitations of its own. The key to determining how much power you'll need is to calculate the total current (listed as either amps or watts) required to make each necessary product go. For instance, the standard RV light draws about two amps (see the following table). Five lights shining brightly at once would use 10 amps. Add to this mix the sporadic use of the TV, the furnace fan, and the water pump left in the "on" position, and that number grows. Can your RV handle it?

Estimated Electrical Requirements of Typical 12-Volt RV Accessories	
Lamp bulb	2 amps
Water pump	5 to 8 amps
Small 12-volt appliance	2 to 8 amps
Forced-air furnace	5 to 8 amps
Powered vent	1 to 7 amps
Roof-mounted air conditioner	2,000 watts
19-inch color TV	30 watts
VCR	50 watts
Stereo	50 watts
Coffee maker	1,000 watts
Medium-size microwave	900 watts
Curling iron	60 watts
Laptop computer	120 watts
Small power tool	450 to 500 watts
Blender	300 watts
Toaster oven	1,200 watts

Again, these ratings are all approximate. Amp or watt draw is usually listed on the product's decal or within the specs of the user's manual.

One for the Road

You're probably wondering why everyone can't just rate his stuff in either amps *or* watts, right? Here's the magic conversion formula.

Watts ÷ volts = amps

Amps × volts = watts

Like amps and watts, volts are listed on the product itself or in the product's owner's manual.

Running Out of Juice

Will your batteries run dry when you least expect it? Can the generator or inverter save the day when hookups are miles away? Is there any limit to the flow of current at the campsite? For answers to these questions, read on.

Hooking Up

Connecting to a shore power source (campsite, home, etc.) means a constant source of electricity. You are, however, limited as to *how much* electricity you have to work with. Connecting to 30-amp service means you have, you guessed it, 30 amps of electricity at any one time, probably enough to run the air conditioner and the microwave at once, as well as a number of smaller items—but don't push it. Of course, you can add up the total amps required so you know for sure. Tripping the circuit breaker lets you know you're asking too much and you'd better turn something off. The same theorem is true in the case of 15-, 20-, or 50-amp power, with these limits governing how much electricity you have to work with at any given moment. Easy, right?

Generators and Inverters

Both generators and inverters work when void of hookups. Both help run larger appliances, and both have their limits. A small generator or inverter producing 3,000 watts of electricity (check the decal or owner's manual for the model's rating) will struggle like a Driver's Ed student at the Brickyard 400 to power a number of power-hungry appliances all running at once. Get a larger unit if your plans call for hot-and-heavy power usage.

Drain in Vain

A battery rated for 100 amp hours means just that. Assuming it's at full strength, it will provide 100 hours of service at one amp per hour. Of course, nobody uses just *one* amp. Most monitor panels update users as to their battery's approximate status, or you can do a little simple math to gauge how long it can go. I'll bet you were hoping for a chance to demonstrate your mathematical acumen, right? Add all devices that will be utilized and multiply that by the number of hours that each device will be used. Leave a little extra room for current "leaks" or "drain" that can and will occur, a sort of electrical embezzlement. This number gives you an idea of how long your fully

Pull Over

Leaving even the tiniest exterior compartment light on can slowly drain a battery over time. Making sure there are no unknown battery drains is important to keeping the charge at respectable levels. Periodically inspect the entire RV, both inside and out, to see if there is any unbeknownst battery drain going on.

charged battery can go until it begins to cry out for help. Sure signs of fading include dimming lights and a grumbling water pump.

Keeping batteries charged is a top priority when away from shore power. Driving is the easiest way to recharge all batteries. In drastic cases, it may take a few hours behind the wheel to bring the automotive and coach batteries back from the dead. For most people with schedules of driving one day and camping the next, you already have a good system of depleting and recharging. Connecting to shore power also energizes a depleted system, as well as running the generator for at least 30 minutes every so often.

Solar Power

Solar power, or photovoltaics, provides a legitimate means to keeping RV batteries charged and appliances humming. In this case, energy from the sun is trapped in solar panels affixed to the roof of the RV and converted into DC power. The more solar panels, the more watts produced. A voltage regulator automatically monitors things, making sure the 12-volt battery is charged but not overcharged. If your RV is equipped with an inverter, the 12-volt DC is transformed for use in the 120-volt equipment, meaning you might not have to run the generator except usually for the largest of appliances (for example, the air conditioner). This is especially nice when it's just a cup of hot coffee you're after, and it is not really worth the effort of warming up the generator or taxing the inverter. Several companies sell all-inclusive kits, with everything needed to get started.

Pull Over

Not all deep-cycle batteries are compatible with solar energy. Be sure your existing batteries are equipped to handle the charge before investing in an expensive series of panels. Fortunately, more and more battery manufacturers are producing versions to support solar applications.

Solar energy is quiet, virtually maintenance-free, and can last and last and last. True, the less sunlight, the less power, but panels trap energy even on overcast days—even when covered in snow. Besides, you didn't take up RVing to hang around the Midwest in December, did you, so you're probably not going to struggle to find Ole Sol very often. Starter kits (without inverter and deep-cycle batteries) run between $300 and $1,000. A 20-year warranty is not unusual. The sunlight—for now, anyway—is free.

Blackout!

I knew I shouldn't have started up my 120-volt chainsaw, you say to yourself just moments after the RV goes dark. You've tripped the breaker. Now what? Immediately turn off all 120-volt AC devices that were in operation. Now to find the problem. It may be the 30-amp breaker at the campsite pedestal, but it's most likely the main 30-amp circuit breaker in the coach that trips. Check them both and reset the tripped breaker (just like at home) to get back on track. You've exceeded your RV's limits, and you might want to find out why. If you're not sure why this happened, re-calculate your amp/watt numbers. Perhaps your wife sneakily plugged in the curling iron, skewing the numbers slightly. It won't take long before you know your limits and learn not to exceed them.

Important Add-Ons

Here are some suggestions for useful accessories to add safety and convenience to your electrical systems.

Extra Shoreline Power Cord

All new RV purchases come with a 30- or 50-amp shoreline power cord for hooking up to 120-volt electricity at the campsite or wherever. Unfortunately, it never seems to be long enough, particularly when asked to snake around the picnic table, under the lawn chairs, around the maple tree, and to the electrical outlet 25 feet away. It's a good idea to make sure you have 50 feet of cord, in two cords of 25 feet each.

Pull Over

Not all shoreline cord is created equal. Use only types of the heavy-duty RV persuasion, made specifically for the rigors of outdoor use. Be sure to match any additional cord's amperage with that of the original (for example, 30-amp with 30-amp). Choose cords with bright colors to avoid tripping over them when walking around the campsite at night.

Surge Protectors

When plugged into a campsite's electrical supply, the system is always at the mercy of potential power spikes and surges. Lightning, faulty wiring at the pedestal outlet, and an overtaxed campground can all contribute to a shocking experience for your RV's sensitive components. Spend a little money for a high-grade surge protector, one with the ability to shut down an incoming power flux before any damage is done.

Polarity Tester

Such a device is cheap insurance against a faulty or potentially dangerous electrical campsite hookup. A polarity tester plugs into a 120-volt AC receptacle and tracks the three legs—hot, neutral, and ground. If all three wires are in the right place, the correct LEDs will light up. If any two are reversed or open, the telltale indicators will reveal the problem. What this means for RVers is that if the polarity tester doesn't like the outlet, avoid it. Consider this a handy and inexpensive necessity before plugging into the campground pedestal.

Voltage Meter

A good, accurate digital voltage meter, or voltmeter, is a nice item to have around. Useful for measuring the AC voltage at the campsite's electrical pedestal, this device helps travelers avoid subpar voltage situations, which are damaging to appliances, particularly the roof-top air conditioner. Anything near 120 volts is okay. Too high (above 130 volts) or low (below 105 volts) and it's best to ask the campground owner for another site. Don't leave home without one.

Ammeter

This handheld device measures your RV's total power draw, in amps. Want to know just how many amps all your onboard equipment is using? An ammeter will tell you, although its $150 to $200 is a pricey alternative to tripping the occasional breaker.

The Least You Need to Know

- An RV relies on three distinct electric systems: engine power, coach power, and shore power. The engine and coach systems are responsible for 12-volt DC equipment; shore power, typically harnessed by plugging into a campsite's electrical outlet or produced via generator or inverter, powers 120-volt appliances.
- Like your home, an RV has its electrical limits, based on the electrical needs of the RV's equipment and how much electricity is available, either stored in the batteries or generated through shore power.
- Electrical hookups offered at campgrounds vary, but include 15-, 20-, 30-, or 50-amp service. Consider this number the limit for your RV's electrical consumption. Most RVs come equipped with a 30-amp shoreline cord; larger rigs feature a 50-amp cord. An adapter may be required to fit outlets of greater or lesser ampages.
- Devices such as generators, solar power systems, and inverters are capable of creating or transforming electricity to your RV's batteries while you're away from a typical energy source. Otherwise, utilize shore power, found at campgrounds, for a constant flow of electricity.

Chapter 11

LP Systems

In This Chapter

- LP gas (propane) as a power source
- Refilling, safety, and operating tips
- Controlling the refrigerator, heat, and cooking functions

Like electricity, your RV's LP system is a very good thing, especially when you know how to wield it. Without LP gas there to work its magic, you and your crew would be mostly out of luck come mealtime, with the burners and oven sitting there in a most useless fashion. When the temperature dips, the thermostat would be powerless to stop it. And forget about that hot shower you relish every morning; that's gone, too. LP is the key behind much of an RV's better functions. With that said, it's important to understand how and why it works, so you're never left out in the cold.

LP: It's a Gas

There's no real mystery to LP (liquefied petroleum), otherwise known as propane. Like Jumping Jack Flash, it's a gas, gas, gas—but it doesn't start off that way. LP is sold in liquid form and stored in a container (or two) outside the RV. Once released, the vapor trapped inside the tanks works its way through the lines to fuel components onboard. LP gas is inexpensive to buy, clean-burning, fuel-efficient, and relied upon by each and every RV on the road today. Like its fellow electrical system, LP gas is the wind beneath the proverbial wings of many of the wouldn't-want-to-live-without-it stuff onboard. However, unlike electricity, sewer, and fresh water, you can't "hook up" to LP at a campsite. Sorry, it must be stored in containers, or tanks, and carried with you. When it's empty, fill it up, and continue on your merry way.

When you think propane, think heat. Love your gas grill working wonders out on the patio? Good, because it provides the perfect working example of the role of LP gas as it relates to life aboard your RV. Check it out the next time you throw a few T-bones on the grill or that mango-encrusted halibut that gets the neighborhood all a-flutter. LP gas, stored in a small tank, meanders up through the supply line to fuel the burning flame beneath that culinary delight. LP gas + flame = a steady heat source. This is an RV's propane system in a nutshell. Unfortunately, for us grilling purists, there are no charcoal-burning RV's in existence ... yet.

Here are the LP appliances onboard your RV:

- Refrigerator (runs off electric, too)
- Furnace
- Range
- Oven
- Water heater (also electric on some models)

The following is a rundown of each LP appliance and how to make it sing.

Refrigerator Madness

Since the RV's refrigerator is the one appliance that necessitates constant operation (unless you want green mayonnaise), newer models are made to be powered by multiple sources, namely 12-volt, 120-volt, and LP gas. A digital mode selector enables owners to switch among the three settings easily; just press a button to make the change. You'll probably find yourself splitting time among each power source, depending on the situations. Or just lay back and let the fridge auto-select (a nifty new feature) do all the work for you. A pre-set priority list switches from 120-volt, LP gas, and 12-volt. (The engine must be running for the 12-volt selection.)

One for the Road

Absorption refrigerators must be level to work properly. The complex mix of hydrogen, ammonia, and water within utilized for the cooling process mustn't be allowed to settle in one end or the other, which risks damage and/or sub-par cooling. Some RVers mount a bubble level when parked to know for sure that their fridge is on the up-and-up. Even on unlevel terrain, the refrigerator works fine when driving, thanks to the rocking motion that adequately moves the fluids back and forth.

Refrigerators have high-end versions, boasting double doors, 10-cubic-feet of storage, and ice maker thrown in just for kicks. An older RV may "only" be capable of delivering a bi-modal power source (usually, propane and 120-volt). On the smaller end, as observed in pop-ups and truck campers, the fridge probably resembles a dorm-room-size model that held bottles of … soft drinks (yeah, right) during your beloved college days.

Mode-Us Operate-Us

Here's a few tips for selecting the proper refrigerator mode. Use the 12-volt electricity, created in abundance by the constantly recharging automotive and coach batteries (thanks, alternator) when heading down the road. Twelve-volt can drain the batteries quickly when parked, however, so switch to one of the other power sources as soon as the destination is reached. If camped away from shore power, conserve the batteries and switch to the propane mode. Otherwise, go with the 120-volt source when plugged in at the local campground, which is free and provides virtually limitless amounts of electricity.

The Heat Is On

Camped in Florida, you needn't worry about staying warm. Mother Nature takes care of that. In places like the Midwest, however, it's a nine-month source of anxiety. Believe me, if you do any type of traveling at all, you're gonna get chilly from time to time. Thankfully, RVs are armed with a heating system to keep you from scurrying to the closest motel.

Two things determine the comfort level onboard during slipping temps: the power and efficiency of your heating system (measured in BTUs) and the quality of your insulation. You can't do much about the latter (although insulation package upgrades are sometimes offered), so it's good to know how the heating system works when it's cold outside. And yes, your mother was right—put on a sweater and keep the door closed. What, were you born in a barn?

Use the Force

Most RVs rely on a forced-air furnace, which is just a fancy way to say an onboard furnace that uses a fan to funnel warm air through a series of ducts. The furnace is a true team effort between the electrical and LP systems; the furnace itself runs off propane, controlled by a thermostat, while the coach's 12-volt battery powers the fans or blower. When a chill is in the air, go to the thermostat, turn it on, set the temperature, and wait for the warm winds to heat things up. You'll need LP gas in the container to make this go and enough 12-volt battery power for the fans to do their job.

Pull Over

As mentioned, catalytic heaters utilize oxygen—the same as you do. Set portable models near an opened window, providing a steady source of oxygen for both you and it. They do not work like a space heater, rather, an air-gobbling device that must be specially treated. Wall-mounted versions should be vented to the outside, eliminating this concern. However, make sure the vent is clean and free from blockage.

Catalytic Heaters

You won't see many of these installed in new RVs, so if you're smitten with catalytic heat, you'll have to add a portable version yourself. Wall-mounted units (on older models) tap into the propane supply; portables are BYOP (bring your own propane), secured in a small container. Simply defined, catalytic heaters utilize a mix of propane and oxygen to create heat. With that said, it's imperative models are run near an open window to provide a steady supply of oxygen. Otherwise, it might take yours. While many swear by them, I'm a little more cautious. Anything that relies on oxygen for its livelihood besides me, my family, and a few house plants makes me a little nervous—especially since there are other viable sources of heat out there.

You're in Hot Water

Hydronic heat uses water instead of air for radiant and semi-convected heat. This heat source is still fairly rare, as only the big boys have them due to their high costs and effects on vehicle weight.

Spaced Out

If the furnace is weak, the night is freezing, or you just have ice water in your veins, feel free to plug in a space heater. This is especially nice when your sleepwalking spouse makes off with all the blankets. True, it won't defrost the entire vehicle, but a well-aimed model can keep you plenty warm and save on LP costs. Space heaters should never be left unattended.

Home on the Range

It's lunchtime and the natives are restless. Surely, there's nothing better than cooking over a campfire, but fancier meals (like mac 'n' cheese!) benefit from the sweet precision of the RV's range. Expect anywhere from two to four gas burners on most decent-size RVs, all propane-reliant, and similar to those found at home. Turn the cooking dial to release the gas, light the flame, and you're in business. Otherwise, the stoic pilot light burns brightly, eliminating the need for a light. Expect to see newer versions equipped with piezzo ingnitors, separate dials that do the lighting work for you. In these cases, turn on the desired burner(s), allow the gas to flow, and crank the ignitor's dial to create the spark. Now you're cookin'.

One in the Oven

You might toil cooking a 25-pound Thanksgiving bird, but an RV oven works well with most creations. Again, there's nothing too out of the ordinary here to get going. Locate the pilot light (inside, and usually at the bottom center of the oven). Turn the oven dial to pilot light, strike a match, and fire it up. Select the appropriate heat setting and get going. Check the manual if the pilot's location proves elusive. Piezzo ignitors can be found on some ovens as well.

Road Scholar

A constantly burning pilot light is an unnecessary waste of propane. Extinguish them when not needed to spare you unnecessary LP costs. They also launch onboard temperatures during the hot summer months, so it's best to keep the flame going only during mealtime.

Water Heater

LP-fueled with push-button activation, the water heater is the difference between a warm shower and a cold one. An electronic ignition switch (or DSI, direct spark ignition) is common, saving you a trip outside with a lighter. Expect your 6- or 10-gallon water heater (the only sizes available) to be fully heated within 30 to 45 minutes. Leave this on when camped or just activate when needed.

Some water heaters are LP/120-volt electric, giving you a couple of options when washing the pooch. (Propane seems to do a faster job warming things up, however.) Some water heaters found on motorhomes may boast a motor-aid feature, with hoses running from the engine through the water heater and back. In this setup, hot engine water is utilized to heat the water in the tank, resulting in hot water just as soon as you arrive and shut off the engine.

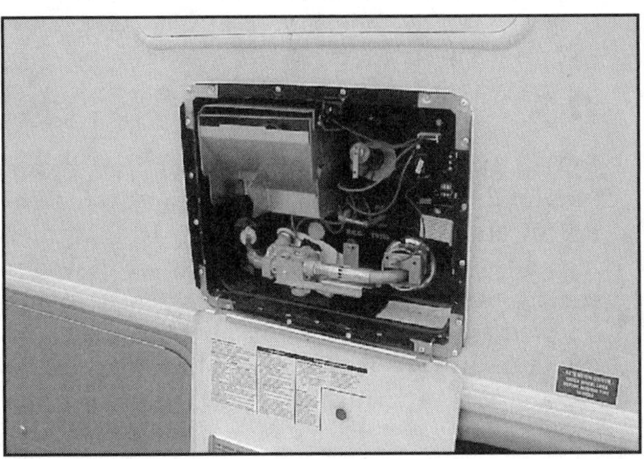

A typical RV water heater, mounted on the outside but controlled on the inside.

RVocabulary

As the supply of LP gas within the containers starts to diminish, the pressure with which it's dispensed could decrease as well. This is the reason behind a pressure **regulator,** to maintain a steady level of LP gas through the lines at all times.

Pull Over

LP containers are mounted horizontally (ASME) or vertically (DOT) for a reason. Re-installing the tanks in a different position can cause the liquid LP (instead of their vapors) to pour into the lines, creating a dangerous situation onboard. The same rule should be honored during transport and re-filling. Keep the containers in the same position as they are mounted at all times.

LP Containers

Let's start our discussion of how the LP system works at the heart of the matter: the LP container(s) themselves. Containers are always stored outside and vary in size and shape on the type matched to the RV. Larger vehicles will probably offer two containers, with larger capacities to match. (See "Typical Specs" in Chapters 4, "The World of Motorized RVs," and 5, "The World of Towables," for a range of sizes per RV.) In these cases, the first one automatically switches over to the secondary container when it runs out of LP.

Turning the tank's valve to the open position unleashes the flow of propane through the lines of the coach and to the appliances it needs to fuel (see the list earlier in the chapter). Otherwise, the valve should remain closed, or in the off position, during travel. A *regulator* maintains the proper pressure of gas running through the lines, so everything inside keeps firing away without a hitch.

Container Types

Not all RVs share the same kind of containers. There are two types used in the RV industry: DOT and ASME. Who cares, right? It's just a lousy container. Ah, not true. The distinction is significant, affecting how they are filled, stored, and handled. It's prudent to learn the differences between the two because there might be a quiz later.

DOT

DOT (Department of Transportation) tanks are usually mounted vertically and installed most often on fold-down campers, truck campers, and travel trailers, both big and small. In most cases, tanks are mounted to the trailer's tongue. DOT containers can usually be unscrewed and removed, enjoying the benefit of taking the tanks in for a refill without having to bring the whole RV along with you.

A pair of DOT LP gas containers, which stores the fuel responsible for much of an RV's heating and cooking elements.

ASME

Nope, the American Society of Magazine Editors isn't in the propane business. The American Society of Mechanical Engineers, now that's more like it. ASME containers are always affixed horizontally, within an accessible exterior storage compartment of most motorhomes and usually located in a front storage area under the gooseneck of fifth-wheel trailers.

An ASME LP gas container, affixed horizontally to the RV.

Who Needs a Refill?

Your RV's LP gas container(s) will periodically (shock!) run empty. This is a finite resource, after all, and unlike the ice cube trays in the freezer, you're definitely going to want to refill them. Of course, Murphy's Law dictates this will occur in the middle of the night when it's cold outside or about a half-hour after you put the roast in the oven. Expect to use a couple of gallons per week during warm weather; more during colder climes, when the furnace is working overtime. This, however, is just an approximate. A gauge on the cylinder lets you know when the supply is running low.

The nice thing about propane is that it's cheap and available all over the place. Most campgrounds sell it, as do propane dealers and outlets, hardware stores, and some service stations. Since you must be licensed to dispense the stuff, all the consumer needs to do is just sit back and let the attendant handle it. It's still a good idea to know a little something about it, just to look smart.

What Do I Do?

Okay, here's a job for you prior to filling up. Extinguish all pilot lights—water heater, stove, and range (if so equipped). Turn off all LP appliances, including the furnace, and switch the refrigerator to 12- or 120-volt—anything but the propane setting. Finally, make sure the container's valve is in the off or closed position. And please, don't smoke.

Gas Crisis

It's not unusual for some LP appliances to act a little goofy after a new batch of propane is added or after periods of dormancy. Your refrigerator might struggle to switch over to the propane mode; the water heater may simply mock you. The usual culprit is air trapped inside the lines, caused by a left-open container valve in most cases. Turn on the stove burners to purge the lines, then attempt to light each one. This is an easy way to correct the problem. It might take a few moments, but they'll eventually ignite, signaling the triumphant return of your LP system.

If it fails to light, double-check the system. Is the valve open far enough to release an adequate supply of gas into the lines? Do you have enough propane in the container? During one deep-woods pilgrimage, I was minutes away from fleeing back to town when I couldn't get the furnace to kick on. It was 30°F outside and falling fast. The crew had murderous looks in their eyes for me and the $100K motorhome with everything but heat. And then I remembered, oh yes, I actually have to turn the valve on, don't I? Not one of my better days.

Safety First

Like gasoline, propane is highly flammable, which is what makes it such a desirable fuel source. Think of it like the Godfather—treat it with respect and it will do you plenty of favors. Capeche? Care must be taken not only when replenishing the supply, but while driving down the road minding your own business. Learn these few rules and learn them well.

Handling the Tanks

As mentioned before, the biggest mistake is manhandling the containers like someone out of the World Wrestling Federation. Don't jostle or invert containers when removing or installing them before, during, or after a refill. This is really only the case for removable types, which some folks treat like a sack of potatoes. Again, vertical containers should stay vertical; horizontal should stay horizontal at all times. Shaking, improper mounting, and general mistreatment might invert the liquid supply, which should rest at the bottom of the tank. Always treat tanks with care.

LP tanks are located outside for a reason: the gas and subsequent vapors are harmful in the event of a leak and better left outside. Never bring containers inside the RV or store in unventilated areas.

Happy Trails

Here are a few propane-related steps to add into your pretrip routine:

Pretrip LP Precautions

- ❑ Turn off all LP appliances.
- ❑ Switch the refrigerator to 12-volt, 120-volt, or leave it off. (The unit's insulation will keep it cool for a reasonable length of time, provided the door remains closed.)
- ❑ Extinguish all pilot lights.
- ❑ Close valve on all tanks to "off" position.
- ❑ Don't use the furnace to warm the RV in transit.

Consider an onboard LP detector a true "must-have." Fortunately, it's standard equipment on all new RVs and common on older models as well. Don't look to the ceiling for its locations, rather the baseboards. LP gas is heavy, staying close to the floor, exactly where the detector should be. Check it often, and replace batteries as needed.

Pull Over

Traveling with container valve(s) open is a bad idea. In the case of an accident or fire, propane-filled lines won't help the situation very much. In fact, the results could be disastrous. Make doubly sure the containers are closed before pulling into a gas station, and turn off all LP appliances as well.

That Rotten Smell

Some describe it as rotten eggs, others say it's more like onions or garlic. In either case it's an odd smell since you're only making peanut butter and jelly sandwiches. Such an odor signifies a gas leak. Put down the white bread, it's time to vacate. Leave the coach immediately, propping the door open behind you to air things out. Again, smoking or any spark-producing activity is a no-no. Don't return until the RV is aired out completely. Shut off the LP valve, extinguish pilot lights, and keep LP appliances turned off until a trained service professional finds the source of the problem.

The nasty smell was added to make the naturally odorless LP gas detectable for situations like these. Every coach also should have an LP gas detector as standard equipment, blasting an alarm when it senses trouble. You'll find such devices low to the floor, which is where the heavy gas likes to linger. Check this and other alarms often to guarantee they're in working order. More on this in Chapter 20, "Playin' It Safe."

The Least You Need to Know

- LP gas, or propane, is a liquid fuel source, with gas vapors delivering fuel to your RV's furnace, stove, oven, water heater, and refrigerator. Exterior containers are mounted, supplying onboard appliances through a series of gas lines.
- Propane powers many of the appliances onboard. Newer refrigerators usually offer tri-modular settings, meaning they can be powered by 12-volt, 120-volt, or propane. A forced-air furnace uses a fan to circulate the heated air through ducts inside the coach. Operating range, oven, and water heater is similar to those at home, requiring manual lighting or electronic ignition of pilot lights.
- For safety reasons, propane containers should be turned off while in transit. Extinguish all pilot lights and discontinue the use of LP appliances. Handle tanks with care, always keeping them in the same position they were mounted in to avoid inverting the liquid and vapors inside.

Chapter 12

Plumbing Systems

In This Chapter

- Enjoying your fresh water supply
- Dumping holding tanks
- Maintaining the various water systems

It isn't enough that a bed, electricity, heat, air conditioning, and a working kitchen are all at your disposal, but some crazy engineer began installing water systems as well. Just think, a cool drink of agua on a hot day. Brushing your teeth without that walk to the campground's bathroom. A warm shower, water for cooking, a private bathroom—all onboard and without needing a degree from your local community college to operate. Hooray, clean dishes for everybody!

Whether camped at the local state park or private campground, heading down the interstate, or parked in a remote stretch of forest, most every recreational vehicle can deliver a healthy supply of fresh water, no matter where you are. Like the old saying goes, there's water, water everywhere—and most of it fit to drink. Impossible? Too good to be true? Far from it. And that's just the tip of the proverbial iceberg in terms of the complex water systems onboard your RV.

But this chapter is about more than just turning the faucet and filling your Batman mug. It's about using the self-sufficient capability of an RV to your advantage and understanding the complex (but easy-to-use) series of fresh and wastewater systems.

On top of that, it's also nice to have an answer for junior when he asks where the water comes from. So prepare the *Nautilus,* Captain Nemo. The exploration of your RV's water systems awaits.

Water World

Essentially, the watery world onboard an RV isn't much different than life at home. Hot and cold water pour from faucets, the showerhead delivers a steady stream every morning, toilets flush, and waiting drains are there to send it all away. The main difference, however, is that 1) unless connected to a constant source, your fresh water supply is finite and must be periodically refilled; and 2) used water, or wastewater, is collected in tanks and must be emptied.

All but the smallest recreational vehicles come with onboard plumbing and holding tanks to facilitate all of these functions, which can be divided into two basic systems: fresh water and wastewater. Let's take a closer look at each.

Fresh Water System

The fresh water system consists of all faucets, including sinks and showers (both inside and out), as well as the water heater and the toilet's water level. As the name implies, the fresh water onboard is the good stuff, ready for drinking, cooking, cleaning, or for loading up the squirt gun and having it out with a grumpy co-pilot.

Pull Over

Traveling through Mexico or South America is an exciting odyssey for some. However, many RVers can attest to the old traveler's tale about not drinking the water. If your itinerary sends you south of the border, take steps to safeguard your water supply. Rely on bottled water for drinking, cooking, and brushing teeth. Keep your mouth closed during showers. Avoid ice.

Water Sources

Since the world is comprised of 70 percent water, finding an adequate supply for fill-ups isn't too much of a challenge. (However, leave the saltwater to the tropical fish.) Fresh water is either supplied via a water inlet (most readily available as part of a campsite hookup) or stored in your RV's fresh water storage tanks, available for when you need it. Although the water in both cases is basically the same, the manner in which each is accessed as well as its limitations are different.

Tapping into a campsite's fresh water hookup means a sweet, uninterrupted flow of H_2O. It's just like the electrical hookups discussed in Chapter 10, "Electrical Systems"—as long as you're connected, it's always on, with RVers enjoying a steady, uninterrupted flow. Hook up to the water outlet outside your house for the same groovy sensation.

Connecting to fresh water is facilitated through a special drinking water hose (supplied by you), running from the campsite's water outlet to the RV's water inlet, which is known and usually labeled as the city-water hookup and found on the driver's side of the vehicle. To activate, simply twist the campsite's faucet to start the flow. All the water faucets inside are now ready to go.

Hose Job

When it comes to the fresh water supply, a hose is most definitely *not* a hose. Don't use the same garden variety you use to water the lawn to connect to and from your RV; only a specially labeled and manufactured "drinking water" version, designed for RVers, will do. Usually white and available in a variety of lengths, these hoses are made to better protect the drinking water while abolishing that stubborn rubbery taste.

Pull Over

How nice, the campsite comes with its own fresh water hose. I'll just use that one. Skip it. Remember, the hose is the conduit for the water you'll be drinking, showering in, and brushing your teeth with. Is the hose clean? Has it been used only for fresh water? Relying on your own equipment guarantees a source you can trust. Heard of the 25-foot rule? A single 25-foot water hose is not always long enough; a 50-foot one is overkill and a tripping hazard. Carrying two attachable 25-foot hoses is considered the best defense against coming up short when attempting to reach an elusive water outlet, which can sometimes be a ways away.

Treat the drinking water hose with the respect it deserves as the pipeline of your fresh water supply. Store it in a clean, dry place. Connect both ends together when not in use to seal the inside against dirt and debris. Storing it in a plastic bag adds yet another layer of protection, especially if you're of the Felix Unger mindset in regards to cleanliness. A new hose should be purchased at the first sign of trouble.

Handling the Pressure

Not all water pressure was created equal. Surely, you've noticed this fact at home when the pressure dips when Grandma decides to do the dishes while you're taking a shower. Unfortunately, water pressure can be unpredictable, a fact of life for RVers relying on a campground's reserve. While too little pressure can be annoying, too much can be problematic for the plastic piping throughout the vehicle. It may seem hard to believe (someone call Ripley's!), but that innocent-looking water valve is capable of unleashing potentially damaging force.

RVocabulary

A **water pressure regulator** combats the elusive and sometimes volatile water pressure when connected to water hookups. Attaching to the drinking water hose to regulate water flow into the RV, such devices help protect delicate piping onboard. The item is relatively inexpensive and available at most RV stores.

Just as a surge protector squashes electrical spikes, a *water pressure regulator* overrides dramatic changes in pressure to establish a steadier stream. The cost is about ten bucks for this small device that runs interference between the water outlet and the end of the hose.

Tastes Great, Less Filling

Many RVers tap into a fresh water supply and never give it another thought. Water is water. Open up the tap and take what's coming to ya. I, on the other hand, take a more cautious approach, preferring a diet free of as much pesticides, bacteria, and lousy-tasting water as I can. Again, it's up to you.

If water purity is a concern, filters are available for both the inside faucets and exterior connections. Even the most deluxe filters and filtration systems, with promises of water quality rarely seen since the times of melting glaciers, are usually fairly inexpensive. But expect to pay considerably less for a run-of-the-mill variety. Such filtering devices are good insurance in an overly polluted world.

One for the Road

You turn on the shower and get only a trickle. A few older campgrounds with antiquated pipes may underachieve in terms of delivering the necessary pressure to your shower or faucets. This can easily occur at newer parks, too, during times when everyone in the park is scrubbing up at the same time (morning, for instance). The best strategy is to wait it out.

Going to the Store

Sailing down the road and dying of thirst? Don't like the looks of the campground's water supply? Parked in the boonies and desperately need to boil water for spaghetti? In any of these situations, water is available by tapping into your very own ready water supply, compliments of the fresh water storage tank. The name says it all—the tank acts as a sort of giant canteen for the passengers onboard. Unlike the limitless supply accomplished by connecting to a fresh water source at the campsite, carrying your own reserve has its limits. Once you consume the last drop, it's time for a refill, best facilitated at the campground, a backyard faucet, or another safe and sanitary source.

An RV's fresh water–holding capacity, like most things, varies from unit to unit, vehicle class to vehicle class. A high-end motorhome or fifth-wheel trailer can reach 100 gallons, granting a more than reasonable period of time between fill-ups. Smaller fold-downs or camper vans require more diligent visits to the water fairy, with each probably storing less than 20 gallons total. Review the "Typical Specs" section of each kind of RV in Chapters 4, "The World of Motorized RVs," and 5, "The World of Towables," for a range of fresh water storage tank sizes.

Fill 'Er Up

"Honey, did you use up the last of the fresh water?" your spouse slyly accuses. Although it's a slightly more serious charge than who ate the last of the Ben & Jerry's, replenishing the supply isn't too challenging. Fresh water is pretty common at most any campsite, the in-laws' house, rest stops, some gas stations, and the like. In the meantime, you can always use bottled water for drinking or shower at the campground's facilities, so it's not the end of the world if you run out.

The connection to the fresh water storage tank varies among the types of RVs. Most will have a simple gravity fill on the side of the vehicle, allowing for a simple attachment of the hose. You're now ready to fill. (Remember, this is a different inlet than what you use for the water hookups.) Once full, the water simply overflows down the side, signaling that your job is complete. Other larger units and high-end coaches might employ a "quick fill" valve that the owner opens while connected to city water, thus filling the tank. This is certainly a convenient alternative to reconnecting the hose directly to the fresh water tank.

Road Scholar

All this talk of water cleanliness making you worry? It's still true that quality water is not the exception in North America, it's the norm. But why take chances? A modestly priced water filter should eliminate most concerns. Other folks stock the fridge with bottled water, a bulky albeit comforting addition to any packing list.

Pumping Up

Possessing a full tank of water means you're only halfway there to a tall glass of refreshment. Hah, I knew it couldn't be that easy, you say. Actually, it's easier. A 12-volt *water pump,* installed in all RVs with a built-in fresh water system, must first be activated to propel the water up through the pipes in a gravity-defying feat. You must use a pump whenever taking water from the fresh water tank; it's not needed when hooked up to an outside water system, with its own inherent water pressure. Switch the pump to the "On" position prior to showering, washing hands, or whatever watery function needed. Better yet, just leave it activated whenever you're around, guaranteeing water will always circulate to its appointed rounds. Leaving the pump on is especially helpful when water needs are at their greatest, such as a busy night of washing dishes, the dog, and muddy preschoolers.

RVocabulary

A **water pump** is the difference between carrying fresh water and actually dispensing it. Flip the water pump to "on" and the 12-volt appliance forces water from the fresh-water storage compartment up through the twists and turns of your RV's plumbing, to the faucets, shower, and marine-style toilet—wherever it's needed. A water pump is found on all RVs with a fresh water system and isn't needed when connected to a pressurized water source.

Pull Over

Turn off the pump whenever you leave the RV. In the event of a leak or watery mishap while you're away, the pump will keep chugging along, doing its job of pushing water through the lines. Only this time, the workaholic pump will send water through the leak, onto the floor, causing a slippery mess. Unnecessary use of the pump also wastes energy, a big no-no especially when relying on finite battery power.

The water pump is usually found in a fairly conspicuous place, often near the kitchen. After a few trips, you should begin to decipher the pump's status by listening for changes in its sounds, kind of like distinguishing between the various cries of a newborn. But unlike junior, the pump won't keep you up at night or spit up on your favorite shirt. A steady hum signals that the pump is activated and functioning correctly. Hiccup-like patterns probably occur as a result of not turning a faucet off completely. Changes in tone occur as the fresh water levels sink, reaching a more frantic pace once the tank nears empty. And you thought you and your RV never talked anymore?

The RV's coach battery is responsible for powering the 12-volt pump, an act that will slowly drain the deep-cycle battery over time. That is, unless you're connected to shore power (campsite electrical outlet, generator, or inverter), in which case, there's probably enough power to go around. Revisit Chapter 10 if you have no idea what I'm talking about.

Again, it is not necessary to activate the water pump when connected to an outside water source.

Avoiding the Cold Shoulder

Although you've probably been told to go take a cold shower from time to time, it's not really something you want to make a habit of. (I speak from experience.) A water heater is the difference between a warm shower and the more displeasing, icy variety. Thankfully, most every RV has one.

Available in either 6- or 10-gallon capacities, most water heaters are large enough to warm a reasonable-length shower—but don't push it. You might need to hustle some with hair full of suds to avoid a chilly reception. This is especially true if morning rituals include a soapy rendition of *The Phantom of the Opera*. It may be a strange adjustment, not having the enormous residential water heaters you've grown used to at home, but you'll get used to it. And so will your rubber ducky.

A showerhead equipped with an on/off switch is the easiest way to conserve water—and hot water, to boot. Your RV may or may not have one, but never fear, showerheads are easy add-ons found in the aftermarket.

A flip of the water heater's switch, or lighting the pilot flame, is all it takes to get things heated up. Water heaters most often run on LP gas, but electric/LP models are becoming more common. It's then just a matter of allowing enough advance time to let the heater do its thing. An hour's head start will suffice to heat the 10-gallon models. Like the water pump, some folks leave the water heater on whenever they're around, creating a warm water reserve at all times. After all, you never know when you might want to shower, need warm water for dishes, or whatever. Again, this taxes your resources, in the form of propane (although at a minimal rate), so keep that in mind. We'll talk more about conserving water and propane in Chapter 17, "Roughin' It." As with most things, it's a good idea to shut it off when leaving the RV for extended periods.

Pull Over

The water heater must be allowed to fill up with water prior to activation. Failure to do so could harm the unit. Turn on the hot water faucets before turning the heater on. A spurting or foamy discharge from the pipes signals that it's not yet filled; a free-flowing water supply suggests the heater is sufficiently topped off and ready to light.

Bathroom Talk

Some mothers insist that if you're going to talk bathroom talk, then go in the bathroom. It's for that reason that I'm typing this chapter in the bathtub, so as not to offend any maternal sensibilities. All but the smallest fold-down campers and camper vans are outfitted with a marine-style toilet, similar to what's found on an airplane. Water levels and flushing are operated through floor pedals, a back lever, or a combination of the two.

Unlike the "head" at home, travelers can add to the existing water levels of the marine-style toilet via one of the pedals after each use. How much more is up to you, but remember that the water supply is limited, and all such wastewater must eventually be emptied from the black water tank. The basin should automatically fill with enough water to safely jettison waste materials throughout the pipes, so there's really no excuse to play with water levels. When not in use, there should be enough water to keep seals lubricated but not enough to spill out during transit.

Pull Over

Be especially careful about what goes into the RV's toilet. Just like a James Taylor song, they can be somewhat sensitive. As a rule, don't add anything to the basin besides, well, you know. Cigarettes, hygiene products, and Legos (don't ask) are no-nos. Rely on biodegradable toilet paper, which is more easily dissolved than regular kinds.

In the absence of a marine-style toilet, expect a small porta-potti in its place. Porta-potties function independent from your RV's plumbing. The water is manually filled; all waste materials are captured in its own basin and must be emptied. These are more common in small towables and Class Bs.

Wastewater Systems

The question still remains: Where does all this fresh water go, anyway? Down the drain and off into oblivion? Does a flush of the toilet dispatch waste straight to the landfill? Well, not exactly—but I'm sure some energetic engineer is working on that. In the case of the RV's plumbing system, the old saying is true: What goes in, must come out. The same is true with "used" fresh water, now suddenly transformed into "wastewater."

Waste water takes two distinctly different forms: gray water holding tanks and black water holding tanks. A look at each is provided next, as well as what to do with them.

One for the Road

Although we advise using the onboard monitor panel only as a guide, many RVers report wildly goofy readings coming from their black water holding tank. In-tank probes report the status of the RV's tanks, which can be corrupted by debris that has adhered to these sensors. A good cleaning should remedy the problem and restore mostly accurate readings.

When Good Water Goes Bad

Again, a self-sufficient RVer can go periods of time in his RV without requiring much assistance from the outside world. RVers can produce and store their own electricity, carry propane for heating, and, more specifically to this chapter, store their own fresh water and collect its remnants (wastewater) for later emptying.

As mentioned briefly in Chapter 3, "Where to Stay?" gray water is what empties down the drain from the faucets and shower. Black water is the water and material waste from your RV's marine-style toilet. A network of pipes delivers each to a specific holding tank, all the while keeping them oh so separate from the fresh water supply and piping. Gray water empties into the gray water holding tank; black water straight into the black water holding tank. When these tanks reach capacity, they must be emptied. Sounds reasonable, right?

RVers have a choice as to where and how they choose to empty the gray and black water tanks, but in either case, they *must* be emptied. Exactly when to empty these tanks depends on the holding capacities of each and your water usage. Review "Typical Specs" in Chapters 4 and 5 for a range of holding-tank capacities by RV.

Runnin' on Empty

For some, purging the holding tanks constitutes the "dark side" of RVing. But really, it's a fair trade-off for the perks of running water and your own private bathroom. As a young RV editor, I avoided the holding tanks on the RVs I took out like one would an angry loan shark after Super Bowl Sunday. I had many self-imposed rules onboard, but Rule #1, the absolute, nonnegotiable mandate of any trip, was "stay out of the bathroom."

Road Scholar

There's no way to sugarcoat it, dumping the tanks is a dirty business. With this in mind, I strongly recommend wearing rubber gloves when engaged in all sewer-related duties. Keep a box of disposable surgical gloves in an exterior compartment, along with a bottle of soap for washing up afterwards. Store the sewer hose in its own compartment to prevent possible contamination of other essentials. And be sure to keep it far away from your fresh water hose.

Emptying the tanks was definitely something I wanted to avoid. All bathroom functions were to be completed at the campground's facilities, the local McDonald's, or the quickie mart. I didn't care—anywhere but in the pristine quarters of the RV. We drank bottled water and made the nightly hike to the campground's bathroom to brush our teeth. Cooking with water was kept to an absolute minimum, which I

Pull Over

Monitor panels should be used as an approximation, not an exact science. There are those who feel they are historically inaccurate and that travelers should always "round up" when factoring in this data. In the case of holding tanks, its best not to wait until the tanks are completely full to avoid any unnecessary plumbing "back ups." Besides, why carry all that extra weight?

never let drain into the tanks for fear of having to later empty them. Rather, it was saved to put out the campfire. In fact, the gray and black water holding tanks would never see a drop, and therefore, no emptying was ever required. The problem was, I was shortchanging the RV experience for all of us, running around like a neurotic loon. You can dodge these tasks like I did or enjoy the full functionality of your vehicle. But here's how to empty the tanks.

Like a beagle barking to go out in the early dawn hours, your monitor panel will tell you when the tanks are nearing capacity. After a while, you'll just sort of know when it's time. In extreme cases, severely full tanks scream "no vacancy" when water refuses to drain. It's time to dump the tanks and do it now.

When it's time to purge the gray and black water holding tanks, RVers have two choices how: through a sewer hookup or at a dump station. The locations are different, but the process for each location is basically the same.

Sewer Hookups

Camping at a site offering a sewer hookup offers the chance to empty the tanks without the long lines of impatient RVers or a special trip to the dump station. The connecting task is performed through a sewer hose (yours), running from the singular sewer outlet underneath the RV to the in-ground sewer opening at the campsite. Be sure to stick the hose a good ways into the sewer opening to prevent it from slipping out unexpectedly.

One for the Road

Water and electric hookups are plainly visible and easy to find. Sewer outlets, on the other hand, may be more elusive since they're sometimes off by themselves at the corner of the campsite. Their in-ground location only complicates matters, occasionally hidden by tall grasses or piles of leaves. An appropriately marked metal cover or a twist-cap lets you know you've hit pay dirt.

You'll notice that the gray and black water holding tanks each have their own individual dump release valve. When pulled, the contents of the tank empties, running through the hose and down the sewer drain. Warning: Opening these valves without a sewer hookup and awaiting sewer hose causes the contents to pour out all over your campsite. I guarantee you won't make this mistake more than once (but try never to make it in the first place).

With a secure sewer connection (always double-check before dumping) and full tanks a-callin', it's time to dump. Follow this exact process every time for best results. Open the black water tank's valve first, allowing it to empty completely down the sewer drain. It's a good idea to give the toilet a couple of flushes here (more, if necessary) to clear out the tank with extra water to remove any accumulated materials. Close the black water tank's valve, and then pull the gray water's release, allowing it to empty out completely. Why this order? This method allows the gray water to push any accumulated heavier black water materials out through the hose. Remember, although there are two valves, the contents of each are going down the same sewer hose. Close the gray water valve. Congratulations. Empty tanks.

With a constant sewer hookup, why not just leave both tank valves open all the time, to empty each tank as you go? Certainly a fair and obvious question. Although empty tanks leave your RV light and lively, a *totally* empty gray or black water tank isn't really a good thing. Leaving both valves constantly open may drain all of the water while keeping materials behind. This can result in an odiferous situation and a costly tank repair if the build-up is large enough. Soap, dirt, and oil remains from showers and handwashings can cling to the tank walls and hose lining long after the liquid is gone. The same is true in the black water tank, although the materials in question are, well, different—but just as potentially damaging. In both cases, having a steady base of water in the holding tanks is a good thing.

Pull Over

Get in the habit of periodically inspecting your various hoses for damage and leaks. Replace as needed. Also double-check hookup connections (water, electric, sewer) every day. With all these cords and hoses lying around, the possibility that one may come unplugged or pulled out of place is a possibility.

Down in the Dumps

Dump stations are clearly marked, usually off by their lonesome at most campgrounds (both public and private), rest stops, RV stores, RV service facilities, and a few gas stations along the way. Most campgrounds offer this as a free service for guests, and may allow nonguest dumping, if you're in dire need, for a modest fee. True, dump stations are not the most pleasant spots on earth, but their availability is a godsend to travelers with bulging tanks.

It's always a good idea to visit the dump station to empty wastewater tanks before leaving the campground. Don't worry, it's not usually fenced in, as this photo shows.

In the absence of a sewer hookup, most travelers prefer to visit the dump station *before* hitting the road on the way to their next adventure. Again, good riddance to that extra weight. It's for this reason that you might wait in line for one, particularly on a Sunday afternoon, a popular checkout time at many campgrounds. Pay special attention to pull up to the dump station correctly, so the tanks match the corresponding side, just as you would match your fuel tanks to a gas pump. Also park close enough that the sewer hose can reach the sewer drain.

Pull Over

This may sound like an oxymoron, but make sure the dump station is clean before departing. Most offer a water hose for cleaning any spilled residue, to aim toward the sewer drain for disposal. Hoses are also there to wash hands and clean off sewer hoses, both good habits. Do *not* use this hose for drinking or to fill up your fresh water holding tanks, for obvious reasons.

Basically, the procedure is the same as the one outlined earlier. If you forget, instructions are usually posted somewhere near the dump station for a quick review. Grab your rubber gloves and locate the sewer opening at the dump station. You'll probably be able to slide the sewer drain's cap open with your foot. Stick one end of the sewer hose down the opening and attach the other end to the tank inlet underneath the RV. Release the black water tank valve until it's empty, as demonstrated by a slowing sound of the black water. Have the co-pilot flush the toilet (sans those dirty gloves!) a couple of times for an additional rinse of the black water tank.

Close the black water valve and pull the gray water's release to let those contents through. When empty, close its valve and disconnect the sewer hose from the RV. Hold the hose up high as you walk back towards the dump station, giving gravity a chance to drain any excess fluids down the drain. Give the sewer hose a quick wash with the dump station's hose (definitely don't use your own) and store it back in its own private compartment. Close the sewer inlet on the RV and slide back the drain cover. Tidy up the dump station if you've made a mess (the true purpose of the aforementioned affixed hose) and get out of Dodge.

Mr. Clean

Even the best-kept holding tanks must be routinely cleaned, for different reasons. Clean and sanitize the fresh water storage tank so your drinking water is bacteria-free and safe for drinking, cooking, and for making that scary gargle sound you do when brushing your teeth. While it's true that gray and black water tanks will never be "clean," a little preventative work eliminates clogs, bad smells, and potential repairs. Here are some ways to keep these tanks as nice as possible.

The best prevention is a periodic purge and cleaning of the fresh water tank. This is also a good idea before long periods of storage and when the current batch isn't your best. The best time for this is when fresh water levels are low. Either let the fresh water tank reach empty or find the tank's drain, usually a simple plastic drain cock at the side of the RV or a full-way gate valve that must be opened, and empty the tank. Most coaches ten years old and newer have two low-level drain valves, one each in the hot and cold lines, supposedly at their lowest point somewhere in the coach. Opening the low-level drain valves, the fresh water container valve, and the water heater drain will quickly empty all the fresh water from the system. Just be sure the city water is not connected and running, or you'll never finish the job.

With an empty (or near-empty) tank, concoct a bleach cocktail to rid the tank and pipes of mold and other evildoers. One cup's worth of bleach to every 15 gallons of water is a proven winner. Let the bleached water stand for a while, or better yet, take the RV out for a spin. The sloshing motion should add a little extra muscle to your sanitizing efforts and coat all those hard-to-reach areas within the tanks. Run the faucets, showerhead, and flush the toilet to clear out the pipes. Rinse the tank, refill, and repeat. Harder-hitting chemicals and cleaning agents are available in the aftermarket, making this chore somewhat easier.

Waste Not, Want Not

No matter how hard you try, the black and gray water tanks will never sparkle. However, taking steps to combat odors and sediment should make for more pleasant and less odiferous travels. Even the most diligent dumping practices create clogs and build-up over time, which must be removed. To do this, attach a "water wand" (found at RV supply stores) to the end of a hose to blast residue throughout the hidden areas of your black water tanks via the toilet. The safest way to protect and treat the holding tanks and to eliminate odors is to then use a nonchemical, enzyme-based product, preferably one that contains live bacteria. The live bacteria actually digest the odor-causing molecules and break down the solid waste. This type of bacteria was used after the Alaskan oil spill to help digest the oil and to aid in the cleanup efforts, so it's more than good enough to be used here.

Pull Over

Do not use bleach, ammonia, detergents, or soaps in the wastewater holding tanks. At one time, many different chemicals were formulated to mask odors and break down the solid materials. For many years, formaldehyde-based chemicals seemed to work the best. However, as technology progressed and the dangers of formaldehyde poisoning came to be understood, other options became a reality. Many RV campgrounds now prohibit the dumping of formaldehyde-laced tanks into their waste systems.

The Least You Need to Know

- An RV contains two different water systems, with two distinct purposes: fresh water and wastewater.
- RVers can connect to water hookups at the campground for a steady supply or carry it with them in the fresh water holding tank. An onboard water heater provides hot water. When relying on one's own reserves, a water pump must be activated to force the water up through the pipes.
- Wastewater comes in two forms: gray water (from sink and shower drains) and black water (water and materials from the toilet). Wastewater relies on a different network of plumbing, and each kind empties into its own holding tank. Tanks must be periodically emptied, either at a campsite with sewer hookups or at a dump station.
- Keeping tanks clean is important. Fresh water tanks should be occasionally drained and sanitized with bleach or specially made cleaners. An effort should be made to eliminate build-up in wastewater tanks through regular cleanings and additives to prevent smells and build-up.

Part 5

Your First Trip

Life on the open road is so close now you can almost smell it. It's now just a matter of fine-tuning your skills, which is exactly the aim of this section. The goal here is to prepare you for that first real trip—first of many, we hope. Since it's always best to begin in the beginning, learning how to pilot that motorhome or tow that trailer is the first order of business. We'll then turn our attention to the importance of weights (the RV's, not yours), how and what to pack, choosing the campground, as well as how to enjoy nights away from civilization—a.k.a. roughin' it.

Chapter 13

Towin' the Line

In This Chapter

- Matching tow vehicles to trailers and vice versa
- Towing trailers, fifth wheels, as well as secondary vehicles behind a motorhome
- Must-have accessories and operating tips

As you may have already decided, through reading the earlier chapters on the subject, perhaps a trailer is the best choice for your family right now. Whether it's the lower costs, variety of floor plans, available living space, or something else that struck your fancy, towable RVs offer many distinct and wonderful advantages. This chapter is for you. But you motorized fans, listen up, too. Just because you're riding high in a camper van, truck camper, or mega motorhome, doesn't mean your towable days are necessarily over. Install a hitch on your motorhome, and you're now free to tow a car, boat, or even a small trailer behind you, thus expanding your options upon arrival. The addition of a separate, nimble vehicle can surely add a whole new dimension to an already exciting lifestyle.

This chapter deals with all things towing. From towing a full range of trailers and secondary vehicles, to the smallest fold-down trailers around. From enormous fifth wheels to a compact car to a pair of snowmobiles pulled behind the motorized RV du jour. Got an existing car, truck, or van you want to match to a shiny new towable? We'll tell you how to make a match made in Heaven (or at least the nearest dealer's lot). Found that great fifth wheel, travel trailer, or fold-down camper you can't live without? We'll show you how to narrow the field to find the right tow vehicle for the job. We'll demystify the confusing towing terminology, break down how to transport most any type of vehicle, and provide a host of tips and accessories to make this task safer and easier. Read on, your chariot awaits.

How Much Can My Vehicle Tow?

For most, this question lies at the very heart of the matter. You have an existing car or truck and you need to know just what—or how much—it can safely tow. It's important not to put the cart before the horse, so to speak, which is why the tow vehicle is a great place to start. The first step is to determine the tow vehicle's *tow rating,* or basically how much it can safely pull. Every vehicle has its limits, and yours is no exception.

RVocabulary

Listed in pounds, the **tow rating** measures the maximum weight a vehicle can safely tow. The larger the tow rating, the heavier the towable a vehicle can safely transport.

How Do You Rate?

Every vehicle has a tow rating. Even the tiniest compact car has one, although it might be embarrassingly low. Just don't count on that two-door coupe to haul around that 40-foot travel trailer you've been eyeing. A number of factors combine to affect tow ratings, including engine size, rear axle differential ratio, etc. And unless these inherent qualities of the vehicle are somehow altered (adding a new engine, for instance), the tow rating will not change, and therefore, the towing limit stays constant. How this rating is determined isn't nearly as important as the sum itself. This information is no secret, determined by the vehicle's manufacturer. Check the owner's manual for the vehicle's tow rating. Otherwise, contact the vehicle's builder for this information.

The Big Three

With your tow vehicle's tow rating in hand, you now know exactly how much it can safely pull. Consider yourself halfway there. The next step is to determine the weight of the trailer that you hope to haul around. Makes sense, right? Although trailer weights are also readily available, an alphabet soup listing of ratings and terms listed throughout brochures and stickers often bombards buyers with lots of information. I've reduced the "need-to-knows" to three important terms to help you match a tow vehicle with a towable.

Unloaded Vehicle Weight

Also listed as the UVW, or dry weight, this figure relates to the weight of the vehicle. No cargo, no fresh water or propane, and definitely no passengers toting heavy fruitcakes—just the *actual* weight of the trailer and nothing else. Provided by the manufacturer, consider this weight somewhat of an approximate number. Why? Because add-ons (sometimes installed after the unit leaves the factory) in the forms of slide-outs, an extra air conditioner, awnings, or other upgrades may not be included in that number, serving only to escalate this figure. Hopping on a truck scale is the only way to know the towable's true UVW, which we'll discuss in Chapter 15, "How Much Does Your RV Weigh?"

Gross Vehicle Weight Rating

Sometimes shortened to GVWR, this is the *maximum* carrying capacity of the fully loaded vehicle. The UVW is what it actually weighs; the GVWR is its maximum weight limit. This rating includes everything onboard—water, propane, food (can't forget the grub!), all passengers, and their gear. Consider this figure nonnegotiable. Exceed it and it's like asking you to give not just *your* child a piggyback ride, but every kid in the neighborhood, bad news for your back and an equally bad situation for a trailer and tow vehicle pushed beyond what they can handle. This is the towable's limit and the magic number for tow vehicle/towable matchmaking.

Gross Combined Weight Rating

Commonly seen as the GCWR, this rating applies to the maximum weight limit for the tow vehicle, the towed object (trailer or secondary vehicle), and all passengers and cargo inside each. Why is this term necessary when we have the GVWR? Because the tow vehicle itself is carrying gear and passengers, which affects its towing abilities as well. Basically, this number serves as the maximum *combined* weight of what the tow vehicle can safely handle, hence the name.

Matchmaker, Matchmaker

All this brings us back to the original question: How do you know what you can safely tow? Look at the tow rating for the tow vehicle you have (or plan to purchase). Compare this number to the GVWR of the trailer you are considering. If the GVWR of the towable is *less* than your vehicle's tow rating, you're in business. Congratulations, the tow vehicle is up to the job. However, if the trailer's GVWR is greater than the tow vehicle's tow rating, you have two choices: Find a lighter towable or find a tow vehicle with a higher tow rating. Don't be tempted to push the envelope here. Always heed these ratings and don't ask a tow vehicle to do more than it can. It's not worth risking the safety of your family or others on the road. More on the perils of overloading in Chapter 15.

Pull Over

Some first-time RV buyers make the mistake of plunking down their hard-earned cash for a trailer on impulse, without doing the proper research. Regrettably, some salespeople are occasionally misleading or uninformed in their assurances that your tow vehicle can do the job. And then, it's too late. You discover that you have a mismatch—a towable too heavy for the vehicle to tow. A costly mistake.

Come on, the numbers are close enough, you say. That awesome travel trailer with the cool floor plan, slide-out entertainment center, and gas fireplace (yes, there is such a thing) is just a couple of hundred pounds more than my vehicle can handle. So what, what's the big deal? Besides, my neighbor has a trailer just like it and his truck's smaller than mine. Again, every case is different. The number-one thing to remember is that weight and tow ratings are there for a reason. Manufacturers didn't just pull them out of the proverbial hat just to cramp your style. There is no gray area here and no room for debate—either you can safely tow that trailer or you cannot.

One for the Road

Make buying decisions based on hard facts, not on what someone tells you that you can handle. Images in brochures and advertisements are sometimes misleading, with pictures of undersized vehicles pulling towables way out of their league. And just because you see someone towing something you believe is beyond them doesn't mean they can safely do so. Each towing situation is different. Avoid trying to keep up with the Joneses here.

The Hitching Post

You think you've got pressure? Try being a trailer hitch, the most vital link in the towing system. Without one, a new trailer is pretty useless, unable to go, and staring at you sadly with those puppy eyes. The purpose of a hitch is to connect the trailer to the tow vehicle, attached either to the bumper or frame (for conventional trailers) or within the bed of the truck (for fifth wheels). As seen in the following table, there are different hitches for different trailer weights, with each rated according to the load it is designed to handle.

Hitch Classes

Class	Weight Limits
Class I (weight-carrying)	For trailers up to 2,000 pounds
Class II (weight-carrying)	For trailers from 2,001 to 3,500 pounds
Class III (weight-distributing)	For trailers from 3,501 to 5,000 pounds
Class IV (weight-distributing)	For trailers from 5,001 to 10,000 pounds
Class V (weight-distributing)	For trailers from 10,001 to 14,000 pounds

Unlike conventional bumper- or frame-mounted versions, fifth-wheel hitches aren't divided into traditional weight classes (Class I, Class II, etc.). In the case of fifth wheels, hitches are segregated and labeled by weight capacity (e.g., a 15,000-pound hitch, a 20,000-pound hitch, etc.). Furthermore, ratings vary from manufacturer to manufacturer.

The Right Hitch

A dealer specializing in towable RVs is the most likely place to obtain the right hitch. He or she should be able to advise you on the correct type for your towable, and install it as well. If you prefer not to go this route, aftermarket service centers and hitch shops specialize in matching tow vehicles to trailers and make their living installing hitches. Prepare to answer questions about what you're towing and its GVWR. Check the Yellow Pages under "Trailer Hitches" for businesses nearby.

One for the Road

Different towing packages, available in the aftermarket or during a new vehicle purchase, can save you a few steps. You can buy a tow vehicle all set up to pull trailers, with the ideal gear ratio, sufficiently powerful engine, an engine brake, and the wiring and perhaps even the hitch already installed.

Choosing the right hitch, like most things related to towing, boils down to weight. Again, the hitch must be able to handle the load of your trailer. For instance, a trailer with a GVWR of 7,000 pounds requires a Class IV hitch rated for the job, which, as seen in the preceding hitch classes table, can handle that load and then some. Like Starsky and Hutch, the hitch and the tow vehicle's tow rating must work together, and you're only as strong as your weakest link. If your truck is rated to tow

10,000 pounds but you find yourself with only a Class II hitch, consider the vehicle's limit now reduced to 3,500 pounds. You'll need a new hitch if you want to tow more. Conversely, a Class V hitch on a small tow vehicle makes little sense since the tow vehicle could never, ever pull such a load.

One for the Road

The RV dealer or hitch shop can install most any type of hitch, along with safety cables and wiring harness that operates a trailer's lights, brakes, and battery.

As stated earlier, most conventional trailers have a uniquely different hitch configuration than fifth wheels. These hitch types are mutually exclusive and can never be substituted for one another. A closer look at each type is provided in the following sections.

Conventional Trailers

Let's start with the hitches found on conventional trailers, namely travel trailers, pop-ups, and for some secondary vehicle towed behind the motorhome. For any one of these scenarios, one of two standard hitches is required: a weight-carrying hitch or a weight-distributing hitch.

Weight-Carrying Hitch

Take another look at the hitch classes table. You'll see that the Class I and II types are of the weight-carrying persuasion. (In a few cases, Class IIs are sometimes a receive-type hitch). Here, the hitch is forced to support the brunt of the trailer's hitch weight. Usually mounted to the bumper, these hitches are only really useful for smaller loads less than 3,500 pounds, limiting the user to very lightweight trailers and pop-ups. However, for those pulling a secondary vehicle behind the motorhome, this allows for a fairly decent selection of automobiles.

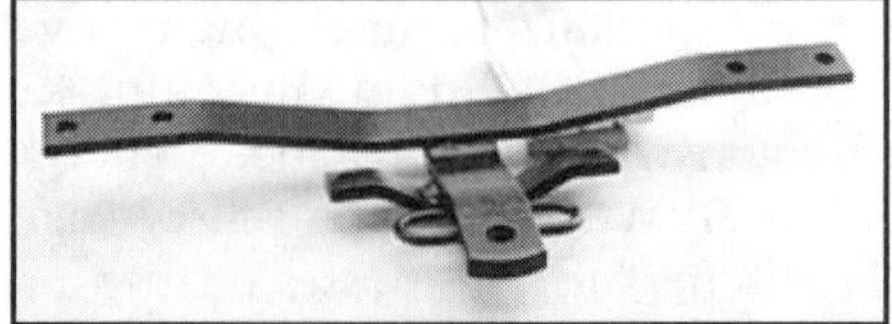

Those towing smaller loads, usually less than 3,500 pounds, can rely on a weight-carrying hitch to do the job.

(Photo courtesy of Draw-Tite)

Weight-Distributing Hitch

Question: Would you rather carry Aunt Gertrude's pool table yourself or have three other people help you? Unless you're Superman looking for a workout, you'd surely rather enlist the help of some buddies, exactly the rationale behind a weight-distributing hitch, sometimes referred to as a load-equalizing hitch. Attached to the frame of the tow vehicle, these hitches are designed to spread the weight around to both axles of the tow vehicle, rather than just the back end. With the weight properly distributed, larger trailers can now be towed.

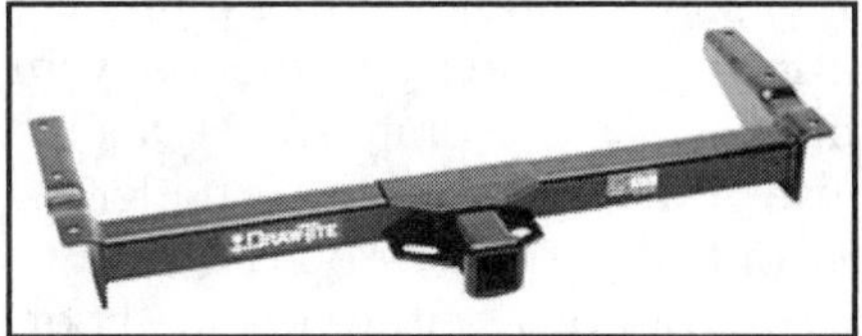

A weight-distributing hitch, specially designed to distribute the load of the towable among the tow vehicle's axles, is the only type of hitch suitable for larger towables.

(Photo courtesy of Draw-Tite)

What's What—Hitches

While the dynamics at work in a weight-carrying hitch are barely more than a ball attached to the vehicle's bumper, the weight-distributing hitch is somewhat more complex, comprised of several important parts. A basic understanding of the purpose of each should help eliminate confusion when the fella at the hitch shop is "talkin' the talk." And since we'll be dropping a few of these terms when it's time to hitch up, better to learn them now.

The typical trailer hitch is made up of three important parts: the *hitch receiver, ball mount*, and *spring bars*.

RVocabulary

The **hitch receiver** acts as the hitch's overall foundation, bolted or welded to the frame of the tow vehicle. The **ball mount** serves as the connection point between trailer and tow vehicle, sliding into the receiver hitch and pinned in place. Proper height and tilt are important for a snug fit, which is best left up to a professional installer to dictate. The ball mount on weight-distributing hitches is removable when not towing to avoid becoming a knee-basher. The **spring bars** are designed to disperse the towable's weight among the tow vehicle's axles for better handling and steering. These are sometimes referred to as tension bars.

Hitching Up

The trailer sits at one end of the lot, the tow vehicle at the other. How are we gonna get these two shy kids to meet? The first step in hooking up a trailer is to raise the trailer's *tongue* (the metal A-frame portion that connects to the tow vehicle) above the level of the ball hitch on the tow vehicle. This is accomplished via a jack found on the tongue, which has the dual purpose of helping level one's trailer after arriving at your destination (so you don't roll out of bed at night). You can easily adjust the height of the trailer by raising this jack up or down, either manually or with the aid of a power jack, if available.

RVocabulary

The **tongue** is the "A"-shaped portion of the trailer frame responsible for hitching up to the tow vehicle, securing the LP containers, and the location for the tongue jack that raises and lowers the front end. The **coupler** is the forward-most component of the trailer's tongue and fits snugly over the ball hitch to make a tight towing connection.

Once you have the trailer's tongue in position above the level of the ball hitch on the back of the tow vehicle, back up the tow vehicle until its hitch is positioned just below the *coupler* on the end of the tongue. It might take you a couple of tries—but we're patient. Take your time, and just pull forward a bit and try again, watching the hitch and trailer tongue as you ease in. If possible, enlist the help of another person to guide you back via a series of hand gestures (no, not *that* one) and voice commands. We're halfway home.

Once in position, use the jack to lower the coupler onto the ball of the hitch, and lock it into position. (Those using a weight-distributing hitch, put the spring bar in before lowering the jack.) Raise the tongue jack slightly to put the weight of the trailer onto the hitch. (The tow vehicle should "sink" a little if a good connection has been made.) Since you won't be needing the tongue jack anymore (not until you unhook the trailer later on, that is), raise it or fold it up against the tongue of the trailer so it is safely out of the way. Well done. At this point, a basic connection has been made. A few finishing touches and you'll be on your way.

Get Wired

Regardless of the type of hitch you use, you will need a wiring harness to go with it. Much or all of this is usually included in the service when having the hitch installed. In simplest terms, it involves running wires from the brakes and lights on the trailer to the brakes and lights on your tow vehicle. The goal here is perfect symmetry between the two, in terms of running lights, turn signals, and brakes. The wires should be bundled together in a neatly accessible manner near the hitch, and the same goes for the trailer. When it's go-time, the wires are easily connected or disconnected near the hitch by simply plugging them together or pulling them apart. (When not in use, make sure both ends of the wiring are tucked up out of the way, so they don't become frayed or dirty.) Once connected, a magical thing happens. The trailer's lights and braking system mimic the actions of the tow vehicle. Not only is this cool, but it'll keep the local police force happy (it's the law)—and is a vital step before towing a trailer of any size.

Road Scholar

Ball hitches come in a few sizes so you need to ensure that you have the right size for your towable. Again, your dealer or hitch shop should help here. If it's too big or small for the trailer's coupler, you must replace the hitch with the correct size. Most hitches allow you to swap out the ball portion for another size, a versatile option for towing different trailers. The correct ball size is usually stamped on the top portion of the coupler.

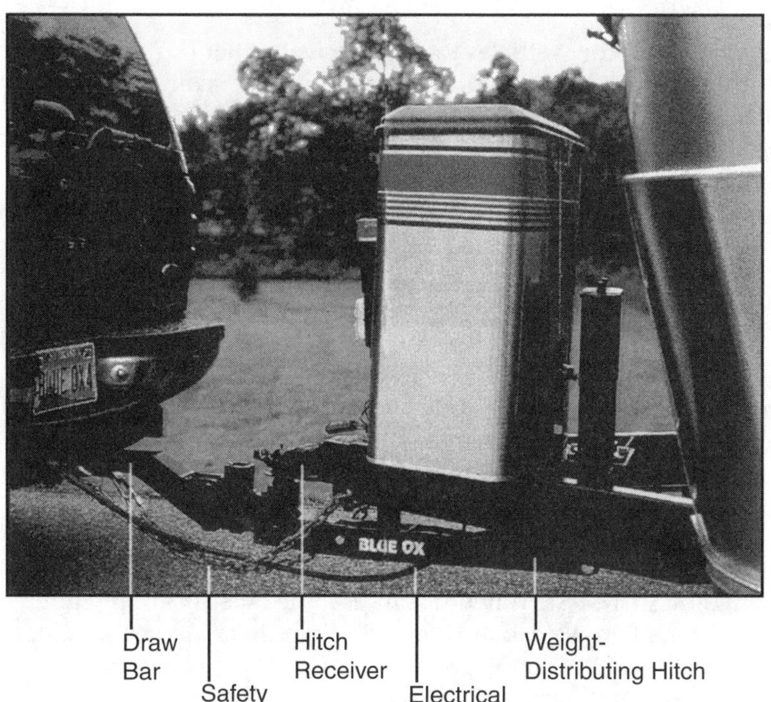

A closer look at all the players involved in a standard hitch-up for conventional towables.

(Photo courtesy of Blue Ox)

Brake Time

A tow vehicle's brakes are designed to stop you and a decent-sized payload—and that's about it. But where does this leave your trailer chugging along behind you? Fortunately, most trailers come equipped with brakes of their own (older trailers should be tested to ensure that they are in working order). This way, you're not dependent on the tow vehicle's brakes to stop the entire load. Now it's up to you to connect the towable's brakes to that of the tow vehicle, as documented in the "Get Wired" section earlier in this chapter.

RVocabulary

The **brake controller** is a device mounted within the tow vehicle to activate the trailer's brakes independently or in conjunction with the tow vehicle brakes.

To match both sets of brakes (the tow vehicle's and the trailer's), wiring must be installed when the hitch is installed. After doing this, simply plug both connections together after hitching up to ensure that both braking systems work in tandem. The trailer brakes should engage automatically when you step on the tow vehicle's brakes. However, they can also be applied by hand through a device known as a *brake controller,* mounted near the steering wheel of the tow vehicle.

Control Yourself

A brake controller is a must on all tow vehicles towing a travel trailer or fifth wheel with electric brakes. (Most trailers feature electric brakes.) The brake controller is added to the tow vehicle at the time all other wiring is done. The brake circuit terminates in the same plug as the lights and charge line, etc. Most controllers have an independent method of activating the trailer brakes without activating the tow vehicle brakes, like when descending a hill or stopping a slight sway situation. The device is installed in the cockpit, usually near the steering wheel.

Safety Chain Gang

Safety chains are a must to keep your trailer from "running away" in the unlikely event it becomes unhooked. As part of the hitch installation, two short chains are attached to the trailer near the tongue. The crossed chains form a basket of sorts to catch the tongue should the trailer ever try to part company with the tow vehicle. The chains are welded to the coupler and connect to rings welded to the hitch receiver on the tow vehicle. Instead of "S" ends, universal chain links with a threaded nut are used. The chains should be long enough to hang loosely, but not touch the ground to prevent an ongoing spark-fest. When not in use, the chains simply hang under the coupler since they remain welded at that end. Wrap them along the trailer tongue to keep them up and out of the way. Again, the trailer dealer or hitch shop is the best source for getting and applying safety chains.

Breaking Up Is Hard to Do

The *break-away switch* adds further peace of mind in the event the trailer and tow vehicle no longer want to see each other. Mounted on or near the tongue, the device is equipped with a pin attached to a cable, which in turn is attached to the ball mount. The connection is wired from the trailer's battery and to the electric brake circuit on the trailer. If the trailer and tow vehicle ever disconnect from one another during transit, the separation pulls the pin and the trailer's brakes are automatically activated to help slow the runaway trailer. It's kinda like pulling the pin on a hand grenade. This is why it's important to have a charged battery on the trailer, so this feature won't let you down in this unlikely, but potentially very dangerous, event. No battery, no break-away switch, no brakes, no stopping the runaway trailer, no good.

RVocabulary

The **break-away switch** is a pin-activated safety device mounted near the trailer's tongue that automatically activates the braking system in case of separation from the tow vehicle.

Conventional Trailer Checklist

- ❑ Coupler and hitch locked into position
- ❑ Safety chains crossed under trailer tongue and attached to bumper of truck
- ❑ Spring bars and sway control (if added) adjusted properly
- ❑ Wiring connected
- ❑ Break-away switch cable connected
- ❑ Running lights, turning signals, electric brakes, and back-up lights working on trailer

Fifth Wheels

Fifth-wheel trailers, due to their unique gooseneck design, require a different kind of hitch, which is mounted in the bed of the truck doing the towing duties. Unlike regular trailers, relying partially on gravity to help reinforce the connection, fifth wheels use a locking hitch mechanism. Here, the *kingpin* on the front of the fifth wheel slides and locks into the hitch mounted in the bed of the truck. Again, the weight of the fifth wheel determines the type of hitch required. Opt for a fifth-wheel hitch that "flexes," as it will allow you to hitch up on uneven ground more easily, while taking stress off the hitch when driving over uneven terrain. Air ride hitches reduce road vibration and trailer sway. All of these configurations are available at RV dealerships or hitch shops.

RVocabulary

The **kingpin** is the part of the fifth wheel that slides and locks into the truck-mounted hitch. It is round and sticks down a few inches below the underside of the front of the fifth wheel, near the very nose of the trailer. Incidentally, this is a common place to bump your head while rummaging through outside storage compartments while parked, so be careful.

RVocabulary

Also known as a safety pin, the **locking pin** secures the connection between the kingpin and fifth-wheel hitch for a tight fit and added safety. Exact methods of locking vary among hitch manufacturers.

One of the benefits of a fifth-wheel hitch is that it can be removed, thereby freeing up the bed of the truck for other things. Different fifth-wheel hitch makers have their own methods of attachment, but most are removed fairly easily by removing the pins holding them in place. Others require unbolting the hitch in several places before lifting it out of the back of the truck. Most RVers only do this when they will not be towing their fifth wheel for a while.

The Big Tow

Hooking up a fifth wheel is a little different, but there's more than a little common ground compared to conventional trailers. First, you must use the fifth wheel's jacks in the front of the trailer to raise or lower the kingpin to the same level as the hitch. (Smaller models might require a hand-crank.) This part is easy—just access the switch inside the small compartment on the driver's side of the trailer (right near the front) and press the switch in the desired direction. This is also a good job for Junior, by the way.

Drop the truck's tailgate and slowly back the truck, aimed right at the kingpin. (You will probably be able to match this connection up perfectly using your rearview mirror as you maneuver in.) Use side mirrors or have someone help you if necessary. When the kingpin is right behind the hitch and properly lined up, simply ease back and lock it into place. There will be a bit of a jolt when this happens, so don't forget to warn the wife inside, who may be just about to down the last cup of hot coffee. Otherwise, lower or raise the hitch if necessary so that it is at just the right level to slide into the hitch. Next, get out and push the *locking pin* through the hole in the kingpin, fastening it into place with the wire clip.

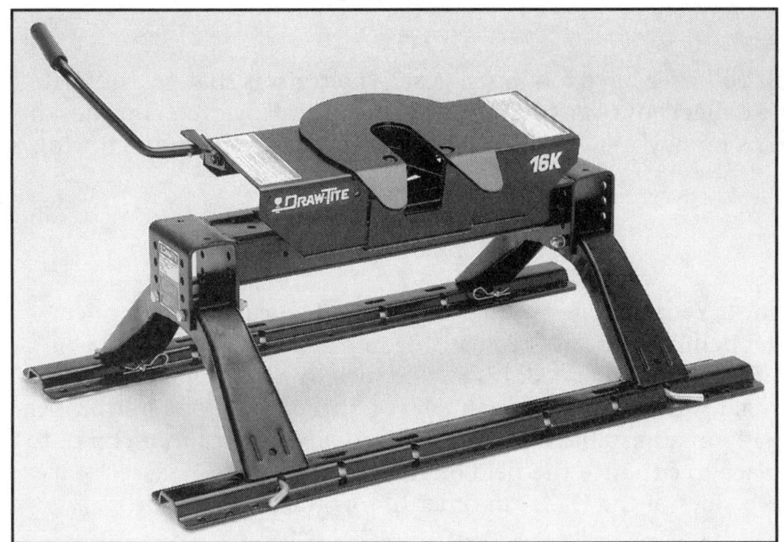

Instead of the bumper- or frame-mounted hitch used for conventional towables, a fifth-wheel hitch such as this one is installed within the cargo bed of the tow vehicle.

(Photo courtesy of Draw-Tite)

Final Steps

Just as we do for conventional trailers, with the hitch connection made, it's time for some final safety features. Plug the wiring from the fifth wheel into the truck connection, so the taillights, turning signals, and brake/reverse lights are in working order. The fifth wheel's braking system will be activated in this manner as well. Safety chains are a nice precaution, but aren't as essential here since you won't be using a ball hitch. Consult your dealer or hitch shop for more information. Finally, lower the trailer until all the weight rests on the hitch of the truck, by raising the trailer's front jacks with the push of a button. Keep raising the jacks until they are fully retracted, then manually slide the jacks up the rest of the way (if necessary). Push the metal pins through the holes in the jacks up near the belly of the trailer, so they don't slide out in transit. When disconnecting the two vehicles, be sure to lower the jacks to support the trailer after the truck is removed.

Final Checklist

- ❑ Kingpin connected into hitch
- ❑ Locking pin in position
- ❑ Wiring connected
- ❑ Safety chains added (if desired)
- ❑ Check braking, lights, and signals on trailer
- ❑ Break-away switch cable connected

Accessorizing

Most men will ask: Can you ever have too much gear? The truth is that yes, unfortunately, one can (see the dangers of overloading in Chapter 15). However, consider the following towing options money well spent, particularly if you're new to the towing game.

Mirror, Mirror

Towing mirrors are a must. Your rearview mirror is going to be nearly useless once hooked up to that trailer behind you, and regular side mirrors won't stick out far enough to give drivers the views they need. It's a good idea to either replace existing side mirrors with ones that slide out (either manually or at the touch of a button); extend existing mirrors with an adjustable mirror bracket; or add mirrors that clip onto the ones currently in place to enhance the field of vision behind you. It is necessary for the driver to see both sides of the trailer in order to tow the trailer safely.

No Sway, No Way

Sway control devices help reduce much of the lateral movement of conventional trailers. This is especially true for longer travel trailers, which are prone to wiggle somewhat behind you as you go (fifth wheels, which rest in the bed of a pickup truck, inherently have a much more stable ride). Gusts of wind and passing semis can worsen the sway problem. An anti-sway device can help keep you on the straight and narrow, so to speak, making your RV travels safer and less stressful.

One for the Road

Excessive sway is generally not a problem associated with fifth wheels, due to their snug fit over the truck bed. In fact, as discussed in previous chapters, this is one of their major advantages over conventional travel trailers.

Anti-Air

An air deflector mounted to the top of the truck reduces air drag when towing tall fifth wheels, noticeably improving fuel mileage over time. The savings could add up to serious dollars over your towing lifetime. These products are available aftermarket through RV supply stores and places that sell custom truck accessories. While some owners object to their strange looks, beauty is in the eye of a beholder. Those who tow fifth wheels extensively throughout the year soon realize that anything capable of cutting fuel costs is beautiful indeed.

Stuff for Loners

There are also nifty products designed to help a solo driver with the hitching-up process. A special convex mirror, mounted between your travel trailer's LP tanks or on the tongue jack post, can enable you to see both the hitch ball and the coupler on the trailer tongue once they are within 12 inches of each other. Navigator back-up lights, installed on a bumper hitch, can be a big help when hitching up in the dark. Fifth-wheel owners enjoy a special level attachment to the side of the fifth wheel geared to "remember" the position of the bubble when the trailer was unhooked. This eliminates the guesswork at establishing the correct hitch height, bypassing a somewhat tiresome step.

Towing Behind a Motorhome

We've said all along that one of the advantages of a motorized RV is not having to worry about towing. Now I'm going to eat those words. The truth is, many motorhome owners discover that towing a separate car or small trailer (also known as a *toad,* auxiliary vehicle, or dinghy vehicle) behind the motorhome is very convenient, adding greater ease in getting around once the destination is reached. After all, it's certainly oodles easier commuting back and forth to town in a compact automobile than in a 40-foot motorhome. Hence, the logic for towing one. Take a day trip into a state park without worrying about narrow, winding roads or finding a suitable parking space. Leave the campsite for errands in a secondary vehicle without having to ready the motorhome, unhook the water, sewer, and electric, and pile the whole family onboard. The advantages are obvious and well worth the effort of mastering a few towing essentials.

What Can My Motorhome Tow?

As is the case with any other vehicle, your motorhome has its own tow rating. To find this, subtract the motorhome's GVWR from its GCVR (both found in the owner's manual or through the manufacturer). The difference is how much weight your motorhome can safely tow—easy, right? Easier still, the tow ratings might simply be listed separately, so no heady math is required. Choose a secondary vehicle that does not exceed that weight, and you're ready to roll—literally. Those pulling automobiles can learn the toad vehicle's weight from its owner's manual or by contacting the manufacturer. Don't forget to add the weight

RVocabulary

Toad is a slang term for the car or truck being "towed" (get it, towed or toad?) behind a motorhome. Another frequently used term for this type of secondary vehicle is a "dinghy," yet another RV term borrowed from the nautical world.

Pull Over

Always consult the owner's manual or contact the manufacturer concerning towing instructions and procedures for any vehicle you wish to pull behind a motorhome. Every vehicle is different, depending on weight, transmission, etc. What works for one may not work for another.

of the actual device used to transport the towed vehicle (e.g., tow bar, dolly, or trailer). When choosing a toad, it makes sense to choose the lightest vehicle that will meet your needs. And remember, don't fill the toad vehicle up with gear—this affects the motorhome's tow rating, too.

Towed Vehicles Come in Threes

There are three ways to tow a vehicle behind a motorhome, truck camper, or van camper. Again, a hitch is required—just like the conventional trailers previously mentioned. After all, something must connect the two vehicles, right? Your three basic options include *tow bars, tow dollies,* and *trailers*. A look at each attachment follows.

Tow Bars

Tow bars connect a secondary vehicle to a motorhome while allowing the car or truck to be towed with all four wheels down. This is generally the most convenient option and gives a streamlined appearance. Tow bars are the most popular choice among RVers since they're easier to store and install than the much larger (and heavier) tow dollies or trailers; most models simply fold up when not in use. Tow bars are more expensive than tow dollies, however, and aren't compatible with some types of vehicle transmissions. The biggest thing to remember is to never back up—not even a little bit—with a tow bar in place. It will wreck the bar and could damage both vehicles in the process. If a backup is necessary, disconnect the secondary vehicle and tow bar before throwing the RV into reverse.

It is important to check with the manufacturer of any vehicle you are considering towing behind your motorhome, to find out whether it is rated to be towed with a tow bar. If the intended vehicle is not approved for towing with all four wheels down, it may still be possible to use a tow bar with the help of aftermarket products such as transmission uncouplers and lockout devices. Otherwise, a tow dolly or trailer is the answer. Just be aware that any modifications you make to the toad may void the manufacturer's warranty, and it can be expensive to have these modifications made safely.

Hooking up with a tow bar is pretty simple. Depending on the type you purchase, you must either align the bar with the motorhome's hitch ball by driving the car forward or line up the baseplate on the toad with the tow bar that is attached to the motorhome. It's simpler if you have a second person directing you while maneuvering the vehicle forward. Telescoping and self-adjusting tow bars are also available to make it easier to hook up for solo travelers. A wiring harness and safety cables must also be connected. Once hooked up, set the ignition key of the car to a position that allows the car's front wheels to turn freely, and put the car in neutral.

For many folks pulling a vehicle behind their motorhome, a tow bar is a lightweight and easy-to-use product to do the job.

(Photo courtesy of Roadmaster)

Tow Bar Checklist

- ❑ Towed vehicle connected to tow bar and motorhome
- ❑ Towed vehicle's steering and transmission set to tow
- ❑ Safety cables crossed and wrapped around legs of tow bar to keep them from dragging
- ❑ Wiring connected
- ❑ Running lights, turning signals, and auxiliary brake device working on vehicle
- ❑ Break-away switch cable connected

Road Scholar

If you decide to use a tow bar, you will need a baseplate or bracket kit, which attaches to the front of the toad. Each type of toad will need its own baseplate, which can be purchased for the most popular toads, or custom-made to fit your particular type of vehicle. A professional installation of the tow bar and base plate is recommended.

Hello, (Tow) Dolly

A tow dolly (such as the kind you rent from U-Haul) is designed to tow a vehicle with two wheels on the dolly and two wheels riding along the pavement. This option is less expensive than a tow bar

Pull Over

Drivers must never attempt to back up the motorhome with a tow bar or tow dolly attached. Doing so could damage the entire set-up, including both vehicles. If you're in a jam, the best remedy is to disconnect the tow bar or dolly and move the towed vehicle separately *before* attempting a backup.

and useful with many different vehicles. No modifications are necessary to the toad, and the dolly may even come with its own braking system. Unfortunately, its size can be a burden, as smaller campsites might struggle to accommodate the motorhome, the secondary vehicle, *and* the tow dolly, too. A dolly also adds more weight to your bottom line (GVCR), about 500 to 1,500 pounds' worth. You will have more maintenance, including two extra tires, and in some states, a tow dolly even needs to be licensed separately. Like the tow bar, never back up while a tow dolly is attached to the motorhome.

If you decide to tow with a tow dolly, a ball hitch must be installed to the motorhome. Hooking up with a tow dolly is a little more involved. First, it must be hitched to the motorhome. This can be done manually, by simply wrestling the dolly into position, to save having to back up the motorhome. Next, connect the wiring harness and safety chains between the two. Finally, drive the car up onto the dolly, and secure it into position with straps designed for this purpose. Rear-wheel drive vehicles can be loaded with the rear wheels on the dolly, front-wheel drive with the front on the dolly. Set the towed vehicle in neutral, and you're ready to go. Again, always consult the towed vehicle manufacturer for safe towing practices.

Tow dollies are useful to transport vehicles ill-equipped to ride with all four wheels on the ground.

(Photo courtesy of Roadmaster)

Tow Dolly Checklist

- ❑ Coupler and hitch locked into position
- ❑ Towed vehicle secured in position, with correct axle on dolly
- ❑ Safety chains crossed under dolly tongue and attached to receiver or frame of motorhome
- ❑ Wiring connected
- ❑ Running lights, turning signals, brakes, and back-up lights working on vehicle
- ❑ Break-away switch cable connected

Trailers

Very few motorhome owners choose the trailer option these days, now relegated for towing expensive vehicles (such as racecars or vintage autos) or if you want to haul other cargo, such as jet skis, motorcycles, or a small boat. In those situations, the extra cost and weight of a separate trailer might be practical. Generally, only the larger motorhomes are capable of handling this much weight. With a trailer, backing up without unhooking is possible, unlike the other two options.

Hooking up a trailer to your motorhome is just like hooking up most towables. Have someone help you back the motorhome into place, aligning the hitch to the coupler on the trailer's tongue. Connect wiring and safety chains before departing.

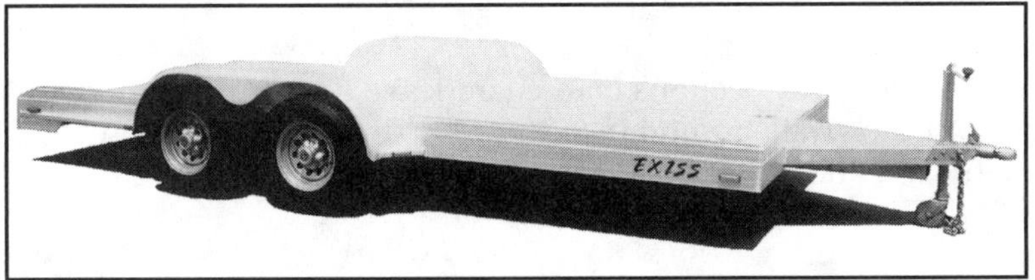

Using a supplemental trailer to haul around a towed vehicle is a reliable, albeit weighty, method of transport.

(Photo courtesy of Exiss Aluminum Trailers)

Trailer Checklist

- ❑ Coupler and hitch locked into position
- ❑ Towed vehicle secured on trailer
- ❑ Safety chains crossed under trailer tongue and attached to frame of motorhome
- ❑ Wiring connected
- ❑ Break-away switch cable connected
- ❑ Running lights, turning signals, electric brakes, and back-up lights working on vehicle

Proper Wiring

As with all towables, the proper wiring for all towed vehicles is a must. Again, this will be part of a professional installation at an RV service center or dealership doing the hard part for you. All you have to do is plug it in. If using a tow bar, you can also use a detachable light bar if you do not want to alter the car's wiring, although this is not as convenient.

Safety Chains

Safety chains or cables are needed regardless of which method of towing one uses—tow bar, dolly, or separate trailer. Some tow bars have the wiring and safety cables inside the frame of the tow bar for a neater appearance.

Give Me a Brake

Adding the extra weight of another vehicle makes your motorhome harder to stop. A secondary braking system is needed to compensate for this fact. If you are towing a trailer, it will generally have its own brakes, and many tow dollies also have independent brakes as well. A separate toad braking system, which activates the brakes in tandem with those in the motorhome's cockpit, is highly recommended for towing with a tow bar. A break-away system that activates the brakes if the toad becomes disconnected from the motorhome is more than a good idea.

Inspections

Get in the habit of checking your connections before you leave on a trip and periodically during the journey. A quick walk-around inspection, with special attention to the connections, lights, brakes, and safety chains, is time well spent.

The Least You Need to Know

- A tow vehicle can safely transport a trailer if its tow rating is more than the towable's gross vehicle weight rating. Otherwise, either secure a larger tow vehicle or a lighter trailer.
- A properly installed hitch facilitates the connection between the vehicle and trailer. Conventional trailers utilize either a bumper- or frame-mounted hitch, with classes based on the weight of the load. Fifth-wheel trailers use a special hitch, mounted in the bed of the truck doing the towing.
- In addition to a suitable tow vehicle and hitch, towing situations mandate safety chains in case of a breakaway and extra wiring to control the towed vehicle or trailer's brakes, turning signals, and brake and back-up lights.
- Towing a vehicle behind a motorhome offers an easy way to commute back and forth from the campsite. This is accomplished through the use of either a tow bar, tow dolly, or trailer.
- Double-check all connections for optimal safety. Periodically inspect wiring, safety chains, and hitch-ups before and during any long trips.

Chapter 14

Drive Time

In This Chapter

- Tips for piloting a motorhome or towable
- Establishing a pretrip routine
- Avoiding common operating errors
- Accessories to make driving easier

A 20-foot trailer hitched up to an SUV adds up to more than 30 feet of vehicle, which is a size at which most Class As *begin*. Pull a car behind the motorhome and these recreational vehicles could easily exceed 50 feet. Even a relatively modest-sized camper van or truck camper presents a few new driving wrinkles. Wide-body designs, lofty exterior heights, and battleship-type weights all factor into the RV driving experience. This merits some attention, particularly from beginners.

As mentioned throughout this book, operating an RV is different, not difficult. Those who have never found themselves behind the wheel of a large motorhome or towing even the smallest trailer should expect a brief apprenticeship of sorts in the cockpit. Backing up, motoring around town, pulling into campgrounds, traversing steep grades, and highway driving are all obviously not as effortless as manhandling the family compact. However, with a little practice and experience it won't be long before it's second nature—or first nature, depending on how seriously you pursue the RV lifestyle. Hopefully, this chapter will aid in that goal as well.

The Only Thing to Fear

Novice RVers might be somewhat daunted at *driving* or *towing* an RV at first, a totally natural and acceptable feeling, and one that should fade over time. After all, the difference between operating most any type of RV and a lifetime of owning small imports, sedans, and sport utility vehicles is significant at first. Relax—with every new skill comes some doubts. Realize, too, that even veteran RVers occasionally jump a curb on a turn, drive too fast for their own good, or fail to back into the campsite in one flawless motion. Want to know the greatest secret of RV driving? RVs are much easier to operate than you think. Shhhhh, don't tell anybody. My Aunt Rite drove a lengthy motorhome well into her 70s—and there are millions of folks on the road right now just like her. Furthermore, if I can do it, anyone can. Adjust your mirrors, fasten seat belts, and remove the German Shepherd from the driver's seat; it's time to learn how to drive.

RVocabulary

The term **driving** will be used throughout this chapter to include operating motorized and towable RVs alike—**towing** your trailer or camper will be referred to as driving. Any caveats to that practice (such as towing specifics) will be listed and explained separately to avoid any generalizations of the text.

Start Your Engines

Regardless if you're towing a fold-down camper or a mammoth diesel pusher, the basic principles of safe driving still apply. None of the unique characteristics of an RV (increased height, weight, length) *adversely* affect the way we drive, rather just require some adjustments.

The biggest difference is to allow more time and distance for stopping and accelerating and more room when turning corners and changing lanes. Hills are a bit more of a challenge—both going up and coming down—because of the added weight. Keep your eyes on the road ahead and try to anticipate the need to stop, slow down, or turn, and always allow a little extra time for any maneuver. You're not in the Corvette, remember.

One for the Road

The most important piece of advice: Learn and respect the limitations of the vehicle. It won't take long before you realize precisely how much time and room is needed to stop, how spunky the engine is in terms of quick starts, and how good your ability to maneuver through traffic, corner, and tackle steep grades is.

Take a Brake

Every RV must be driven differently—motorized and towables need to allow more time to brake than any vehicle you've ever driven. It won't take long to determine how your vehicle stops at different speeds. It will probably take you, oh, I'd say roughly 10 seconds to learn that you're at the command of a pretty big ship. Why do you think they call the driving area the cockpit? Different size loads affect stopping power, too. Coming to a complete stop takes longer with passengers and cargo than when transporting a fairly empty unit with just you behind the wheel. Anticipation is key—but you probably have these instincts well forged from years of driving. Upcoming brake lights, construction, curves and bends, congestion, etc. are all clear signs to begin to slow down.

As mentioned in the previous chapter, it is highly recommended that all towables and towed vehicles feature a braking system of their own. You can never have too much stopping power at your disposal. Whether it's that innocent-looking Saturn pulled behind the motorhome, the smallish travel trailer, or the enormous fifth wheel, each should have its own independent stopping force. Such braking controls are wired through the tow vehicle and activated at the touch of the brake pad within the cockpit. An additional hand control (brake controller) near the steering wheel is sometimes offered for those preferring to control things that way.

Pull Over

We've all heard stories about jackknifed trailers. When the smoke clears, the culprit is usually hard braking, where the tow vehicle stops and the trailer keeps going. Inclement conditions can also share the blame. Avoiding this kind of calamity is just another in the long line of reasons why we wire the trailer's or towed vehicle's brakes to the lead vehicle's.

The largest RVs often benefit from a secondary braking system in the form of a hydraulic or exhaust brake. Also popular add-ons to tow vehicles hauling larger towables, exhaust braking systems (or engine braking systems) are a big help, especially when staring a deep descent square in the face. They come in real handy when going down hills, helping you to slow down without overtaxing the vehicle's brakes. Primary brakes can overheat and fail on long descents, so it's important not to overuse them. If you can actually smell your brakes working, they're getting overused.

Cornering

When cornering, remember to swing wide. The longer the RV, the farther out you need to go to ensure that everything goes where it is supposed to. Seeing how many curbs you can run over is not the goal here. Ever notice how semi drivers do this? Your RV probably isn't that long, but the principle is the same. Wide and slow. Remember, as you turn, your back end will "swing" out somewhat in the opposite direction. Trailer owners should think about where the towable is going to go as you turn the corner—but watch where the front of the tow vehicle is going, too. For motorhomers towing a car, be sure to compensate for the added footage.

Pull Over

Before attempting any risky maneuvers, ask yourself, "What is the rationale behind it?" Are you feeling impatient? Rushed? Looking to make up some lost time? With less room for error, don't push yourself in an RV. Hard driving is just that—hard on you, your crew, and your rig. As the saying goes, if you were in such a hurry, you should have left yesterday.

Lane Changes

Allow more time for lane changes. A motorhome requires more room to complete this move than, say, a Toyota Camry. Although you needn't plan a maneuver like a D-Day invasion, a little forethought always pays off. Check the side mirrors for a nice, wide opening. Signal well ahead of time, look in the mirrors again to make sure there is *plenty* of room, and move on over. Generally, I find other drivers on the road to be quite courteous—either that, or they're terrified of me.

Steep Grades

The extra weight of an RV means more power is required to get you to the top. Anticipate hills and accelerate a bit before you get there. On longer climbs, it is advisable (and courteous) to pull into the far right lane, allowing faster traffic to pass. Don't worry—you'll have plenty of company in the slow lane, such as the big trucks and fellow RVers. Try to use your brakes as little as possible as they can become hot on long descents. Use the trailer brakes or toad brakes (if pulling a car) instead of the tow vehicle or motorhome brakes when possible. (See Chapter 13, "Towin' the Line," for more on braking systems.) Downshift in lieu of hard braking. As mentioned, with very heavy RVs, an engine brake can be a real asset.

Parking

Remember the song, "Don't Fence Me In"? It most definitely applies when docking the rig. Leave yourself plenty of room to get out, especially with a bigger trailer or motorhome. You can forget about getting that parking space close to the main entrance when you are an RVer. Concentrate instead on finding a place with plenty of room around you, preferably at the far edge of the parking lot where you're out of the way. Besides, the extra walking will do you good. When it comes to parking the RV at the grocery store or roadside attraction, think like James Bond and plan your escape ahead of time. Avoid getting into tight spots, forcing an unnecessary back-up to free yourself.

Although very doable, backing up is still best avoided whenever possible. Opt for pull-thru campsites (remember in Chapter 3, "Where to Stay?") at RV parks, especially when toting a larger rig or if you are uncomfortable with life in reverse. Travel centers and truck stops are much more convenient for filling up and other necessary stops, since they're built for larger and longer vehicles—like you. Designed for drive-thru traffic, these stopovers are close to highways and enable RVers to fuel up, park, eat lunch, and then leave, all by driving forward. Presto! No backing up required.

Road Scholar

Here's a great tip courtesy of veteran RV writers Joe and Vicki Kieva. Write down the RV's exterior height on an index card and attach it to the sun visor. This way you'll never forget it and can circumvent any chance encounters with low overheads, such as those found at gas stations. It's a good idea also to include the vehicle's GVWR, giving you a number to shoot for during weigh-ins.

Clearance

It probably won't come into play much when driving anything but the tallest motorhomes and fifth wheels, but knowing your RV's exterior height keeps you out of trouble. Avoid any situations that might call this into question, such as a low overpass, parking garage, or the sheltered top of a gas station. Height should be listed in the owner's manual or brochures, or is available through the manufacturer. Be sure to factor in the added height of any extra items such as rooftop air conditioners, storage pods, and satellite systems to this figure. Remeasure from the ground to the RV's highest point if you're unsure. Always lower TV antennas before departing, a forgotten act that has left more than a few owners to ponder its sudden disappearance during the trip.

Rush Hour

The cutthroat world of rush-hour traffic can quickly sap the thrill of the open road out of even the most exuberant traveler. Passing through a metropolitan area during the teeth of the daily commute is just begging for a wheel-gripping, fist-shaking situation. The best way to handle such bumper-to-bumper bonding is to skip it altogether. Awake early or leave late in the day to avoid times of gridlock. If there's no way around a congested area, take Goldilocks' approach when choosing a lane: The fast lane is too fast, the slow lane too unpredictable. Pick the middle lane, and stay with it. Relax, accept it, watch for sudden stops, give the vehicle in front plenty of room, and take advice from your co-pilot. Leave the chronic lane-jumping for the guy in the Porsche. If things become unbearable, hit the off-ramp, find a spot at a travel plaza or parking lot, and play a game of Go Fish.

Life in the Fast Lane

Highway driving is pretty simple. Just pick a lane and go. Of course, throw in a little construction, traffic, and periods when you have no idea where you are, and things get more complicated. But basically, you've been driving long enough to know how to thrive in this arena. Since speeds are generally at their highest, be cognizant of the buffer zone between you and other vehicles. Avoid unnecessary lane changes and pass with care. Again, the middle lane is best, as it's the best vantage point to make the jump to the other lanes for off-ramps or avoiding trouble.

Road Scholar

A good rule is to add at least one second of distance between you and the vehicle in front of you for every ten feet of vehicle you are operating. Use a roadside marker to count off the time between the two vehicles. For example, if your RV measures 40 feet, (include tow or towed vehicles) pad at least 4 seconds between you. Add more distance when driving at night or when driving during adverse conditions.

Backing Up

The best rule is to avoid backing up whenever possible. However, it's not always possible when that lemonade stand materializes out of nowhere in front of your motorhome. The biggest mistake people make when attempting to back up an RV is getting in a hurry. Take your time, and don't let anyone rush you. If there are people watching, ignore them (well, unless they are screaming and waving fire extinguishers). Motorhomes pulling vehicles connected to tow bars and tow dollies should never, ever attempt a back up—you will damage the connection. If there's no other way around it, unhook the towed vehicle first, and scoot it out of the way. You can back up when towing a vehicle on a trailer, but it is more difficult to see behind the motorhome, particularly if you do not have a rear view monitoring system.

Before you attempt to back up, get out of the vehicle and assess the situation. Sometimes you may not be able to tell for sure whether you are able to drive through or are forced to back out unless you get out and survey the scene. Hop out and have a look-see. Better yet, wake up the co-pilot and have her do it. If someone is there to help guide you back, discuss where you want the RV to end up beforehand. Note any vehicles, mailboxes, or other obstacles you want to avoid. And don't forget to look up—there might be overhead wires or tree branches best left unprovoked. Look for any landmarks—or make one, such as a stick or mark in the gravel—so you know to stop when the object lines up with your wheels. This is especially helpful when backing into an RV site where you want to align the hookups with the corresponding points on the RV.

Get back in the driver's seat and put it in reverse. Use your side mirrors religiously. (Remember, the rearview mirror will probably either be blocked or nonexistent.) Lower the windows to hear prompts from anyone helping you back in. Back up very slowly, using small, quick turns of the steering wheel as necessary. Towable owners should focus on where the back of the trailer is going, rather than the movements of the tow vehicle. Don't hesitate to stop, get out, and walk back to check if things get goofy. If you get too far off course, just pull forward and to one side or the other, and try again. You may need to do this several times, especially if you do not have someone helping you. That's okay, you won't lose Brownie points. Just don't get in a hurry—that's when mistakes are made—usually expensive ones!

Road Scholar

The trickiest part of backing up a trailer is remembering to turn the steering wheel in the opposite direction of where you want the trailer to go. Place one hand on the bottom of the wheel, then move your hand in the direction of where you want the trailer to end up. In the event the trailer starts to veer to one side, turn the steering wheel toward the "problem" to straighten it out again.

It Takes Two

Backing up is like life. It's a whole lot easier with someone to guide you. (Are we sharing a Hallmark moment?) That is, assuming you and your partner can work out a system of hand signals or use handheld radios. Screaming, gesturing wildly, and jumping up and down are not particularly helpful to the driver—but this does make for a popular sideshow. It is also important that the person guiding you back understands exactly where he needs to stand in order to stay within the driver's sight. If you can't see the guider in the side mirror, he most definitely can't see you. Communicating via a pair of handheld radios is a great assist for those with larger vehicles.

The Seven Deadly Driving Sins

It's true, sometimes we are our own worst enemies. The same mistakes made behind the wheel of a car are multiplied in a larger, much heavier RV. The following are some of the more common—and correctable—driving errors.

Pull Over

Always stop immediately if you can't see the person guiding you back, or if she stops talking on the radio (if so equipped). You definitely don't want to end a long day with running over your spouse, which can lead to some ill-will, to say the least.

Rush, Rush

You've dreamt of this trip for weeks. Rushing home from work on a Friday afternoon, you quickly throw the cargo and crew onboard and blast out of the driveway in an effort to make some time. You're burning some serious rubber on the highway, leaving horrified onlookers to eat your proverbial dust. Why is everyone driving so slowly? The stoplights seem eternal, the traffic like miles of flypaper. To get to the campground at a reasonable hour, you push it, tailgating, making hurried lane changes and aggressive maneuvers. RVs aren't high-performance vehicles, and you're no Jeff Gordon. Trying to do too much too quickly is a surefire way to get into trouble. Slow down. Relax. Leave work early instead of forcing an unrealistic schedule. Stay an extra day on vacation to recharge the batteries if need be (yours, not the RV's).

One for the Road

I have found over the years that people do their best to give RVs a wide berth. Other drivers often seem to know that it's unwise to travel in a semi's or RV's blind spot, which is why few linger there. Expect respect for your RV's size, making your job a lot easier.

Car Talk

Most of us have been driving for many, many years, with the skills and experience to match. Obviously, this all serves as good preparation for RVing. However, a recreational vehicle is not a car; towing a trailer is different than anything most of us have ever done. It should go without saying that operating an RV like an automobile is another way to find a certain amount of peril. Failing to compensate for extra braking distances, counting on acceleration that simply isn't there, or darting around town or on the highways like we do with the family sedan is the stuff many novice drivers are made of. Remember the tips given earlier. Take the time to practice, working on backing in, cornering, and stopping. Learn your RV's abilities and limitations.

Nervous Nellie

Passive and nervous driving are nearly as bad as overly aggressive behavior. Slow or erratic speeds, poor decision-making, and an anxious demeanor lead to lousy driving—and could result in an accident. Driving in an overly anxious state is kind of like the athlete terrified of getting injured. And what usually happens? Ultimately, this causes him or her to do just that—call it a self-fulfilling prophecy. Follow speed limits, be confident, and don't worry about what other drivers behind you are thinking. Be courteous and safe, but be assertive. Concentrate on where you're going and the best way to get there. Identify your problem areas and practice those at length in isolated areas, such as a deserted parking lot or country road.

Lost in Space

It's always obvious when driving behind someone who's lost. The signs are always the same—erratic speeds, turning signals that rapidly appear and disappear, thoughtless lane changes, frequent braking, and a lot of frantic head-turnings are all dead give-aways. If that driver is you, then consider those who are struggling in your wake. Hopefully, an observant co-pilot won't let you get into this jam or can bail you out with some clever map working in times of trouble. Since turning around and sudden movements are often burdensome in an RV, it's best to just stop and get your bearings rather than keep driving around aimlessly when lost. Don't steer your rig into a situation that's tough to get out of—dead-end streets, narrow underpass, etc.

Road Scholar

Getting lost for me is as common as knowing where I'm going. A cell phone changed all that, as I now possess the ability to confirm an address or ask directions on the fly. Avoid unnecessary confusion in the first place by relying on mapping services found on the Internet, such as www.mapquest.com or www.randmcnally.com. A good travel atlas is another must. Just make sure the co-pilot can read it.

Danger, Will Robinson

Bad weather is a part of life. Driving through it doesn't have to be. Their higher profiles leave motorhomes susceptible targets to wind; gusts can batter longer travel trailers loopy, especially ones without sway bars (see Chapter 13 for details). Ice, rain, fog, and snow are problems for everyone, but especially for RVers needing more time to stop and being less capable of performing evasive maneuvers in an emergency. The best advice is to sit out extreme weather. If you're driving with doubts, you shouldn't be driving. Find a rest area and play a game of cards. Get off the highway and stop for dinner. With a kitchen, living area, and all the onboard amenities, there's no shortage of things to do while waiting for the weather to calm. You will find more on dangerous driving conditions in Chapter 20, "Playin' It Safe."

Overdoing It

Driving for some is the best part. The ever-changing landscape and the chance to see the scenery up close ranks among the most rewarding experiences of life on the go. Others, on the other hand, just want to get where they're going. Since trips to Florida, national parks, and Uncle Frank in Nova Scotia usually require more than just a few hours behind the wheel, we're all susceptible to overdoing it. Remember the three "As" of safe driving: Alert, Awake, and Active. Anything else puts you at risk. Driving a big rig is more tiring than the family Pinto, so give yourself a break. Better yet, give yourself a lot of breaks, and the time to clear your head, stretch out, and block out the highway hypnosis accompanying hours of nonstop transit.

Pull Over

Factors such as terrain, traffic, weather, and the type of RV all affect one's driving threshold. The most important thing is to know your limits and respect them. Push it and expect concentration and performance to wane significantly. Take frequent breaks. Determine your own abilities, going only so far as your mind and body allow. Switch off with the co-pilot when your momentum subsides.

Driving Under the Influence

As duly noted, RV owners are among the safest drivers on the road. They're usually a little older, more experienced, and respectful of the vehicles under their control. What can I say, we're a thoughtful bunch. Unfortunately, sometimes we unwillingly put ourselves at risk. Prescription medications can deliver side effects that impair our ability to operate a vehicle. Even some simple cold medicines may leave us tired, disoriented, or unnecessarily wired, all lousy traits when piloting a 20,000-pound motorhome or lengthy towing combination. Obviously, those under the influences of various narcotics or alcohol put themselves and their passengers at tremendous risk.

Sleepy, Sleepy

Okay, count this as the eighth deadly sin and one of the most overlooked. I think we've all been there. The crooning of the radio rocking us to sleep like a sweet lullaby. Oncoming headlights in a perpetual blur. The darkness lulling us into a sleep-deprived stupor. Our eyelids are getting oh so heavy. But despite these dangers, we trudge on. Hey, we're only a couple of hours from the ketchup museum, and there's no way we're stopping for the night. It's a waste of time and money, we think. Perhaps this will wake you up: According to a recent study by the National Highway Traffic Safety Administration (NHTSA), more than 100,000 crashes are attributed to drowsy drivers every year. This is a serious and underreported problem, one not to be taken lightly. If fatigue is getting the best of you, pull over. Eat a meal, walk around, switch drivers, find a campground, do whatever it takes to recapture your bearings. If you can't shake the grogginess, find a spot to spend the night.

Practice, Practice, Practice

Like any new skill, driving must be practiced. Remember all those y-turns you did in the driveway when you were getting ready to get your license? I would make the same recommendation whether you were a first-time motorhomer or a novice skateboarder. Practice, practice, practice. Before hitting the road, drive the RV around town to improve your skills and increase your confidence. Set up some cones in an empty parking lot, and work on accelerating, turning, slowing down, stopping, backing up, and parking. (Don't worry—RVers aren't expected to know how to parallel park.) Notice how much longer it takes you to stop with the added weight behind you and how much wider you need to swing around corners. Work at that backing-up technique until you get the hang of it. It's much easier to perfect this in private than at a campground full of onlookers.

A Class Act

Practice makes perfect, but a little instruction along the way doesn't hurt. Although still rare, a few RV dealers take pains to make sure customers know how to operate their new purchase before taking delivery. Take advantage of any driving classes and seminars offered, whether found at a dealership, RV show, or other types of get-togethers. Driving schools are also a good bet, offering practical and behind-the-wheel instruction, usually in your very own rig. Finally, if you ever get involved in the RV rally scene (see Chapter 18, "Travel Planning," for the low-down), driving seminars, classes, and competitions are frequently offered.

The advantages of certified RV instruction are many. For starters, attendees learn the ins and outs of driving and towing, taught by veteran RVers and professional drivers. The best situation is actual behind-the-wheel instruction in your very own RV with an able teacher there to guide you. Some RV insurers provide discounts for suitable coursework or graduation from an accredited class or school, saving you a few bucks over the lifetime of a policy.

Fuel

I find travel plazas and truck stops along the highway are the best places to fill up. Drivers can count on plenty of room to maneuver, lofty clearances, and a fresh supply of diesel, a concern addressed back in Chapter 6, "Narrowing Down Your Choices." Not only that, but there's also never a shortage of nachos, milkshakes, and cheeseburgers the size of your head—but I digress. Of course, no one's limited to just these places to fill 'er up—most anyplace will do.

Fuel costs are among the greatest threats to an RVer's pocketbook. Don't expect more than 20 miles per gallon no matter what you're driving or towing; a large motorhome easily sinks under 10 mpg. Obviously, this is a leggy expense for those driving over the mountains and through the woods to grandmother's house you go. Face it, you're

Pull Over

Frequent gas stations offering enough room to maneuver, particularly when operating a large RV. Keep an eye on clearances and avoid getting yourself into a tricky driving situation at smaller facilities. Make doubly sure no LP appliances are in use, pilot lights are extinguished, and the propane container(s) are shut off before pulling in.

operating a gas-guzzler, and there's not much you can do about it. However, keep weights low and an RV rewards you with a little better fuel economy. Join a travel club or gas chain offering discounts on fill-ups, such as the Flying J Travel Plazas. Even a 10 cent discount per gallon shines brightly when topping off a 100-gallon tank. And it's most definitely true that traveling 55 mph is more economical than a high-speed odyssey across the country. Steady speeds and highway miles are recommended.

Dealing With ...

Careful, there are forces at work to disrupt the cool tranquility of an RV vacation. Some of this baggage you bring with you; others are the cold slap of a world in a rush, where patience and civility are sometimes broadsided—and then backed over for good measure. It seems that not *everyone* is as pleased about your RV purchase as you are. Here's how to deal with the roadway naysayers by taking a look at their various gripes.

You're Big

Imagine the driver of the poor compact car behind you. He or she can't see beyond or around your RV's towering facade. You're probably even blocking out the sun—the oxygen, too. There's nothing you can do about that fact except give fellow drivers as much room as possible. Don't crowd them, leaving plenty of space on all sides. During traffic, find a lane and commit to it, keeping you out of as many people's hair as possible. Maintain a steady speed. Pull over and let others pass when it's safe to do so, especially when climbing hills. Even on two-lane roads, an extra lane is often present in uphill areas for this very purpose.

You're Slow

On the highway, you're fine. It's those steep grades or slow starts around town that get tailgaters steamed. Don't take it personally. These folks are in a hurry and will surely be just as annoyed at the next guy they pass. Don't let others drive your vehicle. Maintain adequate speeds and stay out of the fast lane. If a crowd is forming behind you like the Macy's Day Parade, pull over and let them pass. It's a nice gesture and lessens the anxiety about the mob scene bringing up the rear.

Road Scholar

Drive long enough and you're bound to encounter some sort of road rage. One of the perks of a recreational vehicle is that obnoxious drivers are less likely to mess with you—just one of the benefits of life at the top of the food chain. In the event of a volatile situation, let the vehicle pass. Stay clear. Don't reciprocate antagonistic behavior. In the case of trouble, take down their plates and call the police.

Must-Have Gear

Assuming there's any money left after the big purchase, a few extra accessories are recommended to make driving a tad easier. Specific gear to make the towable owner's life easier is listed in Chapter 13.

Side Mirrors

Invest in a pair of extra wide side mirrors, providing elongated views of the sides and back of the coach or towable. Since the rearview mirror is absent or rendered useless by obstructed views, side mirrors are your lifeline to what's going on behind you. True, all vehicles come with *some* sort of side mirror, but opt for larger, extendable versions found throughout the aftermarket to create bigger, broader sight lines.

GPS/Navigation Systems

Since getting lost is that much more traumatic in a large vehicle, many owners need little rationalizing to drop some money on a global positioning satellite (GPS) or other navigational aids. Believe me, you won't miss all those trip-saving U-turns and quick jaunts off the interstate to get directions one bit. Although not cheap, costs are coming down, and there's a full range of products available, all designed to get you where you're going. Nicer GPS systems pinpoint an exact location, receive up-to-date detours around construction, and identify points of interest such as restaurants, hospitals, and service stations along the way. Of course, for a purist like me, nothing beats a compass and a co-pilot who can read a map (unlike my wife).

Rear View Monitoring System

A rear-mounted camera and cockpit monitor take much of the guesswork out of backing up. Although far from essential, such devices are very helpful, particularly if you are backing up alone. It's also a nice way to learn what's going on behind your vehicle when you hear a bump in the night. Consider it an eye in the sky, if you will. Such systems consist of a camera and perhaps a microphone mounted on the rear of the vehicle. The view from the rear is displayed on a monitor inside near the driver's seat, so you can literally watch where you are going as you back up. These devices aren't substitutes for getting out and checking out the scene first. (They may not reveal low-hanging branches or pieces of broken glass.) Find a camera that works at night for late-night back-ins.

The Least You Need to Know

- Driving and towing an RV is different, not difficult. Respect your weight, height, and width, realizing that stopping, cornering, and accelerating demand more time and patience than the vehicle at home. Practice these skills in a contained area. Attending a licensed driving school, classes, or seminars is also recommended.
- Common operator mistakes include hurried or passive driving, fatigue, influence of medications, pushing through inclement weather, refusing to take breaks, and a lack of awareness of the RV's abilities and limitations.
- There are a number of products (both dealer-installed and aftermarket) to make driving easier, such as side mirrors, navigational aids, and a rearview camera and cockpit monitor.

Chapter 15

How Much Does Your RV Weigh?

In This Chapter

- The importance of following weight limits
- How and where to weigh your rig
- Packing procedures for proper balance
- Dieting tips for a slender RV

Americans are compulsive about their weight. Why did I eat that last slice of pizza? How long must I toil on the treadmill to burn off that chocolate chip cookie? Does my butt look big in these jeans? (Men, don't answer that!) Such obsession with our appearances is probably not such a good thing since it can make you absolutely crazy if you let it. However, keeping tabs on our *RV's* weight regimen is something else altogether. As we'll try to demonstrate in this chapter, one's recreational machine can never be too slim—and an overweight condition can lead to a serious problem.

A portly motorhome or towable is trouble on wheels. Like all vehicles, RVs have their limits as far as what they can and cannot safely transport. With new RVs boasting tons of clever storage compartments, enormous holding tanks, room for numerous passengers, and plenty of space for your spouse's drum set, becoming overloaded is not an exception, rather almost a foregone conclusion for most newbies. At the very least, an overweight vehicle consistently underperforms, increases the likelihood for needing service and repairs, and might earn owners an expensive ticket from the local constable. Worse still, added pounds compromise the safety factor, something that can never be overstated.

So while you take a breather from your aerobics class or compute the caloric content of that chocolate éclair (you don't want to know), ponder the state of a chubby RV. Fortunately, unlike the grapefruit diet you're on, this chapter delivers some amazing weight-loss tips (not for you, your RV), as well as weigh-in strategies and the proper way to pack and load vehicles for proper balance and optimum driver control. The result is a leaner, meaner RV and a lifetime of safer transit.

Weighty Concerns

It doesn't matter if you're towing a lovable little pop-up or hauling around a 20,000-pound fifth wheel. It makes no difference if one finds herself behind the wheel of a camper van, a truck camper, a diesel motorhome, or a custom-made bus. Overloaded is overloaded, and this weight gain never adds up to a positive situation. The chassis, axles, and tires don't want to hear excuses for why you're exceeding their weight limits. They just know that you are and each strains accordingly. The danger is real—an overloaded vehicle is a dangerous condition.

Understanding an RV's weight restrictions is very important for novice and veteran RVers alike. Exceeding these ratings can be problematic for you and your family, not to mention others sharing the roadways with you. This added girth can cost you more in repairs and maintenance, because expensive components such as transmissions, brakes, and tires will wear out prematurely. The strain on the chassis, the very foundation of the vehicle, is also cause for concern, and I guarantee this will come back to haunt you. It will take a heavier motorhome or trailer-tow vehicle combination longer to stop, more muscle to maneuver, and otherwise transform a once road-worthy RV into a sluggish pile if you let it fatten up. Gas mileage suffers, too, costing you plenty of dollars over time.

Road Scholar

Many buyers make the weigh-in the last step in the purchase of a new RV (whether towable or motorhome) *before* the final papers are signed. This ensures that our shiny new toy on the lot really *does* weigh what the sticker or brochure claims, and whether or not it allows you enough extra payload for your family and all your belongings.

But here are a few more reasons not to gamble on these weighty odds. In the event of an accident, an overloaded RV screams "liable" at the top of its lungs. A zealous insurance company can and will refuse coverage, warranties may be voided, and the fallout could spill over to a courtroom, costing you more than you ever imagined. Driving an overweight vehicle is also against the law, and for good reason: It's dangerous and easy to remedy. Have I made this point clear? Keep that vehicle underweight and out of trouble.

Is My RV Fat?

It's bad enough that our spouses need constant reassurance about their looks, but now the RV has a complex, too. Well, in this case, it's a good thing. Routine weigh-ins are the only real way to determine its true weight. No, I'm not talking about weekly Weight Watcher classes. But weighing your rig is very important for safety (yours and everyone else's) and should not be neglected. Here's how.

Weight and See

So where does one weigh a recreational vehicle? The nearest certified scale is probably a lot closer than you think. The most likely place is a truck stop (most have scales) or possibly a grain elevator. Your RV dealer should know where the nearest scale is located. Otherwise, check out the Yellow Pages under "Scales," ask at the next truck stop, or keep heading down the interstate until a weigh station presents itself.

One for the Road

At some point, you will hear someone talking about *wet* versus *dry* weights. This terminology stems from the fact that there are major differences between a fully loaded RV (wet) and an empty one (dry). It's just another way of saying loaded or unloaded.

The beginning of a trip is probably the best time to belly up to the scale, when the volume of provisions (food, particularly), full fuel and fresh water tanks, and LP gas containers are at their greatest. New RVers especially have a tendency to overpack. In addition, it's a good idea to weigh an RV regularly. In time, you'll begin to know what things can come along and what must stay behind—like Grandma and her house full of felines.

Tipping the Scales

None of us likes bellying up to the scale. If you're like me, the results are often dispiriting. Note to self: Cancel my subscription to the Donut-of-the-Month Club. (Goodbye sweet Boston Cream.) But take note, an RV has no such conscience. When you arrive at the scale, simply follow the signs. When prompted by the green light or voice commands, pull ahead very slowly until told to stop, either over the loudspeaker or by the light changing to red. You may have to ease ahead a short distance since some scales are equipped to weigh your rig at different points to ensure that the weight is properly distributed.

Motorhome owners should learn their vehicle's total weight (separate from any towed vehicle), the weight of each axle (accomplished by pulling only the front or back wheels on the scale), and the weight of the vehicle they're towing (if applicable), which is performed separately. Those pulling a secondary vehicle definitely want a tally of the motorhome/dinghy vehicle combination as well. Trailer owners' work is similar. Start by weighing the loaded tow vehicle first. Pull the trailer onto the scale and weigh the entire tow vehicle/trailer combination together, then, just the trailer alone, and finally, each axle.

Pull Over

It is important to weigh in when the RV is at its heaviest, usually after the RV is loaded with everything you plan to take on the road, including filled fresh water, fuel, and LP gas tanks, passengers (including Fido!), and gear. This is to ensure that you did not overdo it during the loading process, which is easier than you might think. After a few trips, travelers quickly learn their limits and how to pack accordingly.

When indicated, drive off the scale and park your rig. Go back inside to get your printout and pay the fee (usually nominal, but money well spent). Now, how did you do? No idea what all those numbers mean? Let's take a closer look.

RVocabulary

The **axle weight,** also known as gross axle weight, or GAW, is the number of pounds that each axle can safely support. Axle ratings are available through the manufacturer, or listed in the owner's manual or in brochures. Proper weighing at a truck scale can detail the exact weight for each axle.

The Tale of the Tape

First, find the total weight. We're looking for two things here: First, the total weight of each vehicle, so we don't overshoot the individual weight limits of each, or GVWR (see Chapter 13, "Towin' the Line," if you're drawing a blank). Secondly, the combined weight of the towing combination so as not to exceed the limitations of the vehicle doing the towing, better known as the GCWR (Chapter 13 again). Compare these numbers with the manufacturer's recommendations. If the scale reports ratings less than the manufacturer's guidelines, you're in good shape. However, if it's greater than your vehicle's weight or towing limit, well, it's time to diet, which we'll discuss later in this chapter.

The printout should also reveal the various *axle weights,* the recommended limit that each axle can safely support. Compare these figures with your RV's axle recommendations (also known as gross axle weight, or GAW), found in the owner's manual or through the manufacturer. Too much, and we have to redistribute the weight (see how in the following section) inside the RV.

The Findings

If these numbers are within the proper limits, you are ready to hit the road, secure in the knowledge of a svelte, sassy vehicle. But if not, you will need to take out a few things—or redistribute them (in the case of inflated axle ratings). Sometimes you can be within the safe limits overall, but overweight in one area, such as over the rear axle. If that is the case, you'll need to lighten the load in that area. Maybe the 23-volume set of encyclopedias needs to go back into the living room. Or maybe you just need to replace it altogether with a CD-ROM version. In the case of extreme overloading, it's time for some serious soul-searching. How did this happen? What stays and what goes? How do I tell my spouse he has to stay home and mow the lawn? Take a deep breath. Let's start at the beginning ...

Packing

A new RV, a wide-open itinerary, and the call of the open road. It's an exciting time, for sure. Don't let this euphoria corrupt the packing stage, as it always seems to doom bright-eyed first-timers. Overpacking is almost a foregone conclusion for the new RVer. You simply want to bring everything you can because, well, the RV looks big enough to handle it. Again, repeat after me: RVs have limits, and overzealous packing is the fastest way to exceed them. Modify behavior in the packing stage, and you shouldn't have problems later on.

When to Say When

Let's be scientific about it. Just how much can an RV hold? Actually, someone's already done most of the work for you, referred to as the RV's *net carrying capacity*. This number reflects the difference between what the RV actually weighs (UVW) and the maximum it can safely hold (GVWR). The net carrying capacity basically refers to the weight of any and all additional items—passengers, gear, fluids, etc.

RVocabulary

You may know it better as the NCC, or the payload. The **net carrying capacity** is how much cargo your vehicle can carry, determined by subtracting the RV's unloaded vehicle weight (UVW) from its maximum capacity (GVWR). This number includes passengers, provisions, full tanks, and the bloated cat. The smaller the number, the less you can bring. The larger the number ... hey, you catch on fast.

Although the NCC is usually common knowledge, most often listed in brochures and the owner's manual, let's just double-check that figure. Take the RV to the truck scale and get the honest truth. First weigh the RV completely empty—no gear, empty tanks, etc., to determine its UVW. Sure, this, too, is listed in your owner's manual, but as belabored in Chapter 13 and previous chapters, consider this rating as an estimate. That original number might have ballooned somewhat from the assembly line to the dealer's lot, affected by every add-on and accessory item, including awnings, an extra air conditioner, and/or a slide-out room.

Next, subtract the UVW from the GVWR (a number that never changes, no matter what happens after the vehicle leaves the assembly line). Bingo, the NCC is born. This number may be sizable or quite paltry. In any event, it's the total weight of passengers, their gear, and tanks full of fuel, fresh, black, and gray water. Write this number down, frame it if you like, as it serves as the absolute packing limit.

Here's a brief example of computing the net carrying capacity. Take a look at the equation, in this case a typical 34-foot motorhome with two slide-out rooms:

GVWR	–	UVW	=	net carrying capacity
20,500 lbs	–	18,000 lbs	=	2,500 pounds

In this case, you have 2,500 pounds to work with. Of course, it's a good idea not to push this number to the brink, in the event that you load up on supplies or extras along the way (like those his and her Elvis busts from Graceland). I'm sure 2,500 pounds sounds like more than enough weight, doesn't it? However, the example that follows should demonstrate just how quickly a typical family can devour that number.

What Weighs What?

With the net carrying capacity in hand, it's time to start loading up. Decisions, decisions. Should I bring along the saxophone? How about the holiday turkey with stuffing, cranberry sauce, and a nice pumpkin pie? How about the kids? Okay, let's bring 'em. I'm certainly not advocating putting every single item on the bathroom scale, but it's good to have at least *some* point of reference as to what you're loading onboard. The following exercise should get you thinking about the cause-and-effect relationship of packing and overloading.

Passengers

Start with the weights of all passengers—and not that suspect number appearing on their driver's licenses either, the *real* number.

Net Carrying Capacity for Your RV

Passengers	Weight
Husband	225 lbs.
Wife	130 lbs.
Child A	100 lbs.
Uncle Frank	210 lbs.
Family Dog	60 lbs.
Total	790 lbs.

Tanks

Next, add up all the fluids. What does a full tank of gas weigh? How about a fully loaded LP gas container(s) or the fresh water filled to capacity? These numbers adversely affect the net carrying capacity, too. Obviously, tank specs vary by the RV type (see Chapters 4, "The World of Motorized RVs," and 5, "The World of Towables," for typical specs). The following weight table should help you compute these numbers.

Weights of Various Fluids

Fluid	Weight
Water	8.4 pounds per gallon
Gasoline	6 pounds per gallon
Diesel	8 pounds per gallon
LP	4 pounds per gallon

In the case of our 34-foot motorhome, you can see how these full tanks add up.

Net Carrying Capacity of a Typical Thirty-Four-Foot Motorhome

Fluid	Capacity	Weight
Fresh water system	50 gallons × 8.4	420 lbs.
Gasoline	75 gallons ×	450 lbs.
Gray water holding tank*	50 × 8.4	420 lbs.
Black water holding tank**	50 × 8.4	420 lbs.
LP gas container(s)	60 gallons × 4	240 lbs.
Total		1,950 lbs.

**Since there's no reason to drive around with full wastewater tanks, subtract this number when applicable. In this scenario, we can easily subtract approximately 800 or more pounds if we drive with near-empty tanks.*

***Revised total: 1,110 pounds (with empty wastewater tanks)*

Gear

As you can see by our example, after passengers (790 pounds) and full tanks (1,110 pounds—without empty waste water tanks), that leaves 600 pounds of gear, or about 50 pounds per person (not including the pooch) until the RV reaches the bloated stage. This number includes all food, clothes, cooking supplies, plates and dishes, laptop computer, lawn chairs, fishing gear—basically, anything else added onboard. Keep these numbers in mind before your next trip.

Road Scholar

This exercise demonstrates how innocently packing can start, only to become potentially overloaded at the end. One of the biggest excesses are the fluids. As noted, full waste-water tanks add hundreds of needless pounds. Get in the habit of emptying tanks before leaving the campground. A fresh water tank filled to capacity is yet another weighty extravagance, particularly if fresh water hookups are available down the road.

The Leader of the Pack

Only you can say what you need on your trip. Of course, a lot depends on where you're going, what time of year, and for how long. You'll pack differently for a weekend a few miles away from home than for a two-month sabbatical through the western states. Full-timers wrangle with different packing criteria than weekend warriors; larger families' things-to-bring list is different than a couple's. So with grain of salt in hand, allow these recommendations to stimulate a little thought. Consider it the mother of all packing lists. Until you've nailed down your own list, go ahead and use ours. And watch those weights.

What to Pack

Cooking

- ❑ Food and drink
- ❑ Spices and seasonings
- ❑ Silverware
- ❑ Plates and dishes
- ❑ Paper towels
- ❑ Skillet
- ❑ Oven mitt
- ❑ Can opener (manual)
- ❑ Bottle opener
- ❑ Baking dish

- ❑ Drinking cups
- ❑ Cooking utensils
- ❑ Cutting knife
- ❑ Recipes
- ❑ Matches
- ❑ Aluminum foil
- ❑ Tupperware
- ❑ Plastic bags
- ❑ Garbage bags
- ❑ Dishwashing detergent
- ❑ Cutting board
- ❑ Coffee maker or percolator
- ❑ Sponge
- ❑ Toaster
- ❑ Pot(s) and pan(s)
- ❑ Dish towels

Sleeping

- ❑ Pillows
- ❑ Blankets
- ❑ Sheets
- ❑ Alarm clock
- ❑ PJs
- ❑ Robe

Bathroom/Shower

- ❑ Towels
- ❑ Soap
- ❑ Shampoo
- ❑ Lotion
- ❑ Prescription medicines
- ❑ First-aid kit
- ❑ Suntan lotion
- ❑ Aspirin
- ❑ Comb/brush
- ❑ Toothbrush
- ❑ Toothpaste
- ❑ Hair dryer
- ❑ Curling iron
- ❑ Deodorant
- ❑ Shaving gear
- ❑ Makeup
- ❑ Vitamins
- ❑ Toilet paper

Personal Effects

- ❑ Watch
- ❑ Cell phone
- ❑ Laptop
- ❑ Music
- ❑ Book
- ❑ Maps
- ❑ Cash
- ❑ Campground directory
- ❑ *The Complete Idiot's Guide to RVing* (shameless plug)
- ❑ Eyeglasses/contacts (with solution)
- ❑ Sunglasses
- ❑ Camera
- ❑ Pen and paper
- ❑ Proof of insurance
- ❑ Swiss army knife
- ❑ Pet supplies (leash, toys, bed)
- ❑ Envelopes and stamps
- ❑ Vehicle registration, proof of insurance, roadside assistance
- ❑ RV and appliance manuals
- ❑ Calling card

Clothing

- ❑ Hat
- ❑ Long underwear
- ❑ Rain gear
- ❑ Shoes (for inside and out)
- ❑ Underwear
- ❑ Jeans
- ❑ T-shirts
- ❑ Jacket
- ❑ Socks
- ❑ Belt
- ❑ Dress shirt
- ❑ Hangers
- ❑ Shorts
- ❑ Swimsuit
- ❑ Laundry bag
- ❑ Laundry detergent

Outside Stuff

- ❑ Golf clubs
- ❑ Fishing poles
- ❑ Lawn chairs
- ❑ Portable grill
- ❑ Charcoal
- ❑ Lighter fluid
- ❑ Cooking grate
- ❑ Bug spray
- ❑ Flashlight
- ❑ Emergency kit*
- ❑ Spare parts kit**
- ❑ Basic tool kit***
- ❑ Tablecloth
- ❑ Frisbee
- ❑ Flashlight
- ❑ Jumper cables
- ❑ Tire pressure gauge
- ❑ Two 25-foot electrical cords
- ❑ Two 25-foot fresh water hoses
- ❑ Sewer hose
- ❑ Cable for cable TV hookup
- ❑ Hand soap
- ❑ Disposable rubber gloves
- ❑ Door mat or carpet swatch
- ❑ Chemicals for tanks
- ❑ Wheel chalks and leveling boards
- ❑ Cleaning supplies
- ❑ Mini vacuum

**An emergency kit is useful in the event of an accident. It should include flares, reflectors, a pencil and paper, flashlight, and disposable camera for capturing the scene of an accident. Compile a list of names (doctor, insurance agent, lawyer) and any medications you're currently taking. Then hope there's never a need to open it.*

***The spare parts kit should consist of the following items: an extra LP regulator; batteries for CO monitor, smoke alarm, LP gas detector; extra battery terminals; fuses; wire-splicing terminals; running/stop/marker bulbs; water pressure regulator; holding tank patch kit; and water hose repair kit.*

****A basic tool kit should consist of the following items: assorted Phillips and flathead screwdrivers; needle nose, 8-inch groove joint, standard slip joint, and locking pliers; duct and electrical tape; socket set (3/8-inch drive); combination wrench set (1/4 to 1 inch); crescent wrenches (6 and 12 inches); tire gauge; flashlight; eye goggles; and polarity tester.*

Never forget any must-have items again by stocking the RV with its own supply of linens, dishes, nonperishable foods, and supplies. Avoid bringing valuable items that could get lost or dirty "out in the wild."

Common Pitfalls

Unfortunately, an RV can't lift weights, swim laps in a pool, or jump rope to shed unwanted pounds (a funny image, though). The only way to maintain its proper physique is to not overdo it in the first place. Too many of us take the home on wheels thing a little *too* seriously, treating our RVs like an endless reservoir for everything we could ever possibly want or need. Scrutinize packing lists and realize that a lot of little things *do* indeed add up. Weigh the rig or trailer/tow vehicle periodically during the season to ensure those numbers aren't creeping up, kind of like our waistlines over the holidays. When overpacking does occur, often one of the following is to blame.

Chow

How many canned goods does it take to effect an RV? How about endless cases of soda, an unusual attachment to canned hams, and a month's worth of meals? Now I certainly don't want anybody to go hungry, but food is a popular overindulgence—both eating it and bringing too much along. First-timers especially seem fearful that their family might become stranded without their Eggos. Tote along only enough food for *this* trip; there's no reason to stockpile here. For shorter getaways, create a menu and buy only those items required. An RV galley isn't like the pantry at home—there isn't the space to keep a lot of provisions onboard "just in case." Think light when grocery shopping. Break the trip down into parts and do the shopping when the cupboards are bare and the natives get restless. It's not prudent to attempt one all-inclusive grocery trip for a lengthy vacation.

Cooking Supplies

Cooking appliances are the slipperiest of slopes. Fortunately, most RV galleys feature everything most of us need for simple camping cuisine, but some of us just like a few more options. If you're gonna bring the Crock-Pot, then the electric skillet has just got to come, too. And the family just loves their Smurf-shaped waffles, so the waffle iron is a definite must. Next thing you know, the popcorn maker, juicer, and wok are jockeying for room onboard, with an A to Z catalog of cookbooks as well. Make a few tough choices to stop the insanity. How many skillets and how many pots? Again, a weekly menu should help determine what cooking apparatus is needed and what will just be gathering dust by week's end.

One for the Road

Drop needless pounds by substituting heavier items with lighter versions. Use paper plates and cups instead of weightier (and more fragile) traditional place settings. Try cans instead of bottles, fast-food-size condiments over bulky containers, single-serving packages instead of bulk goods, stainless steel or aluminum cookware over glass or cast iron. Remove excess packaging and favor dry goods, like pasta and pancake mix. They keep well and are lighter than canned items.

Storage Pods and Nooks

Smaller RVs, where storage for a growing family is sometimes dicey, can certainly benefit from an extra storage pod, usually attached to the roof of the vehicle. More room, more stuff. Problem solved, right? Well, yes and no. Again, just because you have the space, it doesn't mean you should always go and fill it. Since pods are generally outside and out of the way, heavier items always make their way here. I don't need to tell you about the trouble with heavy items, do I? They're heavy! Going the pod route is perfectly fine; just keep tabs on what goes in here, and ask yourself just how important these items really are.

The more storage onboard, the happier must of us are. Most RVers lament that they never have enough space to put things. However, such thinking gives rise to the temptation to fill every available inch. Basement storage floor plans, with cavernous compartments for cumbersome outside goodies, are especially vulnerable to overfilling. A disciplined packing list should help prevent overloading, even when space is abundant.

Child's Play

Squeezing their whole life into a suitcase is especially traumatic for kids. It starts off innocently enough. Yes, you can bring Mr. Snuffles. Sure, Frankie the Bee can come, too. Next thing you know, there's an entire menagerie of stuffed animals and friends in every nook and cranny. A library of favorite books riding shotgun is instant poundage. Those traveling with young girls know that your little diva will demand an outfit for every occasion. Teenagers, with bulkier gear, may be especially hard to de-program. Make ground rules known in advance. Start with one bag or allotted compartment onboard per person and see how that works. Remember, the early days of your RV life is a work in progress. You may look back and laugh about your once pack rat mentality.

Tools

I know how difficult it can be to leave the table saw behind. I, too, have grieved over the thought of my faithful drill at home all alone. Unfortunately, some of us succumb to separation anxiety with our tools, some of the weightiest and least essential weight offenders you can bring along (no offense, fellas). As previously mentioned, a small (yes, small) tool kit is a useful tag-along. Anything more is probably overkill.

The Loading Zone

Yes, there's a right way and a wrong way to load an RV. Too much weight on one side, and your motorhome or trailer might begin to lean like my dad after a 48-ounce sirloin. Too much weight in the rear, and the rear axles might complain, or worse, exceed their ratings. Meanwhile, a proper *hitch weight* is important to keep towables level while reinforcing the connection between the two vehicles. Furthermore, proper placement of gear eliminates breakage and that frantic search for the corkscrew come vino time. A properly loaded RV is more stable and handles better. Gauge hitch weight by lowering just the tongue portion onto a truck scale. A bathroom scale often works here for some lightweight towables.

RVocabulary

The **hitch weight,** also known as tongue weight, is a rating specified by towable manufacturers to aid in ride stability. Generally, 10 to 15 percent of the RV's total weight should be placed near the tongue of the trailer to reinforce the hitch connection. Fifth wheels usually ask for 15 to 20 percent to be placed in the gooseneck portion.

Even Steven

Towable owners should review the hitch weight (found in the usual channels—owner's manual, brochure, or by contacting the manufacturer directly). Distributing approximately 10 to 15 percent of the trailer's GVWR to the front of the trailer is the best thing for the tongue and hitch connection. Fifth-wheel owners should bump that number up to 15 to 20 percent. Too little weight here and expect a little fishtailing; too much and the added weight may buckle the hookup.

As stated above, axles, too, have special needs. Don't overload one or the other. You'll notice that the rear axle weight recommendations are usually heavier than the frontal counterparts for most motorhomes. Follow these instructions by placing more gear aft, which lends greater stability to your ride. Most excess tongue-weight issues arise

Road Scholar

Minimize movement and possible breakage of fragile items by wrapping them up during transit. Sheets, pillows, blankets, and coats make terrific buffers around delicate objects to avoid scratches, dings, and impromptu tumbling demonstrations. Place cardboard sleeves between glassware. Add nonskid material to shelves to keep things from sliding.

when some RVer decides he wants to bolt a generator onto the "A" frame of the trailer, mount a 27-drawer tool box up there, or carry three dirt bikes on the rear of the tow vehicle.

Double-Duty

The more items that can do double-duty, the better off you are and the more room left over. A wastebasket doubles as a bucket come cleaning day. A set of stackable drawers also serves as an end table. Agree on one brand of shampoo for everyone to avoid cluttering the shower. Leave the CD cases at home and store just the CDs in a small case. Use decorative pillowcases to store extra blankets or even clothing when they are not in use. Always be on the lookout for innovative, space-saving products for your RV—like folding dish racks or coffee tables with surfaces that raise up when needed.

The Least You Need to Know

- Exceeding an RV's weight limits leads to sluggish performance, poor stopping and acceleration, unnecessary wear and tear, added maintenance, and generally a dangerous situation for you and fellow travelers. It's also against the law.
- Determine your vehicle's true weight at weigh stations and compare against the manufacturer's recommendations. Scales provide key information such as the total weight and axle weight. Too much weight and it's time to diet.
- Disciplined packing is the best counter to an overloaded vehicle. Passengers and holding tanks comprise the majority of cargo weight onboard. Knowing what these things weigh should keep you and your rig out of trouble. Favor RVs with larger carrying capacities (NCC).
- A balanced RV performs better and creates a more stable ride. Distribute cargo evenly side to side to prevent leaning; add a little more weight in back than in the front. Towable owners should settle 10 to 15 percent of the weight near the front to support the hitch connection. Place lighter items in overhead cabinets and heavier items down low to avoid a top-heavy condition.

Chapter 16

Choosing a Campground

In This Chapter

- Determining the best places to stay
- Setting up and breaking camp
- Following campground etiquette

Campgrounds are a vital part of the RV experience. Without them, we'd have to beach our rigs in a hodgepodge of locales—most of them well off the beaten path, lacking the recreation, safety, and facilities most of us enjoy as part of travel. As you will hopefully recall, we started this discussion way back in Chapter 3, "Where to Stay?" examining the differences between private and public parks, plush resorts and rustic accommodations with minimal development. While that discussion may be a total blur by now, the most important thing to remember is that the choice of campground dictates much of the outcome of any particular trip. So, as the saying goes, let's choose wisely.

This chapter is designed to do just that. Whether you're simply looking for a stopover to spend the night or a place to lounge about for an entire vacation, we've got you covered. With millions of campsites scattered throughout the United States, there are plenty of places to call upon—with prices, views, amenities, and opportunities for fun to match any type of traveler.

And we'll even take that one step further. Once you arrive, you may be puzzled about what to do. So you don't waste time fiddling with awnings, slide-outs, and wondering where all those plugs and cords go, we'll walk you through the setting-up process without delay. You certainly don't need to tell us how precious your leisure time is. When it's time to go—you guessed it—more help is on the way, as we explain the best way to break camp and head on back home—or the next stop on the journey. It's a big country out there, so let's start exploring.

Where to, Bub?

With a fully self-contained vehicle, the spouse, the kids, the family pet, and a week's worth of grub in the fridge, it's hard to go wrong. Unlike the campgrounds themselves, the spaciousness and comforts aboard an RV are constants, a steady environment in an ever-changing world. Touring in such a livable shell, it's now really just a matter of where to park it. Obviously, RVers sift through all sorts of criteria when planning a trip and choosing their accommodations, and only you know what's most important for you and yours. However, let's look at some of the major decision-making factors to stimulate the thought process.

Location, Location, Location

Most campground stays fall into one of two categories: stopovers and destinations. A stopover is just that—usually just a quick overnight stay on the way to your *real* destination. On a long trip, say, from Chicago to the Alamo, expect to spend a couple of nights along the way. And since these stopovers are relatively short—usually just one day or a night's sleep and then away you go—whether or not the place has a swimming pool, mini-golf, or a 7:30 A.M. aerobics class may not be that important. Rather, as long as it's safe, quiet, and isn't nestled at the base of a toxic waste dump, everyone is happy enough. Many folks, eager to make time and get a move-on, look for a quick stopover near the interstate and then leave in the morning.

Pull Over

If chewing up miles is the most important thing to you, choose a stopover just off the highway. Easy in and easy out gets you back on the journey with little fanfare and few trip detours. However, don't pick one that's *too* close to a busy road, or you might experience a sleepless night awash in interstate noise.

Destination stays are entirely different. First of all, we hold them to a higher standard because this is the spot we've been traveling all those miles to reach. These campgrounds are usually near the attraction we've come to see (e.g., Disney World, the Grand Canyon, Cooperstown) and, thus, serve as a launching pad for each day's activities. Sometimes the campground itself *is* the main attraction, especially in the case of deluxe RV resorts or that mountain retreat with the splendid trout fishing. The conditions and offerings of these accommodations therefore become hugely important, since this is where you'll be spending much of your time.

Money Matters

Whereas hotels eat precious dollars from a vacationer's budget, campgrounds are far more forgiving. Even the nicest digs probably won't ever exceed $50—and that's for the finest accommodations in the best places, offering everything a weary RVer could want. On the flip side, a number of federally run facilities are free—yes, free—sparing pocketbooks even further. But most campsites' costs lie somewhere in between, with rates based on amenities, number of passengers, campsite location (pretty views might cost more), season, and discounts/affiliations.

One for the Road

Join one or more of the nation's larger RV clubs and perhaps knock as much as 10 percent off your accommodation bill. Frequent places that honor such affiliations. Seniors, AAA members, and large groups may also earn cheaper rates. Those loyal to national chains such as KOA or Jellystone Parks should obtain a membership card for nightly discounts. See Appendix A, "Resources," for various club information.

Special Needs

If you're one of the 50 million Americans with some form of mobility issue or handicap, it stands to reason that you favor more accessible RV parks. Ramps, user-friendly bathrooms and showers, paved campsites and roads can make all the difference. Of course, special needs come in many forms. Families traveling with pets prefer more animal-friendly settings, with dog runs, walking trails, and hosts quick to dish out a Milk-bone or two. If a pull-thru site is paramount, make sure the campground offers them—and that one is available for you. Kids are bored stiff at "adult-oriented" parks just as some couples quickly tire of the controlled chaos of "family-friendly" campgrounds. Determine your needs, locate accommodating facilities, and make them known when making reservations.

Fun, Fun, Fun

Recreation comes in many forms (see Chapter 3 for a list of possible offerings). One person's pastime is another person's snoozefest, so make sure there's plenty of stuff for everyone to do. Again, if you're only staying the night, this probably won't matter much. Otherwise, it's enormously important and sure beats channel-surfing the day away in your trailer. Want to teach the kids to swim in the pool? Looking for boat or bike rentals? Preferring a more natural vacation consisting of hikes, cross-country skiing, or bird watching? Every campground has its specialties—it's just a matter of matching them up with your preferences.

Road Scholar

Reservations help eliminate surprises upon arrival. Double-check the aspects of the stay in advance that are important to you, for example that the swimming pool is open. Be advised that some recreation and facilities are seasonal. Make needs known, such as a campsite overlooking the water or one near the bathroom. Reconfirm required hookups (water, electric, sewer, etc.) and a pull-thru site if needed.

One for the Road

Many campgrounds facilitate late-night check-in. Most provide a slot and perhaps envelopes or registration cards—you fill them out and put them in the slot with your cash or check. Others instruct campers to choose a site and pay in the morning. If there are no instructions, most RVers can just park in an empty site that meets their needs and take care of business the next day.

Extras, Extras

Most of us bask in enough goodies onboard our RVs and do not have to rely on a campground for a bathroom, shower, or potato chips from the camp store. However, such aspects are important to some, especially those traveling in smaller trailers, truck campers, and camper vans where floor plans are tight. If hot showers or sewer hookups will make all the difference between a good stay and a sour experience, make sure the park has them. Furthermore, if little extras such as a laundry room, planned activities for the kids, modem access, full hookups, and cable TV are vital, use them to narrow down your search for the perfect campground. (See Chapter 3 for a list of possible campground facilities and services.)

Finding Mr. Right

With more than 16,000 campgrounds in the United States and millions of available campsites, I like your chances of finding plenty of great places to say. But how, you may ask, do I find the best of the best, those parks most suitable for me and my crew? Never fear, there are plenty of ways to accomplish such a daunting task.

Campground Directory

Simply the best, most comprehensive, and expedient way to match up campgrounds with customers, a quality campground directory is a major asset in the life of any RVer. Well-known versions produced by Woodall's and *Trailer Life* provide detailed listings of the majority of private campgrounds in the land. Armed with a comprehensive ratings system, these books feature trained evaluators inspecting each park, relaying information on the level of development of facilities and recreation. A good directory is an impartial source of information and ranks high among the best $25 a camper could ever spend.

Here's a sample of typical listings information:

- Brief campground description
- Total number of sites
- Typical campsite dimensions
- Number of full hookup, primitive, and pull-thru sites
- Availability of modem, cable TV, and phone hookups
- Recreational offerings
- Range of costs
- Directions from major highways
- Tenting, cabins, or rental trailers offered
- Dump stations, laundry, groceries, and propane
- Seasonality
- Handicap-access
- RV size restrictions
- Payment options
- Contact information

Road Scholar

When choosing a campground directory, get the biggest book you can. Here size matters, with a quality book often exceeding 2,000 pages. Make sure the campgrounds are personally inspected by trained professionals. Information should be comprehensive and easy to use. Area maps, tourism information, and additional travel resources are nice pluses.

Internet

Twenty years ago, the typical campground employed a rudimentary power grid, relied on a lone pay phone to help travelers stay in touch, and hadn't the faintest clue what a slide-out was. How things have changed—and for the better. That same park today probably boasts a sophisticated phone system, modem access, and its own Web site. And who knows what the next decade will bring? Moon teleportation and jetpack rentals perhaps. The Internet affords many park owners a relatively cost-effective advertising source and the opportunity to lure potential customers from the Web. Spend a few minutes surfing for suitable accommodations, using your search engine du jour to locate prospects. More sophisticated Web sites allow customers to make reservations online and chat with owners via e-mail. While this selection method is a free and relatively easy process, less Internet-savvy campgrounds won't be discovered, thus limiting your choices somewhat.

Tourism Agencies

The folks down at the Chamber of Commerce and other tourism agencies love to hear from vacationers. In fact, it's a big part of what they do, to give you the warm fuzzies about their community and attractions. Contact tourism offices in the area you want to visit for a list of names and numbers of local campgrounds. Give these PR mavens enough notice, and they'll bury you in enough tourism and information packets for a lifetime of bonfires.

Word of Mouth

As we've been told, listening is a skill, and one that never fails to pay off when chatting with fellow RVers. Eventually, the conversation turns to campgrounds. Soon after, the hyperbole starts flying about that free little federal park next to the ocean or the New England resort with the 250-foot water slide. RVers are as opinionated about where they stay as what they drive, so expect lively discord about places to stay—and the ones to avoid. The next time your itinerary leads you into uncharted territory, open up your ears, go online, and ask around—you may just find a can't-miss recommendation.

Your Personal Campground Checklist

Cost

$________ The most I'm willing to pay

$________ Affiliations/discounts honored

Location

________ How many miles from the major attraction?

________ Proximity to the highway?

Special Needs

Important considerations for me or my passengers?

1. ______________________________
2. ______________________________
3. ______________________________

Recreation

Must-have activities/entertainment?

1. ______________________________
2. ______________________________
3. ______________________________
4. ______________________________
5. ______________________________

Campsite

- ❑ Pull-thrus?
- ❑ Full hookups?
- ❑ Water and electric?
- ❑ No hookups?
- ❑ Cable TV?
- ❑ Phone service?
- ❑ Other?

Facilities

- ❑ Bathrooms/showers
- ❑ Dump station?
- ❑ Modem access?
- ❑ Camp store?
- ❑ Laundry?
- ❑ Tenting?
- ❑ Cabins/cottages?

Setting Up Camp

Over the course of countless RV adventures, you will undoubtedly discover all sorts of interesting places to camp. And no two places are ever the same. It's not like checking into a Holiday Inn or other hotel chain where you know exactly how it will be before you even get there. For many, this great unknown is one of the best things about RVing. Indeed, the variety of such accommodations through America has always been what I like best. Snorkeling off the shore of that Florida Keys campground. Bass fishing at that Indiana state park. The conquering views from that little spot within the Colorado Rockies where few travelers dare to tread. I've been floored by the beauty of state- and federal-run campgrounds, enjoyed the extraordinary kindness of a mom and pop stopover, and let my vacation stretch lazily within the premises of an endearing RV resort. The choices, the variety, the uniqueness of each make every trip an adventure. And now that adventure is yours, a novel experience waiting around every bend.

Checking In

Hopefully, you've made the campsite reservations well in advance (summer and holiday weekends fill up fast) and explained exactly what you require—full hookups, a pull-thru site, a shady spot, etc. This should eliminate any surprises at check-in or a bitter case of the "No vacancy blues," the ultimate momentum-buster. At the entry point of every campground—no matter how big or small—is a place to check in—a campground office, a ranger booth, or camp store where the owner mans the cash register. This is your first and best opportunity to get the lay of the land and learn what the place offers, what's fun to do in the area, and what are any rules or restrictions for campers. After that, they're probably going to want some money, too, usually paid in advance.

One for the Road

Customer-friendly parks work hard to help visitors plan their stay. Local maps, videos, and orientation packets help out-of-towners acquaint themselves to a new area. Some RV resorts offer a type of concierge service, available to plan side trips, instruct travelers as to where to get the best blueberry pancakes, and tell you whether or not the fish are biting. Travel guides are for tourists; get the local angle from those in the know.

The campground office acts as a sort of nerve center. This is the best spot to get answers on most anything, get change for the laundry room, or just learn where the best steak joint within 20 miles can be found. Be sure to grab a map of the premises, highlighting facilities, recreation, and the like. I'll never forget the nice owner who, after check-in, hopped on his bike, led me to my campsite, connected me to all the hookups, and came back with firewood later on. I've even heard of a few places more than happy to back-in your rig and do the setting up chores for you. Don't expect this level of service everyplace, however, but it's nice when you get it.

Road Scholar

Unlike hotels and motels, don't expect the campground's office to be open when you saunter in at midnight. If arrival times place you somewhere in the late evening, call ahead and let them know you're still coming. Extend this courtesy to avoid being stuck outside the premises after a long day's drive. Late-night check-ins are often available, with campsite and park information awaiting you.

A Site for Sore Eyes

There she sits, a well-landscaped, grassy campsite on level terrain. Or perhaps it's a level (level is good!) concrete slab set amongst some tall trees producing wonderful shade. If you're lucky, the spot is overlooking the water, the mountains, or carved out of the deep woods for a remote feeling. Campsites differ tremendously, with terrain, views, and proximity to key facilities always up for grabs. The one thing they all have in common, however, is that each requires one last bit of driving ability to match up the vehicle with the hookups. Backing into position is called for in most scenarios. Take your time and do it right. Have your co-pilot get out and help you ease the rig where it needs to go, close to hookups and not butted up against the camper next door. Obviously, a pull-thru site eliminates any "reverse anxiety" since they're designed for you to drive right through and into position.

Road Scholar

Nothing captures the attention of campers like a big rig or trailer combo backing into a campsite. Call it a rite of passage, but expect a few onlookers when doing the deed. Drawing a crowd can unnerve even the most confident drivers. Relax. Plan the course, enlist the help of a spouse (or neighbor), and take it slowly. If it takes a couple of tries, so what?

Initiate Docking Sequence

The first order of business when pulling or backing in is to decide where you want the RV to end up. The proximity of hookups, amount of shade or sunlight, and obstacles to be avoided such as picnic tables, low-hanging branches, and campfire rings all factor into this decision. Be especially careful to allow enough space when settled to deploy slide-out(s) and awnings, which can add a couple of feet here and there. For those pulling cars behind the motorhome, this is a good time to separate the two vehicles and remove the tow bar/dolly from the equation. Remember, never attempt a back-up with either of these two devices in place (see Chapter 13 for the details). When the motorhome is in place, pull the secondary vehicle in behind, since it now serves as the primary transportation.

Road Scholar

A two-dollar investment in a bubble level always lets RVers know if they're on the "up and up." Otherwise, you'll need to guesstimate or see if your wife's casserole slides from the cockpit to the rear bedroom. Attach the level to the fridge so there are no doubts.

On the Level

The back-in or pull-thru was uneventful (the best kind), the RV sits near the vital hookups, and there's plenty of room for the slide-outs and awnings to stretch out. Before we pop the champagne, is the RV level? As mentioned in Chapter 11, "LP Systems," an RV's refrigerator only works properly when the unit is level (or mostly level). Moreover, an even keel prevents inhabitants from sliding around the interior like a Pee Wee hockey team or rolling out of bed in the morning. Okay, maybe that's an exaggeration, but level thinking is the way to go. Most spots are relatively flat, meaning no further action might be necessary. Otherwise, it's usually just a matter of fine-tuning. Although they probably don't sound like much fun, campsites with concrete slabs—inherently level and constructed near hookups—take the guesswork out of the process.

One for the Road

Dirt sites quickly devolve into a muddy mess after a rain, which may cause jacks and leveling systems to sink and maladjust. A hardy board under each "leg" should do the trick to halt any submergence. Just be sure to incorporate the same size board for all sides to keep things even Steven.

Most RVs are outfitted with some kind of levelers to forgo the frustration of moving the entire vehicle over and over into a level plane. Like most things in life, such equipment is as nice and effortless to operate as your wallet will allow. Pricier RVs might feature a built-in leveling system, which does the work for you. The push-button varieties are the best and most expensive—just activate the device (usually near the driver's seat) and enjoy the show as the RV shakes and shimmies its way to the right horizontal plane. Otherwise, consider the budget-friendly, more traditional wooden board route, where the driver levels the RV by pulling onto a couple of 2×8s (or whatever works) to prop up one set of wheels. Carry a few different sizes to create a workable balance.

Towable owners often rely on a tandem of manually deployed stabilizing jacks and the tongue jack to "right the ship," so to speak. It's a good idea not to unhitch the trailer from the tow vehicle until you are confident that the towable is where it needs to be. The final step is to add wheel blocks behind the towable tires, especially in the case of a slope or muddy conditions, to prevent any unnecessary roll.

Hookups

With the RV parked and level, you're ready to set up shop, er, camp. But before baiting up the fishing poles or sticking that pot roast in the oven, it's best to power up the rig's onboard systems, the core of most everything you'll want to do inside. Chances are the kids will attempt to sneak away for some quick fun, but get them involved in the set-up process, too. The sooner you're done, the sooner the leisure begins for everyone. Start with the hookups. The procedure varies based on the number of utilities offered in your site; full hookups require more steps than a more primitive site.

Locate the campsite's various utilities in question. (You should have done this when pulling in so the rig is nice and close and all the cords reach.) A tall metal box houses the electrical outlet and cable TV (if offered); the water faucet should be nearby, sticking out of the ground. You might need to scour the earth a little bit to locate the sewer drain, which is sometimes hidden amongst tall grass, weeds, or leaves. All of these hookups should be relatively easy to find and may be tucked back slightly in the site to prevent any unnecessary run-ins with RVs. Still, stay alert so as to not back over them when pulling in.

Electric

I still like to begin with the electrical hookup (better known as shore power), giving the electrical appliances some needed juice and the batteries a head start in recharging. As evidenced in Chapter 10, "Electrical Systems," this step is, to coin a phrase, as easy as falling in love. Plug in the RV's electric power cord to the campsite's electrical outlet at the pedestal. These days, most campsites offer 30-amp power, a good thing since this is probably what your RV was built for. Fifty-amp power is becoming increasingly popular for bigger rigs with more doo-dads. Consider a campsite with anything less than 30 amps (15- or 20-amp) a trip back into yesteryear. These paltry levels can struggle to adequately power today's RVs, forcing you to tone down your electrical usage onboard.

An adapter is necessary in the event of a mismatch (for instance, a 30-amp power cord and a 20-amp electrical outlet). It's a good idea to have an adapter to fit each of the four kinds of outlets typically offered (15-, 20-, 30-, 50-amps); otherwise, you won't be able to facilitate the connection. Check the site's power flow with a polarity tester first (again, Chapter 10) to reveal any potentially faulty wiring that could damage appliances. Contact the manager if there's a problem, and request another site. If all systems are go, plug in and enjoy a steady supply of electrical juice.

Pull Over

Do things around the campground not exactly resemble the awe-inspiring brochure? Are the facilities rundown? Is the "fabulous playground" a pile of scrap? Does the "wondrous summit" overlook a trash heap? Are the showers something out of a horror movie? Don't accept such deception by staying the night. If you feel the park was misleading, demand your money back. If they don't budge, threaten to consult the Better Business Bureau and the publishers of the various campground directories.

Fresh Water

The nice thing about onboard fresh water tanks is that you can always rely on your own reserves. A flip of the water pump and it's water time. Of course, you can always go with the campground's supply. It's up to you. Attach the fresh water hose from the city-water inlet on the side of the RV to the campsite's water outlet. As previously stated, using an inline water pressure regulator is good insurance when connecting to an outside water source. Some campgrounds may have unrestricted pressures, which can damage internal fittings. I also strongly advise a quality water filter or filtration system to screen out bacteria, molds, and other contemptibles. Most water is perfectly fine. However, give the water a taste—or find some other guinea pig—first before completing the hookup.

Turn the handle and the water is flowing. As long as you are hooked up to the campsite's water source, no water pump is required to propel the water through the pipes. If a shower or other hot-water need is in your future, now's a good time to activate the water heater to heat up a batch. (It might take 30 minutes to an hour, depending on the size of the appliance.) Just make sure the heater is filled before activation since operating it without water in its tank can harm the unit. Open all the hot water faucets first, to make sure water is fully flowing. If this is the case, then you know the heater is filled and safe to light.

Propane

It doesn't get much easier than this. Go outside, turn on the flow of propane at the container, and you're ready to go. Return to the vehicle and set the refrigerator to propane or 120-volt. (See Chapter 11 to determine which setting you might prefer.)

The remaining LP appliances—stove, oven, and/or water heater—are ready to go (although lighting a pilot flame or activating the ignition cycle may first be necessary). It's not uncommon with a new batch of LP for some air to infiltrate the lines, making it difficult to light some appliances at first. This is also likely after periods of extended nonuse. In such an event, ignite the stove burners for a minute or so to purge any air out of the system, and then try to light the remaining appliances. The lines should quickly clear, and you shouldn't have any more problems.

Sewer

Unless the waste water tanks resemble your cousin Al after an all-you-can-eat buffet, I suggest connecting to the sewer drain only when ready to empty—best performed at the end of the stay. (This may not be practical for longer stays, requiring multiple tank purges.) This gives you one less hose to trip over when carrying that plate of hamburgers and prevents the temptation to empty the tanks as you go, a no-no which can cause clogged pipes and tanks as discussed in Chapter 12, "Plumbing Systems." When it's time to dump, put on some disposable rubber gloves and attach the sewer hose from the connection underneath the RV to the (hopefully) nearby drain. Follow the dumping procedures outlined in Chapter 12.

Pull Over

Twenty-five feet of electric cord. A seemingly endless pile of fresh water hose. A sewer, phone, and/or cable TV connection snaking its way through the campsite. With all these potential hazards underfoot, how does one circumvent a nasty fall? Avoid them altogether by establishing a path away from hookups. Coil extra hose and store underneath the RV. Brightly colored hoses work best in avoiding nighttime encounters.

Phone

Like a birthday check from Grandma, onsite phone service is nice when you can get it. In a communication-obsessed age, many travelers are starting to demand such amenities, and campgrounds are complying. However, at this point, overnight phone service is still rather uncommon. Phone hookups are accomplished in two ways. The first method is through the phone company, requiring a pricey activation fee, deposit, and probably a fair amount of time spent on hold listening to Neil Diamond. This

Road Scholar

When camping without cable hookup—and in the absence of a television satellite system—the last resort is to try to pick up some free TV. Hand crank the onboard antenna (look up, it's located in the ceiling) for better reception of local programming. Just remember, to retract it before leaving, or it won't be up there for long.

expensive process only really makes sense for seasonal campers and those planning lengthier stays. The better alternative is an instant-on activation, available mostly at newer parks and resorts. A daily fee, an installed phone jack inside the RV, and, yes, a phone, is all that's required to call the grandkids, check voice messages and e-mails, and surf the Internet in search of a *Star Trek* chat room. A deposit is usually required, and travelers must settle up the bill before checking out. Personally, I think a cell phone is the best answer, but to each his own.

Cable TV

Why oh why would you want to go on vacation and miss wrestling? Of course you wouldn't, which is why cable TV is a nice perk. Like the phone, it's not offered everyplace, but that, too, is changing. You'll need a cable jack installed within the RV and a good length of 75-ohm cable (what else?) to connect to the outlet, usually located as a part of the campsite's electrical pedestal box.

One for the Road

Satellite signals must be received by a dish. Some are obvious; some are inside a bubble-like component mounted on the roof. Some are portable; some are fixed. Some must be manually aimed at the satellite in the sky; some can automatically track the satellite on the move. You can get the satellite signal most anywhere in the continental United States. Possible interference comes from obstructions such as overhanging trees, mountains, tall buildings, and heavy storms.

And then there are those who are waaaayyy past such pre-historic entertainment as that silly cable TV. Satellite TV allows folks to hit the highways with hundreds of juicy channel offerings along for the ride, a costly but oh so plush extra guaranteeing that favorite show is never missed—even when camped in Timbuktu. I'll bet even those tenting purists might be swayed to knock on the door with a batch of Gorp knowing the RV owner next door is the proud owner of a satellite system. Life as a dish-owner isn't as expensive as you might suspect, but does mandate a monthly service agreement and sometimes plunking down a nice chunk of change on the gadget itself.

What's Next?

After hooking up, what you do now is up to you. However, you'll probably want to deploy any slide-out rooms. That's as easy as pushing a button, although there might be a safety bar holding the room into place that must first be removed. Take a walk around the RV first to make sure the extended rooms won't ding a nearby tree, picnic table, or inattentive spouse. The same principle is true with the awnings, useful in manufacturing a little shade. Electric versions are replacing the overly complicated deployment methods of the past, so it probably won't take the aid of the 101st Airborne Division to get it down. With propane and electricity now running through your RV's veins, feel free to regulate the temperature controls inside. Otherwise, consider yourself set up, free to unpack, roam, and start living the good life.

Rules and Etiquette

Despite all the differences from one campground to another, I've found that the attitudes of guests are roughly the same. Like-minded travelers taking control of their vacations. Families and couples reconnecting with one another. Lots of smiles, good-heartedness, and relaxation. I'll bet these are some of the very reasons why you became interested in RVing in the first place. However, in the interest of your camping brethren, there are a few rules that must be followed. Such restrictions are rarely a secret—you'll probably receive a list upon check-in or be notified via posted warnings about possible no-nos. In addition, a number of unwritten rules—a campground etiquette, if you will, that uninitiated RVers might unknowingly shun—should also be observed. We'd better look at these, too.

Road Scholar

Late-night arrivals are a noisy experience for slumbering neighbors. If you check in late, be courteous. Don't slam vehicle doors or argue with the co-pilot about who made whom back into the maple tree. Set up as quickly and quietly as possible, avoiding unnecessary lights and engine noise. Extend others the same courtesy for early morning departures.

Shhhh ... Quiet

By day, sounds of kids playing, music, laughter, and perhaps a random hard-starting engine fill the air. However, nighttime is a different matter, with self-imposed "quiet hours" taking effect. Although you might see campfires and hear light conversation going into the wee hours of the morning (guilty as charged), it's expected that you at least put the banjo and karaoke machine away.

Gone to the Dogs

There's nothing quite as irritating as a chronically barking dog. Even the cutest pooch quickly wears out his or her welcome with excessive noise—and this is a dog lover talking. Most campgrounds frown on the practice of leaving pets unattended, especially those of the loud and edgy variety. Obey leash laws even if your canine is as gentle as Lassie and twice as well-behaved. And always pick up after them, another nonnegotiable.

Generating Ill-Will

Generators are noisy. The carbon monoxide pouring through exhaust vents into the open windows of a nearby coach won't make you any friends, either. There's simply no reason to run a generator when you're connected to an electrical hookup. Save it for the next boondocking escapade. If you must run it for some reason, do so only during the day and for brief periods of time. Never operate a generator at night when folks are sleeping—and may come visit you for a candid midnight discussion.

Don't Get Fired

I couldn't dream of camping without a campfire. It sounds almost un-American to have one without the other. However, a minority of places don't allow them—and usually have sound reasons for such. Dry climates, where fires can quickly spread and spiral out of control (parched western states, for example), might put the brakes on any flame-inspired activity. Sure, it's a bummer, but as the old saying goes, "them's the rules." In other cases, owners put limits on size of fires or what goes in them. Refrain from adding anything but wood—and not the green stuff snapped off from a nearby sapling. A steel fire ring, a fixture at most campsites, corrals campfires and should be used whenever available. Always make sure the fire is completely extinguished before departing, and never leave a blaze unattended.

Trashy Behavior

Economizing and organizing garbage is a test for many campers. Families make quite a lot of waste, and for some reason, RVs never seem to come equipped with garbage cans onboard. When they do, they're usually woefully small—smaller than a Smurf and half as useful. Why, I don't know. Don't let that be an excuse to ruin a nice setting with rampant litter. Items such as cigarette butts, bottle caps, and smaller debris quickly transform a rustic campground into a disappointing mess, so stay on top of the problem. Keep a garbage bag inside and another outside (best stored in an exterior compartment away from critters) to head off a messy condition before it starts. Deliver trash bags and recycling to the proper facilities.

Walking the Walk

True, the shortest distance between your campsite and the rec. room is indeed a straight line. However, don't cut through neighboring campsites to get there. This is considered bad form and equivalent to the masses traipsing through your yard at home. Respect campers by always following the roads and paths meandering through the campground. This little extra distance is good exercise and won't irk the locals.

Road Scholar

Longer trips require many of life's mundane chores that we were vacationing from in the first place, like washing and drying clothes. While laundering is certainly a necessity, with many campgrounds featuring full-service laundry facilities, don't hang clothes at the campsite. This is more of an aesthetic quirk of most owners, but a clothesline could also harm campers fumbling around in the dark.

Kids at Play

Personally, I found the two boys sneaking around the rig and hiding our supply of firewood sort of charming. I certainly did worse as a kid. Others might not enjoy your kid's merry mischief, which is why a chat with youngsters about common courtesy is probably warranted. Keep tabs on kids who may acquaint a campground's wide open spaces with an anarchistic free-for-all. While campgrounds are some of the safest places around, that doesn't mean children should run amok, especially in locations fraught with water, tough terrain, or wild animals. Even rustic areas are subject to vehicle traffic, and there's no shortage of cords and hoses to trip over. Keep an eye on kids at all times, and teach them to respect the rights of others.

Idle Engines Are the Devil's Workshop

Yes, it's a good idea to warm up your rig before take-off. And yes, diesel engines in particular benefit from a little cuddling in the morning. However, excessive idling is loud and polluting, and the exhaust is not much fun to inhale with the morning coffee. Keep this act to a minimum and cut surrounding campers a break.

Breaking Camp

Get in the habit of walking around the outside of the RV looking for anything amiss before take-off. How's the tire pressure? Are the slide-outs retracted? Are you still connected to any hookups at the campsite? I once pulled out of an RV park with the entry door wide open, half my gear unstowed, and lawn chairs sitting back by the campfire. Double-check things inside as well, paying special attention to unlatched drawers, open cabinets, and precious heirlooms that might tumble about during transit. Finally, conform the cockpit to the driver's needs. Struggling with mirrors and seat belts during rush hour traffic is asking for unnecessary trouble.

Pretrip Checklist

Engine

- ❑ Check oil.
- ❑ Check washer fluid.
- ❑ Check battery fluid.
- ❑ Check power steering fluid.
- ❑ Check transmission fluid.
- ❑ Check brake fluid.
- ❑ Check battery terminals.

Exterior

- ❑ Disconnect city water and stow fresh water hose.
- ❑ Dump black and gray water tanks via sewer connection.
- ❑ Disconnect sewer connection, stow hose, and close valves.
- ❑ Disconnect and stow electric power cord.
- ❑ Disconnect phone service.
- ❑ Disconnect cable TV.
- ❑ Turn off LP gas supply.
- ❑ Inspect tires for wear and take pressure.
- ❑ Secure and lock all outside storage compartments.
- ❑ Check headlights, turning signals, brake and back-up lights.
- ❑ Retract stabilizing jacks/stabilizing system.
- ❑ Retract awning(s).
- ❑ Latch storage pods.

Interior

- ❑ Stow all gear; protect fragile items.
- ❑ Latch all drawers, cabinets, and doors securely.
- ❑ Close windows and secure blinds.

- ❑ Close roof vents.
- ❑ Batten down larger items.
- ❑ Position refrigerated items for travel.
- ❑ Secure loose objects.
- ❑ Select 12-volt power mode for refrigerator.
- ❑ Turn off water pump.
- ❑ Turn off water heater.
- ❑ Turn off furnace.
- ❑ Extinguish all pilot lights.
- ❑ Retract slide-out(s) and check/remove surface debris.
- ❑ Lower TV antenna.
- ❑ Retract entry step.

Cockpit

- ❑ Adjust side mirrors.
- ❑ Buckle up.
- ❑ Determine blind spots.
- ❑ Check gauges, particularly fuel.
- ❑ Position seat.
- ❑ Position steering wheel.
- ❑ Position vents and fans.
- ❑ Retrieve maps and directions.
- ❑ Find coins for tolls.
- ❑ Find sunglasses.

Towable Owners

- ❑ Hitch up trailer or towed vehicle.
- ❑ Connect wiring.
- ❑ Attach safety cables.
- ❑ Set break-away switch.
- ❑ Double-check lights.
- ❑ Remove wheel blocks.

Campsite

- ❑ Fully extinguish campfire.
- ❑ Pick up trash.
- ❑ Move campsite fixtures back to original positions.
- ❑ Check site for forgotten items.

Final Steps

- ❑ Check out, if necessary.
- ❑ Visit dump station (unless dumped via sewer connection).
- ❑ Empty garbage/recyclables in dumpster.
- ❑ Provide bathroom breaks for the family.
- ❑ Hook up seat belts for everyone

The Least You Need to Know

- ➤ Campgrounds come in many different shapes and sizes, and it's up to you to decide what's important. Establish a list of must-haves in terms of recreation, facilities, and location to make the selection process easier. Consider a quality campground directory money well spent.
- ➤ Be careful when backing into the campsite to avoid any obstacles. Have the co-pilot or a neighbor help back you in, or opt for a pull-thru site instead. Park near hookups, being careful to gauge the impact of sun or shade, while allowing space for slide-outs and awnings to deploy. A level RV steadies life onboard and is key to the proper operation of the refrigerator.
- ➤ Set up the campsite first, beginning with electrical and fresh water hookups. Sewer hookups are best left to the end when dumping the tanks. Release the flow of LP gas from the propane containers, set the refrigerator to the appropriate setting, activate the water heater, slide-outs, and awnings, followed by temperature controls. Cable TV and phone service are great when offered.
- ➤ Follow the posted rules during campground stays. Respect the rights of fellow campers. Keep children and pets under control and behaved. Honor quiet hours and take steps not to disturb neighbors with excessive noise. Be courteous during late-night arrivals and early morning departures.
- ➤ A comprehensive checklist is the best way to facilitate a fast and orderly departure. Create steps for disengaging utilities, stowing provisions, hitching towables, checking appliances, and preparing the campsite for the next guests.

Chapter 17

Roughin' It

In This Chapter

- The why and where of boondocking
- Preparing for life without hookups
- Conservation tips to preserve systems and supplies

It's hard to imagine "roughin' it" in a recreational vehicle, isn't it? Most of us were probably once counted among the ranks of the tent-camping community and frankly, RVing isn't exactly the stuff pioneers are made of, at least, not with a queen-size bed, kitchen, and that furnace and air conditioner tandem to protect us when the going gets tough. A fully insulated vehicle flowing with electricity, LP gas, and fresh water is a long way from fiddling with a broken sleeping bag zipper, tiny portable stove, and wet socks courtesy of a leaky tent. There's no use denying it, we RVers are pretty pampered.

But that's not to say we don't like to push it now and again. While most RV travelers springboard from campground to campground, full hookups to full hookups, there are those who most definitely prefer the road less traveled. In fact, some folks hardly want a road at all, heading to parts unknown and preferring to camp only in the remotest of areas. We call this spirited effort boondocking, dry camping, or self-contained camping. Whatever term you choose, it basically entails setting up camp where no such camp exists. Good examples include a deserted parking lot for the night, settled outside the in-laws house, a large RV rally void of hookups, or on federal lands open to visitors but short on utilities. Our RVs were designed to work under these "primitive" conditions, and like the old saying goes, "If you got it, flaunt it!" While a certain mastery over hookup-less situations may not finally earn you that elusive Merit Badge, boondocking skills are definitely worth learning for when you need them.

Why Oh Why?

What possible reason could someone have to give up the cushy confines of a campground? Give up the sweet hum of available electricity? Turn down the uninterrupted flow of fresh water? No game room, camp store, or arts and crafts class for the kiddies? It's like forgoing the spoils of a buffet to snack on bread and water. Truth is, many of us were first reeled in by the nomadic lifestyle that RVing provides. We romanticize camping on a deserted beach, waking up to the sounds of the rolling surf. We picture ourselves entrenched deep within a forest of tall pine trees, not another person for miles. We imagine catching trout, parked streamside at the base of a majestic mountain range, with nothing but the sounds of the eagles sailing above. These are exactly the kinds of visions that seduce curious wannabes to come kick the tires at their local RV dealership. And let us not forget that the act of forging our own trail is an American institution, as patriotic as the hot dogs we dream about cooking at our own private retreats. Still, people boondock for all sorts of reasons. Here's a look at the most common.

One for the Road

Boondocking is a prickly issue. Obviously, lots of campground owners hate the practice since it takes money out of their coffers. Local ordinances sometimes prohibit such overnight parking, citing safety concerns or swayed by loss of potential revenue. Some business owners dislike squatters, while others feel that allowing campers to bunk in their parking lots is good for business. Of course, RVers will always lobby hard for their right to camp where they like.

Isolation

A good-size campground swells to several hundred—perhaps even thousands of people—on crowded weekends. Kids running about, enormous motorhomes and trailers congregated in an orderly, although sometimes crowded fashion. A few feet away, the neighbor talks to you passionately about gas mileage. People, people everywhere.

They say there are some of us who can't see the forest through the trees. What if you can't see the forest through the satellite dishes, slide-outs, and awnings of the crowds around you at campground XYZ? Surely it's not hard to appreciate that there are some folks with little patience for such a congested scene. Hop in the RV, head out in the wilderness, and leave breadcrumbs to find your way out. Ah, now that's more like it.

More Than You Paid For

We gladly hand over $20,000 for a decent trailer. We have no problem tapping into the kid's college fund for gas, tolls, and a round of corn dogs and curly fries for the family. But don't you dare ask us to fork over $20 a night for the privilege of parking our RV at a campground. While even an overpriced site is usually a good deal, especially compared to conventional lodging, some travelers just won't hear it. Piloting a recreational vehicle designed to go anywhere, complete with self-sufficient living capabilities, it's little wonder why these folks grin at the prospect of free camping. After all, why pay the campground owner when you can get the milk for free (okay, so I mixed my metaphors here). Boondocking is a lot of things, but it is most definitely free in most cases—and certainly a hard offer to refuse.

Location

A former co-worker of mine broke her foot and found driving exceedingly difficult. Just getting around was even tougher. This didn't bode well for her workload, considering the lengthy commute back and forth to the office. Fortunately, she owned an RV, and it wasn't long before she was living in the company parking lot, dry camping with the best of them. That 20-foot commute to work every morning made all the difference. But more likely, boondockers think they can do better than the area campgrounds. Perhaps the views at the RV park pale in comparison to those offered down the road, just left of the maple tree, and down by the creek bed of that deserted property. Or maybe Grandma just insists that you park in her driveway, so she can be closer to the grandchildren.

No Vacancy

Your spouse told you 1,000 times to make a reservation, and what did you do? You watched Jerry Springer instead. Bad choice, as now there's no room at the inn and it's getting late. As I've extolled more than once in this book, make reservations whenever possible, especially during peak seasons, at popular destinations, or when in need of a special type of amenity (pull-thru site, handicap access, etc.). At the very least, a confirmed site is a nice alternative to driving around in a strange town looking for a place to sleep, a likely scenario when the number of visitors is high and campsite availability is low. Perhaps the national banjo picker's club came to town and gobbled up every site within a 30-mile radius? Hey, it could happen. Next thing you know, you're pulled over for the night, putting those boondocking skills to the test.

Because I Can

Daniel Boone didn't become a legend for his microwave venison and days spent channel-surfing aboard the motorhome. Lewis and Clark didn't make history by relying on their rig's GPS system to map their way across America. No one ever took their recreational vehicle up Everest, down the Nile, or across the Atlantic—but golly, you're gonna try. The pioneer spirit certainly is no stranger to the RV demographic, folks who want to take control of their travels and blaze a trail as unique as they are—or think they are. Follow the pack? Never. Experience the easy life found inside the confines of an RV resort? Are you kidding? Take the easy way out? Don't be silly. Forge your own trails? Ah, now you're talking.

The Path of Most Resistance

Boondocking for the first time is akin to taking the training wheels off the bicycle. Your first wipeout only confirms what you already knew—your easy rider days are behind you. Of course, an interesting new world awaits, so hold on tight and keep pedaling. Sure, during your first dry-camping escapade, you might flirt with draining the coach battery down to nothing or running out of water just when Kool-Aid would hit the spot. I've gotten spooked at every snap of a twig in the forest engulfing my rig in some remote spot and been miles away from a mini-mart when a potato chip craving woke me from a deep sleep at 2 A.M. But such edgy adventures are worth it. When dry camping is good, it's very good. That is, assuming you take this crash course in Survival 101.

An RVer sans hookups is involved in a chess match of sorts against his or her vehicle's capabilities. Without a city-water hookup or a natural stream nearby (as if those existed!), the fresh water supply eventually runs dry. Propane, too, has its limits, and with it goes the heat, many of the cooking capabilities, and the hot water that it's so hard to live without. Generating electricity in the wild is a little easier, thanks to generators, inverters, and solar power—but these, too, depend on outside factors (fuel tanks, battery size, hide-and-seek playfulness of the sun)—and some vehicles won't have them. Those black and gray water tanks are gonna need emptying at some point, too—there's simply no getting around that.

Certainly, there are many ways to boondock. Catching a little shuteye in the back of a deserted parking lot is much different than sequestered deep within a 100,000-acre forest. Parked without utilities in the driveway is an easier concept than life in the Alaskan frontier, toiling with a sinking propane supply and a lone can of beans. However, before tangling with the particulars of where, when, and how, those interested in such boondocking behavior should first always satisfy the following criteria.

Is It Legal?

Contrary to the mantra of the late 1960s, the Earth does not in fact belong to everyone. Otherwise, those in the business of building fences, security cameras, and signs shouting "Keep out" wouldn't have a day job. While free love may still exist, a free stopover may raise the ire of a less than understanding business or property owner. Finding that deep-woods oasis or beachside camping haven is great, but chances are it belongs to someone—and that someone isn't you.

Deciding where to go takes more foresight than pulling off the road to that charming little field underneath the stars. This squatter mentality will almost certainly result in Officer Friendly's nightstick tapping against the doorway at 3 A.M. Some RVers rely on stealth tactics when deciding where to hide out and camp for a few days. They find a remote location and do as little as possible to advertise the fact that they're there. To me, this is little more than freeloading. We can do better than this.

One for the Road

Our tax dollars are hard at work preserving millions of acres throughout this country through federally protected lands. The scenery is majestic. The lands are often wild and spectacular with not a strip mall in sight. Free camping may be provided in lieu of a formal campground, hookups, or abundance of rangers to service your every wish. Bureau of Land Management areas and National Wildlife Refugees are two of the most common examples of such subsidized camping.

The best advice is to always try to secure the owner's permission before putting up stakes for the night, whether it's behind the Wal-Mart or a beautiful plot next to a bubbling stream. Be specific about your intent—how long you'd like to stay, the number of passengers, etc. Offer to pay for the privilege and/or make a purchase from the kind business owner who allowed you to stay when the area campgrounds were overbooked. If this is just an overnight stopover and there's no one around, park the rig well out of the way and leave first thing in the morning.

Is It Safe?

Even hard-core dry campers balk at situations that appear unsafe. I certainly don't advocate camping in unfamiliar parts since it could compromise your family's safety. You just never know. Such uncertainly is especially true in isolated areas, void of other like-minded campers or any semblance of security. In the event you're just looking for a spot to rest heavy eyelids, a travel plaza or truck stop is the best place.

Although probably not ideal in terms of a peaceful sleeping arrangement, consider well-lighted venues with regular traffic flow about as safe as you can find in lieu of a protected campground.

Can the Rig Handle It?

Sure, *you're* up for the challenge, but is your RV? The nimble qualities of a camper van, truck camper, or smaller trailer come in handy when the roads turn to paths, the terrain gets rough, and clearance issues come into full effect. Consider the fact ahead of time that there just might not be a space big enough for a wide-body motorhome with three slide-outs. Only you know where your RV can go, and once it gets there, how long it can hold out with what's onboard. Do you lack a generator, inverter, or solar power? This condition definitely limits one's ability to reinvigorate the electrical system when the batteries read nil. Fresh water tanks a paltry 20 gallons? Then better not schedule a two-week trek to the outback without added water reserves. That back tire plagued by a slow leak? Better fix it before conquering the Amazon.

Ready for Action

As my old fraternity creed goes, "Success and self-reliance are inseparable." However, before you get too impressed, keep in mind that we also used to memorize the back of Budweiser cans. As with that of most any undertaking, the success or failure of dry camping lies in the details. Here are a few things not to overlook before heading out into the great beyond.

Inspection

The most important step is to ensure that the RV and the various systems (electric, LP, plumbing) are in proper working order. The goal here is to avoid a breakdown in a scene straight out of *Heart of Darkness*. That, or make sure your emergency roadside service boasts a helicopter with a heavy-duty crane. For longer, out-of-the-way journeys, have the vehicle inspected by an RV service technician prior to departure.

Practice

If you've never dry camped before, think baby steps. Get a taste of hookup-less living first before testing it in a hard-core environment for real. Camp at an RV park without relying on any of the hookups. Think of it as a dress rehearsal, giving you practice working off the coach battery, fresh water tank and water pump, and trying out some of the conservation practices listed below. The driveway or backyard is another good place to work out the kinks. As with everything in RVing, a little practice goes a long way.

Pull Over

Traveling with full tanks adds a shocking amount of weight. A full fresh water tank can add hundreds of extra pounds, which is why we recommend traveling at reduced capacity. In the case of boondocking, however, you might require every drop of that 75-gallon fresh water tank. To avoid an overweight condition, lighten the load elsewhere to compensate.

All Systems a' Go-Go

Before departing on your backroads adventure, make sure the fresh water and propane containers are filled to capacity, the gray and black water tanks are near empty (remember, we always want a *little* fluid in the tanks), and there's plenty of fuel. After a decent-length drive, the coach battery should be good and charged, meaning you have some amps to play with. (Of course, this depends on how depleted it was in the first place.)

Provisions

Prepare for a boondocking odyssey with the same objectives and planning as any other trip. The toothbrush, prescription medicine, and clean pair of socks are as important here as anyplace else. Rely on the packing list provided in Chapter 16, "Choosing a Campground," to get you started, but be aware that there may not be a camp store on the premises to bail you out when you forget the can opener again. Leave room for a few other "rugged" items to make your list, including firewood, supplemental canned goods, alkaline batteries, charcoal, and extra blankets. For those sitting on the fence about buying a cell phone, a night in relative isolation might finally convince you.

Conservative Thinking

Just how long you can stay away from civilization is up to you and your willingness to conserve resources. Even a tiny RV—with even tinier capabilities—should have little trouble living off itself for a couple of days—longer if you ration reserves carefully and don't use up all the water wetting down the slip 'n' slide. Larger RVs, equipped with a myriad of power sources, gigantic tanks, and useful add-ons, can go much longer. Again, it's up to you and your level of discipline. The following tips won't hurt, either.

Power Outage

The RV's electrical limitations have a major say in most matters, including the quality—and duration—of a shore power-less escapade. Fortunately, the ability to generate your own electricity is, if nothing else, pretty cool. Smaller RVs and many towables are at a significant disadvantage here, usually lacking a generator to finagle more juice when the coach battery starts to wane. Consider a portable model, inverter, or solar power solution if you expect boondocking to become a regular gig. Otherwise, a miserly approach to the stored energy is the best answer.

Road Scholar

Holy blackout, Batman! The battery voltage is beginning to drop, and there's no generator, inverter, or solar power to save the day. Partially recharge the batteries with a turn of the ignition key and let the vehicle idle for a while. Otherwise, take the RV for a spin. A good drive can restore *some* of the charge, extending your dry camping that much longer.

Remember how mad your father got when you left the lights on in the bedroom? How about that blatant disregard you demonstrated for his money as you stood gawking in front of the refrigerator with the door wide open? Assume the same easily agitated approach to energy loss and your electrical supply should go far. Turn off all lights and unnecessary devices such as the water pump, electric step, or water heater when not in use. Those amps add up. Go manual whenever possible—forgo the electric can opener for a hand crank, electric razor for straight edge, blow dryer for a vigorous shake with a towel. We are roughin' it, aren't we?

By parking in the shade on a cool day and dropping the awning, we just may keep the air conditioner at bay, which is among the hungriest of the electrical hogs. Select a sunny spot to taper furnace operation during cold climes, thus saving the output of the electric fans and precious propane. Leave the big appliances at home. Do you really need to vacuum, run the power drill, or gulp down a cappuccino every morning?

Water Logged

Mr. Motorhome Owner could probably never imagine going through 100 gallons of fresh water, but how it does seem to vanish. Just ask Mr. Pop-Up Owner, saddled with a 10-gallon-tank and a bunch of thirsty kids, how popular fresh water is over a long, hot weekend. Protecting the water supply is critical. Fortunately, it's also the easiest to horde and resupply. Obviously, for those perplexed by tiny tanks, a few well-placed jugs of water never hurt. Cumbersome and weighty, yes, but good in a pinch when the natives need a round of drinks and are getting ornery. Extend the reserves with a few behavior modifications. Never leave faucets running (like my wife) when washing dishes and brushing teeth. The same is true for showering. Don't lollygag here. Get in and get out.

Pull Over

I know what you're thinking, because we have all thought it before. Why not just dump those tanks right here in the boonies? Come on, no one's around. Who's to know? The question is not whether you can get away with it, but why? Is this how we show gratitude for a wonderful camping environment, by submerging it in waste water? Come on, you know better.

Waste Not, Want Not

This disciplined approach to dispensing fresh water naturally prolongs the need to empty the gray and black water tanks. If less goes in, less comes out. Mark this down in the two birds with one stone category. The only added suggestion for waste water tanks is to use any available facilities—yes, even that scary porta-potti—whenever possible. Every little bit helps.

Don't Touch That Dial

Shifting some of the cooking operations to natural methods outside is among the best ways to save propane. Substitute a smoldering campfire for the cooking range; a portable charcoal grill for the oven. Spare the LP even further by extinguishing all pilot lights when not in use. Engage the water heater only when necessary. Go easy on the thermostat to lessen the impact of the biggest LP gas-guzzler, the furnace. Like Mom always commanded, wear a sweater and follow some of the insulation practices found in "Cold-Weather Camping" to take the chill out. With all that said, propane is usually the least of your worries (unless it's below zero outside).

Pull Over

Diesel fuel must be blended for use in cold climates, which is why that batch you bought during warmer times might yield lackluster results in freezing temperatures. Fortunately, popular truck stops or travel plazas, where the big boys fill up, should know the difference. The marketplace is also full of additives to protect diesel tanks from the gelling and icing brought on by frigid conditions.

Cold-Weather Camping

Some folks take boondocking to the extreme, favoring an RV trip when the temperatures are ridiculous and snow has enveloped the once-grassy campsite. Winter camping is a strange phenomenon; some do it by choice, in support of seasonal activities such as cross-country skiing, snowshoeing, and snowmobiling (which aren't much fun in the summer). I can attest to winter's power as an incredibly beautiful and remote time of year to camp. Others simply find themselves the victims of an unruly weather pattern, accidental tourists stuck in a winter wonderland. No matter if by choice or by fault, RVing in colder climes is certainly possible and worthwhile, though it does present some unique challenges.

One Cool Customer

The first question poised on your lips should be "Can your RV handle life in such temperature extremes?" Many pop-ups and lightweight travel trailers are really year-round vehicles in name only; they simply weren't built to handle hard-core winter conditions. Remember, there's a big difference between a chilly fall night and a January morning when you awake to the sounds of your own teeth chattering and purple toes. Spartan insulation, thin building materials, and smallish tanks combine to leave inhabitants of less expensive RVs pondering the location of the nearest Holiday Inn. Vehicles constructed with the year-round camper in mind—namely motorhomes and mid-size or larger trailers—are the best bet for cold-weather camping and better constructed to handle variable weather. Look for added insulation packages, enclosed underbellies to heat the tanks, and larger furnaces to keep the chill out.

Pull Over

Snowdrifts can block vents and lead to a dangerous situation. A quick walk-around should reveal the status of heater and refrigerator exhaust. Keep out carbon monoxide by eliminating blockage. Snow piled on the top of slide-outs must be cleared before retracting. De-ice doors and locks when necessary to avoid a lockout.

For those of us who endure six months (nine months in Chicago) of winter every year, the goals are simple: Stay warm and prevent the pipes from freezing. This is doubly true in your RV, even when hooked up to shore power at a campground with winter service. Give your RV a quick test to determine its cold weather aptitude.

Let There Be Heat

Finding a built-in heating system, typically a forced-air furnace, is not the problem. Every RV has one and so will yours. Getting one powerful enough to heat the entire RV when it's 4°F outside and dropping is the challenge. Insulation is a major part of this as well (see the following section). Pay attention to your comfort level on a chilly September night. If jumping jacks are the only thing between you and hypothermia, leave the RV at home for a Minneapolis getaway in February. If you can't seem to stay warm during modest temperatures, don't expect it to perform during the fangs of winter. Supplement a hard-working furnace with a space heater, and set the thermostat at a constant temperature to avoid overworking. And keep that hot cocoa coming.

Insulation

Despite what most of us think, extra insulation isn't just a cold-weather fighter; it pays off year-round. A well-insulated ride acts as a sort of thermos, keeping the RV warm in winter and cool in summer. Consult the manufacturer to gauge the quality of insulation (some are mum on the subject, so as not to draw comparisons to house-type insulation values). The magic "R" rating (R-5, for example) measures these levels, and as Tony the Tiger says, "They'rrrre grrrrreat!" The higher the rating, the better.

A few interior alterations help retain warm air. Weather-strip all doors and windows to combat drafts. Seal windows in plastic and add rugs and carpeting to trap in heat. Park in the sun to soak up the free heat whenever possible. Plug up any holes where nasty breezes could infiltrate your cozy sanctuary. And by all means, keep that door shut. One absent-minded passenger of mine once forgot to shut the door on a particularly frigid night. The next morning, I had to be thawed out with a blowtorch.

Tanks and Pipes

Ever tried to empty a frozen gray water tank? There are certainly better ways to spend an afternoon. The same is true for any of the other holding tanks, which are vulnerable to freezing. Your pipes, too. RVs with exposed tanks and plumbing are prone to more problems during winter camping. Fortunately, engineers are taking cold-weather operation more seriously, implementing a number of safeguards in recent designs. Nicer models offer enclosed tanks to soak in the interior's warm air. Others route heat around tanks and plumbing or insulate pipes for an extra barrier against the elements.

One of the simplest things you can do to protect piping is to leave cabinet doors and drawers open to circulate heat to the pipes. Turn the bathroom faucet so it's at a steady drip to keep water moving and prevent pipes from freezing. Obviously, this hastens the drain on the fresh water tank, so it may not be a practical solution unless you are connected to free city water.

Pull Over

Keep tank levels up so as not to tempt a frozen situation. Adding specially formatted RV (yes, RV) anti-freeze to the wastewater tanks should prevent an icy condition from forming inside. About a quart per tank should do it. Although safe for use with your RV's plumbing system, do not add this to the fresh water tank.

Tank Capacities

The larger the various tank and propane container capacities, the happier you'll be. This is true for two reasons: First, larger and fuller holding tanks are more difficult to freeze; second, expect the furnace to work double-duty on cold days, sapping the LP supply faster than a keg at a Mu Lambda Sigma party.

Winterizing Hookups

Most campgrounds north of the Mason Dixon Line stick to seasonal schedules, when the weather doesn't yet take on arctic conditions. Halloween through tax day is not exactly swimming pool weather in these parts. As such, a dedicated search may be needed to find accommodations with service and open facilities during the cold-weather months up north (or east, for that matter). But, they're out there, offering awaiting hookups if you're bold enough to accept the challenge of a winter retreat. Electricity via shore power (any power, for that matter) can't freeze so winterizing this connection isn't necessary. (A flooded battery, on the other hand, can and will.) Just plug into electrical connections and go, a nice feeling since energy consumption rises dramatically in cooler climes. Workaholic furnace fans, more lights required to compensate for less daylight, and more hours spent inside all contribute to accelerated usage.

Protecting fresh water and sewer connections is another matter entirely. Again, the choice is yours, depending on whether one opts for a hookup or relies on his or her own reserves. Use water from the fresh water tank and purge tanks only when absolutely full via the dump station. Otherwise, enjoy a city-water connection at the campsite and its unlimited resources—provided you prepare them to rebuff the cold temperatures.

Icy Conditions

A separate fresh water hose for winter use is a good idea. Keep it as short as possible (10 feet or so), wrap it in heat tape (available at hardware stores and such), and cover with pipe insulation available in four-foot lengths from the builder supply stores. (It comes split up the middle, so you can insert the hose.) An extra layer of duct tape never hurt, either. The water connection should now be doing its best mummy impression and be completely wrapped. Make sure the faucet itself and water inlet on the RV receive some TLC as well, to prevent these exposed areas from freezing up when they're needed most.

Road Scholar

Most RV parks that leave water turned on in the wintertime provide some type of cover for the water outlet, such as a pail with a notch cut in one side or straw for extra insulation around the water hookup. Otherwise, find something to cover it with for extra protection, especially when it is very cold outside.

A high-quality sewer hose is the only type you want working on your behalf during winter camping. Add a layer or two of insulation wrap here for good measure. Straw acts as a great buffer between it and the frozen tundra. Maintain as steep an angle for the hose connection as possible, to avoid the propensity of water or materials to settle and freeze. Leave release valves closed until you're ready to dump, following the procedures listed in Chapter 12, "Plumbing Systems."

The Least You Need to Know

- Camping without hookups, or boondocking, is a common practice among RVers seeking remote locations or during times when suitable campsites can't be found. Settings range from primitive campgrounds, some government lands, driveways, parking lots, or whenever one might stay for the night—or longer.
- Camping illegally gives RVers a bad name and could raise the ire of property owners and the police. Always get permission before boondocking on unfamiliar lands. Don't compromise the safety factor when parked in unfamiliar areas.
- Your RV's capabilities and your conservation practices dictate the success of any boondocking venture. The fresh water and propane supply is finite; holding tanks must eventually be emptied. RVs equipped with a generator, inverter, or solar power can generate electricity. Otherwise you must rely on the amount of current stored within the coach battery(ies).
- Camping in cold weather, either by design or accident, mandates steps to keep warm and protect pipes from freezing. Proper insulation and heating, as well as design elements to protect tanks and plumbing, are crucial to thrive in frigid conditions.

Part 6

Life on the Road

Life on the road is what you make of it. The reason is because—say it with me one more time—RVing is all about choices. If nothing else, we promise that getting from point A to point B in a shiny new RV has never been this much fun. But don't worry, I'm sure you'll get used to the good life in rapid time. Millions already have, with many more jumping into the RV fold every day. Of course, with such travel flexibility come lots of decisions—where to go, who to take, and how to do so in comfort and safety. But don't worry, you can handle it.

Chapter 18

Travel Planning

In This Chapter

- Considerations for traveling with kids and pets
- The ins and outs of RV rallies and caravans
- Practices for international RVing
- Is full-timing for you?

There are many different ways to enjoy RVing. One woman once told me she couldn't sleep the night before an RV tour through Mexico—she was too excited. A full-timing couple revealed that after spending the week visiting grandkids, they were pointing their rig west for some much-needed R&R. RVing is the only way one family of seven could afford to travel together, said another friend of mine. Meanwhile, my mother and stepfather loved bringing their basset hounds on their adventures, heads hanging out the windows, ears flapping in the wind. (The bassets, that is.)

Such diversity calls attention to different needs while on the road. Life as a full-timer is decidedly unique when compared to that of a weekend traveler—the RV is now their home, after all. Those traveling with large groups, babies, or pets demand a special travel-planning criteria (and comfort level with a certain onboard anarchy) than other journeys. RVing to foreign countries requires a different level of preparation than, say, a jaunt to Mount Rushmore; signing on for an RV caravan, club, or rally dictates new realties as opposed to life as a loner. So many lifestyles, so little time. Fortunately, you've come to the right place.

Kids and Families and Babies, Oh My

Sure, that last car vacation with the kids got a little tense at times. It only took a thousand or so "Are we there yet?"s to drive you stark-raving mad and vow to never do it again. You may figure a better vacation answer might be to hop the fastest jet airplane you can find and pray for strong tailwinds. Before you book a seat next to the toothbrush salesman from Toledo, imagine the family vacation from the kids' perspective. Crammed in the back seat for hour after eternal hour, one child on top of the other like a Dagwood sandwich, uncomfortable, hot, thirsty, hungry, bored, wanting attention and their little brother away from their Etch-a-Sketch. I know this because I was the most impatient back seat passenger you ever saw (and still am not much better). There weren't enough French fries in the world to keep me quiet.

However, consider a recreational vehicle the great equalizer for hyperactive passengers. Kids love them because, well, they're pretty cool and probably not like anything they've ever seen before. If you plan it right, everyone should have his own space, bed, and storage for toys, books, and games to turn those frowns upside down. Mealtime is easily accomplished without a stampede to the roadside fast-food joint; a cold drink is always nearby; and, depending on how coddling you want to be, the gang can melt the miles watching movies or playing video games onboard. (Towable owners can probably add a TV/VCR/gameport for passengers in the tow vehicle's back seat.)

Here are a few more considerations to turn brooding youngsters into happy campers on the next big trip.

Road Scholar

Like Shirley Temple, the very first family RV trip should be short and sweet. An extended weekend is a good start, somewhere within a few hours from home. Remember, your kids need to be sold on the RV experience, too, so don't make their first memories those of endless driving. Increase the distance from home and length of stay slowly over time.

Get Them Involved

Planning a trip that everyone will enjoy can be like an episode straight out of *Mission: Impossible.* This is especially true of older children, whose infatuation with the family vacations—and their overly caffeinated parents—may begin to wane as they get older. Each person has a strong opinion of where the family should go, and everyone wants to bring more and more of his stuff. Your time off is precious, and you want to make the most of it. Mom wants everyone to get along. Dad's secretly praying that he won't have to take on a second job to pay for it. With so many different agendas, how can everyone be satisfied?

Depending on the age of your crew, planning a trip can be as democratic a process as you care to make it. Sure, when the kids were young, the family ran like an eastern block nation—you decided on the itinerary and everyone obeyed. However, older kids have opinions, opinions that must be heard and respected if everyone is to get along. It's important children and teenagers feel a part of the decision-making process, whether it be voting on the destination, choosing places to stay, or each child getting a day to shape the itinerary. This *is* a family vacation, right? Run things like a dictator and there's bound to be a coup.

Pull Over

A baby or infant probably won't be too vocal about what he or she wants to take—as much as they'll just be plain vocal. Again, pack liberally, remembering key items such as car seats, favorite toys, bottles, high chairs, diapers, playpens, and the like. Think long and hard about this list to avoid forgetting a key accessory.

Man Your Positions

There's nothing I enjoy more than settling arguments over who gets to sit where. Render the wrong verdict, and you'd be surprised at how long a kid holds a grudge. RVs and tow vehicles equipped with air bags shape some of these decisions for you—no kids under 12 in the front seats. The potential bag deployment is simply too powerful for youngsters up front. As for divvying up the rest of the RV or tow vehicle? Well, that's a tad trickier. Alternate first-round picks, kind of like an NBA draft, so everyone gets a chance to be top dog. Otherwise, assign seats and be done with it. Fortunately, for those motorized owners, most of the seats are pretty great, comfortable, and offer plenty of room to avoid hundreds of miles of kicking, hair-pulling, and drawing on their baby brother with a felt-tip pen. Regardless of where the kids sit, remember to enforce the number one rule: Seat belts must be worn at all times.

Sleeping arrangements may not be as democratic, depending on the available space. To avoid a logistical situation not seen since the marines stormed the beaches at Normandy, keep bed-swapping to a minimum. Since the whole brood is now sharing one enclosed area, reflect on the decision of who goes where before assigning bunks. The cab-over bed found in Class C motorhomes might not be appropriate for some kids, since managing the ascent can be tricky. Find a spot for infants guaranteeing the most privacy, most likely in with you in the master bedroom. Sequester those who awake early in the morning away from the late-sleepers and vice versa. Of course, in close quarters such as these, when someone awakens, chances are that it's rise and shine for everyone.

Take It Easy

Long trips are hard on everyone. The latent anticipation coupled with the constant confusion over how much farther is doubly hard for kids. If the mood inside turns ugly, take a break. As one RV chum put it, "If Junior ain't happy, ain't nobody happy." Pull off to a rest stop and share a picnic. A little fresh air will do everyone some good. Fifteen minutes throwing the Frisbee or taking a quick hike won't affect the E.T.A. too much, and it gives everyone renewed energy. Keep tabs on everyone's comfort level onboard. In larger RVs, the temperature in the rear is often dramatically different than in the cockpit. Take chants of "we're boiling" seriously. Set temperature gauges accordingly, and run the air conditioner if necessary. The dashboard A/C is rarely good enough to cool down those in back of a larger motorhome.

One for the Road

Families traveling for extended periods should opt for bunk beds for the kids. They're fun, space-efficient, and don't require transforming back into a sofa or dinette every day. These also give every youngster a place to call his own. Kids like to hang pictures around their bunks, and these quarters can easily be curtained off for more privacy. Small bookshelves or even a TV can be installed at the foot of these bunks.

Rules of the Road

As family-friendly as it is, an RV still has many of the same potential dangers of home. The easiest and most high-strung response is to prohibit children from touching anything. A better alternative is to explain how things work—that the refrigerator is like the one at home, the stove and burners do indeed get hot, and exactly how the bathroom operates to keep water works to a minimum. Deep entryway stairwells bear watching as kids come and go, and doors can be difficult to open and shut for smaller folks. Assist with bed conversions to avoid pinching fingers, and under no circumstances are children allowed up from their seats while the vehicle is in motion.

Pull Over

Take special caution with platform steps in the entryway, used to help minimize the distance between the RV and the ground. A handrail is a good idea, too. Remember to lower manually deployed steps upon arrival to prevent falls. Electric models should deploy whenever the door opens and retract when closed. Watch out for shins, sometimes bruised if standing too close to the entry door.

Heavy Petting

I'll admit it, I'd do just about anything for my dog. Unfortunately, the rest of the world isn't always so pet-friendly, which is why RVing is such a great compromise. A bed, food and water bowls, and a toy or two are all that's needed to turn a furry friend into an exuberant (albeit slightly drooly) co-pilot. Planes stick anything but the smaller breeds of dogs in the cargo hold; hotels frown on pets like a Hell's Angels convention. And you know how a couple kids and a cat or two in the car for eight hours goes—a tad feisty, for sure. I don't know how many people have told me that their pet is the reason they took up RVing in the first place, but it ranks right up there.

For the purposes of this chapter, pets are limited to dogs and cats. Hey, nothing against the rodent, reptile, winged, or aquatic set, it's just that it's easier to focus on the "big two." In many cases, this advice is prudent for any animal.

Pack Animals

Fortunately, our pets aren't nearly as materialistic as we are, so you won't go bonkers packing their things. (And unlike your spouse, if you forget something, they probably won't give you a hard time about it.) A food and water bowl, leash, a few toys, a bed, and an adequate supply of chow is almost all they require. That, and their usual 18 hours of beauty rest. Also, I would recommend talking with your vet about your travel plans in case any vaccinations are recommended. For example, I heard of a case where an RVer nearly lost his puppy recently due to parvovirus, which is not a problem in their northern state but a serious threat in warmer climates. Keep collars on animals at all times, with your home address and phone number in case they get lost. Ask your vet about other ways to safeguard your pet while traveling.

Cat Call

Spend a few days helping pets acclimate to their new RV surroundings prior to the big trip. Let them get accustomed to the sights and smells for a couple of hours inside each night as you read a book or pack the RV. Cats are notoriously slow for getting their bearings in a new space, so be patient with them. It took Rocky, my six-toed feline, a week just to come out from under the bed whenever we moved to someplace new. Add a second litter box, bed, and a few new toys to make the transition easier. A few sniffs is all it takes most dogs to get up to speed. Make life onboard as similar to home life as possible. If they sleep in a cage, have one onboard. If they have a favorite blanket to cuddle up on, make sure that's available for a little extra security. It might help to even feed them inside the vehicle a couple of nights before you leave to set up a routine. It won't be long before they, too, appreciate the second home on wheels as much as you do.

It's a Dog's Life

Once in the swing of things, most pets have few complaints with their roving bed with the exception of maybe your being a little tight with that extra cookie or wad of catnip. The biggest concerns for them are adequate hydration and general comfort. There are a few water bowls on the market that stay full without sloshing out onto the floor of an ever-shaking vehicle. Make sure it's full and that there's plenty of circulating air to keep animals cool. Those fur coats get hot, and remember, animals tend to get overheated when they're excited.

Campground Behavior

Dogs and cats are welcome at most public and private campgrounds. However, always call ahead and double-check before making a reservation. Some owners are wary of certain breeds, such as pit bulls, while others might prohibit animals exceeding a certain weight. It's not unusual for pet owners to be assessed an extra fee for the privilege, usually one or two dollars more a night. Nearly everyone admits cats, although they, too, may be subject to additional costs.

The fastest way to turn Mr. and Mrs. Campground Owner against animals is to violate their rules. Most are adamant about not leaving dogs unattended, so where you go, so does your pooch. This is for the animal's protection (see the following section), as well as cutting down on the inevitable barking that seems to accompany a lonely dog. Leash policies are another big one. I'm always surprised when certain people cower from my happy-go-lucky little beagle, with wagging tail and smiley face. Truth is, not everyone likes animals (cute or not), which is why the leash rule is enforced just about everyplace you go. Furthermore, a cavalier response to picking up after your pets all but guarantees campgrounds won't be so pet-friendly in the future.

Road Scholar

Here are a few extra items to consider for pets. Medicine to ward off fleas and ticks is a good idea. Make sure they wear a collar with identification and a home number at all times in the event they get lost. Proof of rabies vaccination is worth toting along, as you might be asked to show it from time to time. This could come into play when visiting other countries, such as Mexico and Canada.

Abandoned Ship

There's a reason dogs break out the ole puppy-dog eyes trick whenever you leave them—they don't like it. Given their druthers, they'd much rather socialize with you than that squeaky toy that looks like a miniature mailman. I have yet to meet a cat that gets worked up over my departure, but leaving any animal alone in the RV for any length of time can be problematic. The best thing to do is to take him or her with you. However, if you can't, take steps to keep them safe and comfortable. Temperature is the first thing to consider. Even on mild days, make sure windows and vents are open. Warmer temperatures require air conditioning. A word of warning: Dogs get overheated quickly. Just because you don't think it's too warm, your animal may disagree. Be sure to leave out plenty of water and toys as well. Keep time spent away to a minimum. Again, those with busy itineraries outside of camp should consider boarding their animals instead.

Road Scholar

Pets get carsick the same as some travel-intolerant humans do. As a rule, it's best not to feed them immediately before a long drive. Overfeeding and frequent cookie breaks only worsen matters. Hopefully, as they get more roadworthy, pets should settle down. Taking frequent breaks with plenty of fresh air should help, too. See your veterinarian for medication to ease their queasiness if problems persist.

The Group Mentality

Although goin' solo is common among the RV community, many travelers find comfort and solidarity in the group setting. RV clubs are extremely popular for novices and experienced journeymen alike. Memberships can open up a world of regular outings, insightful publications, a network of affiliated campgrounds and resorts, and tremendous group buying power, with discounts on everything from insurance to mail-forwarding services to roadside assistance for its members.

The Good Sam Club, for example, boasts a membership base of more than one million members. Other group benefits are more specific, such as Coast to Coast, which offers a network of membership campgrounds. Camping World's President's Club treats members to heavily discounted camping and RV supplies, while the Family Motor Coaching Association (FMCA) was created and run for motorhome owners only. Chances are good that there's a local RV chapter near you. See Appendix A, "Resources," for a list of clubs.

Whether big or small, local or national, enrollment in one or more RV clubs is a great idea, especially for beginners. You should never pass up an opportunity to learn from experienced travelers, and the discounts alone can easily eclipse the annual dues. Of course, it's the intangibles that seem most worth it—making friends, sharing tips and resources, and uniting in a similar RV passion.

Rally Ho

Most clubs feature regional or nationwide events, or rallies, giving the various state and local chapters a few days to meet and mingle. Activities such as these invoke the rare opportunity to share ideas, experiences, and practical know-how not always found in the pages of your favorite publication, book, or Web site. And they can be plenty fun, too. Rally-goers represent different lifestyles and backgrounds, but all are united in their affection for RVing—and the desire to improve their pastime. For some, rallies are the best and most looked-forward-to reason to join an RV club.

If you've never attended such an event, you're missing out on a memorable experience. Just imagine, hundreds or thousands of RVers, camped out for a week's worth of bonding and fellowship. Food, entertainment, bathrooms, dump service, plenty of campfire chatter—and, of course, a spot to spend the night (with or without hookups)—are usually included in entry costs. You can also probably count on a few seminars, led by industry experts and lifestyle mavens, to help you get the most out of all your adventures. Exhibitors are sometimes on-hand to showcase the latest products, ranging from the newest $300,000 diesel pusher to that $2 item that might prove indispensable onboard your rig. And then, hopefully, everyone departs a little wiser and thankful that they made the decision to buy an RV in the first place.

Road Scholar

Audition prospective tour companies as you would any trip provider. Have they organized trips to these locales before? Exactly what is and isn't included in the price? How many years have they been in business? Are the guides experienced RVers? Have they led previous tours to the area? Does the company have references? Remember, you're paying for *their* experience and expertise.

Tours and Caravans

An RV tour or caravan is a hoot. If you've never done one, you definitely should, since it's one of those great throwback experiences of a lifetime. Like the wagon trains of old that once meandered their way through the Old West, RV caravans are designed to deliver safe, organized, and enjoyable trips to a host of intriguing destinations. Tame Alaska, follow the NASCAR circuit, journey to South America, or take a trip Northeast to experience some amazing fall foliage. A number of companies specialize in the planning and guiding of such journeys, with packages as simple or complex, lavish or bare-bones as you demand. Trips range from a few days to a couple of months. Of course, there's nothing stopping you from forming a caravan of your own, with some close friends tagging along for the ride.

Such trips aren't cheap, but can be a good deal in lieu of planning it yourself. Once the check clears, all you need to do is tag along and enjoy, knowing that everything is taken care of. Meals, admission costs, and campsites are usuallyincluded in the price. (Fuel and spending money is up to you.) Tour-goers meet at a designated location, which serves as the springboard for the journey. Experienced guides, sometimes under the manly moniker of "wagon masters," lead the group, make the arrangements, and double as cheery activities directors in the process. Expect plenty of side-trips along the way. Nights are usually spent in pre-selected campgrounds and offer a nice setting for everyone to get acquainted and reflect on the day's events. Quality companies work diligently to load up trips with as much entertainment and novel experiences as possible. A list of tour and caravan operators can be found in Appendix A.

Border Patrol

It's safe to say you could travel a lifetime and never quite hit all of America's truly interesting hot spots. Consider it another one of the benefits of living and touring in a country as diverse and dynamic as ours (cue the "Star Spangled Banner"). But over time, you might be tempted to play the role of tourist in another country, fraught with new languages, customs, and perhaps the dreaded metric system. Yikes! "How many kilometers to the Queen Mum's palace, honey?" Space prohibits us from discussing the individual laws and RVing practices of every single country on the globe (it's a big world, don't you know), so we'll stick to trips to the most popular border crossings, Canada and Mexico.

One for the Road

Is there such a thing as a recreational vehicle in other countries? Sure there is, with a few differences. Although chiefly an American art form, RVs—in some form or another—are found throughout the world. Building practices, size restrictions, and many interior systems are different, meaning the RV that rolled out of the Indiana assembly line might puzzle our European, Australian, or Asian counterparts. Contact an overseas tour company for help arranging trips abroad.

Oh, Canada

The United States and Canada have long enjoyed a symbiotic relationship. Canada exports us a steady supply of hockey stars, stand-up comics, and Ann Murray, while we reciprocate with Mountie jokes and tourists wondering just how cold it gets in Winnipeg. While Alaska gets most of the attention as the "last frontier," parts of Canada make our fiftieth state look almost urban by comparison. Moreover, the country delivers some of North America's most beautiful cities and unique cultures all its own. It's no joke—Canada is a wonderful destination.

For their part, our neighbors to the north act as willing hosts, and the border crossing is rarely much of an event. A passport isn't required, but proof of insurance and vehicle registration will likely be called into play. Call your insurer to see if coverage follows you up to these parts. The family pet might have to cough up a rabies certificate. (No growling, please.) An upstanding citizen like yourself probably won't be submitted to a vehicle search, but if it does happen, don't panic. Answer their questions and don't pull any of that "My country could beat up your country" stuff. Firearms will probably be confiscated, so declare them and show permits to avoid any hard feelings—and legal wranglings. The return trip should go much like the first, with the exception of an opportunity to declare any loot purchased on the journey.

Mexico

Crossing the Mexican border is easy and usually uneventful. The guards seem only a little more curious than their Canadian counterparts, with the biggest concern being proof of citizenship. Don't forget your passports—it's a long drive back home to fetch them. Otherwise, a copy of your birth certificate and photo ID should suffice for American travelers. You must also present proof of Mexican insurance if your policy lacks adequate coverage in Mexico. Fortunately, insurance companies lace many border towns for just this event. Vehicle registration, proof of rabies vaccination (for pets, not you), and an absence of weapons is all that's left, at which time you'll be given a free Mexican Tourist Card. Keep this with you at all times.

Traveling throughout Mexico is like riding through a history book one day and a festival atmosphere the next. Where else can you explore staggering Mayan ruins and then revel among the jet set at Acapulco or Puerto Vallarta? Beautiful beaches, amazing fishing, and predictably hot weather are yours year-round. Hard-core adventure-seekers shouldn't resist the chance to zigzag the Baja Peninsula's 1,000-mile trail from Tijuana to the southernmost tip of Cabo San Lucas. After an RV escapade such as this, consider yourself in the advanced category.

Such journeys are not without their challenges. Even the most PR-savvy Mexican tourist centers confirm problems of unpurified water in undeveloped areas. Obviously, toting along one's own water supply alleviates much of this concern, but be careful when you refill the water tank. Drink bottled water when out and about. Keep your mouth closed when showering, avoid ice, and wash off fruits and vegetables (with bottled water) to avoid a trip-altering encounter with a vengeful Mr. Montezuma.

Purity problems are less of a concern in upscale establishments, but caution is still merited. The ceaseless hot weather requires other adjustments. Take it slow and wear plenty of sunscreen. Safety is a concern in some outlying areas, especially in remote parts of the country or throughout areas of unrest. Taking part in an established RV tour is recommended for inexperienced travelers.

The Full-Timing Life

I don't know if RVing is up there with baseball and apple pie, but it's truly an American concept. We created it, we perfected it, and our citizenry continues to explore this way of life in record numbers. Recent estimates put those who full-time, or live year-round in their recreational vehicles, at approximately one million. I would go as far as to wager that each and every one of us has, at some point, dreamed of cashing in our chips, pulling up stakes, and living full-time, RV-style. Come on, admit it. You're just a tad curious what the year-round life would be like, aren't you?

It may be too early in your RV career to be talking about this level of commitment, but a little chat wouldn't hurt. Surely, full-timing is the biggest plunge of them all, but is it right for you? On one side, there's no yard to mow, house payments, or laborious commute to work. Every day yields a new view, a new town, and plenty of sights unseen to propel adventures even further. On the other, it's a radical change. Are you ready for this kind of wanderlust, residing in a home on wheels, traveling the byways like a modern-day gypsy? The full-timing experience has been met with praise and disaster alike. Couples believing they were ready for such ultra simplicity and take-charge freedom quickly wilted under the strain of tight quarters, money troubles, and lack of purpose. The flip side reveals couples lamenting that they should have tried it sooner, rejoicing in the new vigor that only a wide-open itinerary provides. How will you react if given the opportunity to try it out for a while? Hmmm?

Can I Afford It?

The carefree life sounds inexpensive, but it isn't necessarily. Living on the go can be a pricey proposition. One full-timer recently told me he needed a holster for his credit card because he was pulling it out so much. Just how expensive things get is up to you. If you're the type who moves around constantly, expect to pay a decent premium for these nonstop adventures. Fuel, campgrounds, and life as a perpetual tourist can add up. However, those who spend months in one location—such as at a sunny seasonal campground off a Florida beach—reap considerable long-term savings and avoid much of the heart-stopping fuel costs.

There are those who sell all their worldly possessions—home, cars, and their collection of shot glasses from every state—with that cash influx going straight into the travel fund. For them, full-timing means good-bye to mortgages, property taxes, maintenance, and the usual costs of the sedentary life. Others maintain a residence, holding on to the mortgage or lease for if and when they decide to return to their previous lives.

One for the Road

There are lots of ways to full-time and none has to be a permanent solution. Many full-timers spend a few years traveling, until they find a spot to retire. Others RV year-round "just to get it out of their system," and return to their "normal" lives. And for some, this is it—the way they want to live as long as they are able.

Road Scholar

One of the most popular employment opportunities for RVers is as work-campers, with positions available at many larger private campgrounds. In exchange for a salary and a free campsite, work-campers assist in the campground operation, such as in maintenance, construction, or desk help. The work is usually seasonal. It's not unusual for workers to return to the same campground every year.

Just because your home shrinks from a 3,000-square-foot colonial in the suburbs to a 35-foot trailer and tow vehicle doesn't necessarily mean an escape from the high costs of living. A smaller kitchen might not equate to smaller food bills. A month's worth of $30 campsites can sting as badly as some mortgages. Eight miles per gallon goes fast when motorhoming across the country. Tolls, insurance, phone bills, entertainment, and the ongoing costs of owning and operating a recreational vehicle all add up. Of course, there are some breaks. Little space for superfluous possessions means you won't buy them. The budget-breaking vacations of the past are assimilated into everyday expenses, so subtract those as well. And if you do it right, you'll be surprised at how far you can stretch a dollar. Only you know how long you can milk a buck and what type of full-timer you might be. Crunch the numbers, and make sure you have a decent nest egg before proceeding. Otherwise, think about ways to make money as you travel.

Many RVers supplement their savings by working on the road. Thankfully, earning a living in the Information Age is easier than ever, thanks to cell phones, voice mail, e-mail, the Internet, and the trusty laptop community. (More on these things in Chapter 19, "Staying in Touch.") Perhaps the best solution is to keep working your regular job, taking advantage of telecommuting and consulting opportunities. Despite being camped 3,000 miles from the office, with the right setup you're really only a phone call or mouse click away. Freelancing is another great gig and a perfect match to the RV lifestyle. I've known plenty of writers, artists, photographers, and graphic designers who get along smashingly in a roving office. And there's certainly nothing stopping you from finding employment wherever you land, whether seasonal, full- or part-time.

What Is My Purpose?

The fastest way to hate what you're doing is to lack a reason for doing it. Full-timing is no different. Traveling around from mountains to beaches, in-laws to grandkids is great—but is it enough for you? At the end of the day, is this a satisfying way to live? What, if anything, do you hope to accomplish out there? Do you plan to keep on working, taking advantage of telecommuting, freelancing, or finding employment to supplement savings? Are you looking for a place to retire, hoping to catch a baseball game in every Major League park, or driven to tour the sights in every state? Can too much recreation be a bad thing? Think about a schedule and how you'll fill your day. Is this full-time experience a brief interlude or something you might want to pursue long-term?

Will I Strangle My Spouse?

One lady articulated her relationship with her husband onboard their trailer as a kind of ongoing dance. According to her, it takes a while to learn the rhythm needed for both of you to co-exist in a space much smaller than you're accustomed to. Some of us are just better dancers than others, she said. Consider a few lengthy trips beforehand as the best indicators as to your "dancing" abilities. If cabin fever quickly sets in, or you simply can't stand your husband's idiosyncrasies on a trial getaway, chances are a prolonged journey of a year or two might not be such a good idea. Remember that you won't be able to retreat to the "man room" in the basement like you once did at home when your wife's amusing herself with her John Wayne impressions again. Unless you engage in separate hobbies or work, most of your time will be spent together.

Road Scholar

Giving away the 8-track player is easy; parting with your great, great grandmother's rocking chair from the Civil War days is hard. Store important items in one of thousands of self-storage facilities to eliminate such impossible decisions. Pay in advance so you know your items are safe. Otherwise, loan keepsakes to friends, children, and grandkids, clearly stating that you may want these articles back someday.

Can I Give It All Up?

You spend half your life working to provide security, a stable home life, and money to buy a pair of shoes for every occasion. Consolidating a home into an RV is a tough business, an emotional shipwreck for many trying to reconcile one life into another. Space is tight and hard decisions must be made about what comes along and what must stay behind. If you can afford to RV *and* keep the house, then this process is much less traumatic. However, for most, it's one way of life or the other. There's no room to bring along a den full of bowling trophies. Your favorite easy chair, power tools, and precious art must be stored, given away, or sold. Loads of family heirlooms and keepsakes can't make the trip; closets full of clothes shrink down to a suitcase or two. Still, there are those who can't part with these possessions fast enough. Many have told me about the true freedom this streamlined approach provides. Are you of the less-is-more persuasion or too deeply entrenched within a materialistic society to give it all up?

How Do I Stay in Touch?

Bill paying, mail-forwarding, and communicating with friends and loved ones is addressed in the next chapter.

What RV Do I Need?

The short answer is the biggest one possible. Believe me, you'll find use for every inch of available space, for you and your stuff. Sure, some full-timers make smaller towables, truck campers, and van campers work, but realistically, consider 30 feet the minimum-size vehicle for year-round living. A slide-out or two won't go to waste, either. Remember, this is now your home—where you'll spend most every day and night—so don't skimp on size, floor plan, or features. Gravitate toward vehicles with higher NCC (net carrying capacity, remember?) ratings, meaning more weight left over for you, full tanks, and cargo. Workstations or office-type add-ons found on some models are useful for those keeping a day job. A secondary vehicle is a must, for commuting to work and running errands. Towable owners can simply use the tow vehicle; motorhomers should seriously consider towing a car.

The Least You Need to Know

- Appreciate the needs and concerns of children and younger passengers. Honor their opinions by getting them involved in trip planning and helping out around camp. Be especially careful to pack items that are important to them. Explain the rules of the campground and set a good example of conduct for them to follow.
- Allow pets to adjust to the RV before bringing them along. Help them acclimate by setting up beds, food and water bowls, litter boxes, and toys, just like home. Set temperatures for their comfort, and avoid leaving them unattended. Most campgrounds accept cats and dogs, assuming they're quiet, on a leash, and picked up after.
- RV clubs offer a great way to learn about the lifestyle and make friendships with those with similar interests. Product and travel discounts, informative publications, and rallies are just some of the advantages. Joining an RV tour or caravan is an enjoyable and hassle-free way to enjoy complex trips.
- A few lengthy journeys and a careful self-examination should help you decide if full-time RVing is for you. Define goals, evaluate finances, and make peace with space, livability, and cargo restrictions before undertaking this radical lifestyle change.

Chapter 19

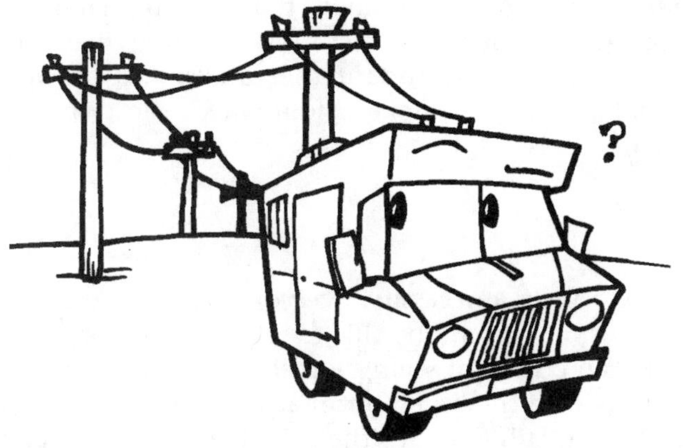

Staying in Touch

In This Chapter

- Remaining a phone call away, no matter where you go
- Tips for e-mail and other online activities
- Procedures for sending and receiving your mail

Hey, did you hear the word? We live in the Information Age. Surely, you got the memo, voice message, e-mail, or fax about the good news? Still need proof? Ask any teenager proudly sporting a cell phone, laptop, his own Web site, two-way pager, and a mailbox full of voice messages from giddy friends about the sale at the mall. Of course, adults aren't immune to communication overload, either. Most of us can now be reached in a multitude of ways, at home, the office, our vehicles—and even out in the great beyond.

Fortunately, this always-accessible way of life gels nicely with RVing, where the challenge is how to get away from it all without getting away from *everyone*. Staying in touch is important. No matter where we're camped out, we still want to hear how our grandson liked his first T-ball game. And it's always nice to get the heads-up concerning a work-related emergency, so there's an actual job to come back to. Suppose the Publisher's Clearing House Prize Patrol is waiting on the doorstep back home with a $1,000,000 check? A call from the neighbors would certainly be appreciated, wouldn't it?

But even in a world as technologically dependent as this, staying in the loop is more complicated than giving friends and family the cell phone number. You could easily go in-communicato if you travel out of range. And what about that stack of mail piling up at home? How will the bills get paid while you're bicycling Martha's Vineyard? Are you able to send and receive e-mail, dance about the Internet, and still say howdy-do to loved ones while motoring about Alaska, the Smokey Mountains, or lost on a country road in Nowheresville? The answer is yes. Here's how.

Phone Home

Staying in touch on the road isn't a luxury, it's a necessity. Everyone from loved ones to the home office needs to know where you are and be able to reach you—even when camped in Parts Unknown. Agreed, it's an odd sight seeing someone with a cell phone in one hand and roasting marshmallows with the other, but that's modern living. Until someone says otherwise, the phone is still king. It's the fastest, easiest, and most flexible way to communicate, which is why I've championed the cell phone cause throughout this book. However, these little wonders can come with a certain amount of baggage—unruly costs, unpredictable signal availability, and service contracts, just to name a few. And if the cellular way was the great end-all, this chapter would be pretty short. Fortunately, there's more than one way to make a call these days.

Cell Out

As much as I hate to see some guy yapping away on his "cellie" in the restaurant, having one is simply a no-brainer for RVers everywhere. Contact roadside assistance in case of a flat tire. Get directions to that elusive campground. Give the kids a stable number to call in case of trouble, or ring up the movie theatre for a list of show times. All this without ever leaving the driver's seat. What could be better?

One for the Road

Cell phones can get expensive, especially when traveling outside of normal areas. Some travelers discipline themselves to only use them when absolutely necessary. Limit outgoing and incoming calls (you pay for these, too) to keep bills down. Watch roaming and long distance charges carefully. Full-timers should customize their service plans to match their nomadic lifestyles, finding plans with flat rates and expansive coverage areas.

Considering that most of us already have a cell phone anyway, it's no wonder why they've become the ultimate accessory item for roaming about the country.

You've probably been around the block enough times to know that all this convenience comes at a price. For starters, there's the service plan and contract (required in many cases) waiting for your John Hancock. The calling plan you choose can make or break the cell phone experience. The best advice is to comparison shop and find the service best suited for your lifestyle, whether designed for home use or life on the road. Unchecked roaming charges, the heightened usage fee assessed when traveling out of the cellular provider's area of coverage, has wreaked havoc on more than a few RVers' bottom line.

Which calls are long-distance and which ones are local? Check your plan for the territorial differences. Since I do most of my traveling in the Midwest, I opted for a plan targeting the states surrounding my home. Nationwide coverage plans are best suited for those always on the go, thus eliminating separate long-distance and roaming fees. Nip costs wherever you can. How many minutes do you have each month? Can you do with less? The phone itself may be free (depending on the plan) or a pricey number if you go with a fancy version, like something out of *Star Trek*. Cellular technology ranks high among the most competitive marketplaces around, with new technology popping up all the time. Be patient and great deals can be had. Be selective, watch for sales, and opt for plans that fit your lifestyle.

Pull Over

A cell phone is only as useful as its signal strength, determined by your carrier's coverage areas. That's why it's harder to place and receive calls in remote areas than metropolitan ones. As such, it's a good idea to have a calling card or other means of communication waiting as a backup in case your signal takes a prolonged siesta.

Calling Cards

For those who want next to a sure thing (no, not that trifecta the cabby told you about), tuck a calling card away in the event of an underachieving cell phone. They're also a good way to avoid seeing a chiropractor, eliminating that terrible kink caused by folks driving around with a phone constantly propped between their head and shoulder. A plentiful supply of pay phones means you can always count on a steady land line—and no signal fluctuations. Just dial the telephone number on the card, insert your code or user number, and chat away. Since this practice is a one-way street—you call them, but they can't call you—you'll need to work out a system to collect messages. Advise loved ones to leave a voice mail or message on the answering machine to reach you. A number of private voice mail services are available for those lacking such message services.

Pull Over

Be wary of the person hustling prepaid calling cards up and down the block. The deals are unbelievable—that is, until you try to use one of these phonies. While I'm sure some sellers are legit, many are not. These cards look the part, but are really only useful to scrape ice off the windshield—not too good when you need to make a call. Buy only from reputable sources to prevent such wrong numbers.

Calling cards are available from the phone company and long-distance carriers, with charges usually directed right to the monthly bill. Another option is a prepaid calling card, offered just about everywhere, which delivers a flat amount of long-distance service at a one-time price. As the name suggests, buyers purchase a block of minutes in advance, available for use anytime, anywhere. This route guarantees no unexpected charges and no strings attached—when you're out of time, the card is defunct. That is, unless you buy more time, which is another nice option. Generally, the more minutes you buy, the cheaper the per-minute rate. Check around for the best deals and be aware of possible expiration dates.

Campsite Hookup

Most campsites aren't like hotel rooms, which all but guarantee a dedicated phone line, modem line, and message service. The campground industry is moving in that direction, but it's still a ways off. As detailed in Chapter 16, "Choosing a Campground," onsite phone service is still pretty rare for overnight stays. For an activation fee and deposit, long-term guests can go directly through the phone company to set up service. This option really only makes sense for stays of a month or longer and requires a phone jack in the RV.

Collect Calls

Unless you're penniless and stranded (or a freshman in college), there's really no reason to resort to placing a collect call. Sure, the folks on the other end want to hear from you, but must they really pay for the privilege?

E-Mail

Phones are just half the battle now. The ability to e-mail documents, pictures, lengthy attachments, and fun chain letters to Uncle Frank adds to one's accessibility when away from home. For your part, online access is key for home and business life. Getting the latest on the stock market, directions to the alligator farm the next town over, or just to see how the Red Sox played last night are all a matter of utmost importance. For those still unconvinced, the online world isn't a fad or the most recent incarnation of the eight-track player. It's here to stay, and the RV industry is taking note.

RVocabulary

What exactly does **modem friendly** mean? Definitions vary from place to place. For some campground owners, it's a lone phone line left unplugged so a camper can go online. A slightly larger definition is in play at other facilities, perhaps taken to mean special computer rooms or instant-on campsite phone hookups. Question owners about their online access beforehand if this is important to you.

A quick tour of nicer recreational vehicles supports this theory. You may see a computer workstation with space for a printer and hard drive, and installed phone jack(s), serving as an onboard passport to the Cyber World. "*Modem friendly*" graces ads and billboards of some campgrounds. Meanwhile, travelers lug laptops, Palm Pilots, online-ready phones, and Internet appliances around with them, always ready to surf for answers along the information superhighway.

Campers stymied by online-intolerant campgrounds have other allies. Public libraries, travel plazas, truck stops, and businesses such as Kinko's are known to be pretty Internet-friendly, providing modem lines and a comfortable environment to conduct one's affairs. For your part, you'll need to change the dial-up number of your Internet Service Provider (ISP) on your computer to forgo a long-distance charge. Call your ISP's (American Online, Earthlink, Microsoft, etc.) toll-free number for a list of local dial-up numbers in that area.

The best part of e-mail is that it travels well and can be every bit as useful as a phone when checked regularly. The question then becomes how to access this information. A laptop computer is the most common method; RVers lugging around their computers to the campground office are a pretty common site. However, a whole new subgroup of Internet devices has recently taken hold in our dot-com universe, with unique benefits of their own. For those confused about which online apparatus is best, a closer look at each type is provided.

Computers

Spend enough time away from home, and you'll most likely find plenty of use for an onboard computer. They're great for going online, doing work, keeping track of finances, storing photos and important data—well, I'm sure I don't need to hype what these babies can do. There's something about writing the great American novel on a laptop in the middle of nowhere that seems almost downright sinful. Computers also hold a lot of stored information, saving us precious weight onboard. Look up directions to the next attraction or that prized family recipe for Goulash without cumbersome cookbooks and atlases. Play games, track expenses, and—more closely related to this chapter—send and receive e-mails to and from friends or that boss who can't run the place without you.

One for the Road

Onsite modem access and full-fledged computer centers are beyond the means of most ordinary campgrounds. To compensate, a complimentary line reserved for sending and receiving e-mail is often found in the office for use by guests. To avoid a logjam of e-mail-happy customers, it's requested that guests follow some simple etiquette. Limit your time online. Compose messages in advance, and use these connections only for sending/downloading messages.

But like the people who love them, not all computers are created equal. Simply put, some travel better than others. While I've seen clunky desktop computers on desks inside the abodes of a few full-timers, for the most part, the laptop is king. It's portable, lightweight, and saves precious space onboard, aspects that never fail to impress. Whatever you use, make sure to bring a phone and extension cord, a printer, a rugged case (for laptops), spare ink cartridges, and a secondary source to back-up information if necessary, such as a zip drive and disks. Some cellular phone users can buy an adapter for direct link with their laptops. The unit's modem does the rest.

Internet Devices

Once upon a time, online functions necessitated traveling with a computer. Thankfully, the laptop had already made the bulky PC overkill, doing everything the big boys could do in a nice, portable package. Not that we've heard anybody complaining, but recently a rash of new Internet appliances, handheld PCs, and mobile organizers scaled things down even further. Some devices are multifunctioned (such as the Palm Pilot series), chiming in with word processing, address books, and calendar functions. Others are the proverbial one-trick ponies, possessing only the ability to compose, send, and receive messages. Sizes vary from a matter of ounces to just under

10 pounds, with information input through a pointer stylus, attachable keyboard, or other twenty-first-century manner. Most offer a cheaper, more mobile communication tool to most any laptop computer.

Connecting to the Internet or e-mail applications is usually fairly tame. A wireless modem grants users online access in some cases; others still rely on an interior modem and outside phone hookup. At the forefront of some of the fastest moving technology around, the handheld PC market is experiencing rapid growth. Increasingly dazzling applications are blowing away tech-lovers seemingly every day. Can't afford the thousands of dollars for a laptop? Searching for a wireless solution? Looking for a simpler way to go online and send and receive e-mails? Lighter weights and manageable costs ($100 to $1,000, based on capabilities) mean these mobile solutions may be leading us to the forefront of another computer revolution.

Pagers

Today's line of pagers are as sophisticated or as basic as you wish them to be. At the heart of the matter is still an attention-getting buzz, ring, or song informing wearers that they are in demand. (That, or there's a hornet's nest in your pants.) The caller's phone number is displayed, and newer units invite them to leave a brief message, as well. In my opinion, a pager is only slightly less useful than a cell phone or voice message service, but to each his own. Like the trusty cell, pagers rely on a service provider, monthly fees, and are prone to coverage lapses in some cases.

CB Radio

At hearing the news that CB radios are still around—and even enjoying a resurgence in popularity—some folks are genuinely surprised. They must have thought these macho devices peaked with the *Smokey and the Bandit* movies. Their limited ranges and niche appeal make CB (citizen band) radios useless for talking with the kids at home or making reservations at the seafood joint down the street, but many travelers swear by them for their roadworthiness. (Unfortunately, a few users swear *on* them as well, preserving their reputation as a slightly crude apparatus for some folks' tastes.)

Think of them as a chat room of sorts, with 40 designated channels for RVers, truckers, and the obligatory HAM operators relating traffic tales, points of interest, and, of course, where the smokies are hiding. The rousing dialog is also pretty entertaining, especially when trying to interpret the loads of jargon bantered about. RVers use CBs as a mix of companionship, entertainment, and more practical matters, such as getting directions, weather updates, and the whereabouts of a good roadside diner. Channel 9 is reserved for emergency use, an often useful aid in case of an accident or other trouble. Members of caravans often share a designated channel to communicate with each other as they motor along.

Road Scholar

Taking advantage of automatic bill paying placates creditors in your absence. Everything from mortgages to utilities to credit card balances can be paid on a regular, consistent basis—all without awaiting a bill, writing a check, and fumbling around looking for stamps. Contact creditors directly for automatic payment options or utilize accounting software to run your empire on your behalf.

One for the Road

Most campgrounds are glad to receive your mail—assuming you're still a guest there. Just saunter up to the office for mail call. However, others indulge guests by offering mailbox service and onsite delivery for those enjoying a longer stay. As a courtesy, check with management ahead of time before having any correspondence sent to that address.

Mail Call

If you're like me, your life just isn't complete without that daily dose of catalogs, advertising flyers, and love letters from creditors. While you're off gallivanting across the country, your mail at home piles up. Bills go unpaid, pen pals unanswered, and important packages sit idle on the doorstep, taking a beating from the elements and the neighborhood kids looking for a substitute soccer ball. Even the mail carrier's getting a complex over your absence. Trips limited to a week or two shouldn't foul up the bill-paying schedule and important correspondence. However, receiving and processing mail for full-timers, seasonal travelers, and the family touring away their summer vacations can be a major nuisance—with problematic consequences. No one likes to return home to disconnected utilities and late charges incurred as a result of failure to address overdue bills and invoices.

Short of enlisting NASA technology to laser-beam mail directly to RV travelers on the go-go, a little crafty planning is all that's needed to rendezvous with important cards and letters on the way. A number of services do exist, useful for anyone who isn't on the Pony Express route.

Mail-Forwarding Services

Going south for the winter? Your friendly neighborhood post office is more than happy to forward mail to any address you give them. The service is free, usually takes about two weeks to get things started, and is good for up to one year. The advantage is that junk mail (in theory, anyway) won't bother being sent, so you only get the important stuff. A host of private mail-forwarding companies (designed especially for RVers) also exist, and may be more flexible and offer a larger range of services. Thumb through RV publications for a list of companies. Utilizing such a service makes sense for anyone spending at least a few months away from home, assuming they have a steady address or two to receive items along the way. Send mail directly to the RV resort (if they allow that kind of thing), a local post office box, or other place where you can pick up the goods. Make sure this new address can receive packages and overnight deliveries, a well-known limitation of a PO Box.

General Delivery

I first discovered the post office's General Delivery program through a friend hiking the Appalachian Trail. At a few predetermined spots off the trail, he orchestrated his affairs so that packages containing fresh supplies were waiting for him at the local post office. This type of forwarding service is good for those on the move, as long as you have a good handle on your travel itinerary. For example, if you're spending March sunning in Tucson, April gambling away the nest egg in Las Vegas, and the summer riding the cable cars in San Francisco, you can arrange mail to be sent to a post office in each location. Mail should be sent to: Your Name, c/o General Delivery, city, state, and zip code.

Road Scholar

It is a good idea to use the General Delivery address of a smaller town rather than a downtown post office of a larger city. Navigating downtown traffic and parking restrictions can be troublesome in an RV, and you will probably receive more personal attention in a small town post office anyway.

It's a good idea to call that post office ahead of time and let them know you're coming. There's no postal box to pay for, and when you're ready to leave town, just fill out another form to hook up with another mail batch at the next place.

The Buddy System

Remember the neighbor who borrowed that cup of sugar? How about the 34 hours spent in labor delivering your firstborn? These folks owe you, and it's time for some payback, don't you think? Whether through love or guilt (or just a pal who's easily conned), arranging for someone to pick up and forward your mail is probably the most flexible solution—for you, at least. A weekly visit to your home to sift through the pile is all you ask—bills and letters go in the forwarding envelope; junk goes into the recycling. Leave a few large envelopes and plenty of stamps, along with word of where you are so they know where to send the goods.

Address Unknown

What about the full-timer without a home address? They may have sold their home to bankroll this extended vacation, so now what? You can't have things sent to a license plate number, right? True, mail without an actual residence is a tricky thing. The best advice is to employ the services of a flexible mail-forwarding service, one capable of keeping up with your travel plans. The question of residency also creeps in for those constantly on the move. Without a permanent address, where do these persons really live? Where do they vote, to whom do they pay any state taxes, etc? Residency is a hot issue right now, with requirements varying from state to state. Full-timers and wannabes should check with their home state—or a future home state—to determine residency requirements. In some cases, the address of a mail-forwarding service determines one's residence for them. Therefore, using that Florida mail service may mean the Sunshine State is now your "official" residence.

The Least You Need to Know

- RV life is made easier with a steady form of communication, namely the cell phone. This is simply the best means of two-way communication on the road. Pagers, calling cards, and CB radios are useful, although limited ways to stay in touch.
- Most campgrounds devise some manner to go online for guests. Laptops are the most common method to send and retrieve e-mail, although a full line of Internet devices and person organizers are making the job even simpler.
- A good mail-forwarding service, whether it be the U.S. Postal Service, a private company, or a willing friend or relative, is a must for anyone traveling for longer periods of time.

Chapter 20

Playin' It Safe

In This Chapter

- Overcoming bad weather, breakdowns, and medical problems
- Avoiding crime, accidents, and potential road hazards
- Must-have emergency equipment

Think of this chapter as that big brother, around to keep you out of trouble. In this case, it's not the school bully we're worried about; rather, any number of troublesome scenarios prowling about to complicate an otherwise pleasant journey. Bad weather, mechanical breakdowns, and succumbing to an avoidable spill at the campsite are chief among them. Travel by RV long enough, and we're bound to encounter some unsavory foe. Accidents can indeed happen, even to the best of drivers in the wrong place at the wrong time. Crime is a fact of life. And just because we may be on vacation doesn't make us immune to medical problems. Unfortunate but true, situations such as these don't just happen to "the other guy."

However, getting nervous and uptight about the "what-ifs" isn't the answer. Nor is rampant paranoia or a doomsday approach to one's travels—there's no sense engaging in any of that. This chapter isn't here to scare you. "Honey, RVing is fraught with danger. Go back to the dealership and sell that rig immediately!" Hardly. The steps outlined here are designed to enlighten and empower—not prod your anxiety like smacking a beehive with a stick. As always, knowledge is power and preparation is king. Playing it safe is easier than you think.

Weather or Not (Here I Come)

The ever-changing weather patterns are life's greatest sideshow. Like the bearded lady and lobster boy at the carnival, they never cease to surprise and amaze. One day it's calm and beautiful, the next we're running for cover. We can't control it, we can't affect it, and, if your meteorologist is anything like the guy on my local station, can't hardly predict it. Unless you're camped year-round in San Diego (78° and sunny), weather is somewhat of a crapshoot.

Road Scholar

A number of Web sites relay the most current conditions and forecasts. One of the best is www.weather.com. Simply type in the city or zip code and up comes the status on everything Mother Nature is up to. For those on the go, a scan through the local AM radio stations should uncover a news channel with constant updates. If you're really concerned, a portable weather radio warns of emerging nasty weather.

A great falsehood of operating a large vehicle is the belief that you're better insulated from the effects of the elements. It's simply not true. In fact, it's just the opposite. Towables can struggle mightily with big winds and wet pavement. Motorhomes require more diligence in icy conditions, and their size makes them harder to stop and maneuver out of trouble. But bad weather is bad weather, no matter what you drive. It's just a matter of knowing how to handle it.

Wind Breaker

Wind is an insidious threat, the one weather condition we can't see coming. But when it arrives, you know it, slapping the side of the RV with vicious intent. Most automobiles breeze (pun intended) right through it. Meanwhile, RVers are battling for control, since taller vehicles and trailer combos only serve to make us a bigger and more tantalizing target. But just because wind is invisible, it's approach isn't. Watch the landscape for signs of unsavory updrafts—shaking tree limbs, leaning crops, etc. are all clues that wind is on the prowl. When the winds swirl, hearken (yes, hearken) back to your Driver's Ed days and grip the wheel tightly at 10 and 2.

Give fellow travelers—especially larger vehicles—plenty of room. Pick a lane and stay put; this is no time for your Richard Petty impression. Rebuff gusts with subtle steering in that direction to compensate, but don't overdo it. If things get ugly, find an exit, and fly a kite.

The Perfect Storm

Nasty rain often packs a one-two punch: wet conditions matched with low visibility. Wind, thunder and lightning, and the zealous pelting of drops against the rig can all serve to rattle the driver's confidence even further. Step one: Turn on your lights, to help you see and be seen. Add an extra cushion (no, not a pillow) between you and other vehicles for extra stopping, and be doubly alert for brake lights and vehicles parked on the shoulder. If the afternoon skies turn green and the winds pick up, put the co-pilot on tornado patrol. Things might get worse in a hurry, so start looking for shelter and a place to dock.

Pull Over

Take caution when traveling over bridges, as they are particularly prone to windy conditions. Be on the lookout for posted cautionary signs denoting well-known trouble spots. Put the cell phone down and grip the wheel with both hands. Find a middle lane (if offered), maintain a steady speed, and stay the course.

Snow Day

I know, avoiding the white menace is why you purchased an RV in the first place. Fair enough. But coming from someone who has attended snowy Cubs games in April and got hit by a blizzard in Colorado in June, I'm not sure the stuff is *totally* avoidable. Our warm-weather friends insulated from such winter wonderlands don't always know how to react when first confronted with it—kind of Close Encounters of the Flurried Kind. A little snow is like rain, only prettier and easier to use when constructing snowmen. Take it slow, be ultra-faithful to one lane, and opt for major highways, usually first to convalesce with Mr. Plow and his magical salt dispenser. Unplowed roads are tricky and best avoided if the snow is sticking and starting to add up. Turn on lights if visibility suffers and stop for the night if things get icy and dicey.

Pull Over

If conditions deteriorate to the point that you're wondering whether or not to get off the road, then by all means do so. Follow your instincts, not the vehicle next to you. The downsides of an accident or being caught in ugly weather far outweigh any gains made by pressing on.

Ice Capades

I'd mess with Texas before going toe-to-toe with a slick roadway covered in ice. In a rogue's gallery of driving villains, it's arguably the worst. Difficult to detect, uncompromisingly tough to negotiate, and unapologetically deadly under the worst circumstances, icy conditions deserve our fullest attention. While the folks in Palm Springs may have no idea what you're talking about, any time spent in northern climes will bring you face-to-face with the stuff. Take it slow. Excessive braking is not the answer here; this locks the wheels on a slippery dance floor. The better remedy is allowing a wide berth for fellow vehicles, and decelerating—the limbo zone between accelerating and braking—to slow your progress. Downshifting gears is a useful maneuver to slow the RV steadily. Ice only worsens at night (when temps sink), so limit travel to daylight hours and only in conditions you can safely handle.

Road Scholar

How do you know conditions are bad enough to pull over? Watch the pros. Semis lining the sides of the highway or congregating in truck stops are good indications that the roadways have lost their friendly demeanor. If the 18-wheelers, known for their "just drive through it" attitudes, fear to tread, you should have been off the highway long ago.

Pea Soup

Great to eat, not so great to drive through, a pea soup–like fog is a driving faux pas. Fortunately, unless you're a 49ers fan, fog isn't terribly common. Most common in the morning, it tends to burn away as the day heats up. A light, low-lying batch is meddlesome, but driveable. Keep the lights on (skip the ineffective high beams), speeds low, and watch those around you like a hawk. If you can't tell if that's an 18-wheeler or a horse and buggy in front of you, it's time to find a place to sit this one out.

Natural Disasters

The truly big hitters—hurricanes, tornadoes, earthquakes—require slightly different coping tricks but all have one thing in common: You don't want 'em. No one will call you chicken for fleeing the scene like the locals did when Godzilla trounced Tokyo. In any event, an RV isn't where you want to be. Even inside a locked rig, sitting in the bathtub with blankets over your heads, you and your family are unbelievably vulnerable. Say adios to your vehicle and find real shelter—a basement, ditch, or underpass for tornadoes, away from structures during earthquakes, and as far away as possible from that 100-foot wave that accompanies a hurricane.

The Accidental Tourist

I remember the older gent who proudly exclaimed that he had never been in an accident, no simple feat considering some 50 years of driving. After letting the group praise him accordingly, his wife leaned in and said, "Yeah, but he's *caused* a hundred of them." Unfortunately, the world is full of so-so drivers. Some are downright awful, seemingly aiming their vehicles like heat-seeking missiles rather than driving them. As a whole, RVers continually earn praise for their abilities behind the wheel. Accidents throughout this segment are wonderfully low, thanks mostly to mature operators heeding their limitations. However, the rest of the world is not always as skilled. Accidents happen and sometimes, despite our Herculean efforts, we're stuck in the crossfire. Here's what to do.

Pull Over

Parking on the shoulder during times of low visibility is like painting a bulls-eye on your back. In the event of a roadside breakdown, pull off as far as possible. Activate hazard lights, and set up flares and reflectors to warn on-comers. Vacate the RV and get away from the road. Contact roadside assistance immediately; a dangerous circumstance like this may merit a call to 911.

Avoid 'Em

They say an ounce of prevention is worth a pound of cure. It's also worth forgoing a costly repair job, medical bills, legal problems, and all the other yucky baggage stemming from an accident. Let's skip it altogether, shall we? We discussed the seven deadly driving sins in Chapter 14, "Drive Time," aggressive and passive driving, pushing it in bad weather, and fatigue—among others. Eliminate this troublesome behavior and—poof!—you cut down your risks considerably. Give drivers lots of room, avoid irate drivers like the plague, and take frequent breaks to recharge your faculties. Be especially diligent in parking lots and close quarters, the most common sites for an inexplicably high number of collisions every year.

Oh-Oh

It's extremely hard not to take things personally when a Sunday driver derails the family's vacation with a mindless collision. How dare he? Your first reaction is probably to throttle that person's … calm down, it's not worth it. Don't get angry. Rather, devote that energy surge to making sure you and everyone are all right—and stay that way.

Protect Valuables—You

People—yes, even the one who hit you—are the most important thing right now. Safeguarding the involved parties takes two forms: treating those in the accident and making sure you don't add to their numbers by involving any oncoming traffic. Don't press injured passengers to move unless there's a risk of fire, explosion, or danger from other vehicles—further movement could add to their injuries. Treat yourself first; if you're okay, move on, ascertaining the status of passengers. If everyone can walk and is okay, get them away from the scene. Call 911 and explain the situation. Do your best to provide the location and await authorities.

Pull Over

Place the following acts in the don't-do category: Get in a shouting match with the other driver. Dash to the RV to get a favorite possession. Hang around the roadway, appraising damage. Investigate where that smoke is coming from. Trivialize the injuries of others.

Don't Be a Hero

There are some who believe it's your duty to "secure the area" after such an occurrence. I disagree. Scurrying around a fast-moving highway, setting up flares and reflectors after an accident is an easy way to end up getting hit by another vehicle. Only take these steps if it's safe to do so. Frankly, your crew is the primary responsibility, so I say stay with them and await authorities. The police may want to investigate the scene, so it might be best to leave it alone. For accidents of the fender-bender variety, where the damage is minimal, get vehicles off the thoroughfare and onto the shoulders or other out-of-the-way area.

Motion Sickness

No, we're not talking about that queasy feeling you get after two baskets of fried calamari. You're on your own with that. However, the RV might need more than a few antacids to get righted in case of a roadside breakdown, another of life's annoying little adventures. Maybe it's a wobbly tire, a glowing "E" on the fuel gauge, or an overheated state brought on by August in Death Valley. No matter the cause, your vehicle isn't going to stand for it another minute. Find somewhere to pull over and do so quickly. And when the spouse and children look at you with those worrisome expressions, be cool. You know just what to do.

Okay, that's a big lie. You have no idea what to do. Changing a motorhome's tire is a tough, dirty job. A dead battery 50 miles from the nearest service station shakes the confidence of any soul. Worse yet, maybe the rig just went dead on you, succumbing to a malady beyond your range of expertise. Is that a coyote I hear in the background? Are those vultures circling above? Is the sun setting on your last ray of hope? Now what?

Circle the Wagons

Again, a sizeable tow vehicle/trailer combination sticks out when disabled along the side of the road. A motorhome is no small thing, either. Do oncoming traffic a favor by setting up reflector triangles and/or flares (skip it if oil or gas leaks are present) to direct them to other, safer lanes. If you can fix the problem, then get fixing. A blaze orange vest or other reflective clothing (don't worry about appearing on the worst dressed list) heightens one's visibility when tinkering about. Keep passengers off the road and away from the scene just in case.

Road Scholar

Presumably, a police offer should pass your whereabouts and hopefully stop by to look in on you. Don't spring out from behind the vehicle and scare the officer into drawing his weapon like I once did. They don't surprise well. Put the "to serve and protect" mantra to work, and place a nonemergency call for help if you're stranded and unable to find help.

Road Worrier

Assuming you can't cure what ails you, someone has to come and play doctor. Hopefully, you'll take my advice and sign up for a comprehensive roadside assistance service, where help is just a toll-free number away. For those who decided to skip it and save a few bucks, you're the next contestant on Dial-a-Date. Take out the cell phone (you do have one, right?) and call around for assistance. More easily remedied problems, such as running out of gas or a dead battery, can usually be handled by the local service station. RV-specific setbacks—tires, towing, and mechanical maladies—require some advanced assistance. Get on the phone and find an RV service station with towing capabilities. Otherwise, it's time to use that secondary vehicle. What vehicle, you ask?

Road Scholar

The good news is that most breakdowns are preventable. The worn tread on the now flat tire was trying to tell you something. Running the tank to empty is taking a chance in a gas-guzzler. Routine maintenance both curtails and corrects mechanical problems. Don't be stingy with service procedures, or you may find yourself stewing about it while waiting for the tow truck.

Twice as Nice

We've preached the benefits of enlisting the tow vehicle or auxiliary auto as a bailout in case of trouble. Here's where it pays off. If the trailer has a bum tire, the tow vehicle stands ready to shuttle passengers into town or directly to the nearest tire store. Motorhome acting funny? That dutiful secondary vehicle you've been pulling behind is more than just a pretty face, there to save the day and provide reliable transit to wherever you need to go.

Mr. Fix-It

Want to see an unscrupulous mechanic cry for joy? Show up on the lot with your RV pulled behind a tow truck. If you don't like their inflated prices or dubious track record, well, it's their way or the highway—and you've already *done* the highway. Like the song goes, "Breaking down is hard to do." You're at the mercy of an unknown service center, with both your home *and* transportation up on blocks. Not anyone's best moment, to say the least.

Enrolling in a roadside assistance club offers consumers at least some protection. In theory, only reputable technicians and businesses are used to comprise the service network. Shoddy repairs and con artists reflect badly on the club, so—again, in theory—such contemptibles are hopefully weeded out. When deciding what service center to do the work, try calling the factory that built your RV. They can help you locate the nearest technician who does work on your type of unit. You can also check the Yellow Pages, where the display ads may show which dealers sell and service which different brands. Campground directories may also have information about nearby service centers.

Alas, emergency repairs are chancy. If you feel you're being taken for a ride (and not a fun ride like those at Disney World), buck the trend by calling for a tow truck to take you elsewhere. Otherwise, throw the dice and take your chances, and have a trusted service center at home review the work.

One for the Road

The pendulum swings back to the consumer when requiring service closer to home. Establish a good relationship with a local RV service center. During warranty coverage, it will probably be with the selling dealer, but after that, many RVers seek out the best professional service facility they can find. Nurture that relationship by patronizing that facility for regular maintenance. The closer the relationship, the higher the priority when crisis repairs arise.

Camping Calamities

Unlike you and the kids, safety never takes a vacation. Care must be taken even when the destination is reached, whether it's preventing falls in the shower to overcoming a grease fire in the galley to thwarting that squirrel with a mean attitude hopping around the campsite. At the risk of sounding like an alarmist, a surprising number of RV calamities occur when happily parked at the campground. Why? Who knows. Perhaps our guards are down or maybe the outdoors really *is* a place where only the strong survive. Whatever the reason, it doesn't mean we should go willingly to the emergency room. Here's how to nip potential problems in the bud.

Pride Goeth Before the Fall

Hide-and-seek with the kids is going well until—boom—you trip over the fresh water hose. You throw open the entry door to take the dog for an early morning walk and—crash—no platform step ready to greet you. Setting foot on a rubber roof covered with early morning dew and—well, I'm sure you can use your imagination here. Either someone's doing their best Three Stooges routine or you need a visit from the Safety Patrol. It may sound like a little thing, but falls inside the RV and around the campsite account for numerous traveler follies—and injuries. This problem is exacerbated for those who don't get around as well as they used to and within vehicles jam-packed with passengers, running around in a sort of daze.

Short of telling you to trade in those two left feet, a little forethought and a couple of prudently installed items should take care of many of these rapid descents. First, identify problem areas: that partially exposed tree root, the misplaced skateboard, that extra length of hose. Pick up loose items around the campsite, which take on a land-mine persona when you are stumbling around in near darkness. Curl extra hose and cords under the RV, away from traffic areas. Discourage running, keep walkways clear, and award an extra s'more for the safest camper.

Counter slippery areas such as the entryway, steps, ladder, rooftop, and shower/bathtub with nonskid mats. If it's a decent drop between the RV and the ground, add a platform step (available in both electric and manual versions, although usually included with the RV purchase) to smooth this transition. Get in the habit of looking down to see if it's deployed (an onboard power failure may leave the automatic step retracted when you're counting on it). Hand-rails along the inside and outside of the entryway are a must; another in the bathtub/shower is another brainy idea.

One for the Road

Some well-placed reflector tape can virtually eliminate most causes of nighttime falls. Wrap a few lengths over the plugged-in cords, a water faucet looking to grab an ankle, or along the base of an unlit entry step.

The Criminal Element

I would doubt very strongly that RVers are any more susceptible to crime than anyone else. In fact, I would worry more about taking steps to protect your home while (we'll get there in a moment) you're away than your RV. Most campgrounds are extremely safe. Many offer some kind of onsite security, controlled gates, an abundance of lighting, staff working on your behalf, and the eyes and ears of watchful campers nearby. Generally, campground owners are pretty restrictive about nonguests coming and going, and, let's face it, the average RV is not as lucrative a target as, say, the mini-mart on Route 6. The doors and windows onboard recreational vehicles lock, and security systems, motion-sensing lighting, and an outside camera to determine potential mischief are plentiful in the aftermarket world.

With that said, as visitors in unfamiliar turf, travelers are always at a disadvantage. We don't known the area, and may unwittingly take a wrong turn into a rough part of town or spend a night in a campground parked next to a family of kleptomaniacs. However, the biggest threat to our safety is the belief that nothing bad could possibly happen on vacation. This tourist mindset lowers our guard and may make us an attractive target to those with questionable intentions.

Troubling Behavior

Ever hear the cautionary phrase to "avoid looking like a victim"? Stay alert, constantly survey the scene, and watch the behavior of those around you. Flashing cash and valuables is a good way to draw the attention of the wrong element. Nighttime is more dangerous than the day; remote locations more prone to problems than locations with lots of activity; traveling alone riskier than as a part of a group. Presenting yourself or your vehicle as an easy mark just might make that a reality. Keep RVs locked at all times, even when staying in the quaintest little campground. While it's tempting to leave cooking items, lawn chairs, and other benign-sounding exterior items out when you're away, don't. Lock gear in exterior storage compartments, so there are no surprises upon arrival.

Road Scholar

Take a few moments to prepare the campsite before leaving to run errands or visit the local attractions. Completely extinguish the campfire. Store and lock gear inside the vehicle or in exterior compartments to prevent thievery and/or damage from wind or storms. This is doubly true for any awnings, which should always be retracted while you're away. Lower the shades, lock the doors, and leave a light on to illuminate the scene.

The best way to keep trouble out of the RV is to, well, keep trouble *out* of the RV. Don't let strangers in, and ask for identification from police or other visitors during matters of official business. If safety is a top consideration—and why shouldn't it be?—audition campgrounds regarding their precautions. What are their policies for visitors? Is there a security staff? Is the park fenced-in, monitored via cameras, and/or well lit? When boondocking, ask yourself: Will I feel safe here? As always, there's safety in numbers.

Crime Fighter

Those looking to commit a crime at a crowded campground are pretty high up on the stupid scale. Break-ins are pretty rare, and theft usually is the act of mischief more than the work of some evil genius. But, let's not make it easy for those with sticky fingers. While the best deterrent is a hungry rottweiler that gets mighty upset when an intruder awakes him from his afternoon nap, this isn't always practical. The good news is that full-blown security systems are fairly common on nicer RVs. The bad news is that they can't fetch a ball or roll over like your faithful doberman. Install a theft-deterrent device if you're carrying a nice array of cargo. Otherwise, security comes in pretty inexpensive forms. Day/night shades and windshield covers shield the interior from prying eyes. Outside scare lights and onboard timers send would-be-thugs scurrying. A safe is common on more than a few high-end RVs.

One for the Road

A number of vehicle locators are available for the RV owner nervous about thieves making off with his or her prized possession. Authorities, working from the device's signal, can often locate the vehicle promptly. Hitch locks stifle attempts of those looking to simply connect *your* trailer to *their* tow vehicle.

Medical Emergencies

Top on my "Things-Not-to-Do" list is getting sick or hurt away from home. A quick poll of the room might suggest many of us share the same concern. Obviously, the fluctuating state of our healthcare system matched with the particulars of one's insurance carrier make this a difficult subject to tackle, to say the least. Running to the emergency room with a pain in your chest *without* contacting your primary doctor first might mean the bill is yours to absorb. It can happen and does all the time. Since my advice *may* run counter to the procedures outlined by the insurance company, let me just say this: Your health is the most important thing. If you're in a serious medical emergency, I don't advise waiting around for an HMO to say it's okay to visit that doctor who falls "out of the network."

One for the Road

How does one handle getting medical care away from home? In a nonemergency, ask your doctor. Since the insurance company ultimately has a role in paying the tab, get their input if you're unsure if you're covered. What are the procedures required by your insurance carrier? Must you first get a referral from a doctor? Can you choose your own provider and get reimbursed in full? What is and what isn't deemed an emergency? As always, it's best to get the answers *before* a medical problem arises.

Finding a doctor for those allergies that won't go away or a dentist for that tooth that doesn't like ice cream as much as you while away from home is a challenge. You're probably going to have to rely on the advice of a total stranger or by leafing through the Yellow Pages. For emergencies, the local ER is the place to go. If needed, get an ambulance to take you there. Otherwise, if you can wait to receive medical care from your doctor at home, that eliminates much of the problem. It's important, however, to be honest in assessing an emergency condition. Don't delay in getting medical care when it's necessary.

Road Scholar

Call your regular doctor for advice when you aren't sure if something can wait till you get back home or not. Some hospitals have a number to call for advice on symptoms and to ask questions. Some communities have an urgent-care facility that takes walk-ins and the cost is much less than for an emergency room visit—a great option for non-life-threatening emergencies.

Don't leave home without the contact information for both your primary doctor and insurance company. Pack additional medications for longer trips. Local pharmacies are nice, but switching prescriptions to a national chain makes refills on the road that much easier. In the event a medical condition leaves you incapacitated, can your spouse or co-pilot drive the RV back home? Those travelers constantly relegated to the passenger seat may struggle when it's finally time to drive the big rig or trailer. Sharing the driving duties keeps both parties fresh and prevents becoming stranded if the main driver gets hurt or sick.

Sound the Alarm

Ask anyone who has smelled LP gas in his rig to describe the odor, and you'll get a number of responses: overcooked onions, potent garlic, bad eggs, or the first dish your roommate made in college. Although its presence is indeed a stinky one, we should be thankful LP has any smell at all because liquid petroleum is naturally odorless. The lousy aroma was added to give our noses a chance to catch this airy intruder in the event of a leak. An installed LP gas detector, standard in all new RVs, does that one better. As previously noted, many RVers say they notice a faint whiff of LP just before the container goes empty or right after a fill-up.

Carbon monoxide is known as the "silent killer" for a reason. Virtually undetectable without a monitoring device, this gas is colorless, odorless, and strikes without warning. Fortunately, a CO detector stands ready to alert us of any signs of infiltration, whether caused by a leak, clogged vent, or camper next door aiming his generator your way. Onboard smoke alarms often suggest the obvious—that the drapes are on fire—but are important protection, nonetheless.

At the first bell, buzzer, or shriek of an onboard detector, make plans to scatter. In some cases, it's a false alarm, but don't bet on it. (Some RVers report a faint smell of propane upon receiving a new batch or after long periods of storage.) Gas leaks are not worth waiting around for—get everyone to safety, out of the RV, and then deduce a plan of action. Let the houseplants and mother's crystal fend for themselves. Leave the door open to ventilate the interior. Don't create a flame or spark, as it could ignite LP gas into the world's biggest bonfire. Be careful not to induce metal-to-metal contact during a hasty retreat. Turn off the propane supply at the container (some LP gas detectors automatically shut down the tanks on your behalf). Ventilate, ventilate, ventilate. Do not return until the alarm shuts off. Turn off any and all appliances and systems relating to the problem—we don't want a repeat performance. If the source of the leak is unknown, have the rig inspected by a professional.

Pull Over

To keep these onboard sentries in working order, be sure to feed them a fresh supply of batteries, inspect them periodically, and follow the maintenance procedures (if any) outlined in their owner's manuals. Have safety devices inspected at the first sign of abnormality.

Pull Over

Never run the generator as you sleep. While there are several candidates for a possible carbon monoxide leak, generators rank highest among them—particularly, antiquated models. Of course, the culprit may not be your own, but someone's close by. It's possible to suffer secondhand affects from the camper's generator next door, usually triggered when wind blows exhaust back into the rig. Keep windows near the generator's position closed (yours and neighbors') to avoid this blow-back effect.

House Warming

You don't need to reroll the footage of the *Hindenburg* to see how quickly fire can spread. An RV with propane and gasoline/diesel running through its veins doesn't lack fuel for the proverbial fire, which is why you probably shouldn't stick around to battle a formidable blaze. My personal mantra? If the fire is bigger (and meaner) than you, run. Grab the passengers and pets, and get away—as far as possible in case of an explosion. Do your neighbors a favor and give them a lifesaving heads up as well. The overhead smoke detector watches over you as you sleep—if you hear its piercing scream, chances are smoke has filled the interior. Repeat the same drill as above—high-tail it out of there if the fire is taking over.

Fortunately, despite the combustible elements onboard, RV fires aren't very common. And when they do occur, the same mishaps that burn down conventional dwellings are to blame—cooking gone awry, a wayward cigarette, a candle left unattended, a bum space heater, or kids playing with matches. Prevention is the answer here. RVers should adopt a Frankenstein-like attitude to any sort of flame, controlled or otherwise, onboard: "Fire bad!" Leave the torched shish-kabob recipe at home. As mentioned routinely in Chapter 11, "LP Systems," being on-the-go with flowing propane containers puts you at further risk. Be sure to extinguish pilot lights and shut off the propane supply while on the go, and especially when filling up at the gas pump. Store a fire extinguisher both inside and outside the vehicle to squelch possible blazes. Devise a series of escape routes inside and review them with passengers. In some cases, the best way might be through an emergency exit, a window. or a side door.

One for the Road

RV code mandates an "alternative means of egress," or another door or hatch on the opposite side of the entry door, on the roof, or rear window. Older RVs were designed with a wider roof vent or a hinged rear window to allow escape. Check the workability of these devices annually. Newer coaches usually come equipped with a driver's side door to satisfy this requirement.

Animals and Critters

Prevent furry campsite invaders by putting away all food and garbage at night. Take special precautions when camping "where the wild things are," such as in the middle of bear country. Don't let children or pets wonder off alone where they could find trouble. Always make your presence known, whether onsite or walking a secluded path, to avoid startling or antagonizing anything with sharp teeth and a short temper. Boondocking in such an environment can be a risky proposition.

Bugs are a more insidious threat. How do you think they got the name "pests"? A few well-placed mosquitoes aboard the motorhome or an ant trail leading that watermelon from the icebox out through the front door is a real headache. And since you're not looking for any hitchhikers, get rid of these tag-alongs now before they become like family. Create an impenetrable barrier around the RV by spraying bug spray around the perimeter. (A ring of Ajax is another popular option against ants.) Spray bugs and set traps onboard if they begin to congregate like Green Peace at a nuclear power plant.

A clean and orderly campsite and interior also makes for a less attractive target. Don't let trash build up, keep dishes and countertops clean, and don't park in the middle of Ant Colony, USA. At the first sign of serious infestation, launch a thorough search-and-destroy campaign. A deep-down cleaning—yes, even the scary closets and under the sink—and adequate spraying should tame the problem. If problems persist, enlist the aid of a professional exterminator.

Trouble at Home

The pop-up trailer with three kids, dog, and pair of goldfish onboard might not be that alluring a target to criminals, but the five-bedroom Colonial house you left behind with two cars in the garage and priceless art on the walls is. Peace of mind on the road starts with taking the necessary precautions before you leave. The goal here is to make your home look like you never left, a clever ruse performed by taking a few simple steps. Do your best Fort Knox imitation. Lock all doors and windows, and pull the shades/curtains to prevent clear views into your home—and its contents—by prowlers. Next, tie up loose ends. Enlist a friend or neighbor to pick up mail and the morning paper. (They can water the plants and feed the iguana while they're there.)

A scattering of on-again, off-again lights, perpetrated by an installed timer, should keep anyone casing the joint guessing. And no matter how bad you want to gloat, don't change the phone message to beaming about the family's vacation plans. My parents always included one final step before we left on vacation, and that was to call the police. We'd state that we'd be away from home for the week, and ask if they wouldn't mind driving by and checking up on things once in a while. Did our local constable step up patrols or camp out in our driveway? Who knows, but I always liked the idea of the coppers staking out my comic collection in my absence.

Here is a checklist of important equipment to make sure you have in your RV.

Emergency Equipment

- ❑ Cell phone
- ❑ Important phone numbers (insurance, roadside assistance, doctor, etc.)
- ❑ Road flares
- ❑ Reflective triangles
- ❑ Fire extinguishers
- ❑ Seat belts
- ❑ Child safety seats
- ❑ Air bags
- ❑ LP gas detector
- ❑ Carbon monoxide detector
- ❑ Smoke alarm
- ❑ First-aid kit
- ❑ Jumper cables
- ❑ Spare keys
- ❑ Flashlight
- ❑ Extra prescription medications
- ❑ Spare tire
- ❑ Basic tool kit
- ❑ Reflective tape
- ❑ Ice and/or heat packs
- ❑ Extra batteries
- ❑ Spare LP regulator

The Least You Need to Know

- Bad weather takes many shapes, but generally the same rules apply when driving: take it slow, give those vehicles around you plenty of space, stay visible, and know when to stop and find a place to sit this one out.
- Alert, rested, and prepared drivers are more likely to avoid accidents. However, in the event of a collision, the most important aspect is the well-being of those involved. Immediately call the authorities. Move injured parties only if their location puts them at greater risk. Don't worry about vehicles and possessions—they're replaceable.
- A comprehensive roadside assistance program is the best defense against breakdowns. A secondary vehicle or towed vehicle is useful as well. Cell phones can rescue travelers from life at the side of the road.
- Crime happens, even on vacation. Know your surroundings and stay alert. Keep valuables locked up at all times, and utilize such accessories as onboard security systems, motion-sensitive lighting, and day/night shades to ward off criminals.
- Action taken for a medical problem depends on the severity of the condition and the advice of your care-provider. Prevention techniques, common sense, and a few safety devices minimize the likelihood of such events.

Chapter 21

Basic Care

In This Chapter

- The why's and how's of storing an RV
- Procedures to get it back into service
- Cleaning and preventive maintenance tips

Sadly, for many of us, RVing is only a seasonal exercise. That nasty foe known as winter often puts a cap on our adventures just when things are getting interesting. Although I did my best to tout the virtues of winter camping earlier on, it's just not for everybody. Furthermore, most campgrounds north of the Mason Dixon close up shop after October, making it sometimes difficult to find a place to hang your hat when the frost hits. Sure, at the onset of those little black storm clouds and sinking temperatures, full-timers and snowbirds can simply point their rigs south. Alas, for the rest of us, it's time to prepare our RVs for a long winter's nap.

Long-term storage isn't as easy as unhitching the trailer and placing a "Do Not Disturb" sign on the door. There's a little more to it than that. And once spring does eventually roll around, getting the rig back into fighting shape requires some diligence on your part as well. Of course, basic care is warranted year-round. In between trips visiting long-lost relatives, caravans, rallies, and lazy days camped beachside, a little preventative maintenance keep things looking and running great. But don't worry, we're talking pretty simple stuff here. Even those who don't know a crescent wrench from a croissant should have no trouble following along. Your RV will thank you.

Storage

The onset of winter acts as the proverbial wet blanket for most RV adventures. Cold, snow, ice, campground closures, fear of frostbite—take your pick—all serve to dampen most folks' enthusiasm for life on the road. Hypothermia instead of a sun tan? A snowsuit instead of a swimsuit? No thanks, say most of us, we'll see you in the spring. Warm-weather residents, too, subject their vehicles to long periods of nonuse. Maybe work's been crazy, and you can't get away for months at a time. A family crisis keeps everyone at home when normally they'd be out and about. You docked the rig in the Rose Bowl parking lot, and it takes you two months to find it. Whatever the reason, periods of dormancy come with the territory.

An Idle World

RVs weren't meant to sit; they were designed to go and go and go. They just weren't made for the sedentary life. An idle vehicle gets old before its time—kind of like us. Tires distort under the unmoving pressure. Batteries discharge and corrode. Engine components clog, fluids go stale, and hoses crack. Pests and critters build abodes inside, seeing a nice place to live and no rent to pay. Oxidation and damage from the sun can ravage a docile RV's once good looks, while winter may freeze pipes, leading to costly repairs. Before you know it, that once fine investment isn't looking—or acting—so fine. Whatever one's reasons for putting the RV away for a while, fortunately, an afternoon of elbow grease is about all it takes to tuck in your home on wheels for an uneventful rest. The biggest challenge is probably finding a place to put it.

Where Do You Want It?

Where your RV goes during periods of nonuse depends primarily on its size and one's given situation. Ideally, vehicles should be shielded from the elements, temperature extremes, pollution, blowing sand, salty air, and other troublemakers. Inside is preferable to outside. Homeowners may be able to devote some or all of the garage to pop-ups, truck campers, van campers, and maybe *some* low-profile Class Cs and trailers. With enough room in the driveway or yard—provided neighbors or local ordinances won't be irked—an RV might fit there nicely. In this case, some kind of covering is strongly recommended. (A number of companies produce specially designed canopies and covers to fit the contours of any size RV.) Otherwise, seek the aid of a professional storage facility. Some campgrounds, RV dealerships, and service centers rent space for such occasions. The best of the best will do the necessary prep work (as outlined in the following section) for a fee in order to get the vehicle ready, if you'd rather skip the work.

Winterizing

Upon finding a comfy spot for the RV, the task then becomes how to negate the possible damaging effects of such inactivity on one's vehicle. (If only the fifth wheel would use that health club membership.) This practice is usually referred to as *winterizing,* regardless of the temperatures the unit faces during its down time. At this point, industrious owners roll up their sleeves and prepare the vehicle, both inside and out. Although slightly more involved for those vehicles facing cold-weather climates, the process is basically the same for everyone. A few extra steps are required for motorized vehicles.

RVocabulary

Follow a list of procedures for **winterizing** your RV that are designed to safeguard and preserve an RV's interior systems, automotive functions, and exterior features during times of storage or periods of nonuse.

Everybody Out

Start by removing all food, even nonperishables. For one thing, the inside of a closed-up RV can get very hot or cold, depending on the season, and items can surely spoil, become stale, attract bugs, etc. Also, anything canned or bottled could potentially freeze and burst. There's nothing like a can of soda exploding in the middle of the RV to make a sticky mess of things.

Remove clothes, blankets, and linens for laundering. Unless the vehicle is on your premises, there's no reason to leave any valuables aboard, so take home any key items or anything you'll need while the RV is away. Since dirt and debris only get more stubborn over time, a good cleaning—both inside and out—is recommended before storing. Follow the tips in the following "Clean Machine" section to keep your RV looking its best.

Plumbing

A lengthy sabbatical is harder on the pipes and holding tanks than any other system onboard. Stagnant water turns nasty and pollutes holding tanks. Remaining liquids can freeze and burst the pipes during frigid temperatures. The end result is the same: unnecessary costs and a headache come spring. Fortunately, a few simple steps eliminate this mess. Start by emptying both the fresh and wastewater tanks at a nearby dump station or during the last campout of the year. You won't get out every drop, but it's a good place to start. Unlatch tank drains to purge any remaining fluids and turn faucets and shower on to clear the lines as much as possible. (Refer to the exact procedures in Chapter 12, "Plumbing Systems.") Don't forget any water left in the toilet and the water heater, which must both be emptied.

Empty holding tanks provide a great opportunity for a thorough scrub-down. Remember our mantra: Clean is good. Close any opened faucets and drain plugs before beginning. A water wand (an attachment that delivers high-volume water pressure) is best for rinsing black water tanks, allowing users to access the inner reaches of the tank via the toilet and blast tough corners and force loose any accumulated materials. Gray and fresh water tanks require a more subtle approach, since there's no straight shot inside like most black water models. While a few cleaning agents can do the job (most RV supply stores are full of remedies), it's just as easy to fill the emptied tank with fresh water, add some baking soda or bleach (one cup per 15 gallons of water), and drive down the bumpiest road in town for a few miles. The sloshing motion will coat the tank walls and do the dirty work for you. Once accomplished, drain the tanks completely, and close all water escape points (faucets, valves, etc.) before signing off.

Mr. Freeze

Of course, you and I both know you that didn't get *every* bit of water out of the lines and tanks, a problem if your storage location experiences a yearly deep-freeze come January. Of course, if you're sitting out possible bad weather in a warm tropical paradise, no problem. However, for the rest of us facing winters that would put Washington and his Valley Forge exploits to shame, those extra drops will assuredly freeze and cause trouble on our plumbing. What to do, what to do?

You could always blow out any collected water in the lines with compressed air. RV supply stores offer numerous devices up to the task. While the pipes will most definitely be voided of water, this high-pressure procedure could damage weaker plumbing and antiquated systems. A better solution might be to add a few gallons of RV anti-freeze (yes, *RV anti-freeze*) to the fresh water tank. Activate the water pump, open the various faucets, and let the stuff work its magic through the plumbing system. Like its name suggests, anti-freeze won't go cold on you, acting as an overzealous babysitter for the plumbing system while you're away. As a further precaution, adding an additional cup into each drain afterward (sinks, shower, toilet, etc.) guarantees 100 percent protection.

A water heater bypass kit eliminates the middleman, in this case, the water heater, which would otherwise require having to fill six or ten gallons of RV anti-freeze into the unit as well. Pricier RVs probably already have such a device. Otherwise, it's a cheap alternative to excessive anti-freeze.

Impenetrable Fortress

The biggest precaution concerning your LP gas system isn't so much the appliances, propane container(s), or fuel lines, but rather the vents used for many of the LP appliances. Various members of the animal kingdom have been known to use these open avenues such as intake and exhaust vents to set up a homestead aboard your

RV. And you thought your nephews were annoying? Mesh screens should already be in place for everyday use to keep out birds and varmints, but we're talking total lockdown here. To ward off potential freeloaders, cover any vents and openings with cardboard, aluminum foil, or the material du jour. A little duct tape here goes a long way, too. Mice are particularly partial to a dormant RV, making their home via unchecked openings and sometimes bringing along the spouse and kids. Birds are especially keen to exposed roof vents; ants and spiders are attracted to sweet smells onboard. Spray the perimeter with bug spray for an added layer of protection.

One for the Road

No, it's not a misprint—RV antifreeze goes down the drains. This isn't the lethal, automotive-type you're accustomed to, but rather a product designed for use throughout the RV's water systems. It's specially formulated, nontoxic, and cheaper than a plumber come springtime.

Remember, you're not going for style points here, so shore up the exterior by any means necessary. This includes going underneath the RV and making the chassis impenetrable. Visit the roof and cover the air conditioner (special covers are made for this very purpose) and repair any exposed seams with sealant (available at RV supply stores.) Go inside and turn off the dashboard temperature controls and close vents, thus shutting off a potential rodent freeway in the making. Keep windows closed. In the event things get a tad buggy onboard, call an exterminator or use conventional pest-ridders.

LP Gas

Propane container(s) should be topped off before storage; a fuller tank weathers dissipation better than a half-empty version. Shut off the LP supply completely, and cover the tanks to eliminate dust, debris, the elements, etc. from premature wear. Removable tanks can be taken off, covered, and stored—but should never be placed in the RV, which is the last place you want LP gas fumes. If you remove the fitting to remove a DOT LP cylinder, be sure to cover the open end with a baggy and rubber band to keep critters from intruding. Also, always plug the fitting on the tank outlet with the appropriate plug. Finally, all LP appliances (ranges, oven, refrigerator, furnace, water heater, etc.) should be turned off.

Pull Over

RV refrigerators are more heat-intolerant than residential models. Avoid the old blow-drying trick to hasten the thawing out process, which could damage components.

Prop open the refrigerator door, empty out the contents (yes, even the mustard), and allow it to thaw out (if so equipped with a freezer) completely. Enlist a few pots and pans to catch any drippings. This is a golden opportunity for a quick scrub-down with warm, sudsy water to remove the memory (and odor) of your spouse's hot dog goulash. Leave the door open for the remainder of the storage, unless you have a penchant for mold. An opened box of baking soda tucked away inside gives smells the boot.

Assault and Battery

During storage, the 12-volt battery system is like a mobster in the witness protection program—it's safe, but not particularly happy. It misses the high-rolling action of the old days. Short of taping episodes of *The Sopranos,* there's little you can do to improve its mood. However, a fully charged battery handles this incarceration best, most easily accomplished by connecting to shore power (a weekend camping trip, for example) prior to storage. Top off the battery's water levels, which dissipate over time. In colder climes, it's best to remove the battery altogether, storing it in a dry, warm location for its protection. Otherwise, disconnect the cables (negative cable first) to safeguard them electrically during storage. All this may seem like a lot of work, but remember, these batteries are the heart of the 12-volt electrical system. Do them a favor, and you're a made guy.

Flip the off switch on the RV's main breaker panel (see owner's manual for location) to safeguard the 120-volt system. All electrical appliances should be unplugged, and dry cell batteries, which can corrode over time, should be removed from alarms, detectors, and any devices inside. Follow the manufacturer's directions for the onboard or portable generator (if so equipped). At the very least, the unit should be cleaned and the exhaust pipe covered to prevent unwanted intruders. Draining the fuel filter, changing the oil, and adding rush inhibitor is also advisable.

Tired Out

Anyone who's ever tended bar, worked retail, or suffered through an afternoon as a store mannequin at Bloomingdales' (it's a long story), knows how hard it is to stand on your feet all day. Take this lesson to heart, and consider the plight of your RV's poor tires, enduring thousands of pounds of pressure all day, every day. Storage worsens the effects considerably, since the weight is stationary, resting squarely on one rubbery spot. A few months of this torture, and even the finest treads may begin to resemble a donut with a Homer Simpson–size bite out of it.

Those lucky dogs with leveling systems should consider using them to support the vehicle's weight on the jacks instead of the tires. Always consult the device manufacturer and review the owner's manual regarding long-term jack use. Otherwise, incorporate a set of outside jacks or blocks for each axle, money well spent considering the expense of replacing messed up tires. A cost-free but more doting method is to periodically move the RV one-half revolution (once or twice over the winter should do it) to distribute the weight over other portions of the tire's surface.

Engine

That taunt you're hearing is probably from the towable owner relaxing in the shade as the motorized community contemplates a few more steps. Since we want our motorhomes to act just as sprightly when we call on them again, a little work must still be done to the engine. As previously mentioned, inactivity is hard on any vehicle, but most taxing on the motor—particularly in harsh climates. Start by protecting the fuel source by topping off the gasoline or diesel tanks. A fuel stabilizer, found at most any automotive or RV supply store, is a must. Just be sure to add the right one for your engine type (gasoline or diesel). Idle the engine to allow the additive to make its rounds throughout the system.

As always, strive for full tanks and fluid compartments in the engine, to lessen the chances of them freezing or drying out. Top off the radiator with anti-freeze matched for your climate; flush and replace with a batch suited for Siberia-like temperatures if that is indeed the case. Inspect levels throughout the engine (windshield wiper, oil, brake fluid, etc.), and refill as needed.

Spring Shakedown

Those of us still making snow angels in March call it a spring shakedown. However, run these drills whenever you're reuniting with your RV after a period of storage. The primary goal when prepping the vehicle back into service is to undo everything we did to get it ready for hibernation in the first place. Once that's done, there are a few added steps to get back into the swing of things. After all, the vehicle will certainly be busy trying to keep up with all the adventures you've planned during the off-season.

A Quick Look Around

Like a third-grader on the first day of school, there's plenty of work to be done to get ready for the new season. For starters, the interior might be a tad musty from being cooped up. Open windows to air things out. Check for any signs of leaks or trouble or just anything amiss. Assuming everything is as it should be, start by rectifying the paste-up job you should have done on the vents and various openings throughout the coach. Start on the roof and work your way down underneath the chassis. Put on your inspector's hat and tear away any makeshift blockades installed last time to ward off bugs and varmints. Don't forget any—a blocked vent is very dangerous.

Road Scholar

This is the best time for you to take an inventory of necessary work onboard. Do any hoses, cords, or seals need replacing? When was the last time curtains, fabrics, clothes, and blankets were laundered? Spray for pests, deep clean the carpet, and add a new shower head if the old one leaks. A little extra work now reduces would-be annoyances later on.

Check seals around doors and windows for leaks or wear. Reinstall new ones at the first signs of trouble since these are popular avenues for water to slip inside. How are the seams on the roof? Check around the air conditioner, vents, antennas, etc. Reseal with aftermarket products if necessary to dissuade a season's worth of weather from sneaking around onboard. Crawl underneath the unit, looking for any irregularities. Colorful puddles, dangling wires, and gremlins asleep in the wheel wells are all red flags. Inspect the tires for wear, and air up as necessary. Take the unit in for service if problems developed underneath. Nip concerns in the bud now before you're a thousand miles from home.

Systems Check

Reinstall and/or reconnect the 12-volt battery terminals, and top off water levels. Plug the electric cord into an electrical outlet (if available) to revamp the coach batteries while you work. Despite their inactivity, voltages probably dropped fairly dramatically. Plug in all needed appliances, add wet cell batteries to alarms, detectors, and any devices onboard. Inspect safety devices (smoke alarm, LP and CO detectors) to guarantee working condition. Follow the owner's manual for a yearly checkup of the RV's generator (if so equipped). Let motorized RVs warm up for a few minutes. Test appliances one at a time, and follow their various owner's manuals for yearly preventative maintenance while you're at it. Now is as good a time as any to undertake these procedures. Contact the manufacturer if you're unsure of how to proceed.

Uncover and/or reattach any propane containers. If LP container(s) were removed, just before reconnecting them to the system, quickly open and close each tank valve to expel any contaminants that may have settled in the throat of the valve where it can definitely block an orifice. And you know what it's like to have a blocked orifice. Like your boss, the fuel lines will probably be full of air, so a quick purge is in order. Turn the stove burners on to expel air out of the fuel lines, and light each one. Assuming the refrigerator is level (and many RV storage yards are not), close the refrigerator door and set to 120-volt or LP operation.

Attach your fresh water hose and connect to city water if possible. Otherwise, take the rig someplace where you can fill and drain the tanks. Although nontoxic, the RV anti-freeze in the line isn't quite as refreshing as your favorite cocktail, so drain, refill, and repeat. Fill the fresh water tank and water heater, activate the water pump, and open up the faucets, including the shower. This should clear out the lines. Flush the toilet, too. Repeat these steps as necessary to guarantee proper cleansing. Look carefully for any possible leaks. Freshen up tanks with cleansers as detailed in Chapter 12.

Road Scholar

A shakedown trip, such as the one recommended in Chapter 9, "After the Sale," is the best way to test out all the appliances and systems. Secure a full hookup campsite close to home, spending one day operating off the park's utilities, the next using the RV's self-contained features. Rely on the coach batteries, generator, inverter, and/or solar panels for electricity; the storage tank for the water supply. Be satisfied everything is working before embarking on longer trips.

Motor City

Anything with an engine requires periods of TLC. If you're of the Type A persuasion, you probably know the exact intervals of when to change oil and flush the radiator, as well as the harmful effects of a dirty air filter, by heart. The rest of us have a tendency to let these things slide. Unfortunately, an RV has a long memory, and may penalize you in the form of a needless breakdown later on. As with spring training for ballplayers, consider this the time to tune up your RV's mechanical prowess. It's a long season ahead. Again, manufacturer recommendations reign supreme here, but here are a few to get you started. Some tips won't apply for owners of diesel engines.

RV Tune-Up Checklist

- ❑ Check fluids; change if necessary.
- ❑ Check oil levels.
- ❑ Check brake fluid.
- ❑ Check transmission fluid.
- ❑ Check radiator fluid.
- ❑ Check power steering fluid.
- ❑ Check windshield wipers.
- ❑ Check hoses and belts for wear.
- ❑ Inspect air filter.
- ❑ Change spark plugs.

Trailers

Although spared the extra work underneath the hood, towable owners also have some work to do. Carefully eyeball the hitch, the trailer tongue, wiring, safety chains, and all accessories used to facilitate connections for any signs of distress. This is especially true of any places undergoing metal-on-metal contact, which promotes rust, scratches, and dents. Look for defects in the spring bar assembly, coupler, receiver, and ball mount. Tighten bolts and lube components as suggested by the manufacturer. A few rodents like to cleanse palettes by munching through electrical wires, so pay special attention to their condition.

Drive-Thru

Once satisfied things are as they should be, hitch up the trailer or start up the motorhome for a quick fact-finding mission around town. Start by checking all exterior lights (brakes, headlights, turning signals, etc.) before throwing it into gear. Have a pal jump out and give you the thumbs up on the light situation behind you, spot-checking that everything is in working order. Test the brakes before hitting the road.

Motor through the city, paying special consideration to any unusual sounds, smells, and quirks (coming from the RV, not your spouse) picked up since you last drove it. How are the breaks, steering, and acceleration? Operate the full gamut of dashboard controls and doo-dads. A jaunt on the expressway reveals any problems at higher speeds. Book an appointment with a qualified service center if things aren't as they should be, or if recommended preventative maintenance is more than you can (or want to) handle.

Clean Machine

I'm not your mother, but a clean RV yields many advantages. For starters, it just looks nice, and you won't be embarrassed when the neighbors lobby for an impromptu tour. Keeping the roof and exterior washed makes it easier to spot subtle damage, minimizes the potential oxidizing effects of the sun, and is bound to turn heads when you pull into camp. But washing, drying, and waxing a 35-foot fifth wheel isn't your idea of a great day off. Of course not. Thankfully, it only takes a few days' worth of work during a season to keep things looking nice. In between scrub-downs, park the vehicle under a tarp or canopy to ward off salt, sand, dust, and debris.

Exterior Care

The first step when cleaning up is to identify what kind of materials you're dealing with. The roof is generally made of a different composite than the sidewalls, so adjust your cleaning agents accordingly. The needs of a rubber roof are considerably different than an aluminum version, and vice versa. Always use products designed for the material in question. Most would agree that RV-specific cleaners are usually better than automotive or household products. A hose with a large extension and/or brush is warranted to take the strain out of washing taller, wider, and longer vehicles. Again, the aftermarket is full of products to help you. Tough sap, tar, black dirt streaks, and bird droppings (why do they always find me?) usually require additional muscle to remove. Overachievers should finish the job with a wax made especially for their type of sidewalls, usually aluminum or fiberglass.

Survey the roof and sidewalls for rust, scratches, dents, or (gasp!) holes as you go. Low-hanging branches are likely to blame for roof damage; that picnic table you ran over probably explains the dent in the bumper. Nip body damage early before it saps resale dollars from the unit. A faded appearance is generally indicative of sun damage, which may or may not be remedied by oxidation fighters. Find a quality body shop to restore lost luster. Backyard mechanics find plenty of help in the aftermarket sector with roof repair kits and other godsends. Tighten screws and check seals around doors and windows as you go. Lube joints on outside storage compartments, awnings, entry steps, doors, and the like periodically for easy motion.

Pull Over

Cleaning the roof is a challenge. Many taller vehicles feature a rear-mounted ladder to access the top. Equip each rung with a non-skid material to avoid slipping, and always wear appropriate shoes to prevent falls. Start clean-ups at the front of the roof and work your way back toward the ladder, using only as much water and suds as necessary. Stay low, on hands and knees if possible. Take it to a carwash designed for RVs when available.

It's worth stating again that tires are the most forgotten aspect of any RV. And they are among the most crucial. Like Rodney Dangerfield, they get no respect. Too bad, considering the heavy loads we ask them to carry with rarely a second thought. Check for uneven wear, tread, cuts, etc. Using a tire gauge always lets you know where you stand, so take pressure readings before any trip. (Pressure readings must be taken when the tire is "cold," or anytime when driven less than a half-mile.) Know how much pressure should go in each by weight. Dealers have charts based on size, etc. to help you. Keep them clean and use protectants to repel ozone and UV damage, which can damage tires over time.

Interior Care

The battle for the tidiness onboard usually comes down to the care of fabrics, upholstery, and carpeting. Models with the popular cream, white, and beige color schemes wage this war seemingly full-time, with every smudge, crumb, and speck of dirt shining for all to see. Keeping messes outside is tougher than you think. As always, prevention is the key here. Going from the campsite to your pristine interior involves shaking off more than your share of dust, dirt, and sand. I recommend one pair of shoes for outside, another for inside. Aristocrats should refer to them as house slippers.

Vacuum often to deter dirt from settling. Larger house vacuums just aren't practical to bring along, taking up useful space and electricity. A small, 12-volt model should work okay, especially if you run it often to prevent dirty build-ups. A deep-down industrial vacuum (a.k.a. Rug Doctor), available for rent at numerous places, gets the original color and charm back in a hurry. Launder curtains and removable upholstery annually. Always follow cleaning directions to avoid inadvertently creating fabrics now only useful for Barbie's Dream House. As with the exterior, pay special mind to the materials used in countertops, cabinets, sinks, and throughout the interior. You'd be surprised at the variety. Make sure the cleansers jive with where each is applied. Review the owner's manuals for appliances for care and cleaning instructions.

We could write another book just on preventative maintenance, cleaning tips, and basic care. This is just the tip of the proverbial iceberg, depending on your mechanical aptitude and willingness to give up a Sunday or two to do the work. I'm always surprised at the numbers of RVers who do many of these jobs themselves, but you may fall out of that category. Don't feel bad, I'm not much with a socket wrench either. Follow guidelines in manuals for routine care, troubleshooting, and check-ups. Seek the services of a quality RV service center or dealership if you're uncomfortable working on the vehicle yourself.

The Least You Need to Know

- Recreational vehicles must be properly stored during longer periods of nonuse. A sheltered, temperature-controlled area is best. Turn off all systems and appliances, and patch any openings to keep out pests. Take special precautions against freezing temperatures, including prepping the battery, draining the tanks, and adding RV anti-freeze to the drains and plumbing fixtures.
- Undo the work you did prior to storage to get the RV back into shape. Reconnect and recharge batteries, drain and refill the water supply, and take the vehicle out for a test drive. This is a good time of year to clean, perform preventative maintenance, and troubleshoot appliances and onboard systems for signs of trouble.
- A variety of materials are employed to make up an RV's exterior and interior features. Always use RV-specific products, being careful to match cleansers to the appropriate materials. Clean roofs, sidewalls, and tires help ward off oxidation and enhance their appearance. Routine vacuuming, laundering, and tidying up inside eliminate stains and build-ups of dirt.

Appendix A

Resources

Camping Clubs

Camper Clubs of America
1-800-369-2267
www.camperclubs.com

Escapees
1-888-757-2582
www.escapees.com

Explorer RV Club
1-800-999-0819
www.explorer-rvclub.com

Family Campers and RVers (FCRV)
716-668-6242

Family Motor Coaching Association (FMCA)
513-474-3622
www.fmca.com

The Good Sam Club
1-800-234-3450
www.goodsamclub.com

Handicapped Travel Club
916-966-7090
www.dbyeaw.com/htc

Loners on Wheels, Inc.
1-888-569-4478
www.lonersonwheels.com

National African-American RVers Association
856-784-6897
www.naarva.com

Camping World President's Club
1-800-616-2267
www.campingworld.com/pc

Recreational Vehicle Owner's Association of BC (RVOABC)
604-532-7636
www.rvoa.bc.ca

RV Elderhostel
617-426-7788

RVing Women
1-888-55-RVing
www.rvingwomen.com

S*M*A*R*T
850-478-1986

Campground Clubs and Franchises

Camper Clubs of America
1-800-243-2267
www.camperclubs.com

Coast to Coast Resorts
303-790-2267
www.coastresorts.com

Kampgrounds of America (KOA)
406-248-7444
www.koa.com

Jellystone Park Camp-Resorts
1-800-558-2954
www.campjellystone.com

National Association of RV Parks and Campgrounds (ARVC)
703-241-8801
www.gocampingamerica.com

Ocean Canyon Resorts
805-595-7111

Outdoor Resorts of America
1-800-541-2582
www.outdoor-resorts.com

Resorts U.S.A. Outdoor World
717-588-6661

Thousand Trails/NACO
1-800-328-6226
www.thousandtrails.com

Federal Campgrounds

Bureau of Land Management
202-452-0300
www.blm.gov

National Forest Service
202-205-1706
www.fs.fed.us

National Park Service
1-800-365-2267
www.nps.gov

U.S. Army Corps of Engineers
202-761-0001
www.usace.army.mil

RV Rentals

Cruise America
1-800-327-7799
www.cruiseamerica.com

Cruise Canada
1-800-327-7799
www.cruisecanada.com

Recreational Vehicle Rental Association (RVRA)
1-800-336-0355
www.rvra.org

RV Dealer Associations

Recreation Vehicle Dealers Association (RVDA)
703-591-7130
www.rvda.org

RV Industry Associations

Go RVing Canada
1-888-GO-RVING (1-888-467-8464)
www.gorving.ca

Go RVing Coalition
1-888-GO-RVING (1-888-467-8464)
www.gorving.com

Recreation Vehicle Industry Association (RVIA)
703-620-6003
www.rvia.org

Recreational Park Trailer Industry Association
770-251-2672
www.rptia.org

Driving Instruction

RV Driving School
909-984-7746
www.rvschool.com

RV Caravans and Tours

Creative World Rallies and Caravans
1-800-732-8337
www.creativeworldtravel.com

Fantasy Caravans
1-800-952-8496
www.fantasycaravans.com

Good Sam Caraventures
1-800-664-9145, ext. 358

Meadowlark Tours
306-354-2434
www.meadowlarktours.com

Overseas Motorhome Tours
1-800-322-2127
www.omtinc.com

President's Club Tours
1-800-626-0042
www.campingworldrvtours.com

Reli RV Tours
1-800-409-7354
www.relirv.com

Tracks to Adventure
1-800-351-6053
www.trackstoadventure.com

Wagon Train Travelers Association
1-888-762-3278
www.interlog.com/~rvtours

Woodall's World of Travel
1-800-346-7572
www.woodalls.com/onroad/tours/tours.html

Publications

Camping Life
310-537-6322

Camping Today
716-668-6242

Caretaker Gazette
715-426-5500

Coast to Coast
1-800-368-5721
www.coastresorts.com

Escapees
1-888-757-2582
www.escapees.com

Family Motor Coaching
513-474-3622
www.fmca.com

Highways
1-800-234-3450
www.goodsamclub.com/highways

MotorHome
1-800-678-1201
www.motorhomemagazine.com

Out West
1-800-274-9378
www.outwestnewspaper.com

Pop Up Times
703-938-3722
www.popuptimes.com

RV Companion
970-663-3295
www.rvcompanion.com

RV Gazette
1-800-999-0819
www.explorer-rvclub.com

RV Lifestyle Magazine
1-800-461-9128
www.rvlifemag.com

RV Times
604-857-8828
www.rvtimes.com

RV View
1-800-616-2267
www.rvview.com

RVing Women
1-888-55-RVing
www.rvingwomen.com

Trailer Life
1-800-825-6861
www.trailerlife.com

Western RV News
541-318-8089
www.westernrvnews.com

Woodall's Camperways
1-800-323-9076
www.woodalls.com

Woodall's Florida RV Traveler
1-800-323-9076
www.woodalls.com

Woodall's Midwest RV Traveler
1-800-323-9076
www.woodalls.com

Woodall's Northeast Outdoors
1-800-323-9076
www.woodalls.com

Woodall's Southern RV
1-800-323-9076
www.woodalls.com

Woodall's Southwest RV Traveler
1-800-323-9076
www.woodalls.com

Woodall's Texas RV
1-800-323-9076
www.woodalls.com

Workamper News
501-362-2637
www.workkamper.com

Web Sites

www.busnut.com

www.campnetamerica.com

www.gorp.com

www.gypsyjournal.com

www.journeylink.com

www.motorhomereviewonline.com

www.newrver.com

www.recreation.gov

www.rv.net

www.rv.org

www.rvadvice.com

www.rvamerica.com

www.rv-busconversions.com

www.rvclub.com

www.rvdoctor.com

www.rversonline.org

www.rvhome.com

www.rvnet.com

www.rvnetlinx.com

www.rvrent.com

www.rvsafety.com

www.rvusa.com

www.schoolbusconversions.com

www.workersonwheels.com

Glossary

adult-oriented park Campgrounds catering activities and recreation to adults only.

aftermarket Segment of the industry that provides products and services available to all RVers after the initial purchase of any RV.

alternator Engine-mounted device that produces 12-volt DC electricity for battery charging and other 12-volt functions while the engine is running.

ammeter device Device that measures an RV's total power draw, in amps.

anti-sway device Accessory designed to stabilize and restrict motion between a tow vehicle and travel trailer.

automotive battery Provides the power to start the RV's or tow vehicle's engine and run 12-volt dashboard equipment.

auxiliary vehicle *See* towed vehicle.

backup monitoring system Combination rear-mounted camera and in-cockpit display monitor designed to aid the driver in backing up larger RVs.

ball mount Serving as the connection point between trailer and tow vehicle, the ball mount slides into the receiver hitch and is pinned in place.

basement models RVs with a separate storage section between the chassis and the floor of the interior space.

black water Water and waste materials predominantly from the RV's toilet.

black water holding tank Tank where black water is deposited and stored until later emptied.

boondocking Camping without hookups of any kind (electric, sewer, or fresh water). Also known as dry camping or self-contained camping.

bounce-aways For use with truck campers. Shock-like devices attached below the cab-over section to the truck in order to reduce turbulence while in transit.

brake controller Device mounted within tow vehicle to activate the trailer's brakes independently or in conjunction with the tow vehicle brakes.

break-away switch Pin-activated safety device mounted near the trailer's tongue that automatically activates braking system in case of separation from the tow vehicle.

cab Another name for the driver's area or cockpit.

cab-over area Inhabitable space built over the cockpit of some recreational vehicles. Found on Class Cs and truck campers.

camper van *See* Class B.

campground directory Resource guide providing evaluations and comprehensive listing information of private campgrounds.

campsite Plot of land where RVs park within a campground. Usually comes equipped with various hookups.

caravan Group of vehicles traveling together.

catalytic heaters Wall-mounted or portable heaters utilizing a mix of propane and oxygen to warm the interior.

Class A Motorhomes built on a specially designed chassis, ranging in size from 25 to 45 feet. Can be gas- or diesel-powered.

Class B Also known as camper vans. These smaller, fully self-contained motorhomes share the same chassis and sizes as most traditional vans.

Class C Also known as mini-motorhomes. Smaller motorhomes built on a traditional van chassis, with a specially manufactured frame added later. Sizes generally range from 20 to 32 feet.

Class I hitch Weight-carrying hitch for trailers weighing up to 2,000 pounds.

Class II hitch Weight-carrying hitch for trailers weighing up to 3,500 pounds.

Class III hitch Weight-distributing hitch for trailers weighing up to 5,000 pounds.

Class IV hitch Weight-distributing hitch for trailers weighing up to 10,000 pounds.

Class V hitch Weight-distributing hitch for trailers exceeding 10,000 pounds.

clearance Distance between a vehicle's exterior height and possible obstructions, such as an overpass.

coach power Also known as the auxiliary battery system. Powers the majority of the 12-volt DC equipment onboard an RV, excluding functions controlled by the automotive battery.

conversion bus Also known as a custom-made bus or coach. Deluxe RVs made from a typical bus shell, with sizes between 40 and 45 feet.

conversion vehicle Any vehicle undergoing a dramatic alteration to its chassis or interior. Examples include modified heavy-duty haulers and van conversions.

converter Transforms 120-volt AC into usable 12-volt DC electricity for use onboard an RV.

coupler Apparatus located at the forward-most point of the trailer's tongue connecting to the tow vehicle's ball mount.

deep-cycle battery Also known as a marine-style battery or coach battery. Stores and supplies power for the RV's 12-volt electrical system.

diesel pushers Motorhomes powered by a rear-mounted diesel engine, equipped to propel rather than pull larger vehicles. Generally found in motorhomes exceeding 34 feet.

dinette conversion Table and two bench seats that transform into a sleeping area.

dinghy vehicle Also known as an auxiliary vehicle, toad, or towed vehicle. Nautical term used to describe a car or truck pulled behind a motorhome via a tow bar, dolly, or small trailer.

direct spark ignition (DSI) Method of electrically controlling the LP combustion cycles in RV appliances, eliminating the need for a pilot light.

dry camping *See* boondocking.

dump station Septic area where black and gray water can be emptied via a sewer hose.

electrical connectors Electrically connects the RV to the tow vehicle in order to operate running lamps, turn signals, trailer brakes, and other 12-volt functions. For use with truck campers, fifth wheels, and conventional travel trailers.

electric hookup Connection made from the RV to an outside 120-volt electrical outlet, common at most campsites.

engine power Twelve-volt DC power generated from the RV or tow vehicle's engine.

fifth wheel Most evident by their goose-neck design, trailers relying on a fifth-wheel hitch mounted within the bed of a truck. The largest of all towable RVs, with sizes reaching up to 40 feet in length.

fold-down camper Also known as a pop-up or folding trailer. The smallest towable RVs, known for their boxy shape in transit. Sides expand and must be deployed upon arrival at destination, usually via a hand crank or push-button activation.

forced-air furnace Onboard heating source utilizing a fan to blow heated air throughout the ducts of the RV's interior.

fresh water hookup Connection made from the RV to an outside fresh water source, common at most campsites.

fresh water storage tank Where fresh water is stored during transit until ready for use.

fresh water system Clean water running from all faucets, including sinks and showers, as well as the water heater, and used to maintain the toilet's water level.

full hookups Campsites with water, electric, and sewer connections. Some campgrounds also include cable TV and phone service in this definition.

full-timer Refers to an RVer who lives and travels year-round in his or her RV.

galley Another name for the RV's kitchen.

generator Device driven by an internal combustion engine that produces 120-volts AC electricity for RV use when other power sources are not available.

global positioning satellite (GPS) Onboard device capable of pinpointing a vehicle's exact location and provide navigational functions.

gooseneck Area of a fifth-wheel trailer that fits into the bed of a pickup truck or conversion vehicle to make a connection for towing.

gray water Used water from an RV's sinks and tub/shower.

gray water holding tank Tanks where gray water is deposited and stored until later emptied.

gross axle weight (GAW) Amount of weight each axle can safely support.

gross combined weight rating (GCWR) Used for towing combinations. Rating applies to the maximum weight limit for the tow vehicle, the towed object, and all passengers, cargo, and liquids inside each vehicle.

gross vehicle weight rating (GVWR) Also known as the wet weight. The maximum weight limit of an RV, including all gear, passengers, and liquids.

hitch Device that facilities the connection between a tow vehicle and a towable.

hitch receiver Part of the hitch bolted or welded to the frame of the tow vehicle.

hitch weight Also known as tongue weight. Specified by towable manufacturers, this is the recommended weight to rest on the hitch for greater stability.

hookups Term used to describe a situation when an RV relies on outside utilities, such as electricity, water, sewer, cable TV, or phone.

hydronic heat Onboard heating source using circulating water instead of air for radiant and semi-convected heat and for instantaneous water on demand.

inverter Opposite of a converter. Inverters turn 12-volt DC into 120-volt AC power for use in running typical RV appliances and devices.

isolator Maintains battery separation between automotive and coach batteries, to prevent one from taxing the reserves of the other.

jackknife Serious condition where the tow vehicle ends up perpendicular to the trailer.

kingpin Portion of the fifth-wheel trailer that slides and locks into the truck-mounted fifth-wheel hitch.

leveling jacks Manually or electronically deployed apparatus used to level and stabilize an RV once the destination is reached.

lightweight travel trailers Trailers usually weighing less than 4,000 pounds (unloaded). Sizes rarely exceed 25 feet.

load equalizing hitch *See* weight-distributing hitch.

locking pin Also known as the safety pin. Secures the connection between the kingpin and fifth-wheel hitch for added safety.

LP gas Also known as liquid petroleum or propane. Fuels many of the appliances onboard an RV.

marine-style toilet Similar to those found in airplanes, a toilet that operates via floor pedals or a flush mechanism.

membership campground RV park belonging to a larger private network, where members receive discounted stays.

mini-motorhome *See* Class C.

mobile home Small dwelling with limited mobility designed for stationary living.

modem-friendly Term used to describe a campground offering some kind of modem access, either at the campsites or in a special area within the park.

monitor panel Interior display unit providing important information about the various levels of the RV's onboard systems, including tank levels and battery voltage.

motorhome Motorized recreational vehicle built on a special or traditional chassis. Includes Class A, B, and C vehicles.

motorized RV Also known as a self-propelled RV. A recreational vehicle relying on its own engine for mobility. Includes motorhomes, camper vans, and truck campers.

net carrying capacity (NCC) Maximum amount of weight in the form of passengers, cargo, and fluids an RV can safely transport.

120-volt electrical system *See* shore power.

park model Residential-style structure, capable of being towed but designed for set up in one location for greater lengths of time.

patio-hauler *See* sport utility trailer (SUT).

pickup camper *See* truck camper.

polarity tester Device designed to test 120-volt AC receptacles to determine proper wiring and output.

pop-up *See* fold-down camper.

pop-up or fold-down truck campers Truck campers that lay flat in transit and must be deployed, usually by use of a hand crank, once the destination is reached.

primitive sites Campsite predominantly known to feature electric and water hookups only. Term also may describe campsites with no hookups of any kind.

propane *See* LP gas.

pull-thru site Campsites with access from more than one direction, allowing RVs to drive right through the site thereby avoiding backing up.

rally Large get-together of RVers, often associated with a specific type or brand of RV or travel club.

rear bumper extensions For use with truck campers. May be needed so the truck's license plate is visible from underneath the camper.

recreational vehicle (RV) Motorized or towable vehicle providing a place to sleep, basic cooking functions, and livable space.

regulator, LP Also known as a two-stage regulator. An adjustable device that regulates the fluctuating container pressures, delivering an even flow of fuel to all LP appliances.

RV show Gathering of the latest recreational vehicles and RV-related products and services for sale.

safety chains Vital towing attachment that prevents the trailer from veering off in case of separation during transit.

seasonal Describes a person who stays in a campground long-term, usually at least a month but most likely a season or more.

seasonal sites Campsites reserved for longer-term tenants, those willing to stay at least a month or possibly year-round.

sewer Connection made from the RV to an outside septic system, common at most campsites.

shore power Also known as the 120-volt AC electrical system. A term used when receiving electricity from an AC outlet such as those found at most campsites.

site *See* campsite.

slide-out room Section of an RV's interior that expands several feet outward at the touch of a button, thus creating more space for those onboard.

snowbird RVer who heads off to warm-weather climates to avoid the winter months.

sofa conversion Also known as a pull-out sofa bed.

solar panel Apparatus installed on some RVs' roofs to capture the sun's energy and transform it to usable 12-volt power.

solar power Using the sun's energy as a power source.

sport utility trailer (SUT) Also known as patio-haulers or toy box models. Towable RV with a ramp and special cargo space for smaller motorized vehicles, such as jet skis, motorcycles, and snowmobiles.

spring bars Also known as tension bars. Part of the hitch designed to properly disperse the weight among the axles.

stick and tin Term used to describe an RV built on a wood frame and covered with an aluminum exterior.

suspension coverage Type of insurance that allows policyholders to cancel or reduce vehicle coverage during periods of dormancy, including storage.

sway bar *See* anti-sway device.

12-volt DC electrical system Onboard electrical system powering the 12-volt appliances via the coach and engine batteries.

tie-downs For use with truck campers. Attachments that secure and fasten the camper to the bed or frame of the truck.

toad *See* towed vehicle.

tongue Two diverging frame members that form the trailer's "A" frame, for use in towing.

tongue weight *See* hitch weight.

tow bar Device used to connect a secondary vehicle behind a motorhome.

tow dolly Designed to tow a secondary vehicle behind a motorhome with two of its tires off the ground and two tires riding on the pavement.

tow rating Listed in pounds, measures the maximum weight a vehicle can safely tow.

tow vehicle Vehicle responsible for transporting a towable RV.

towable Any recreational vehicle that relies on a primary vehicle to tow it.

towed vehicle Also known as a dinghy, auxiliary, or toad vehicle. A secondary vehicle pulled behind a motorhome for easier transport once the destination is reached.

travel trailer Most common towable RV, with sizes ranging from 20 to 40 feet. Subclass is the lightweight travel trailer.

truck camper Hard-sided camper affixed to the cargo area of a pickup truck.

unloaded vehicle weight (UVW) Also known as the dry weight. Actual weight of the RV, without passengers, cargo, or liquids.

voltage meter Also known as a voltmeter. Used to measure the exact AC voltage at the campsite's electrical pedestal.

walk-around Final check of the RV prior to departing. Inspection includes the interior and exterior of the vehicle, as well as possible check of the surrounding area.

water pressure regulator Device that maintains even water pressure when hooked up to a water outlet.

water pump Device designed to force water from the fresh water storage tank through the pipes of the RV.

weight-carrying hitch Hitch configuration where the tow vehicle's back bumper and axles bear the majority of the towable's weight. Best reserved for towables weighing less than 3,500 pounds.

weight-distributing hitch Attached to the frame of the tow vehicle, type of hitch disperses towable's weight to vehicle's axles.

wet weight *See* gross vehicle weight rating (GVWR).

wide body Any recreational vehicle wider than 96 inches, with 102 inches being the most common measurement.

winterizing Steps taken to prepare an RV for storage or periods of nonuse.

Index

Symbols

12-volt DC (direct current)
  automotive systems, 190
  coach systems, 191
    coach batteries, 192
    isolators, 192-193
120-volt AC electrical systems, 192-193
  converters and inverters, 194-195
  generators, 195-198
  hookups, 193-194

A

AAA discounts, 45
AARP (Association of American Retired Persons) discounts, 45
accessories
  global positioning systems (GPSs), 265
  rear view monitoring systems, 266
  side mirrors, 265
  towables, 93
  towing, 244
    air deflectors, 244
    mirrors, 244
    solo driving, 245
    sway control devices, 244
  truck campers, 84
accidents, 346-348
accommodations
  boondocking, 53-55
  campgrounds, 32-33, 46
    accessibility, 38
    activities, 40-41
    adult-oriented parks, 39
    costs, 43-44, 53
    discounts, 44-45
    facilities, 41-42
    franchises, 47
    government campgrounds, 48-53
    hookups, 34-38
    private campgrounds, 46-47
    recreation offerings, 39-40
    restrictions, 45-46
    RV resorts, 47-48
    seasonal sites, 38
    services, 42-43
    typical campsite description, 33-34
  hotel parking, 55
activities, campground, 39-41
add-ons. *See* accessories
adult-oriented parks, 39
after-the-sale proceedings
  final walk-thru, 176-177
  first time out plans, 178-179
  follow-up meeting, 178
  insurance considerations, 179
    company selection, 179-180
    coverage options, 179-180
    discounts, 181-182
    finding the best deals, 181
    full-timers' policies, 182
    out of the country coverage, 181
  roadside assistance plans, 182-184
  taking delivery, 176
aftermarket devices. *See* accessories
agencies, tourism, 286
air deflectors, 244
alarms
  activation measures, 355
  carbon monoxide, 355
  fire, 356
  LP gas, 355
  maintenance, 355
alternators, 190-191
aluminum roofing, 124-126
American Association of Retired Persons (AARP) discounts, 45
ammeters, 204
anti-sway devices, 93
appliances
  inspection criterion, 150
  LP-powered, 206
    heating systems, 207-208
    range ovens, 208-209
    refrigerators, 206-207
    water heaters, 209
Army Corps of Engineers Projects, 51
ASME (American Society of Mechanical Engineers) LP tanks, 211
assistance, roadside, 182-184
associations (contact information)
  dealer, 375
  industry, 376
automotive batteries, 190-192
axle weights, 270

B

backing up, 258-260
ball mounts, 237
bars, tow, 246-247
basement models, 65-66
bathrooms
  Class A motorhomes, 68
  Class B motorhomes, 73
  Class C motorhomes, 78

considerations for RV selection, 142-143
fifth-wheel trailers, 96
fresh water systems, 221-222
lightweight travel trailers, 106
pop-up campers, 111
travel trailers, 101
truck campers, 83
batteries
coach, 192
deep-cycle, 191-192
isolators, 192-193
winterizing, 366
benefits, 11-12
comfort, 16
cost, 13
environment stability, 15
hotel avoidance, 14-15
independence, 12
meal preparation, 14
outdoor enjoyment, 16
simplicity, 16-17
special needs accommodations, 17
togetherness, 13
travel arrangements, 15
Better Business Bureau Auto Line program, 185-186
black water, 35
dump stations, 225-227
holding tanks, 222-223
cleaning, 227-228
purging, 223-224
sewer hookups, 224-225
blackouts, 202-203
BLM (Bureau of Land Management), 50-51
boondocking, 53-55, 302
advantages, 302-304
cold-weather camping, 309-310
heating systems, 310
insulation, 311
RV capablities, 310
tanks and pipes, 311
winterizing hookups, 312
criteria, 304
legality, 304-305
RV capabilities, 306
safety, 305-306
pretrip suggestions, 306
practice, 306
provisions preparations, 307
RV inspection, 306
systems checks, 307
resource conservation tips, 307-308
cooking methods, 309
electricity, 308
fresh water, 308-309
wastewater, 309
bounce-aways (truck campers), 84
brakes
controllers, 240
conventional trailers, 240
secondary braking systems, 250
braking tips, 254-255
break-away switches (conventional trailers), 241
breakdowns, safety issues, 348-350
breaking camp, 298-300
building materials, 123-124
aluminum, 124
exterior "skin," 125
frame construction, 124
insulation, 125
roofing, 125
aluminum, 126
fiberglass, 126-127
rubber, 126
steel, 124-125
wood, 124
Bureau of Land Management (BLM), 50-51
buyer's guides, 132
buying process
after-the-sale proceedings
final walk-thru, 176-177
first time out plans, 178-179
follow-up meeting, 178
taking delivery, 176
choosing a seller, 158
private sellers, 158
RV dealers, 158-163
common pitfalls, 163
choice paralysis, 164
emotional decision-making, 164
falling for the hype, 164
hurried decisions, 163
salesperson intimidation, 164
unreasonable expectations, 164
deal negotiations, 165
acting interested, 167
creative bargaining, 167
fifteen percent rule, 166
practicing patience and persistence, 166
price talk, 165
insurance considerations, 179
company selection, 179-180
coverage options, 179-180
discounts, 181-182
finding the best deals, 181
full-timers' policies, 182
out of the country coverage, 181
option inclusions, 167-170
payment options, 172
financing, 172-174
roadside assistance plans, 182-184
trade-ins, 170
value determination, 170-171
warranties, 171
claim procedures, 171-172
extended warranties, 172
voiding circumstances, 171

C

cable TV (campground hookups), 36, 294-295
calling cards, 335-336
campers
pop-up, 11, 108-113
truck, 8-9, 80-82, 85-86
add-ons, 84
bathrooms, 83

cooking amenities, 82
costs, 85
driving features, 83-84
living space, 82-83
pop-up, 83
sleeping capacity, 82
specifications, 84-85
campfires, campground etiquette, 296
campgrounds, 32-33
accessibility, 38
activities, 40-41
adult-oriented parks, 39
breaking camp, 297-298
departure/pretrip checklist, 298-300
checking in, 288-289
checklist for wants and needs, 286-287
clubs, contact information, 374-375
costs, 43-44
government campgrounds, 53
discounts, 44
AAA, 45
American Association of Retired Persons (AARP), 45
franchise clubs, 44-45
length of stay, 45
RV clubs, 44
facilities, 41-42
federal, contact information, 375
franchises, contact information, 374-375
hookups, 34, 291
backing into the campsite, 37-38
cable TV, 36, 294-295
electric, 34-35, 291
fresh water, 292
LP gas, 292-293
satellite TV, 294
sewer, 35-36, 293
telephone, 36-37, 293-294, 336
water, 35
locating, 284-285
directories, 285
Internet, 285-286
tourism agencies, 286
word of mouth referrals, 286
"modem-friendly" sites, 337-338
pet policies, 322
recreation offerings, 39-40
reservations, 284
restrictions, 45-46
rules and etiquette, 295
campfires, 296
children, 297
dogs, 296
garbage, 296-297
generators, 296
idling engines, 297
laundry, 297
"quiet hours," 295-296
walking through other campers' sites, 297
safety issues, 350-351
crime, 351-353
seasonal sites, 38
selection considerations, 282
costs, 283
facilities and services, 284
location, 282
recreation offerings, 283-284
special needs accommodations, 283
services, 42-43
setting up camp, 288
settling in, 295
site parking, 289
achieving level status, 290-291
docking sequence, 289-290
types, 46
franchises, 47
government campgrounds, 48-53
private, 46-47
RV resorts, 47-48
typical campsite description, 33-34
camping clubs, contact information, 373-374
Canada
campgounds, 52
travel considerations, 326
caravans
contact information, 376-377
travel planning, 324
carbon monoxide detectors, 355
catalytic heaters, 208
CB radios, 339
cellular phones, 334-335
certified RV instruction, 263
changing lanes, 256
chassis, inspection criterion, 150-151
check-in process (campgrounds), 288-289
children
campground rules and etiquette, 297
travel planning considerations, 318
accommodating needs, 319-320
packing considerations, 319
planning process involvement, 318-319
seating arrangements, 319-320
supervision and discipline, 320
Class A motorhomes, 6-7, 64-66, 70-71
basement models, 66
bathrooms, 68
cooking amenities, 66
costs, 70
diesel pushers, 66
driving features, 68-69
living space, 67-68
sleeping capacity, 66-67
specifications, 69
wide-body models, 66
Class B motorhomes, 7, 71-72, 75
bathrooms, 73
cooking amenities, 73
costs, 74
driving features, 74
living space, 73
sleeping capacity, 72-73
specifications, 74

Class C motorhomes, 8, 75-76, 79-80
  bathrooms, 78
  cooking amenities, 77
  costs, 79
  driving features, 78
  living space, 77-78
  sleeping capacity, 76-77
  specifications, 78-79
cleaning tips, 370
  exterior care, 370-371
  fresh-water storage tanks, 227
  holding tanks, 227-228
  interior care, 371-372
clearance, 257
clubs
  campground, 374-375
  camping, 373-374
  discounts
    AAA, 45
    American Association of Retired Persons (AARP), 45
    franchise clubs, 44-45
    RV clubs, 44
coach power, 191
  coach batteries, 192
    automotive batteries, 192
    deep-cycle batteries, 191-192
  isolators, 192-193
cold-weather camping, 309-310
  heating systems, 310
  insulation, 311
  RV capablities, 310
  tanks and pipes, 311
  winterizing hookups, 312
collect calls, 336
communications
  CB radios, 339
  computers, 337-338
  e-mail, 337-338
  Internet devices, 338-339
  mail, 340
    forwarding services, 340-341
    full-timers, 341-342
    general delivery, 341
    neighbor assistance, 341
  pagers, 339
  telephones, 334
    calling cards, 335-336
    campsite hookups, 336
    cellular, 334-335
    collect calls, 336
computers, 337-338
containers (LP), 210
  ASME (American Society of Mechanical Engineers) tanks, 211
  DOT (Department of Transportation) tanks, 210
  fill-up procedures, 212
  mountings, 210
  regulators, 210
conventional trailer hitches, 236
  brakes, 240
    controllers, 240
  break-away switches, 241
  checklist, 241
  component functions, 237
  safety chains, 240
  set-up process, 238-239
  weight-carrying hitches, 236
  weight-distributing hitches, 236-237
  wiring harnesses, 238-239
converters, 194-195
cooking amenities
  boondocking tips, 309
  Class A motorhomes, 66
  Class B motorhomes, 73
  Class C motorhomes, 77
  considerations for RV selection, 141-142
  fifth-wheel trailers, 95
  lightweight travel trailers, 105-106
  pop-up campers, 110
  travel trailers, 100-101
  truck campers, 82
cords, shoreline power, 203
cornering, 255
costs
  campgrounds, 43-44, 283
    discounts, 44-45
    government campgrounds, 53
  Class A motorhomes, 70
  Class B motorhomes, 74
  Class C motorhomes, 79
  determining budget parameters, 116
  fifth-wheel trailers, 98
  fuel, 263-264
  lightweight travel trailers, 107-108
  pop-up campers, 113
  towables, 88
  travel trailers, 102-103
  truck campers, 85
couplers, 238
crime
  behavioral precautions, 352-353
  campground safety, 351-352
  prevention techniques, 353

D

day trips, 27
dealers
  advantages, 158-159
  associations, 375
  locating, 159
  selection parameters, 159-160
    delivery process, 162
    location, 161
    price comparisons, 160
    quality of sales personnel, 162
    reputation, 160-161
    service, 161
    trade-in policies, 162-163
dealerships, visiting, 130
deep-cycle batteries, 191-192
delivery, 176
detectors
  activation measures, 355
  carbon monoxide, 355
  LP gas, 355
  maintenance, 355
  smoke, 356
diesel engines, 122-123
diesel pushers, 65-66
dinghy vehicles, 6
directories, campground, 285

discounts, 44
- AAA, 45
- American Association of Retired Persons (AARP), 45
- franchise clubs, 44-45
- insurance, 181-182
- length of stay, 45
- RV clubs, 44

dogs (campground etiquette), 296
dollies, tow, 246-249
DOT (Department of Transportation) LP tanks, 210
driver's education, 30, 263, 267
driver's licenses, 29
driving, 254
- accessories, 265
  - global positioning systems (GPSs), 265
  - rear view monitoring systems, 266
  - side mirrors, 265
- accidents, 346-347
  - attitude, 347
  - avoiding, 347
  - involving the authorities, 348
  - safeguarding involved parties, 348
- backing up, 258-260
- braking tips, 254-255
- certified RV instruction, 263
- clearance, 257
- common mistakes, 259
  - driving during extreme weather, 261
  - driving like a car, 260
  - drowsy driving, 262
  - getting lost, 261
  - impaired driving, 262
  - nervous driving, 260-261
  - overdoing it, 262
  - rushing, 260
- cornering, 255
- dealing with other drivers, 264-265
- getting gas, 263-264
- highway driving, 257-258
- lane changes, 256
- parking, 256-257
- practicing, 263
- rush hour, 257
- steep grades, 256

driving features
- Class A motorhomes, 68-69
- Class B motorhomes, 74
- Class C motorhomes, 78
- truck campers, 83-84

dry weight. *See* unloaded vehicle weight (UVW)
dump stations, 35, 225-227

E

e-mail, 337-338
education, driver's, 30, 263, 267
electric hookups
- boondocking tips, 308
- campgrounds, 34-35, 291
- shore power, 34

electrical connectors (truck campers), 84
electrical systems
- add-on suggestions, 203
  - ammeters, 204
  - extra shoreline power cords, 203
  - polarity testers, 203
  - surge protectors, 203
  - voltage meters, 204
- backups and alternatives, 201-202
  - solar power, 202
- blackouts, 202-203
- converters and inverters, 194-195
- electricity sources, 190
  - coach power, 191-193
  - engine power, 190
  - shore power, 192-198
- generators, 195-198
- hookups
  - determining what type you have, 194
  - outlet types, 193-194
- monitor panels, 198-199
- RV accessory requirements and system limitations, 199-200

emergencies, medical, 353-355
emergency equipment checklist, 358
engine power, 190
engines
- gas versus diesel, 122-123
- winterizing, 367

etiquette, campground, 295
- campfires, 296
- children, 297
- dogs, 296
- garbage, 296-297
- generators, 296
- idling engines, 297
- laundry, 297
- quiet hours, 295-296
- walking through other campers' sites, 297

events (travel planning), 324
expectations, 17-18
extended vacations, 28
extended warranties, 172
exterior care, 370-371
"exterior skin," 125

F

facilities, campground, 41-42, 284
federal campgrounds, contact information, 375
fiberglass roofing, 126-127
fifteen percent rule, 166
fifth-wheel trailers, 10, 94, 98
- bathrooms, 96
- cooking amenities, 95
- costs, 98
- hitches, 241-243
- living space, 94-96
- sleeping capacity, 95
- specifications, 97
- towability, 96-97

filters (fresh water systems), 218
final walk-thrus, 176-177
financing, 172
- avoiding borrow sorrow, 173
- interest, 174
- rate shopping, 173
- service offerings, 173

fires, 356
flooring (inspection criterion), 148
fog, 346-347
fold-down campers. *See* pop-up campers
follow-up meetings, 178
foreign travel, planning considerations, 325
  Canada, 326
  Mexico, 326-327
frame construction, 124
franchises
  campgrounds, 47, 374-375
  club discounts, 44-45
fresh water systems, 216
  bathroom water, 221-222
  boondocking tips, 308-309
  campground hookups, 292
  filters, 218
  hoses, 217
  pumps, 219-220
  sources, 216-217
  storage tanks, 218-219
    cleaning, 227
    filling, 219
  water heaters, 221
  water pressure, 217-218
    regulators, 218
fuel, 263-264
full hookup sites, 43
full-time travelers, 28
  mail issues, 341-342
  planning considerations, 327-330
furnaces, 207
furnishings (inspection criterion), 149

G

garbage (campground rules and etiquette), 296-297
gas (LP power), 205-206
  appliances, 206-209
  campground hookups, 292-293
  heating systems, 207-208
  LP containers, 210-212
  safety measures, 213-214
gas-powered engines, 122-123
GCWR (gross combined weight rating), 233
generators, 195-198, 296
global positioning systems (GPSs), 265
goosenecks, 10
government campgrounds, 48
  Bureau of Land Management (BLM), 50-51
  costs, 53
  membership parks, 52
  national parks, 50
  Parks Canada, 52
  state parks, 49
  U.S. Army Corps of Engineers Projects, 51
  wildlife refuge areas, 52
GPSs (global positioning systems), 265
gray water, 35
  dump stations, 225-227
  holding tanks, 222-223
    cleaning, 227-228
    purging, 223-224
  sewer hookups, 224-225
gross combined weight rating (GCWR), 233
gross vehicle weight rating (GVWR), 233
group travel planning, 323-324
  events and rallies, 324
  tours and caravans, 324
GVWR (gross vehicle weight rating), 233

H

heating systems, 207
  catalytic heaters, 208
  cold weather camping, 310
  furnaces, 207
  fresh water heaters, 221
  hydronic heating, 208
  space heaters, 208
highway driving, 257-258
hitches, 234-235
  classes table, 235
  conventional trailers, 236
    brake controllers, 240
    brakes, 240
    break-away switches, 241
    checklist, 241
    component functions, 237
    safety chains, 240
    set-up process, 238-239
    weight carrying hitches, 236
    weight distributing hitches, 236-237
    wiring harnesses, 238-239
  fifth-wheel trailers, 241-243
  finding the right hitch, 235-236
  receivers, 237
  weight, 279
holding tanks. *See also* storage tanks
  fresh water systems, 218-219
    cleaning, 227
    filling, 219
  wastewater, 222-223
    cleaning, 227-228
    dump stations, 225-227
    purging, 223-224
    sewer hookups, 224-225
hookups, 34
  backing into the campsite, 37-38
  campgrounds, 291
    cable TV, 294-295
    electric, 291
    fresh water, 292
    LP gas, 292-293
    satellite TV, 294
    sewer, 293
    telephone, 293-294, 336
  considerations for RV selection, 146
  determining what type you have, 194
  electric
    campgrounds, 34-35
    shore power, 34
  outlet types, 193-194
  sewer, 224-225
  telephone, 36-37
  water, 35
  winterizing, 312

hoses (fresh water systems), 217
hotel parking, 55
hydronic heating, 208

I

"I-Wish-I-Had" list, 155
ice, 345-346
industry associations, contact information, 376
inspection criterion, 147-150
  appliances, 150
  chassis, 150-151
  flooring, 148
  furnishings, 149
  proper sealing, 149
  sidewalls and roofing, 151-152
  tires, 151
  under the hood, 152
  woodworking, 148-149
insulation, 125, 311
insurance, 179
  company selection, 179-180
  coverage options, 179-180
  discounts, 181-182
  finding the best deals, 181
  full-timers' policies, 182
  out of the country coverage, 181
interior
  care, 371-372
  considerations for RV selection, 144
Internet
  devices, 338-339
  resources, 285-286
inverters, 194-195
isolators, 192-193

J–K–L

jacks (truck campers), 84

kingpins, 242

lane changes, 256
laundry (campground rules and etiquette), 297
"lemons," 184
  Better Business Bureau's Auto Line program, 185-186
  defining "lemon" parameters, 184-185
  documentation guidelines, 185
  ruling decisions, 186
licenses, 29
lightweight travel trailers, 11, 99, 103-108
  bathrooms, 106
  cooking amenities, 105-106
  costs, 107-108
  living space, 105-106
  sleeping capacity, 105
  specifications, 107
  towability, 106-107
livability tests, 140, 145
  awnings, ladders, and steps, 146-147
  bathrooms, 142-143
  cooking amenities, 141-142
  hookups, 146
  interior, 144
  living space, 143-144
  sleeping capacity, 140-141
  storage capabilities, 142, 145
living space
  Class A motorhomes, 67-68
  Class B motorhomes, 73
  Class C motorhomes, 77-78
  considerations for RV selection, 143-144
  fifth-wheel trailers, 94-96
  lightweight travel trailers, 105-106
  pop-up campers, 109-111
  travel trailers, 100-101
  truck campers, 82-83
locking pins, 242
LP gas, 205-206
  appliances, 206
    heating systems, 207-208
    range ovens, 208-209
    refrigerators, 206-207
    water heaters, 209
    winterization tips, 364-366
  campground hookups, 292-293
  containers, 210
    ASME (American Society of Mechanical Engineers) tanks, 211
    DOT (Department of Transportation) tanks, 210
    fill-up procedures, 212
    mountings, 210
    regulators, 210
  detector mechanisms, 355
  safety measures, 213
    pretrip precautions, 213
    smell detection, 214
    tank handling, 213-214

M

mail, 340
  forwarding services, 340-341
  full-time travel tips, 341-342
  general delivery, 341
  neighbor assistance, 341
maintenance tips
  cleaning, 370
    exterior care, 370-371
    interior care, 371-372
  spring preparations, 367-368
    systems checks, 368-369
    test drives, 370
    trailers, 370
  winter storage, 362-363
    batteries, 366
    engine, 367
    LP gas systems, 364-366
    plumbing systems, 363-365
    tires, 366
manufacturers, 127
manufacturing process, 123-124
  aluminum, 124
  "exterior skin," 125
  frame construction, 124

insulation, 125
roofing, 125
aluminum, 126
fiberglass, 126-127
rubber, 126
steel, 124-125
wood, 124
marine-style batteries, 191-192
medical emergencies, 353-355
membership parks, 52
Mexico (travel considerations), 326-327
mirrors, 244, 265
"modem-friendly" campgrounds, 337-338
monitor panels, 198-199
motorized RVs, 6
advantages, 60
"all-in-one" vehicle convenience, 60
boondocking, 61
ease of travel, 60-61
in-motion access, 61
one-time costs, 61
towing capabilities, 62
Class A motorhomes, 6-7, 64-71
basement models, 66
bathrooms, 68
cooking amenities, 66
costs, 70
diesel pushers, 66
driving features, 68-69
living space, 67-68
sleeping capacity, 66-67
specifications, 69
wide-body models, 66
Class B motorhomes, 7, 71-75
bathrooms, 73
cooking amenities, 73
costs, 74
driving features, 74
living space, 73
sleeping capacity, 72-73
specifications, 74
Class C motorhomes, 8, 75-80
bathrooms, 78
cooking amenities, 77
costs, 79
driving features, 78
living space, 77-78
sleeping capacity, 76-77
specifications, 78-79
disadvantages, 62-64
breakdowns and repairs, 62-63
cockpit space, 63
depreciation, 64
driving, 63
limited interior choices, 63-64
sticker shock, 62
towing behind a motorhome, 245
determining towable items, 245-246
inspections, 250
safety chains, 250
secondary braking systems, 250
tow bars, 246-247
tow dollies, 246-249
trailers, 246, 249
wiring, 250
truck campers, 8-9, 80-82, 85-86
add-ons, 84
bathrooms, 83
cooking amenities, 82
costs, 85
driving features, 83-84
living space, 82-83
pop-up, 83
sleeping capacity, 82
specifications, 84-85
mountings (LP tanks) 210

N–O

national parks, 50
natural disasters, 346
net carrying capacity (NCC), 271-273
new versus used vehicles, 133-135

off-season storage, 362
spring preparations, 367-368
systems checks, 368-369
test drives, 370
trailers, 370
winterizing process, 363
batteries, 366
engine, 367
LP gas systems, 364-366
plumbing systems, 363-365
tires, 366
out of the country travel. *See* foreign travel
ovens, 208-209
owner demographics, 20
35 to 54 age group, 21
active lifestylers, 22
athletics fans, 26
business travelers, 25-26
couples, 21
disabled travelers, 23-24
families, 22-23
hobby enthusiasts, 26-27
motor heads, 23
park campers, 24-25
pet-lovers, 24
retirees, 22
snowbirds, 25

P

packing, 271
children's belongings, 319
common pitfalls, 277-279
loading tips, 279-280
net carrying capacity (NCC), 271-273
pets' belongings, 321-322
suggested items, 274-277
tracking weight load, 272-274
pagers, 339
panels, monitor, 198-199
parking, 256-257, 289
achieving level status, 290-291
docking sequence, 289-290
parks
national, 50
state, 49
Parks Canada, 52
payment options, 172
avoiding borrow sorrow, 173
interest, 174
rate shopping, 173
service offerings, 173

pets (travel planning considerations), 24, 321
 allowing pets to get acclimated, 321
 campground behavior, 322
 hydration and general comfort, 322-323
 leaving unattended, 323
 packing, 321-322
phones. *See* telephones
planning, travel
 boondocking, 302
  advantages, 302-304
  cold-weather camping, 309-312
  criteria, 304-306
  pretrip suggestions, 306-307
  resource conservation tips, 307-309
 campgrounds
  breaking camp, 297-300
  check-in process, 288-289
  checklist for wants and needs, 286-287
  hookups, 291-295
  reservations, 284
  resources for finding campground listings, 284-286
  rules and etiquette, 295-297
  selection considerations, 282-284
  setting up camp, 288
  settling in, 295
  site parking, 289-291
 children, 318
  accommodating needs, 319-320
  involving in the planning process, 318-319
  packing considerations, 319
  seating arrangements, 319-320
  supervision and discipline, 320
 communications
  CB radios, 339
  computers, 337-338
  e-mail, 337-338
  Internet devices, 338-339
  mail, 340-342
  pagers, 339
  telephones, 334-336
 foreign travel, 325
  Canada, 326
  Mexico, 326-327
 full-time travelers, 327-330
 group planning, 323-324
  events and rallies, 324
  tours and caravans, 324
 pets, 321
  allowing pets to get acclimated, 321
  campground behavior, 322
  hydration and general comfort, 322-323
  leaving unattended, 323
  packing, 321-322
plumbing systems, 216
 fresh water, 216
  bathroom water, 221-222
  filters, 218
  hoses, 217
  pumps, 219-220
  sources, 216-217
  storage tanks, 218-219, 227
  water heaters, 221
  water pressure, 217-218
 wastewater, 222
  dump stations, 225-227
  holding tanks, 222-223, 227-228
  purging, 223-224
  sewer hookups, 224-225
 winterizing, 363-365
polarity testers, 203
pop-up campers, 11, 108-109, 113
 bathrooms, 111
 cooking amenities, 110
 costs, 113
 living space, 109-111
 sleeping capacity, 109-110
 specifications, 112
 towability, 112
pop-up truck campers, 83
pressure (fresh water systems), 217-218
pretrip checklist, 298-300
primitive sites, 43
private campgrounds, 46-47
private sellers, 158
propane power. *See* LP gas
publications, 377-379
pull-thru sites, 37-38
pumps (fresh water systems), 219-220

Q–R

qualifications, 4-5
"quiet hours" (campgrounds), 295-296

radios, CB, 339
rallies, 324
range ovens, 208-209
ratings, tow, 232
rear bumper extensions (truck campers), 84
rear view monitoring systems, 266
recreation offerings (campgrounds), 39-40, 283-284
Recreation Vehicle Industry Association (RVIA) Web site, 129
recreational vehicles. *See* RVs
refrigerators, 206-207
regulators, 210, 218
rental companies, 130-131
rentals, contact information, 375
reservations, campgrounds, 284
resorts, 47-48
resources
 buyer's guides, 132
 campground clubs and franchises, 374-375
 campgrounds, 284-285
  directories, 285
  Internet, 285-286
  tourism agencies, 286
  word of mouth referrals, 286
 camping clubs, 373-374
 caravans and tours, 376-377
 dealer associations, 375

driving instruction, 376
federal campgrounds, 375
industry associations, 376
publications, 377-379
rentals, 375
Web sites, 379
Recreation Vehicle Industry Association (RVIA), 129
restrictions, 29
campgrounds, 45-46
driver's education, 30
licensing, 29
roadside assistance, 182-184
roofing, 125
aluminum, 126
fiberglass, 126-127
inspection criterion, 151-152
rubber, 126
rubber roofing, 126
rules, campgrounds, 295
campfires, 296
children, 297
dogs, 296
garbage, 296-297
generators, 296
idling engines, 297
laundry, 297
"quiet hours," 295-296
walking through other campers' sites, 297
rush hour driving, 257
RVIA (Recreation Vehicle Industry Association) Web site, 129
RVs
benefits of RVing, 11-12
comfort, 16
cost, 13
environment stability, 15
hotel avoidance, 14-15
independence, 12
meal preparation, 14
outdoor enjoyment, 16
simplicity, 16-17
special needs accommodations, 17
togetherness, 13
travel arrangements, 15
buying process
after-the-sale proceedings, 176-179
choosing a seller, 158-163
common pitfalls, 163-164
deal negotiations, 165-167
option inclusions, 167-170
payment options, 172-174
warranties, 171-172
club discounts, 44
dealers
advantages, 158-159
locating, 159
selection parameters, 159-163
driving, 254
accessories, 265-266
backing up, 258-260
braking tips, 254-255
certified RV instruction, 263
clearance, 257
common mistakes, 259-262
cornering, 255
dealing with other drivers, 264-265
getting gas, 263-264
highway driving, 257-258
lane changes, 256
parking, 256-257
practicing, 263
rush hour, 257
steep grades, 256
expectations, 17-18
insurance, 179
company selection, 179-180
coverage options, 179-180
discounts, 181-182
finding the best deals, 181
full-timers' policies, 182
out of the country coverage, 181
"lemons," 184
Better Business Bureau's Auto Line program, 185-186
defining "lemon" parameters, 184-185
documentation guidelines, 185
ruling decisions, 186
motorized, 6
advantages, 60-62
Class A motorhomes, 6-7, 64-71
Class B motorhomes, 7, 71-75
Class C motorhomes, 8, 75-80
disadvantages, 62-64
towing behind a motorhome, 245-250
truck campers, 8-9, 80-86
owner demographics, 20
35 to 54 age group, 21
active lifestylers, 22
athletics fans, 26
business travelers, 25-26
couples, 21
disabled travelers, 23-24
families, 22-23
hobby enthusiasts, 26-27
motor heads, 23
park campers, 24-25
pet-lovers, 24
retirees, 22
snowbirds, 25
qualifications, 4-5
restrictions, 29
driver's education, 30
licensing, 29
resorts, 47-48
roadside assistance plans, 182-184
selection considerations, 116-119
amenities, 118
budget, 116
building materials and manufacturing process, 123-125
comparison shopping, 128-133
destination plans, 117

driving preferences, 118
gas versus diesel engines, 122-123
"I-Wish-I-Had" list, 155
inspection criterion, 147-152
livability tests, 140-147
manufacturing companies, 127
motorized versus towable, 116-117
new versus used, 133-135
passenger count, 117
roofing, 125-127
slide-out rooms, 119-122
space requirements, 117-118
test drive guidelines, 152-153
warning signs, 153-155
wide-body designs, 127-128
shows, 129
towable, 9, 93
accessories, 93
advantages, 88-91
disadvantages, 91-93
fifth-wheel trailers, 10, 94-98
hitches, 234-243
lightweight travel trailers, 103-108
matching with a tow vehicle, 232-234
pop-up campers, 11, 108-113
towing accessories, 244-245
travel trailers, 10-11, 99-103
trading-in, 170
value determination, 170-171
trip types, 27
day trips, 27
extended vacations, 28
full-time travel, 28
weekend getaways, 27-28

S

safety chains
conventional trailers, 240
towing behind a motorhome, 250
safety
accidents, 346-348
alarms and detectors
activation measures, 355
carbon monoxide, 355
fire, 356
LP gas, 355
maintenance, 355
"back at home" safety, 357-358
breakdowns, 348-350
campgrounds, 350-351
crime
behavioral precautions, 352-353
campgrounds, 351-352
prevention techniques, 353
emergency equipment checklist, 358
fire, 356
LP gas, 213
pretrip precautions, 213
tank handling, 213-214
medical emergencies, 353-355
smell detection, 214
weather, 344
fog, 346-347
ice, 345-346
natural disasters, 346
snow, 345
storms, 345
wind, 344-345
wild animals, 357
satellite TV, campground hookups, 294
seasonals, 38
seating arrangements, 319-320
secondary braking systems, 250
selection considerations, 116-119
amenities, 118
budget, 116
building materials and manufacturing process, 123-124
aluminum, 124
"exterior skin," 125
frame construction, 124
insulation, 125
steel, 124-125
wood, 124
comparison shopping, 128-132
borrowing from a friend, 131-132
buyer's guides, 132
dealership visits, 130
manufacturer research, 132-133
rental companies, 130-131
RV shows, 129
test drives, 131
word of mouth recommendations, 133
destination plans, 117
driving preferences, 118
gas versus diesel engines, 122-123
"I-Wish-I-Had" list, 155
inspection criterion, 147, 150
appliances, 150
chassis, 150-151
flooring, 148
furnishings, 149
inside, 147-148
proper sealing, 149
sidewalls and roofing, 151-152
tires, 151
under the hood, 152
woodworking, 148-149
livability tests, 140, 145
awnings, ladders, and steps, 146-147
bathrooms, 142-143
cooking amenities, 141-142
hookups, 146
interior, 144
living space, 143-144
sleeping capacity, 140-141
storage capabilities, 142, 145

manufacturing companies, 127
motorized versus towable, 116-117
new versus used, 133-135
passenger count, 117
roofing, 125
aluminum, 126
fiberglass, 126-127
rubber, 126
slide-out rooms, 119
advantages, 119-120
disadvantages, 120-122
space requirements, 117-118
test drive guidelines, 152-153
driving performance, 153
prior to take-off, 153
terrain grades, 153
warning signs, 153-154
barely driven vehicles, 154
incomplete information, 155
leans, 154
rental re-sales, 154
water leaks, 154
wide-body designs, 127-128
sellers, choosing, 158
private sellers, 158
RV dealers, 158-163
services, campground, 42-43, 284
sewer hookups, 224-225
black water, 35
campgrounds, 35-36, 293
dump stations, 35
gray water, 35
shore power, 34, 192-193
converters and inverters, 194-195
generators, 195-198
hookups, 193-194
shows, 129
side mirrors, 265
sidewalls (inspection criterion), 151-152
sinks (fresh water systems), 221-222
sleeping capacity
Class A motorhomes, 66-67
Class B motorhomes, 72-73
Class C motorhomes, 76-77
considerations for RV selection, 140-141
fifth-wheel trailers, 95
lightweight travel trailers, 105
pop-up campers, 109-110
travel trailers, 100
truck campers, 82
slide-out rooms, 119
advantages
extra space, 119-120
resale value, 120
disadvantages, 120
campground restrictions, 121-122
extra costs, 121
malfunctions, 121
weight factors, 120
snow, 345
solar power, 202
sources (electricity), 190
coach power, 191
coach batteries, 191-192
isolators, 192-193
engine power, 190
shore power, 192-193
converters and inverters, 194-195
generators, 195-198
hookups, 193-194
space heaters, 208
special needs (campground selection factors), 283
specifications
Class A motorhomes, 69
Class B motorhomes, 74
Class C motorhomes, 78-79
fifth-wheel trailers, 97
lightweight travel trailers, 107
pop-up campers, 112
travel trailers, 102
truck campers, 84-85
sport utility trailers (SUTs), 23
spring bars, 237
spring preparations, 367-368
systems checks, 368-369
test drives, 370
trailers, 370
state parks, 49
stations, dump, 225-227
steel, 124-125
"stick and tin" construction, 124
storage
considerations for RV selection, 142, 145
off-season, 362
spring preparations, 367-368
systems checks, 368-369
test drives, 370
trailers, 370
winterizing process, 363
batteries, 366
engine, 367
LP gas systems, 364-366
plumbing systems, 363-365
tires, 366
storage tanks. *See also* holding tanks
fresh water systems, 218-219
cleaning, 227
filling, 219
wastewater, 222-223
cleaning, 227-228
dump stations, 225-227
purging, 223-224
sewer hookups, 224-225
storms, 345
surge protectors, 203
suspension coverage, 181
SUTs (sport utility trailers), 23
sway control devices, 244

T

telephones, 334
calling cards, 335-336
campsite hookups, 36-37, 293-294, 336
cellular, 334-335
collect calls, 336
television (campground hookups), 36, 294-295
test drives, 131, 152-153
driving performance, 153
prior to take-off, 153
terrain grades, 153
tests, livability, 140, 145
awnings, ladders, and steps, 146-147

bathrooms, 142-143
cooking amenities, 141-142
hookups, 146
interior, 144
living space, 143-144
sleeping capacity, 140-141
storage capabilities, 142, 145
tie-downs (truck campers), 84
tires
inspection criterion, 151
winterizing, 366
"toad," 245
toilets (fresh water systems), 221-222
tongues, 238
total weight, 270
tourism agencies, 286
tours
contact information, 376-377
travel planning, 324
tow bars, 246-247
tow dollies, 246-249
tow vehicles
matching with an RV, 232-234
gross combined weight rating (GCWR), 233
gross vehicle weight rating (GVWR), 233
tow ratings, 232
unloaded vehicle weight (UVW), 233
towing accessories, 244
air deflectors, 244
mirrors, 244
solo driving, 245
sway control devices, 244
trailer hitches, 234-235
classes table, 235
conventional trailers, 236-241
fifth-wheel trailers, 241-243
finding the right hitch, 235-236
towability
fifth-wheel trailers, 96-97
lightweight travel trailers, 106-107
pop-up campers, 112
travel trailers, 101-102
towable RVs, 9, 93. *See also* trailers
accessories, 93
advantages, 88
costs, 88
inhabitable space, 90
longevity, 89
residential styles, 89-90
"second home" uses, 90-91
separate vehicles, 88-89
variety, 90
disadvantages, 91
driving precautions, 91-92
passenger transportation, 92
tow vehicle specifications, 92-93
fifth-wheel trailers, 10, 94, 98
bathrooms, 96
cooking amenities, 95
costs, 98
living space, 94-96
sleeping capacity, 95
specifications, 97
towability, 96-97
hitches, 234-235
classes table, 235
conventional trailers, 236-241
fifth-wheel trailers, 241-243
finding the right hitch, 235-236
lightweight travel trailers, 103-104, 108
bathrooms, 106
cooking amenities, 105-106
costs, 107-108
living space, 105-106
sleeping capacity, 105
specifications, 107
towability, 106-107
matching with a tow vehicle, 232-234
gross combined weight rating (GCWR), 233
gross vehicle weight rating (GVWR), 233
unloaded vehicle weight (UVW), 233
vehicle tow ratings, 232
pop-up campers, 11, 108-109, 113
bathrooms, 111
cooking amenities, 110
costs, 113
living space, 109-111
sleeping capacity, 109-110
specifications, 112
towability, 112
towing accessories, 244
air deflectors, 244
mirrors, 244
solo driving, 245
sway control devices, 244
travel trailers, 10-11, 99-100, 103
bathrooms, 101
cooking amenities, 100-101
costs, 102-103
living space, 100-101
sleeping capacity, 100
specifications, 102
towability, 101-102
towing (behind motorhomes), 245
determining towable items, 245-246
inspections, 250
safety chains, 250
secondary braking systems, 250
tow bars, 246-247
tow dollies, 246-249
trailers, 246, 249
wiring, 250
trade-ins, 170-171
trailers. *See also* towable RVs
conventional hitches, 236-241
fifth-wheel, 10, 94, 98
bathrooms, 96
cooking amenities, 95
costs, 98
hitches, 241-243
living space, 94-96
sleeping capacity, 95

specifications, 97
towability, 96-97
hitches, 234-235
classes table, 235
conventional trailers, 236-241
fifth-wheel trailers, 241-243
finding the right hitch, 235-236
lightweight travel trailers, 103-108
bathrooms, 106
cooking amenities, 105-106
costs, 107-108
living space, 105-106
sleeping capacity, 105
specifications, 107
towability, 106-107
towing accessories, 244
air deflectors, 244
mirrors, 244
solo driving, 245
sway control devices, 244
towing behind a motorhome, 246, 249
travel, 10-11, 99-103
bathrooms, 101
cooking amenities, 100-101
costs, 102-103
living space, 100-101
sleeping capacity, 100
specifications, 102
towability, 101-102
travel planning
boondocking, 302
advantages, 302-304
cold-weather camping, 309-312
criteria, 304-306
pretrip suggestions, 306-307
resource conservation tips, 307-309
campgrounds
breaking camp, 297-300
check-in process, 288-289
checklist for wants and needs, 286-287
hookups, 291-295
reservations, 284
resources for finding campground listings, 284-286
rules and etiquette, 295-297
selection considerations, 282-284
setting up camp, 288
settling in, 295
site parking, 289-291
children, 318
accommodating needs, 319-320
involving in the planning process, 318-319
packing considerations, 319
seating arrangements, 319-320
supervision and discipline, 320
communications
CB radios, 339
computers, 337-338
e-mail, 337-338
Internet devices, 338-339
mail, 340-342
pagers, 339
telephones, 334-336
foreign travel, 325
Canada, 326
Mexico, 326-327
full-time travelers, 327-330
group considerations, 323-324
events and rallies, 324
tours and caravans, 324
pets, 321
allowing pets to get acclimated, 321
campground behavior, 322
hydration and general comfort, 322-323
leaving unattended, 323
packing, 321-322
weather considerations, 344
fog, 346-347
ice, 345-346
natural disasters, 346
snow, 345
storms, 345
wind, 344-345
travel trailers, 10-11, 99-103
bathrooms, 101
cooking amenities, 100-101
costs, 102-103
lightweight, 103-104, 108
bathrooms, 106
cooking amenities, 105-106
costs, 107-108
living space, 105-106
sleeping capacity, 105
specifications, 107
towability, 106-107
living space, 100-101
sleeping capacity, 100
specifications, 102
towability, 101-102
truck campers, 8-9, 80-86
add-ons, 84
bathrooms, 83
cooking amenities, 82
costs, 85
driving features, 83-84
living space, 82-83
pop-up, 83
sleeping capacity, 82
specifications, 84-85
tune-up checklist, 369

U–V

U.S. Army Corps of Engineers Projects, 51
unloaded vehicle weight (UVW), 233
used vehicles (versus new), 133-135
UVW (unloaded vehicle weight), 233

vehicles
matching with an RV, 232-234
gross combined weight rating (GCWR), 233
gross vehicle weight rating (GVWR), 233

tow ratings, 232
unloaded vehicle weight (UVW), 233
towing accessories, 244
air deflectors, 244
mirrors, 244
solo driving, 245
sway control devices, 244
trailer hitches, 234-235
classes table, 235
conventional trailers, 236-241
fifth-wheel trailers, 241-243
finding the right hitch, 235-236
voltage meters, 204

W-X-Y-Z

warning signs, 153-154
barely driven vehicles, 154
incomplete information, 155
leans, 154
rental re-sales, 154
water leaks, 154
warranties, 171
claim procedures, 171-172
extended warranties, 172
voiding circumstances, 171
wastewater systems, 222
boondocking tips, 309
dump stations, 225-227
holding tanks, 222-223
cleaning, 227-228
purging, 223-224
sewer hookups, 224-225
water
campground hookups, 35
heaters, 209
pressure regulators, 218
types
black water, 35
gray water, 35
systems, 216
fresh water, 216-222
wastewater, 222-228
weather considerations, 344
fog, 346-347
ice, 345-346
natural disasters, 346
snow, 345
storms, 345
wind, 344-345
Web sites, 379
weekend getaways, 27-28
weight
gross combined weight rating (GCWR), 233
gross vehicle weight rating (GVWR), 233
issues, 268-269
packing, 271-280
weigh-in process, 269-271
when to weigh in, 269-270
where to weigh in, 269
unloaded vehicle weight (UVW), 233
weight-carrying hitches, 236
weight-distributing hitches, 236-237
wide-body designs, 65-66, 127-128
wild animals, 357
wildlife refuge areas, 52
wind, 344-345
winter storage, 362
spring preparations, 367-368
systems checks, 368-369
test drives, 370
trailers, 370
winterizing process, 363
batteries, 366
engine, 367
LP gas systems, 364-366
plumbing systems, 363-365
tires, 366
wiring
conventional trailers, 238-239
towing behind a motorhome, 250
wood, 124
woodworking (inspection criterion), 148-149
word of mouth referrals (campgrounds), 286